The Hejaz Railway and the Muslim Pilgrimage

The Hejaz Railway and the Muslim Pilgrimage

A Case of Ottoman Political Propaganda

by Jacob M. Landau

Wayne State University Press   Detroit   1971

Published simultaneously in Canada by The Copp Clark Publishing Company, 517 Wellington Street, West, Toronto 2B, Canada.

Library of Congress Catalog Card No. 78-121918

ISBN 0-8143-1422-8

Contents

Illustrations

Illustrations follow p. 64 of Text

Introduction

RAILWAYS

Railway construction in the Ottoman Empire is one of the most fascinating aspects of its later economic and political history. The success or failure of railway schemes accurately reflects financial transactions as well as political pressures and responses. This is all the more true, since most of the construction, expansion, and exploitation of Ottoman railways were both initiated and executed by non-Turks, chiefly Germans, Austrians, Frenchmen, and Britons.

As early as the 1830s British public opinion was responding favorably to private proposals for the construction of a railway linking the eastern Mediterranean to the Persian Gulf. This would be shorter than the long sea route around the Cape. However, it was not until the Crimean War that the lukewarm attitude of the Ottoman Empire towards railways changed as a result of its unavoidable temporary alliance with Great Britain and France. In 1854 an edict of the sultan recognized the beneficial effects of railways; two years later the first railway concessions were granted to British companies. Meanwhile, various publications encouraged the British public to support the idea.[1]

The first railway concessions were granted for relatively short stretches: Konstanza to Tcherna-Voda in the northern Balkans and Izmir to Aydin in Asia Minor. Later, in 1863 a line from Izmir to Kasaba was built. However, these were all side lines, connecting important ports to inland towns, while Istanbul, the capital, was bypassed. In other words, economic interests were preponderant; since foreign concessions were financing the railways, the fairly general practice of making the capital the heart of the railway network was hardly considered seriously.

For the most part the Ottoman railways constructed during the last third of the nineteenth century were in the Balkans, and hence outside the scope of our discussion.[2] Many of the railways in European Turkey were built with Austrian capital, promoted by Baron de Hirsch.[3] In 1888 the first train rolled all the way from Vienna to Istanbul.

In Asiatic Turkey, in the meantime, small stretches of the projected Istanbul–Ismid–Ankara–Sivas–Baghdad Railway were built.[4] As early as 1872 this line was envisaged by the Austrian engineering expert von Pressel, as a statewide railway network based in Istanbul.[5] German experts had published projects about the desirability of connecting the Mediterranean shore to the Dead Sea and Damascus by rail via Jerusalem.[6] However, the retreat of

1. E.g., Macdonald Stephenson, *Railways in Turkey: Remarks upon the Practicability and Advantage of Railway Communication in European and Asiatic Turkey* (London 1859).
2. A detailed account and analysis is in R. M. Dimtschoff, *Das Eisenbahnwesen auf der Balkan-Halbinsel: eine politisch-volkswirtschaftliche Studie* (Bamberg 1894); an app. treats of the railways in Asiatic Turkey (pp. 257–66).
3. Kurt Grunwald, *Türkenhirsch: a Study of Baron Maurice de Hirsch, Entrepreneur and Philanthropist* (Jerusalem 1966), ch. 5. Cf. Kurt Zander, "Das Eisenbahnwesen der Türkei mit Berücksichtigung der wirtschaftlichen Entwicklungsmöglichkeiten der Bagdadbahn," in Josef Hellauer (ed.), *Das türkische Reich* (Berlin 1918 [=Veröffentlichungen des Instituts für Internationale Privatwirtschaft, 1]): 49–51, esp.
4. For a good account and analysis, see M. Hecker, "Die Eisenbahnen der asiatischen Türkei," *Archiv für Eisenbahnwesen* 37 (Berlin 1914): 744–800, 1057–87, 1283–1321, 1539–84; see also Max Schlagintweit, *Verkehrswege und Verkehrsprojekte in Vorderasien* (Berlin 1906 [=Schriften der Deutsch-Asiatischen Gesellschaft, 2]).
5. He repeated the main points and detailed them in a later work; see Wilhelm von Pressel, *Les Chemins de Fer en Turquie d'Asie: Projet d'un Réseau Complet* (Zurich 1902).
6. C. F. Zimpel, *Strassen-Verbindung des Mitteländischen mit dem Todten Meere und Damascus über Jerusalem* (Frankfort on the Main 1865).

the Ottoman ruling circles from earlier reformist policies, a decline of the economy to the verge of bankruptcy, foreign wars and internal revolt, all served to delay the progress of railway construction. The Ottoman government's modest attempts to build the Anatolian railways by itself were soon abandoned. German capital and engineers stepped in to lay the projected Baghdad Railway, and French, to construct the railways in Syria and Palestine. Foreign companies as a rule demanded Ottoman guarantees. While British companies usually insisted on a minimum security for the capital invested, the Germans generally required guarantees of a minimum revenue for each kilometer of railway.[7] Either way, the already insufficient financial resources of the Ottoman Empire were strained further by these guarantees.[8]

By the end of the nineteenth century railway construction in the Ottoman Empire—mainly in Asiatic Turkey—had ceased to be an economic and financial matter (which, strictly speaking, it has never been completely)[9] and political and military considerations became increasingly important. Perhaps the only point on which the closely concerned European powers—Great Britain, France, Germany, Austro-Hungary, Italy, and Russia—agreed was that any type of investment which would contribute too much towards the economic and military strengthening of the Ottoman Empire was to be avoided.[10] Railway tracks run, of course, in both directions; Turkish reinforcements could be rushed by rail, but so could invading troops. In almost every other matter each power competed with the others, taking a different approach to support rival interests. Each power weighed the projected advantages and disadvantages for itself and its rivals in every step of railway development. In practically every instance each power acted (or tried to act) independently.

This situation was astutely exploited by the Ottoman Sultan

7. Direction Générale de la Presse [Turquie], *La Politique Ferroviaire en Turquie* (Ankara 1941): 15–18.
8. See D. C. Blaisdell, *European Financial Control in the Ottoman Empire* (New York 1929).
9. Amply discussed by Yaqub Nasif Karkar, "Railway Development in the Ottoman Empire: an Economic Interpretation" (Ph.D. diss., Indiana Univ., 1964; repro. University Microfilms, Ann Arbor, Mich.). For another view, see Orhan Conker, *Les Chemins de Fer en Turquie et la Politique Ferroviaire Turque* (Paris 1935): 1–82, esp.
10. On the conflicting interests of the powers, see L. D. (= Leon Dominian), "Railroads in Turkey," *Bulletin of the American Geographical Society* 47 (1915): 934–40.

Abdul-Hamid II (1876–1909) for his own purposes. On his accession to the sultanate there were only a few hundred miles of railway tracks in all the empire He needed railways, however, as well as telegraph lines, to increase his hold on far-flung provinces and to be able to rush troops there, as required. Also, he liked the idea of foreign investment in the Ottoman Empire, as long as it was distributed among the powers. In this way no one power could get a stronghold, thereby alienating the others. Consequently, most of the railways were constructed, operated, and owned by foreign companies. Different gauges were used, which later led to difficulties in linking the systems.

Germany's part was probably the most important, at least politically. Its serious participation in the construction of railways in the Ottoman Empire dates from 1888, when a German company obtained a concession to extend the Istanbul–Ismid Railway farther east and southeast into Anatolia, in the direction of Ankara, with several side lines. When it became evident, with further concessions to the Germans in 1893 and then in 1902–1903, that Baghdad and possibly the Persian Gulf were to be reached by this railway, the issue became one of international politics.[11] Wilhelm II, the new kaiser, young, ambitious, and actively interested in Ottoman affairs, did nothing to allay international suspicion of German intentions. Thus, the Baghdad Railway problem was of concern to major European foreign ministries up to the First World War. This is not the place to dwell on diplomatic history, which in any case has been extensively researched elsewhere.[12] Very briefly, Russia was unhappy about the added life this railway might afford the Ottoman Empire; Great Britain became increasingly apprehensive about

11. For German railway construction in Asiatic Turkey, see Carl Mühlmann, "Die deutschen Bahnunternehmungen in der asiatischen Türkei, 1884–1914," *Weltwirtschaftliches Archiv* 24 (1926): 121–37, 365–99. Cf. Tevfik Manavoglu, *Die Aufgaben und Entwicklungen der Wirtschaftspolitik des türkischen Eisenbahnwesens nach 1918* (Berlin n.d. [1938 ?]): 32–40, esp.

12. E.g., Robert Le Coq, *Un Chemin de Fer en Asie Mineure* (Paris 1907); Paul Rohrbach, *Die Bagdadbahn* (2nd ed., Berlin 1911); Georges Mazel, *Le Chemin de Fer de Bagdad: Etude Economique et Internationale* (Montpellier 1911); Ewald Banse, *Auf den Spuren der Bagdadbahn* (Weimar 1913); Abel Muratet, *Le Chemin de Fer de Bagdad* (Aurillac 1914); C. A. Schaefer, *Die Entwicklung der Bagdadbahnpolitik* (Weimar 1916); Emile Aublé, *Bagdad: son Chemin de Fer, son Importance, son Avenir* (Paris 1917); E. M. Earle, *Turkey, the Great Powers and the Baghdad Railway* (Columbia, Mo., 1936); Reinhard Hüber, *Die Bagdadbahn* (Berlin 1943); G. L. Bondarevskii, *Bagdadskaya doroga i proniknoveniye germanskogo imperializma na Blijnii Vostok* (in Russian, Tashkent 1955).

German designs on Iraq and the Persian Gulf, which it considered its own sphere of influence; while France's reaction, although varying, seems to have been mainly conditioned by its general attitude towards Franco–German relations in Europe. Despite British and Russian opposition, work on various sections of the Baghdad Railway continued simultaneously. This was slowed down, however, by lack of funds, as the construction was largely dependent on the availability of German capital. Although the Young Turks, who seized control and ruled the empire in 1908–1909, were favorably disposed towards the completion of the railway network, the 1911 Turco–Italian War and subsequent troubles hindered the construction, so that by the outbreak of the First World War in 1914, the line had not yet reached Baghdad.

On a smaller scale and less flamboyantly, French know-how and capital were active in building railway lines in Syria and Palestine during the later years of the Ottoman Empire.[13] Two companies with French capital, and representing French interests, constructed two railway lines: one from Damascus to Muzayrib in the Hawran, 64 miles south of Damascus (completed in 1894); the other from Damascus to Beirut, a stretch of 92 miles (completed in 1895). The railways brought these places considerably closer to one another. For instance, the first train from Damascus to Muzayrib reached its destination in three hours; formerly the trip had taken two-and-a-half days. The other railway was more important, however, linking Damascus, a great center of inland trade, to Beirut, which was soon to become a major port. The two companies merged, grew, and started work on a more ambitious project. They obtained a concession for a projected railway to link Damascus, Homs, Hamah, Aleppo, and Birejik (on the Euphrates River). Financial and administrative difficulties delayed the execution of this ambitious project for some years, and it was completed only as far north as Aleppo, with a side line from Homs to Tripoli (Lebanon), in 1911. Two years later the French company obtained yet another concession, to link its lines to the Jaffa–Jerusalem Railway at Ramleh. However, when the Ottoman Empire entered the First World War on the side of Germany and Austro-Hungary, the government took over the administration of these railways for the duration of the war. In 1919 the same French company was again

13. For a good account, see Eleuthère Elefteriadès, *Les Chemins de Fer en Syrie et au Liban: Etude Historique, Financière et Economique* (Beirut 1944): 37 ff., esp.

granted the management of the railways, this time under the rule of the French Mandate in Syria and Lebanon.

There was, however, one railway line that the Ottoman government decided, rather surprisingly, to undertake with its own funds—that is, with Muslim donations—the Damascus–Medina line, often referred to as the Hejaz Railway. Despite the substantial use of German engineers, technicians and managers, as well as some foreign foremen and several hundreds of Italian, Montenegrin, Greek, and Syrian workers, this was to be an Ottoman railway par excellence.[14] The originator of the idea is not certain. The whole concept of a railway line to Medina, Mecca, and the Yemen was allegedly first raised in print during 1897, in India, by the editor of the Urdu journal *Waṭan* (Lahore).[15] This possibly had some connection with the project, discussed at the same time in Great Britain, of constructing a railroad from Port Said, the Sinai Peninsula, and northern Arabia, to some port on the eastern coast of the Arabian Peninsula. This would have strengthened Great Britain's position in Egypt and points east. Nothing seems to have come of this plan, but one may conjecture that even the very discussion of such a project may have alarmed the Ottoman ruling circles.[16] In 1898, when the influential Cairo daily *al-Mu'ayyad* tried to espouse the cause of a railway in Arabia, it was rebuked by the Turkish language daily *al-Ma'lūmāt* (Istanbul), as well as by the religiously oriented *al-Manār* (Cairo).[17]

Meanwhile, the official Ottoman attitude was undergoing a subtle change. In 1898 the imam of Yemen had revolted against the authority of the Ottoman sultan. Abdul-Hamid II, who was occupied in the Balkans, was in no position to fight for any length of time in a remote southwestern corner of the Arabian Peninsula.

14. Auler Pascha, *Die Hedschasbahn* (Gotha 1906 [= Ergänzungsheft, nos. 154 (1907), 161 (1908), zu Dr. A. Petermanns Mitteilungen]); H. Guthe, *Die Hedchasbahn von Damaskus nach Medina, ihr Bau, ihre Bedeutung* (Leipzig n.d.); Richard Henning, *Die deutschen Bahnbauten in der Türkei, ihr politischer, militärischer und wirtschaftlicher Wert* (Leipzig 1915 [= Hugo Grothe (ed.), *Länder und Völker der Türkei*, 12]). Victor Bérard, *Le Sultan, l'Islam et les Puissances: Constantinople—La Mecque—Bagdad* (Paris 1907): 124–95, esp. 129–30. Angus Hamilton "The Story of the Hedjaz Railway," *Problems of the Middle East* (London 1909): 273–92, esp. 278.
15. Muhammad Inshaullah, *The History of the Hamidia Hedjaz Railway Project, in Urdu, Arabic and English* (Lahore 1908): later Inshaullah was decorated by Abdul-Hamid II for his zeal in supporting this railway project and in raising funds (see *Revue du Monde Musulman* 4 [Paris 1908]: 425).
16. Inshaullah: 17.
17. Ibid.: 1–2.

He therefore gave in and recognized Yahya as the "Imam of the Muslims." Not coincidentally, the aggressive, puritanical Wahhabi tribes of the Arabian Peninsula were rebelling again in the eastern part. Their leader Abd al-Aziz Ibn Saud defeated the Turks in several skirmishes. He later endangered Ottoman rule in the Arabian Peninsula even more than the imam of Yemen. Arabia, with Mecca and Medina, the Holy Cities of Islam, was one area the Ottoman Empire could not afford to lose.[18] Its religious and strategic significance is obvious.[19] Izzet Pasha Hilw, a Damascene Arab on the secretarial staff of the sultan's palace in Istanbul, was ordered by Abdul-Hamid II to prepare a report on the insurrection in the Arabian Peninsula and to recommend measures against its spreading. He suggested the construction of a railway to link Damascus with Medina and Mecca; this in turn was to be connected with the main arteries of Turkish railways, in Anatolia or Iraq.[20] For the next few years Izzet was to be the prime mover and coordinator of this railway.

The main reasons for initiating the Hejaz Railway were, then, military and political, to strengthen the sultan's authority in the Arabian Peninsula, chiefly in the Hejaz and Red Sea area. Evidently, the distance from Istanbul, the difficulties of the terrain, and the unruly character of the Bedouins, all pointed to the need for speedier communications. Moreover, in this area (as in some other parts of Asiatic Turkey) it was conceivably possible to keep the railway functioning in winter, when many roads became impassable.[21] The sultan and his advisers did not want just another railway line, financed by European capital and administered by foreign personnel, as this would have guaranteed Ottoman interests only in part; nor was it conceivable to them, taking into account the particularly religious character of Hejaz and the annual pilgrimage, that non-Muslim railroadmen and technicians could be allowed to work and travel near Medina and Mecca. They therefore decided to emphasize

18. Paul Imbert, "La Ligne de la Mecque," *La Rénovation de l'Empire Ottoman: Affaires de Turquie* (Paris 1909), ch. 4.
19. Max Roloff, *Arabien und seine Bedeutung für die Erstärkung des osmanisches Reiches* (Leipzig 1915 [= Hugo Grothe (ed.), *Länder und Völker der Türkei*, 5]).
20. Eduard Mygind, *Syrien und die türkische Mekkapilgerbahn* (Frankfort on the Main, n.d. [= Angewandte Geographie, ser. 2, 11]): 1–11, esp.
21. Charles Godard, "L'Importance Militaire des Voies Ferrées dans le Proche Orient" (Aleppo 1933 [mimeo.]): 102 ff., esp.

the religious aspects of this railway, rather than its military, political, or economic aspects.

In May 1900, on the twenty-fifth anniversary of his accession, Abdul-Hamid II issued an irade appointing two commissions to take care of the projected Syria–Hejaz Railway. One of these, in Istanbul, dealt with the financial aspects; it was headed by Izzet Pasha, the Damascene mentioned above. The other, in Damascus, was executive in function, and was directed by the wali (governor) of Syria. Members included, among others, Mushir (Marshal) Kazim Pasha, chief inspector of works for the projected railway, and Sadiq Pasha, who had formerly been in charge of laying the telegraph lines between Damascus and Medina.[22] The importance of Damascus in all those appointments is evident, as it had been a major point of departure of pilgrimages for generations.

The Muslim press and special publications hailed the projected Hejaz Railway as a major Ottoman and Muslim enterprise, as will be explained below. People throughout the Ottoman Empire and Muslims everywhere were urged to donate funds. Abdul-Hamid II himself and the shah of Iran contributed substantial sums, as did many Muslims in India, Burma, and elsewhere. Donations were collected and the names of donors publicized throughout the Ottoman Empire during the period of the construction of the Hejaz Railway.[23] To stir up philanthropic zeal, the donors received tin, silver, or gold medals, according to the sum contributed. When it turned out that the donations, though impressive, were insufficient, all civil and military personnel were requested to contribute a month's salary, then 10 percent of their annual wage. Also customs and stamp duties were imposed and earmarked for the construction of the railway.[24] If one may believe the evidence of contemporary sources in this respect, none (or almost none) of the collected funds were diverted to other purposes.[25]

The initial maps of the route for the projected railway, as well as

22. For further details, see *Hicaz demiryolu laihası* (Istanbul 1324/1906–7): 1–2, 33–43; see also Marcel Castiau, "Le Chemin de Fer Damas—La Mecque," *Revue Economique Internationale* 2 (Paris 1905): 372.
23. E.g., *Ikdam* (May 24, 1907), quoted in *Revue du Monde Musulman* 2 (1907): 525; *al-Mu'ayyad* (June 20, 1907), *Ikdam* (July 8, 1907), both quoted, ibid. 3 (1907): 141; cf. ibid. 5 (1908): 165, 381; 9 (1909): 478.
24. For the expenses, see *Hicaz demiryolu laihası* [n. 22]: 8–12; see also Z. H. Zaid, "Ḥidjāz Railway," *Encyclopaedia of Islam* (2nd ed.). The most complete account (chiefly financial and technical) in Arabic appears to be Muḥammad Kurd ʿAlī, *Kitāb khiṭaṭ al-Shām*, 5 (Damascus 1927): 187–202.
25. See Augustus Ralli, *Christians at Mecca* (London 1908): 272–73.

the more detailed plans for each stretch, were in Turkish.[26] The avowed intention of the sultan was to use only materials provided by the Ottoman Empire and work supplied by Muslims. This was mostly but not wholly adhered to, since the tracks and cars had to be ordered from abroad, and some foreign experts, chiefly German, were employed—but not within the sacred precincts of Hejaz. The administration appears to have remained Turkish, at least up to the outbreak of the First World War.[27] The labor was provided largely by Turkish soldiers who increasingly took over the unskilled jobs in the construction of the railway. While in 1900–1901 some 2,600 Turkish soldiers participated, their number jumped to 5,650 the following year, and reached about 7,500 in 1907.[28] Most probably, the large number of soldiers was also needed as protection against the attacks of Bedouins opposing the project.[29] In September 1900 construction started on the Damascus–Der'a line from both ends. This, as well as the Der'a–Amman stretch, was completed by 1903; a noteworthy feat, considering the short time it took. A side line was constructed from Der'a to Haifa during the years 1903–1906, thus connecting the projected Hejaz Railway to the Mediterranean Sea. In 1904 the railway reached Ma'an, in the south of what is today the kingdom of Jordan. In 1906 Mudawwara was reached, and a year later the tracks reached Mada'in Salih. This was the farthest the German chief engineer Meissner was allowed to go. The work in Arabia proper was directed by Muslim engineers.

In September 1907 a festive gathering in 'Ula celebrated the completion of the thousandth kilometer of the railway.[30] A year later, in September 1908, eight years after its beginning, the line arrived at Medina, and then to close-by Rabigh. During the same month the Damascus–Medina Hejaz Railway, covering a stretch of over eight hundred miles, was officially inaugurated. It was an impressive achievement, executed despite financial difficulties and technical obstacles. Although it closely followed the pilgrimage

26. What is apparently the first route map is preserved in Ms. in the sultan's collection, Library of Istanbul University, no. 93423. For several other Ms. plans, dated A.H. 1320–22, see ibid., nos. 93836–40.

27. Data and figures may be found in a Turkish Ms. report, dated July 10, 1913, prepared by the Ottoman Company for the Hejaz Railway and its side lines ("Şam Hicazi Timur Yolu Şirket-i Osmaniyesi"), ibid., no. Türkçe 9235b.

28. Guthe [n. 14]: 17.

29. Cf. René Tresse, *Le Pèlerinage Syrien aux Villes Saintes de l'Islam* (Paris 1937): 60.

30. *Revue du Monde Musulman* 3 (1907): 290–93, 524–32.

road and the water reservoirs, it passed mostly through arid, sparsely inhabited land.[31] Some of the work in the construction of the railway had been done hastily and was technically imperfect; however, it functioned well enough.[32] The sultan took full credit. Everybody referred to it as the Hamidian Railway (in Arabic, *al-sikka al-Ḥamīdiyya*, which also means the praiseworthy railway), an allusion to Abdul-Hamid II; in Hejaz it was popularly nicknamed *Jaḥshat al-Sulṭān* (young female donkey of the sultan). However, because of economic difficulties, the deposition of Abdul-Hamid II by the Young Turks (April 1909), and the opposition of the local Bedouin tribes, who sustained economic losses as a result of decreases in camel hiring, the line was not extended to Mecca.[33] In any case, the Damascus–Medina stretch was increasingly used in the years preceding the First World War. The following is a table of official Ottoman figures for the first five years of the railway's operation:

NUMBER OF PASSENGERS ON THE HEJAZ RAILWAY[34]

	Civilian	Military	Total
1908–1909	168,448	77,661	246,109
1909–1910	171,101	27,390	198,491
1910–1911	182,662	47,941	230,603
1911–1912	232,563	43,484	276,047
1912–1913	213,071	147,586	360,657
1908–1913	967,845	344,062	1,311,907

One of the reasons for its frequent use was the comparatively low fare for pilgrims: two Turkish pounds (then around three and a half pounds sterling), about a tenth of the pre-railway expense. Other factors include the relative comfort and time-saving. Under

31. See F. R. Maunsell, "The Hejaz Railway," *Geographical Journal* 32 (London 1908): 570, esp.
32. *Revue du Monde Musulman* 4 (1908): 158.
33. The Bedouins attacked and killed workers on the stretch intended to connect Medina with Mecca, and even besieged some localities. Cf. Guthe [n. 14]: 35; A. J. B. Wavell, *A Modern Pilgrim in Mecca and a Siege in Sanaa* (London 1912).
34. Based on *Hicaz demiryolunun 1327 senesi ve sairesini mübeyyin rapor* (Istanbul 1328/1910–11): 7; *Hicaz timur yolunun varidat ve mesarifi ve terakki-i inşaatı ile hattin ahwal umumiyesini hakkında malumat ihsaiya ve izahat lazimeyi muhtevidir. Beşinci sene 1330* (Istanbul 1334/1916–17): 2, 5.

optimum conditions the trip took only seventy-two hours.[35] There is an interesting description of travel on this train from Damascus to Medina at the end of 1908, soon after the inauguration of the line. It was written by A. J. B. Wavell, a Briton who had lived in East Africa and was familiar with the Near East. Dressed as a Muslim, he made the pilgrimage, and one of the most interesting chapters in his account describes the ride on the Hejaz Railway.[36] The journey took only four days; the train was not punctual and the wagons were crowded, but the mood was one of camaraderie, even of gaiety; the only apprehension was caused by fear of Bedouin attacks. The last point is confirmed by other sources, which report the Turks' rushing in military reinforcements, as soon as the trains started rolling, to little avail.[37]

As it was, the Hejaz Railway and its side lines served Muslim pilgrims in considerable numbers during the years immediately preceding the First World War. The low fares for passengers and merchandise competed successfully with the French-owned Damascus–Muzayrib line, which ran very close to the Damascus–Der'a line (the first leg of the Hejaz Railway). French protests were to no avail, and later on, negotiations broke down completely. The Hejaz Railway was in operation for too short a period before the war to fulfill expectations for the economic development of the inland areas. However, like other railways in the Ottoman Empire, it was operated by the Turks and Germans during the war for the transport of troops and supplies. The British were fully aware of this and, indeed, T. E. Lawrence and his Arab associates damaged the tracks of southern parts of the Hejaz Railway during the later years of the war. One wonders whether the Bedouins who assisted Lawrence in sabotaging it were not motivated in part by their discontent with the railway's encroachment on their livelihood. After the First World War the tracks in Syria and Transjordan (up to Ma'an) were used by the new administrations, while Saudi Arabia insisted that other states pay for repairing its share of the Hejaz Railway. Pro-

35. *Revue du Monde Musulman* 6 (1908): 264; Charles-Eude Bonin, "Le Chemin de Fer du Hedjaz," *Annales de Géographie* 18 (1909): 416–32 (Bonin went to analyze the railway and its problems soon after its completion). See also Zander [n. 3]: 72–75.

36. Wavell [n. 33], ch. 3. The same year Maunsell took the trip as far as Tabūk ([n. 31]: 570 ff.), and a year later, again for the Damascus–Tabūk stretch only, Douglas Carruthers ("A Journey in North-Western Arabia," *Geographical Journal* 35 [Mar. 1910]: 225–26).

37. *Revue du Monde Musulman* 5 (1908): 381; 6 (1908): 262–63.

tracted negotiations have not succeeded in reestablishing the operation of the line to Medina. Only the stretch from Damascus to Maʿan remained serviceable and has been used regularly. The railway, as a pilgrimage road, passed into history. But it still aroused nostalgia among Muslim oldtimers and served as the subject of at least one novel in Arabic, *Riwāya ʿalà sikkat al-Ḥijāz* (*A Novel on the Hejaz Railway* [Jerusalem 1933]) by Jamāl al-Ḥusaynī.

OTTOMAN PROPAGANDA AND THE ARABS

Ottoman propaganda among the Arabs with regard to the Hejaz Railway is but one facet of the complex of Turkish–Arab relations in the years immediately preceding the First World War. These relations are still somewhat obscure, since so much is as yet unexplored in the Ottoman archives, as well as others, and furthermore, since what occurred was often kept secret and never recorded. What has been investigated and published has been largely influenced by George Antonius' *The Arab Awakening*,[38] which stressed the role played in Turkish–Arab relations by Arab nationalists, be they champions of decentralization, autonomy, or statehood. Even later historians, such as Zeine N. Zeine,[39] although often disagreeing with Antonius in their methods and conclusions, used some of his work as a starting point.

Little research, if any, appears to have been devoted to the attitudes and activities of those Arabs who were partial to Turkish rule, whether out of Islamic conviction, socio-economic considerations, or personal interest. Such research was evidently of less concern to the twentieth-century historians interested particularly in the origins and growth of the Arab national movement. This consideration, however, seems only superficially relevant, for the Ottoman authorities must have continued to enjoy some support among at least a segment of the population in order to perpetuate their none-too-effective rule up to the First World War.

From the little one knows, one may gather that Arab officialdom in the Ottoman Empire, represented by such dignitaries as Izzet Pasha Hilw, the champion of the Hejaz Railway, supported Ottoman interests of a religious or super-national character, as

38. (London 1938); there are later eds.
39. *Arab–Turkish Relations and the Emergence of Arab Nationalism* (Beirut 1966): 56–58, esp.

against Arab nationalist ones. The former interests were based on some of the larger and richer Arab families in Syria and elsewhere, which identified with Ottoman policy out of religious convictions or a conservative anti-radical stance. These were the Arab elements supporting the project of the Hejaz Railway, which they thought important for the Ottoman Empire. Few of them, if any, read and considered the brilliant thesis of the German orientalist Martin Hartmann, apparently the only observer at the time who noted that the whole stretch of this railway was populated by Arabs, and concluded that it might bring them together sooner or later against the Turks, culturally and politically.[40] In the final analysis, Hartmann may have been closer to the truth than many of his contemporaries. After all, Husayn, sharif of Mecca and ally of the British in their anti-Turk fighting, had been strongly opposed to the project of the Hejaz Railway.[41]

Ottoman propaganda was intense during the more than thirty years of the reign of Abdul-Hamid II and met with varying success. Some of it was directed towards Europe and aimed to present the sultan as reform-minded and therefore deserving of political and financial assistance.[42] Most of the Hamidian propaganda, however, was Muslim oriented. Originating in the nineteenth century, it was put to political use by Abdul-Hamid II.[43] His posing as a caliph spearheading a panislamic campaign was an astutely conceived plan, which was perseveringly carried out. Because of him and some of his assistants, nationalist sentiment continued to be expressed largely through Islamic loyalties.[44]

What is less known, but pertinent too, is the exact nature of the methods employed by Hamidian propaganda to enlist Arab support and buttress Ottoman authority in Arabic-speaking lands. Such action was, of course, very urgent in the early twentieth century, with Arab nationalist activity on the increase.[45] The telegraph,

40. "Die Mekkabahn," *Orientalistische Litteratur-Zeitung* 11 (Berlin, Jan. 15, 1908): 1–7.
41. *Revue du Monde Musulman* 6 (1908): 262–63.
42. E.g., J. M. Landau, "Un Projet de Réforme dans l'Empire Ottoman en 1883," *Orient* 10, no. 40 (Paris 1966): 147–67.
43. Bernard Lewis, *The Emergence of Modern Turkey* (London 1961): 121, 138–39, 334 ff.; "The Ottoman Empire in the Mid-Nineteenth Century: a Review," *Middle Eastern Studies* 1 (London, Apr. 1965): 291–94.
44. Cf. N. R. Keddie, "Pan-Islam as Proto-Nationalism," *Journal of Modern History* 41 (Mar. 1969): 17 ff.
45. For early signs, see S. G. Haim, *Arab Nationalism: an Anthology* (Berkeley 1962), intro.; Francesco Gabrieli, *The Arab Revival* (London 1961): 51–52; Fritz Steppat, "Eine Bewegung unter den Notabeln Syriens," *Zeitschrift der Deutschen Morgenländischen Gesellschaft* 119 (1969): 631–49.

which was introduced in the Ottoman Empire during the Crimean War and expanded rapidly thereafter, enabled Abdul-Hamid II to keep in close touch with the main towns; and the increasingly frequent reports of anti-Turkish agitation no doubt disturbed him considerably, as they were later to disturb the Young Turks who succeeded him as the rulers of the empire.[46] However, while the methods employed by the Young Turks' specially established Bureau of Special Affairs (*Teşkilât-i Mahsusa*), for propaganda and spying, are well known, similar information is as yet not readily available about the Hamidian era.[47]

Hence the propaganda campaign for the Hejaz Railway during 1900 as an overall effort to recruit the support of Muslims, including the majority of Arabs, is of great significance. In August 1900 it was announced that a special book on the Hejaz Railway had been published in Turkish, Arabic, and French.[48] The choice of these languages, particularly Turkish *and* Arabic, was no doubt intentional. Most likely, other publications of the same genre were issued. However, it was the press that seemed the main vehicle for gaining sympathy and funds for the Hejaz Railway; much of this in Turkish, and even more so in Arabic, was directed towards the Arabs. Letters to editors praised the advantages of railroads in Turkey, with particular reference to the Hejaz Railway.[49] *Al-Rā'id al-miṣrī* (Cairo) compared the economic importance of the projected railway to that of the Suez Canal. *Thamarāt al-funūn* (Beirut)[50] was even more specific; the railway would assist in repopulating southeastern Syria, pacifying the nomadic tribes and halting their raids, developing agriculture, exploiting natural resources, reaffirming the sultan's authority and enabling Muslims from all over the world to make the pilgrimage.[51] This last argument was supported with considerable enthusiasm in the Muslim press in India.[52] The hesitation expressed in the European press about the feasibility of the project

46. Zeine [n. 39]: 54 ff.
47. See P. H. Stoddard, "The Ottoman Government and the Arabs, 1911 to 1918: a Preliminary Study of the Teşkilât-i Mahsusa" (Ph.D. diss., Princeton Univ. 1963).
48. Its Turkish name was *Hicaz Şmendüferi*, evidently a Turkicized form of *chemin de fer*! Cf. Istanbul daily, *al-Ma'lūmāt* (Aug. 28, 1900).
49. See ibid. (July 26, 1900), for a letter by an unnamed correspondent.
50. No. 1281 (1900).
51. Both quoted by Elleftériadès [n. 13]: 157–58, probably based on H. Slemman, "Le Chemin de Fer de Damas—la Mecque," *Revue de l'Orient Chrétien* 5 (Paris 1900): 507–18.
52. Inshaullah [n. 15], *passim*.

and its chances of success, if at all noticed in the East, did nothing to dampen the ardor of Ottoman propaganda.[53]

MUḤAMMAD 'ĀRIF'S WORK

A hitherto unpublished manuscript, deposited in the Yildiz Palace Library in Istanbul, supplies interesting new information about Ottoman propaganda aimed at the Arabs, relating to the Hejaz Railway.[54] Its author is Muḥammad 'Ārif Ibn al-Sayyid al-Munīr al-Ḥusaynī'l-Dimashqī. He was a member of a well-known Damascus family, his father being a Shafiite imam who had reached a certain eminence there.[55] According to Sarkis' bibliography, Muḥammad 'Ārif was provisional chairman of the *majlis al-ma'ārif*, that is, of the board of education in the Sanjak of Damascus, one of the committees founded as a result of the internal reforms of the Ottoman Empire during the latter part of the nineteenth century.[56] Otherwise, little is known about him, although he must have been in the good graces of the Ottomans to rate such an appointment. The manuscript supports this assumption, showing the author to be a dedicated, public-minded personality. Fifteen years before composing this manuscript he had already presented to the wali of Syria a memorandum on how to improve the lot of the inhabitants and simultaneously increase the revenue of the Ottoman treasury (no mean feat, of course). He contributed several articles to various Arabic journals, such as *al-Ma'lūmāt* (Istanbul), and is known to be the author of at least four books, all written before the manuscript under discussion:

1. *Asmā'l-rutab fī'l-'aql wa'l-'ilm wa'l-adab* (*The Highest Degrees, Intellectually, Scientifically and Literarily*), published in 1883.
2. *Ḥusn al-intihāj bi'l-isrā' wa'l-mi'rāj* (*The Excellence in Taking the Road of Travel by Night and Ascent to Heaven*), published in 1889.[57]

53. Cf. H. Slemman, "Où en est le Chemin de Fer de la Mecque," *Revue de l'Orient Chrétien* 6 (1901): 144–45.
54. I found the Ms. in the Library of Istanbul University, Arab Ms. 4790.
55. For a biographical notice of 'Ārif's father, Aḥmad al-Munīr, see Muḥammad Jamīl al-Shaṭṭī, *Tarājim a'yān Dimashq* (Damascus 1948): 7–8.
56. Yūsuf Ilyān Sarkīs, *Mu'jam al-maṭbū'āt al-'arabiyya wa'l-mu'arraba* (Cairo 1928), cols. 1258–59.
57. Allusion to the midnight ascent of the Prophet Muhammad to the Seven Heavens.

3. *Ḥamīdiyyat al-zamān bi-afḍaliyyat rasūlinā'l-a'ẓam bi-naṣṣ al-Qur'ān* (*The Praiseworthiness of Time in the Predilection of Our Greatest Messenger for the Text of the Koran*), unpublished?

4. *Aqrab al-qirab fī tafrīj al-kurab* (*The Nearest Waterskin for Relieving Worries*), unpublished?[58]

'Ārif writes that he visited Istanbul in August 1900. This was the time when the idea of the Hejaz Railway was being aired, and as a Damascene, he was very interested in a railway that would connect Damascus with the Holy Cities of Arabia. Then and there he learned that some people in Mecca and Medina were agitating against the projected construction of the railway. Their intrigues (*iftirā'āt*, 'Ārif terms them) were brought about by religious opposition to this innovation and the fear of unemployment or loss of business and income as a result of the future functioning of the railway. Some Bedouins opposed the plan on general principles, since they were, according to 'Ārif, uncouth and uncivilized (*mutawaḥḥishīn*). Then 'Ārif composed this book, admittedly in a hurry, to refute the opposition and advocate the advantages of the Hejaz Railway for all concerned, most probably during the latter part of the year 1900.

While the exact use to which this manuscript was put is not yet ascertainable, its author intended it to serve Hamidian propaganda for the projected railway in Syria and Hejaz. This would certainly have been in line with other pamphlets and articles on the subject, as already explained. In this work the author mentions that during his visit to Istanbul he was in touch with Arab circles. One wonders whether the idea of composing the book was 'Ārif's, or whether he was encouraged by the Ottoman authorities during his visit. The fact that he included detailed information suggests possible official assistance in the preparation of the book. Interestingly, the detailed table of contents is written in Turkish, presumably to enable the decision makers in Istanbul (not always fluent in Arabic) to estimate the propaganda value of the work. Again, the very fact that 'Ārif submitted his manuscript to the authorities in Istanbul (who placed it in the Yildiz Library) would suggest that it was meant as Ottoman propaganda directed at dispelling local Arab apprehension about the new railway scheme. There is no evidence of its being used; but then, other pamphlets had already been published. Also, the dis-

58. Nos. 3 and 4 are mentioned in 'Ārif's Ms.: 19, 126. I have been unable to find out whether either one has appeared in print.

order in some branches of Ottoman officialdom at the time may have prevented its publication.

'Ārif was a dedicated Arab apologist for Hamidian rule. He was writing in an era that might be called "the early infancy of the Arab national movement." Not once, however, does he mention the existence of Arab nationalists opposing the Ottoman government of the area on patriotic grounds, although it is rather difficult to conceive of a lifelong Arab resident of Damascus' being wholly ignorant of it (particularly as Arab opposition was gradually becoming less conspiratorial at the time).

He named this book *al-Sa'āda al-nāmiya al-abadiyya fī'l-sikka al-ḥadīdiyya al-Ḥijāziyya* (*The Increasing and Eternal Happiness—the Hejaz Railway*).[59] The manuscript numbers 157 pages, of which the frontispiece and another 152 pages make up the book itself. It does not include a colophon, but appears to be either an autograph or—more likely—the work of a professional scribe, based on the author's draft. It is written in fairly clear Arabic, in black and red ink. The handwriting, close to *nasta'līq*, is actually of the *dīwānī* type, frequently used in the Ottoman Empire during the nineteenth century. Although its point of departure is the railway controversy, it also contains interesting material on several other matters. These, however, are discussed only in relation with the railway. The good points of the railway are summed up as follows: "The [Hejaz] Railway has many obvious advantages for populating the country, restoring life to the servants [of Allah], serving the Two Shrines [Mecca and Medina], assisting those desirous to visit both of them, promoting the scope of profitable commerce, bolstering the planning of superior agriculture, and maintaining the political balance in the wide, extensive Arab lands."

Such arguments, although often repeated in the manuscript, were not regarded by its author as exhaustive. It is one of his more significant complaints that an increasing number of Muslim pilgrims were bypassing the land route through Syria, and taking ship directly to Jedda. The financial loss to the Syrians was obvious and 'Ārif, as a resident of Damascus, defended the need for a railway on economic grounds, too. The pilgrimage had been one of Syria's commercial and financial mainstays for generations, as our author

59. Apparently the only printed catalog that mentions this Ms. is Bagdatli Ismail Paşa's *Keşf-el-Zunun Zeyli*, ed. Şerefettin Yaltkaya and Kilisli Rifat Bilge (Istanbul 1947), 2, cols. 15–16; however, it does not indicate where the Ms. is located.

aptly points out; he would have liked to see it continue, or even increase, thanks to the new railway.[60]

However, 'Ārif tries to persuade the inhabitants of Hejaz in particular as to the worth of the railway. While he enjoins every Muslim to contribute money for this enterprise, with the sultan's donation set forth as a shining example, he is especially forceful when addressing the Hejazis. More Muslims would be able to reach the holy places rapidly and comfortably; this increase in numbers would be to the credit of the pious, and to the advantage of farmers, businessmen, and Bedouins. Education would be within general easy reach. The search for minerals and metals would be feasible and bring everybody undreamt of prosperity. The prices of imported commodities—food and clothes—would fall. The people of Mecca and Medina could sell their excellent fruit effortlessly in more remote markets. Those residing near the railway tracks, everywhere, would discover new business opportunities. The Bedouins could market their hides and wool far away, and get better prices; also, they could sell their surplus dairy products, now wasted, in the railway stations. True, their camels would be hired by pilgrims for shorter distances, but due to the expected arrival of multitudes by train, the Bedouins and others would certainly earn a large profit in future years ('Ārif then carefully calculates this profit). In addition, employment servicing the trains would be forthcoming for the Bedouins.

This approach indicates that the Bedouins were, doubtlessly, among the strongest opponents of the railway schemes.[61] Naturally, they were apprehensive about the eventual drying up of their three major sources of livelihood: (*a*) hiring out beasts of burden to the pilgrims, and selling them supplies, such as fodder and staple foods; (*b*) raiding, which provided a fair, if somewhat risky and irregular, income; and (*c*) the tribute paid annually by the Ottoman sultan to the strongest tribal chieftains, albeit disguised as gifts, disbursed by a specially designated official accompanying the pilgrimage caravan. All this is discussed in detail by 'Ārif, who went to great lengths to reason away the Bedouins' antagonism with figures and other data. Evidently, this was easier to do on the religious and economic planes

60. Cf. C. P. Grant, *The Syrian Desert: Caravans, Travel and Exploration* (New York 1938): 80 ff.
61. The most useful work on the Bedouins of Syria and Hejaz in the 20th century is still Max von Oppenheim, *Die Beduinen* (Leipzig 1943), esp. 2. For those of Transjordan, see Peake Pasha, *A History of Jordan and its Tribes* (Coral Gables, Fla., 1958): 139–253, esp.

than on the military. It must have been as apparent to the Bedouin in Hejaz, as to the author of the manuscript, that the new railway was bound to strengthen Ottoman rule in Hejaz. Indeed, 'Ārif himself could not but emphasize this aspect, by stressing the element of added security, in an attempt to enlist the support of merchants and others interested in the growth of the pilgrimage. By a considerable tour de force, however, 'Ārif then tried to persuade the Bedouins that, militarily, the railway was not directed at them, but rather intended against a common enemy (or invader). When these arguments are added to the others, the new railway—according to 'Ārif—was to provide all things to all men.

Besides being an instructive example of Hamidian propaganda directed at the Arabs in Syria and Hejaz, and of the writing of an Arab apologist for Turkish rule, Muḥammad 'Ārif's work is revealing about the conditions of those two lands at the very beginning of the twentieth century. True, the West was becoming better acquainted with the Ottoman Empire through increased travel.[62] Syria was fairly well known then, due partly to the growing tourist interest in Palestine.[63] Arabia, however, was to a large degree still *terra incognita*, infrequent exploration having been limited mostly to its fringes.[64] The early unveiling of Arabia was not systematic, but rather a piecemeal process, undertaken by each explorer according to his interests, means, ability, and the dangers he was willing to brave. The age of the scholarly exploration of Arabia by Thesiger, Philby, Wendell Phillips, and others, would come only after the First World War.

'Ārif's manuscript is particularly valuable in its description of and comments on the pilgrimage from Damascus to Medina and Mecca. While the rites of the pilgrimage are well-known,[65] this is not the case with the route of the pilgrimage caravan and the customs and procedures related to it. Few (if any) Muslims at the time

62. Cf. Bernard Lewis, "Some English Travellers in the East," *Middle Eastern Studies* 4 (April 1968): 296–315.
63. Michael Ish-Shalom, *Maṣṣa'ey nōṣrīm bĕ-Ereṣ-Israel* (in Hebrew, Tel-Aviv 1965).
64. D. G. Hogarth, *The Penetration of Arabia* (London 1904); R. H. Kiernan, *The Unveiling of Arabia: the Story of Arabian Travel and Discovery* (London 1937); Jacqueline Pirenne, *A la Découverte de l'Arabie: Cinq Siècles de Science et d'Aventure* (Paris 1958); A. V. Shvakov, *Probujdenye Aravii* (in Russian, Moscow 1969).
65. For an excellent summary and evaluation, see G. E. von Gruenbaum, *Muhammadan Festivals* (N.Y. 1951), esp. ch. 2. For a good recent description by a Muslim, see Aḥmad Ḥusayn, *Al-Ḥajj: asrāruh wa-manāsikuh* (Cairo 1965).

bothered to describe it, and members of other faiths were forbidden to participate, of course, and reached only the fringes of northern Arabia, such as Archibald Forder, who got to the Jawf.[66] J. L. Burckhardt, a Swiss, apparently in 1811 the first European scholar to penetrate Hejaz, was prevented by illness from a long visit and a thorough exploration of Medina.[67] In 1814 he was followed by Giovanni Finati, and in 1841–1842 by Léon Roches.[68] An even more famous traveler, Richard Burton, performed the pilgrimage in Muslim garb in 1852, and related his exploits in a highly entertaining narrative.[69] However, Finati, Roches, and Burton all traveled to Arabia by sea from Egypt, as did Charles Didier very soon thereafter, and in about 1894 another Frenchman, J. C. Gervais-Courtellemont.[70] In 1893 an Egyptian Muslim had followed much the same route and left a detailed account.[71] Other Europeans, such as von Maltzan and Keane, also penetrated Arabia during the second half of the nineteenth century, and more information about Mecca and Medina became available in European languages, particularly in the years immediately preceding the First World War.[72] In the period following the war, other Europeans, such as

66. One of the last good descriptions, that of Ibn Baṭṭūṭa, dates from 1325 C.E. or soon after; see original and French trans. in *Voyages d'Ibn Batoutah*, ed. C. Defrémery and B. R. Sanguinetti (Paris 1874) 1: 254 ff. Forder, *With the Arabs in Tent and Town* (London 1902), *Ventures Among the Arabs* (Boston 1905).
67. *Travels in Arabia* (London 1829).
68. See Ralli [n. 25], chs. 12–13, for details.
69. *Personal Narrative of a Pilgrimage to al-Madinah and Meccah* (first publ. 1855; there are later eds.). See also T. J. Assad, *Three Victorian Travellers: Burton, Blunt, Doughty* (London 1964).
70. Didier, *Séjour chez le Grand-Chérif de la Mekke* (Paris 1857); he met Burton (pp. 12 ff., 32). Gervais-Courtellemont, *Mon Voyage à la Mecque* (Paris 1896).
71. Saleh Soubhy, *Pèlerinage à la Mecque et à Médine* (Cairo 1894).
72. H. von Maltzan, *Meine Wallfahrt nach Mekka* (Leipzig 1865). T. F. Keane, *Six Months in Mecca* (London 1881), *My Journey to Medina* (London 1881); the latter treats of a trip from Mecca to Medina, then back to Mecca, and thence to Jedda. See, e.g., C. Snouck Hurgronje, *Mekka* (The Hague 1888); a condensed English tr. by J. H. Monahan of this important work appeared as *Mekka in the Latter Part of the 19th Century* (Leiden 1931); see also his "Le Pèlerinage à la Mecque," in G. H. Bousquet and J. Schacht (eds.), *Selected Works of C. Snouck Hurgronje* (Leiden 1957): 171–213. See also Wavell [n. 33]; Godefroy Demombynes, *Le Pèlerinage à la Mekke* (Paris 1923); A. Le Boulicaut, *Au Pays des Mystères: Pèlerinage d'un Chrétien à la Mecque et à Médine* (Paris 1913). For northern Hejaz, Alois Musil, *Im nordlichen Hegâz: Vorbericht über die Forschungsreise 1910* (Vienna 1911), is still valuable.

Eldon Rutter, made the pilgrimage and of course, more Muslims began publishing descriptions of the Holy Cities of Islam.[73]

It should be stressed, however, that very few Europeans ever attempted to join the Syrian pilgrimage caravan with Damascus as the starting point, probably a more difficult, although a more colorful and interesting route. Even C. M. Doughty, who did so in 1876 and lived to describe it in his inimitable style, joined the caravan for only part of the way—from Damascus to Mada'in Salih in Hejaz—since he was so obviously a non-Muslim.[74] On the other hand, there seems to be little doubt that Muḥammad 'Ārif himself must have made the whole pilgrimage with the Syrian caravan from Damascus to the two Holy Cities, and he described all the preparations and proceedings in great detail, which he wrote with the knowledge of an insider.

'Ārif's description may be compared only to that of Burckhardt, apparently the first and only nineteenth-century European explorer to have joined the Syrian pilgrimage caravan for all of its way and to have left a fairly extensive account. Ninety years after Burckhardt, 'Ārif recorded in detail the whole course of the pilgrimage route (*darb al-ḥajj*), listing for the first time in recent years the exact location of the Bedouin tribes on the Damascus–Medina–Mecca route. This is particularly valuable for the Hejaz tribes, of which we know much less at that time than of the Syrian tribes. He details the names and positions of small Bedouin ramifications, some of which are unknown from other sources and cannot be identified with certainty. Also, some of the place names mentioned by 'Ārif are not immediately identifiable; many differ from those listed by Burckhardt.[75] Some Bedouin encampments and other small places most likely were abandoned during the nineteenth century, and others chosen as temporary sites. This is evident, also, from various travel accounts and from a perusal of *Cook's Tourist Handbook for Palestine and Syria*, published in 1900; unfortunately, there is no Cook's handbook for Hejaz!

73. Rutter, *The Holy Cities of Arabia* (London 1928). See bibl. in Bernard Lewis, "Ḥadjdj," *Encyclopaedia of Islam* (2nd ed.); Gamal-Eddine Heyworth-Dunne, *Bibliography and Reading Guide to Arabia* (Cairo 1952); Eric Macro, *Bibliography of the Arabian Peninsula* (Coral Gables, Fla., 1958).
74. *Travels in Arabia Deserta* (Cambridge 1888); see also his "Travels in North-Western Arabia and Nejd," *Proceedings of the Royal Geographical Society*, n.s., 6 (London 1884): 382–94. The most recent book on the Syrian pilgrimage caravan seems to be René Tresse [n. 29], 1937; Tresse was unacquainted with 'Ārif's work.
75. App. 3, "The Hadj Route from Damascus to Mekka" [n. 67]: 656–61.

Moreover, the merit of 'Ārif's book is not only in being a more detailed, almost complete account of the Syrian pilgrimage route and of the Bedouin tribes adjoining it. It seems to be one of the very few complete accounts of the Syrian pilgrimage itself written by a Muslim in modern times. In addition, it is also apparently *the very last Muslim account of this pilgrimage*, still using camels and donkeys for transportation and ceremoniously adhering to the accustomed pomp. Indeed, very soon after this account was composed, pilgrims began riding the railway from Damascus for part of the way; after the year 1908, with the completion of the Damascus–Medina Railway, practically everyone starting from Damascus used the train. After the First World War, with parts of the railway destroyed and others shared by new states, Damascus was used less as a starting point of the pilgrimage. The bulk of the pilgrims increasingly used the seaways.

In other words, 'Ārif actually wrote the epitaph of a period. He may have sensed it, for modernization was making inroads even then into the customs of the Syrian pilgrimage caravan. In several instances, which are most enlightening, he compared old and new practices, such as the diminishing importance in the role of several pilgrimage officials, the manner of hiring camels, disbursing funds via money-orders, or the carrying and distribution of mail. One of the highlights is his likening the socio-economic functions of the Muslim pilgrimage to those of international fairs in Europe.

The manuscript treats in detail the pageantry and stylized ceremonies in Istanbul and Damascus, and along the way to Medina and Mecca; the gay festivities in Damascus before the caravan's departure and after its return,[76] which were the social events of the year; the different roads and distances, as well as their relative merits in terms of ease of travel; the business transacted on the way and the behavior patterns; the religious rituals in Medina and Mecca; the Bedouin tribes, their location, customs and economic conditions; and the mails during the pilgrimage, stereotyped in their arrangements and so venal that the author feels he has to suggest ways of reform. Indeed, 'Ārif's lengthy discussion of the mails is truly enlightening, as much less is known of them than of the foreign posts in the Ottoman Empire (British, French, Austrian, German,

76. 'Ārif's account is much more detailed and accurate than others of the same period; e.g. Mrs. Mackintosh, *Damascus and its People: Sketches of Modern Life in Syria* (London 1883): 39–40.

Italian, Russian, Polish, and Roumanian).[77] In addition, he not infrequently quotes prices, and discusses and appraises the climate, topography, flora, and crops. Special interest attaches to the vivid description of the means of livelihood in each "station" where the Syrian pilgrimage caravan stops. Muslim traditions or hadiths, as well as legends (some fairly well known, however), are quoted to make a point, as are bits of Arabic poetry (some of them not so well known).

Despite a tendency to repeat himself, 'Ārif provides us with interesting reading, due to his easy-flowing style, well-marshaled facts, and shrewd arguments. His manuscript not only offers new information, but reveals some of the methods employed by Hamidian propaganda among the Arabs, stressing the religious bond of Islam to achieve political, military, and economic ends. The work is also an edifying portrait of the range of interests of an Arab intellectual early in the twentieth century, who was a pious Muslim but not insensible to the process of change and to the merits of business logic.[78]

To sum up—several factors combined in prompting Muḥammad 'Ārif to write this book in the year 1900 and to present it to Istanbul: his affection for Damascus and his obvious interest in promoting its economic interests; his strong Muslim sentiment; and his desire to promote Hamidian propaganda and thereby advance himself in the graces of the Ottoman hierarchy.

The following pages contain the text of 'Ārif's manuscript and an English translation. I have added facsimiles of the manuscript and several relevant photographs from the Sultan's Library. The text is in literary Arabic prose (sometimes rhymed), with a few syntactic slips and inconsistencies in spelling, noted in the transcription but generally not in the translation. Similarly, the material given in the footnotes to the translation is not repeated in the footnotes to the transcription.

The translation is as literal as possible, though occasionally minor adjustments were necessary in order to render into English

77. See H. W. Hazard, "Islamic Philately as an Ancillary Discipline," in J. Kritzeck and R. B. Winder (eds.), *The World of Islam: Studies in Honor of Philip K. Hitti* (London 1959): 230, esp.

78. I have been unable to uncover further details of Muḥammad 'Ārif's life; he died in 1342/1923–24 (Shaṭṭī [n. 55]: 8). Possibly, the Young Turks may have demoted him, along with Izzet Pasha Hilw and other officials who had been serving Abdul-Hamid II.

both the content and the spirit of the original. Thus, for instance, I have divided the translation into chapters and paragraphs, and added punctuation marks which the Arabic text consistently ignores. In several places I have filled in explanatory words in English, using square brackets. This has been done, for instance, when 'Ārif follows the often used practice of employing the term *al-Sha'm* for both Syria and Damascus, and *Miṣr* for both Egypt and Cairo. Several frequently used pious formulas are represented by dashes in parentheses, as indicated in the footnotes when they first appear.

In order to render into English the Koranic quotes, adduced by 'Ārif to clinch an argument, I have used Mohammed Marmaduke Pickthall's translation, *The Meaning of the Glorious Koran*; the citations in brackets are to his division, chapter and verse. Arabic and other foreign words that have been incorporated into the English language are spelled as they appear in *Webster's Third International Dictionary*. Otherwise, transliteration follows the literary rather than the colloquial Arabic form throughout, for the latter varies so much as to make consistency difficult, if not impossible. Arabic and Turkish words and other terms are defined in the Glossary, which is meant to assist primarily the non-Arabist students of twentieth century Middle Eastern history and of modern Islam. The table of contents was compiled from the text and is not a translation of the one in Turkish.

The notes to the Introduction afford a fairly extensive bibliography. The following brief forms have been used for works often cited in the translation and its footnotes.

BBW. J. L. Burckhardt, *Bemerkungen über die Beduinen und Wahby* (Weimar 1831).

EI. *Encyclopaedia of Islam* (2nd ed.).

HDM. Hermann Guthe, *Die Hedchasbahn von Damaskus nach Medina, ihr Bau, ihre Bedeutung* (Leipzig n.d.).

K. The Koran.

Kaḥḥāla. 'Umar Riḍā Kaḥḥāla, *Mu'jam qabā'il al-'arab al-qadīma wa'l-ḥadītha*, 3 v. (Beirut 1968).

MLPNC. C. Snouck Hurgronje (tr. J. H. Monahan), *Mekka in the Latter Part of the 19th Century* (Leiden 1931).

PNP. Richard Burton, *Personal Narrative of a Pilgrimage to al-Madinah and Meccah* (London 1893).

PSVSI. René Tresse, *Le Pèlerinage Syrien aux Villes Saintes de l'Islam* (Paris 1937).

SIP. Victor Bérard, *Le Sultan, l'Islam et les Puissances: Constantinople–la Mecque–Bagdad* (Paris 1907).
TA. J. L. Burckhardt, *Travels in Arabia* (London 1829).
TS. J. L. Burckhardt, *Travels in Syria* (London 1882).

My sincere thanks go to the staffs of the University Library, the Süleymaniya, and the Municipal Library, all in Istanbul; and to Professor Harold A. Basilius, director of the Wayne State University Press, and his staff for their unfailing courtesy and patience.

J. M. L.

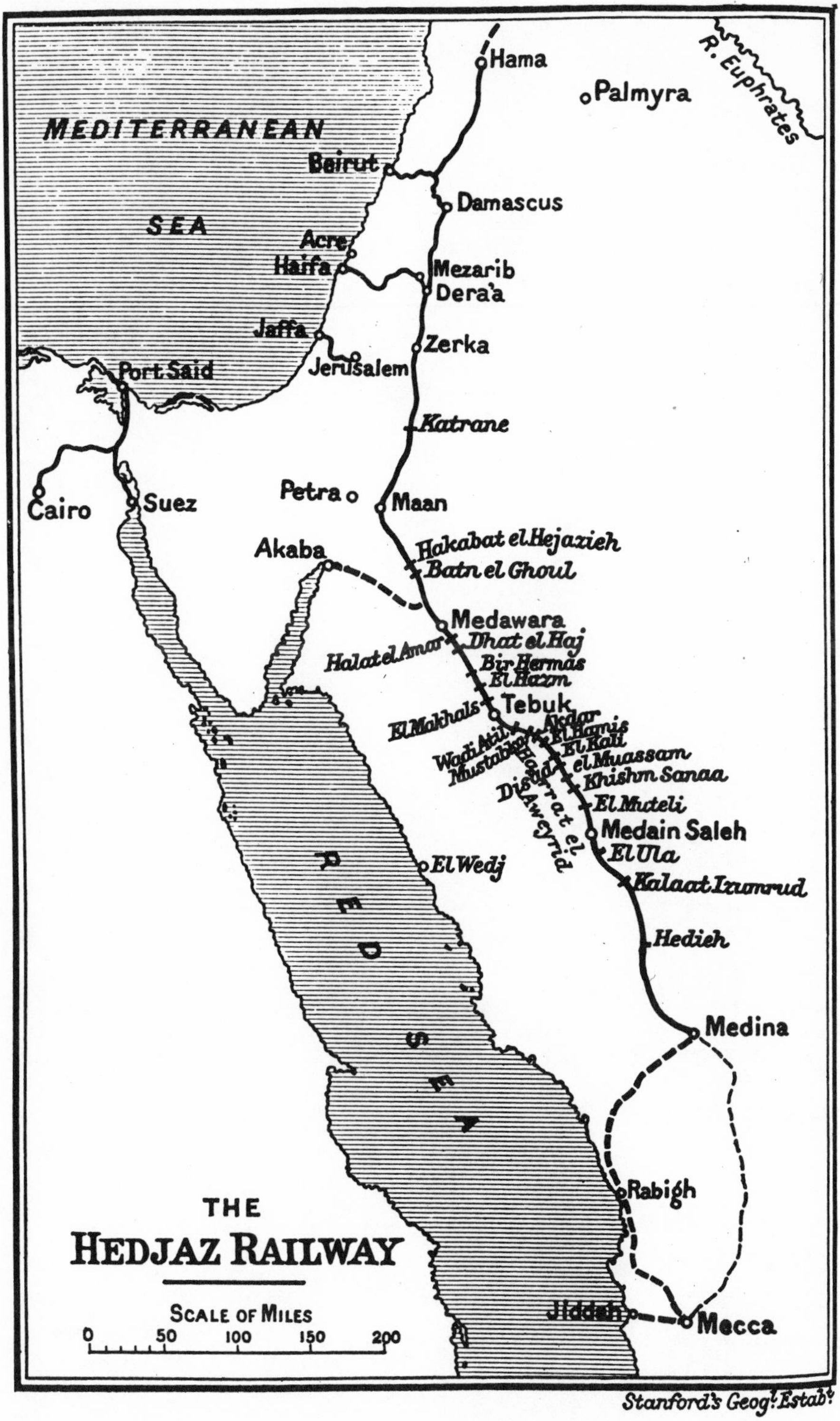

(*From* Hamilton, *Problems of the Middle East*)

The Book of the Increasing and Eternal Happiness —the Hejaz Railway

by al-Sayyid Muḥammad ʻĀrif Ibn al-Sayyid Aḥmad al-Munīr al-Ḥusaynī'l-Dimashqī

May Allah Forgive the Sins of Both, Amen!

English Translation

Contents

* Page numbers of the manuscript are inserted in the text in italic. These numbers are used in the Glossary and Index unless otherwise indicated. Headings added in the translation are not indicated.

Foreword

[*1*] In the name of Allah, the Compassionate, the Merciful!

We praise Thee, O God, Thee Who hast cleared the road for the poor and straightened it for the righteous. We ask Thee—Who hast ordered the Major and Minor Pilgrimages, assigned the Visit,[1] and initiated industry, agriculture, and commerce—to bless him who gave us the canonical law of Islam, founded the right policy, and laid down laws and regulations, Thy very strong and very straight authority, that is, Muhammad, the compassionate, the best one to show the right way. Bless also his Companions who conquered the land, islamized the people, arranged state affairs, and introduced the orders to be complied with. Bless also their followers who go in their ways. Amen!

Now to our main subject. I, al-Sayyid Muḥammad 'Ārif, son of the late al-Sayyid Aḥmad al-Munīr al-Ḥusaynī, an imam of the Shafiite School in Syria, say: Allah inspired His servant, our

1. 'Ārif frequently uses the terms pilgrimage (pilgrims) and visit (visitors) in conjunction, the former referring specifically to the pilgrimage to Mecca, the latter to visiting Muhammad's tomb in Medina.

master, the Commander of the Faithful, the caliph of the authorized Prophet, [*2*] of whose existence we are proud and in the shadow of whose justice and bounty we revel,[2] the Sultan al-Ghāzī 'Abdul Hamid Khān, the son of our master, the late Sultan 'Abdul Majid Khān. May our era continue to enjoy him, whose luck is lit by the stars, to adorn the throne of the Islamic caliphate with him, and to be proud of the achievements of His Majesty and his success in initiating the Hejaz–Syria Railway.

The [Hejaz] Railway has many obvious advantages for populating the country, restoring life to the servants [of Allah], serving the Two Shrines [Mecca and Medina], assisting those desirous to visit both of them, promoting the scope of profitable commerce, bolstering the planning of superior agriculture, and maintaining the political balance in the wide, extensive Arab lands. The sultan (may Allah make his reign eternal) donated 50,000 gold pieces [Turkish pounds] from his private purse for the initial stage. He then repeated this, contributing another 100,000 from the fund for public works (*ṣundūq al-manāfiʿ*). Also, bonds for 1,000,000 [pounds] were issued. Now it was too late to retract. An imperial irade ordered the work on the railway to start. Voluntary societies were founded to handle the matter. Muslims everywhere competed in assisting it, personally and financially. Evil-minded rumormongers saw that the construction of the railway was to come about anyway, God willing. For their personal purposes they spread rumors that constructing a railway is forbidden by the Koran and that the pilgrimage is permitted solely on foot, or riding on the backs of grazing livestock or beasts of burden. This they did, fabricating lies of their own, calumniating the most righteous Book [the Koran].

During this evil, slanderous, obvious, and fertile campaign of rumors, I was [*3*] in Istanbul, the sublime, the capital of the Islamic caliphate, the residence of the Ottoman sultanate (may Allah preserve it from the intrigues of its enemies and any misfortune). That happened on Wednesday, 26 Rabi II 1318 of the Hegira [22 August 1900], which fell on 8 August 1316 of the financial (*mālī*) year of the Hegira.[3]

2. The Ottoman sultan was sometimes described as Allah's Shadow on Earth.
3. At that time the Turks figured dates by the Muslim calendar and by the financial year. The latter was introduced early in the 19th century by adopting the solar calendar year of the Eastern Orthodox Church and the solar months, but continuing to count the years according to the Hegira. Due to the shorter lunar year of the Hegira calendar, by 1900 there was a difference of over two years between them (1318 vs. 1316); there were other minor discrepancies: 26 Rabi II 1318 fell on 23 Aug. 1900, while 8 Aug. 1316 fell on 21 Aug. 1900.

I wrote an article, well-expressed, in which I congratulated His Majesty (may Allah support his reign with justice, beneficence and security). I published it in the Arabic journal *al-Maʿlūmāt*, printed in Istanbul. In it I maintained that the greatest of His Majesty's splendid feats—indeed, the greatest of the feats achieved by the sultans of the Muslim community in those magnificent lands—was this Hejaz–Syria Railway. I refuted the rumormongers' arguments and I decried their deeds and behavior. I explained to the people their intention, corruption, and iniquity, insofar as the situation brooked proof, in my most eloquent style. I proved conclusively that constructing the railway at this time was one of the major tasks for the most necessary means of transportation, for preparing all possible strength, for the most important favors with Allah (may His name be exalted)[4] and obedience to Him, as enjoined in the Koran, in an evident text which may not be interpreted to have any other meaning and which does not need any instruction for [further] clarification of its purport.

A few days later several arguments were spread among the notables and the common people, one of which—and the most significant—was that the Arabs of the Hejaz desert and some of the inhabitants of Mecca and Medina would not assist in the construction of the railway but, on the contrary, would oppose it; that they would not accept it quietly but, on the contrary, would resist it, [*4*] according to what evil-intentioned persons enticed them to do and masters of intrigue wormed into them: that this railway would injure their trade and harm their livelihood, as their profits were based on carrying pilgrims, visitors, and traders on the backs of their riding animals into these lands; that this railway would cause their animals to be idle and their gains to dwindle; that they would become destitute and their spirits crushed. We shall list these arguments at the end of this book and refute them with the finest reply for people of heart and intellect.

Since whoever hears something imperfect, and is liable to improve [gainsay] it, may indeed drive away the falsehood; since uncouthness is prevalent among these Bedouins and ignorance growing and enveloping them; since their alarm comes close to undermining [the plan of the railway]; and since one should be wary of their following a course of lies and falsehood—Muslims should be warned not to lend an ear to this evident incitement and perfidy. I was certain of the general affection for the Ottoman

4. Hereafter this formula is indicated by a dash in parentheses (—).

government and the people's praying for it, morning and evening, as is enjoined on members of the Muslim community; and they, if they understood the truth of the matter, would not let their ears listen when they learn the truth of the outcome.

Islamic zeal moved me, Arab gallantry seized me, my sincere affection for my Muslim brethren attracted me, and my loyal service to His Majesty the sultan of the Muslims roused me to advise those uncouth Bedouins; to awaken whomsoever might be duped from among the rest of the Muslims; to encounter and curb those with inauspicious designs. Therefore, I have written this treatise, or rather book, perforce with great speed, answering in it the flimsy opposition and sapless allegations; explaining in it the benefits of this railway and its advantages for the country—such as the preparation [*5*] of force, stabilization of security, and smoothing of travel in that land and its neighborhood; proclaiming in it the immensity of the benevolence of His Majesty, our master, to his servants, and particularly to the lands of Hejaz and their inhabitants. To this I shall add a description of its affairs and merits, to be found—despite all the obdurate, deluded, and envious—in populating the two Great Mosques and the Two Shrines, increasing their edifices, enlarging the scope of their commerce and farming, introducing civilization, spreading education in all their areas, saving them from the fangs of assassins and the claws of tyrants that are impeding their progress. Then they would live free, in comfort and wealth, enjoying a life of luxury, satisfaction, peace of mind, and pleasure.

I have named this work *The Increasing and Eternal Happiness —the Hejaz Railway*. I beg of Allah (the Noble One, may He be exalted) to make it a source for public use. I raised it from the above-mentioned article [in *al-Maʿlūmāt*] to the gate of the Supreme Islamic Caliphate, hoping that both of them would be accepted by it. This is the apogee of my hope and grace.

1. The Bedouins to Whom This Railway is Relevant

Know that the Bedouins to whom this railway is relevant, from the Damascus gate, formerly known as the Gate of Egypt [or Cairo] and now as the Gate of Allah, to Mecca, are divided into two parts—the Bedouins of Hejaz and the Bedouins of Syria.

THE BEDOUINS OF HEJAZ

One refers by this term to those Bedouins who inhabit the desert and the villages of Hejaz between Mecca and Medina, and the villages in their neighborhood. Since the latter, even if they are villagers, are descended from the desert Bedouin tribes and are their kinsmen in characteristics and traits, [*6*] and since their savageness is the same, indeed more uncouth and ignorant, we have called them Bedouins, classified them among the same, and listed them in the same category—some difference notwithstanding.

As for the Bedouins inhabiting the area north of Medina and

in its vicinity, although they are Bedouins of Hejaz and their interests are not identical with those of the Bedouins of Syria concerning the construction of this railway, we have nevertheless discussed them together, because the Bedouins living north of Medina, in the direction of Syria, do not rent their camels for the Syrian pilgrimage caravan, except when it has to rent [the means of] carrying merchandise one way only from them. This does not apply to the transportation of either the pilgrims [themselves] or the provisions supplied by the government. The reason for this is the Syrian caravan takes along from Syria whatever it needs in the way of riding animals and beasts of burden. When the need arises for [more animals] to bring over the provisions and store them in the usual places, they are rented from the Bedouins of Syria. In the same manner, merchants rent [animals] from the Bedouins of Syria to carry their loads to Medina. On their return provisions are ready for them in strongholds and other places suitable for [safe] deposit. Via the jurdī they get from Syria the [additional] stock they require [for the trip] from Madā'in[1] to Damascus, according to practice and need. Insofar as the merchants are concerned, indeed they do not have to rent [animals] at all, since if their merchandise does not find a ready market and some of it sells badly, either on the road or at the Two Shrines, they may leave it either in Mecca, if it applies to [the needs of] its inhabitants, or in Medina, if it fits into the place's commerce. This the merchants may do, either by way of warranty and deposit for the following year, or by empowering someone they trust [7] to sell it—be it from among their agents or others—or by not showing up for the return trip and remaining behind to sell it [themselves]. Therefore, the Bedouins north of Medina do not share the renting of camels for the Syrian caravans or any other, and this is why we have considered them in the category of the Syrian Bedouins, and not those of Hejaz.

Description of the Bedouins of Hejaz

The tribes of the Bedouins of Hejaz are numerous. We do not intend to investigate all of them here, or describe their tribes and ramifications. We intend to mention solely those having a connection with this railway, in order to draw a useful lesson. Hence, we say:

1. This is not Madā'in on the site of Seleucia-Ctesiphon, but a small place on the road from Damascus to Medina.

The tribes which have to do with the railway are numerous, some full-fledged tribes, others ramifying in branches. It is believed that all of them have auspicious signs. They are the Ḥawāzim, Aḥāmida, Juhayna, Masrūḥ, Muṭayr, 'Utba, Surayḥī, Ḥajala, Qarrāf, Riḥala, Hammādiyyīn, Fuḍaylī, Shawārib, Baḥyawiyya, Dakara, 'Amrawiyya, Timam, Awlād Muḥammad, Sahlī, Luhaybī, Ṣawā'id[2] [or Sawā'id[3]], Zabīdī, Banū 'Amr, Ibn Mūqid, 'Awf, Jahm, Raddāda, Tarājima, Lahaba, Banū Ayyūb, Ṣubḥ, Zubayd, Quraysh, Bilī, Hudhayl, 'Usūm, 'Aṣāliyya, the tribes of the Sharifs and the Sayyids—the Ḥasans and the Ḥusayns—two tribes which are not counted among those listed, nor are they ramifications thereof. Indeed, both these tribes are the noblest as to lineage and the most magnificent of all as to descent [and claim relationship to Muhammad's family]. We have mentioned them here only because they have a connection with this railway; so we have referred to them all together due to these circumstances and to the fact that these two tribes now resemble the others in their characteristics and tastes.

[*8*] THE BEDOUINS OF SYRIA ALONG THE HEJAZ ROAD

The Bedouins of Syria are numerous, their tribes many, their ramifications uncounted, their families joining and breaking up, their frontiers extending from Damascus to Madā'in. [Southwards] to Medina there are the Arabs of Hejaz, but we are referring to them together with the Bedouins of Syria due to their identity of interests, as already mentioned. Since there is no point in investigating them here and no gain in relation to the purpose of this treatise, we have limited ourselves to mentioning [solely] those who have some connection with the pilgrimage road. These are the 'Anaza, Wuld 'Alī, Banū Ṣakhr, Labīda, Fuqarā', Sharārāt, Ḥarābsha,[4] Sa'ādīn, Aḥrāsh, 'Aṭiyya, Banū Shāma, Muṭayr, and Juhayna. The last two are Bedouins of Hejaz, but we have linked them with the Syrian Bedouins, as noted above, since they both inhabit the area north of Medina and their interests are identical with those of the latter. These two tribes are foes of several others; savagery, ignorance,

2. Kaḥḥāla (2:653) concurs. Not all my identifications of names of Bedouin tribes are certain.
3. *BBW*: 604.
4. *BBW*: 604; I prefer this reading.

aggressiveness, plundering, and raiding are prevalent among them. Sometimes they lay siege to Medina, which thus remains invested for a month or two, or more; consequently, prices rise in Medina, fear spreads, and nobody may leave it, even to [visit] the grave of our Sayyid Ḥamza (may Allah have mercy on his soul),[5] which is about half an hour away from Medina. People have undergone insufferable misery at their hands. The Ottoman government has taken innumerable steps to punish these two tribes. Consequently, they often give up renting their camels to the Syrian pilgrimage caravan, which the Bedouins of Syria carry to Medina, as will be related later.

5. Hereafter this type of "mercy" formula with the names of venerated persons is indicated by a long dash in parentheses (——).

2. The Road from Damascus to Mecca

[*9*] Know that the road from Damascus to Mecca passes through Medina, this being one and the same road. When it reaches Medina, however, it branches into two: a western branch, through Rābigh, with four different ways leading to Rābigh, and thence to Mecca; and an eastern branch [to Mecca], which does not cross Rābigh.

DESCRIPTION OF THE ROAD FROM DAMASCUS TO MEDINA

Know that there is one road from Damascus in Syria to Medina, as we have said.[1] Its length in hours [of travel] is 342. Its stages [or legs] are 28½ [in theory], when calculated at usual camel speed with every stage accounting for 12 hours. The road is 684 miles, or 228 parasangs, or 57 posts (*barīd*). A mile takes half an hour, a parasang equals three miles, a post equals four parasangs. The number of

1. *SIP:* 112–23; cf. *HDM:* 5 ff.

stations on this road, considering the journey of the Syrian pilgrimage caravan, is now 31 [32] as is the number of the stages [31], although the latter differ in the amount of required travel hours, as may be learnt from the following list:

1. Damascus–Dhū'l-Nūn 4 hours
2. Dhū'l-Nūn–Katība 10 hours
3. Katība–Muzayrīb 8 hours

[*10*] 4. Muzayrīb–Ramtha 4 hours

5. Ramtha–Mafriq 12 hours
6. Mafriq–Zarqā' [Zerqa'[2]] 8 hours
7. Zarqā'–Balqā' [Belqāʿ[2]] 15 hours
8. Balqā'–Qaṭrāna 12 hours
9. Qaṭrāna–Ḥasā [or Ḥassā] 12 hours
10. Ḥasā–'Anaza 10 hours
11. 'Anaza–Ma'ān 8 hours
12. Ma'ān–'Aqaba 8 hours
13. 'Aqaba–Mudawwara 14 hours
14. Mudawwara–Dhāt Ḥajj 10 hours
15. Dhāt Ḥajj–Qā' 15 hours
16. Qā'–Tabūk 7 hours
17. Tabūk–Ẓahr al-Mughr 10 hours
18. Ẓahr al-Mughr–Akhḍar 8 hours
19. Akhḍar–Janā'in al-Qāḍī 10 hours
20. Janā'in al-Qāḍī–Muʿaẓẓam 10 hours

[*11*] 21. Muʿaẓẓam–Ẓahr al-Ḥamrā' 15 hours

22. Ẓahr al-Ḥamrā'–Tabrīka 14 hours
23. Tabrīka–Madā'in 6 hours
24. Madā'in–Badā'iʿ 10 hours
25. Badā'iʿ–Zumurrud 16 hours
26. Zumurrud–Jadīd 8 hours
27. Jadīd–Barrāqa 14 hours
28. Barrāqa–Hadiyya 6 hours
29. Hadiyya–Iṣṭabl ʿAntar 18 hours
30. Iṣṭabl ʿAntar–Biyār Nāṣīf 10 hours
31. Biyār Nāṣīf–Medina 20 hours

Or a total of 332 hours, 31 stages, and 31 [32] stations [including Damascus and Medina (terminals)].

2. *TS* (app. 3): 657.

DESCRIPTION OF THE ROAD FROM MEDINA TO MECCA

It is actually two roads, a four-branched western one through Rābigh, and a single one by-passing Rābigh [via Ṣafīna].

The Western Road to Mecca

[*12*] The western road from Medina to Rābigh has four branches, joining into one at Rābigh. The first branch is called the Sultan's road[3] (*al-sulṭānī*) [Kingsway?]; the second, the Low road (*al-ghā'ir*); the third, the Branch road (*al-far'ī*); and the fourth is called the Winding road (*al-milaff*) by the Hejazis, or the Middle road (*al-wāsiṭa*) by the Syrians.

The first branch, the Sultan's road, is the nearest to the sea, which is on its west, the Low road on its east. Its length from Medina to Rābigh is 75 hours, and $6\frac{1}{4}$ stages at usual camel speed, or 7 stages according to the Syrian caravan, as follows:

1. Medina–Biyār 'Alī 3 hours
2. Biyār 'Alī–Shuhadā' 12 hours
3. Shuhadā'–Judayda[4] 10 hours
4. Judayda–Ṣafrā' 10 hours
5. Ṣafrā'–Badr 8 hours
6. Badr–Mastūra 20 hours
7. Mastūra–Rābigh 12 hours

There are several wells in Biyār 'Alī, and another, named Bīr 'Abbās, in Shuhadā'. [*13*] This is the smoothest of all the roads, as well as the most populated one; it is shorter than the Branch road. We shall mention further that one can pass it only with difficulty; therefore the Syrian caravan does not use it at all, due to the impracticability of borne litters passing there.

The second branch, the Low road, lies between the Sultan's and the Branch roads, the former being on its west, the latter on its east. Its length is not known exactly, for the distances we have been mentioning for other roads are determined by those joining the Syrian caravan; however, the Medinese and Meccan caravans have not estimated its length accurately, because they vary in pace and

3. Described in *TS:* 656 ff.
4. *PNP* (1893) 1: 262 (n. 1); *TS:* 660.

organization. Let us, nevertheless, list the main places on the road. They are Biyār 'Alī, Bīr Māshī, Jabal Ghā'ir, Bīr Ḥufāt, 'Ayn Tabra, and Bīr Mubayrīk. This road is the shortest of them all. People from the Two Shrines who have used it repeatedly have estimated that it saves 18 hours on the time of other routes. Nonetheless, it takes about 44 hours to ride it from Medina to Rābigh.

The third branch, the Branch road, is east of the Low road and west of the Winding road. The distance it covers from Medina to Rābigh, is 78 hours, or 6½ stages, according to usual camel speed. According to the actual pace of the Syrian caravan it too has 7 stages:

[*14*] 1. Medina–Biyār 'Alī 3 hours
2. Biyār 'Alī–Bīr Māshī 10 hours
3. Bīr Māshī–Ṣamt [Ṣamd] 16 hours
4. Ṣamt–Rayyān 14 hours
5. Rayyān–Ibn Ḍibā' 10 hours
6. Ibn Ḍibā'–'Aqaba 15 hours
7. 'Aqaba–Rābigh 10 hours

This road is second to the Sultan's road in pleasantness and smoothness, but it is three hours longer.

The fourth branch is the Winding road. This is its appellation by the Hejazis, but the Syrians call it the Middle road, as it lies between the Branch road and the Eastern road [from Medina to Mecca not via Rābigh], to the east of the former and west of the latter. The distance it covers from Medina to Rābigh is 62 hours, or 5⅙ stages, according to usual camel speed. It has 6 stages, as well as 6 [7] stations [according to the pilgrimage caravan]:

1. Medina–Bīr 'Urwa 1 hour
2. Bīr 'Urwa–Shi'b Ḥajj 15 hours
[*15*] 3. Shi'b Ḥajj–Bīr Khilṣ 12 hours
4. Bīr Khilṣ–Bīr Ḥiṣān 14 hours
5. Bīr Ḥiṣān–Bīr Shaykh 8 hours
6. Bīr Shaykh–Rābigh 12 hours

All four branches end in Rābigh. This is a large town, in proportion to the neighboring villages, lying about one and a half hours east of the sea. Its main food is vegetables and its climate is very bad. Juḥfa faces Rābigh on its east; there is a distance of approximately an hour between them. Rābigh is the rendezvous where the pilgrims to Medina adopt their ihram. Among those who have visited it were the Imam Abū Ḥanīfa (——) and his followers, and others not from Medina. Juḥfa's climate is worse than that of Rābigh. When the Messenger of Allah [Muhammad] (may Allah bless him, his Family and his Companions)[5] reached Medina, it was glaring hot, so that he prayed for the heat to be transferred to Juḥfa; Allah (—) granted his wish: Medina escaped from the heat, which moved to Juḥfa since that time, and the climate of Medina improved. Muhammad referred to the excellence of Medina's climate by naming it Ṭība and Ṭāba [the good].

Then all four branch roads join into one, leading from Rābigh to Mecca. The distance it covers is 48 hours, or 4 stages according to the [*16*] usual camel speed; according to that of the Syrian caravan, it also has 4 stages:

1. Rābigh–Qaḍīma 14 hours
2. Qaḍīma–ʿAsfān 14 hours
3. ʿAsfān–Wādī Fāṭima 14 hours
4. Wādī Fāṭima–Mecca 6 hours

In ʿAsfān one finds Bīr Tufla, the well whose water was salty and bitter. Then the Messenger of Allah (——) spit (*tafala* [hence the name]) into it, and as a result its water became pleasant and sweet, easy to swallow and drink for everyone. This is one of Muhammad's clear, evident miracles.

The Second Road from Medina to Mecca

It is called the Eastern road (*al-sharqī*).[6] This is the road which does not pass through Rābigh. It is to the east of the Winding [Middle] road. The residents of Medina do not use it on their caravan way to perform the pilgrimage to Mecca, nor on their return. The Syrian caravan, however, uses it considerably. The distance from Medina to Mecca is 140 hours, 11⅔ stages, according to usual camel speed; but according to the pace of the Syrian caravan, it has 12 stages, whose stations are as follows:

5. Hereafter this type of formula "blessing" the Prophet is indicated by a long dash in parentheses (——).
6. Also described in *PNP* (1893) 2: 58 ff.

1. Medina–'Ariḍ 2 hours
2. 'Ariḍ–Khanaq 10 hours
3. Khanaq–Ghurāb 12 hours

[17] 4. Ghurāb–Biyār Ḥajar 12 hours

5. Biyār Ḥajar–Malḥa 12 hours
6. Malḥa–Ṣafīna [Safīna[7]] 12 hours
7. Ṣafīna–Jabalatayn 12 hours
8. Jabalatayn–Bīr Ḥādiba 12 hours
9. Bīr Ḥādiba–Zubayda 12 hours
10. Zubayda–Maḥrūqa 12 hours
11. Maḥrūqa–Wādī Laymūn 14 hours
12. Wādī Laymūn–Mecca 18 hours

GENERAL TABULATION OF THESE ROADS

From Medina to Mecca, according to the pace of the Syrian caravan:

Road	*Travel hours*	*Stations*
Sultan's	123	10
Low	92	10
Branch	126	10
Winding	110	9
Eastern	140	11

From Damascus to Mecca:

[18]

By way of	*Travel hours*	*Stations*
Sultan's road	455	41
Low road	424	41
Branch road	458	41
Winding road	442	40
Eastern road	472	42

7. *TS:* 660.

3. The Geographical Features of the Hejaz Road, Detailing the Stations

Our description of the stations on the Hejaz way is now subdivided into two parts: [1] between Damascus and Medina, and [2] between Medina and Mecca. The stations in the first part, between Damascus and Medina, are of three types [legs].

ROAD STATIONS OF THE FIRST TYPE

This relates to Damascus, Dhū'l-Nūn, Katība, Muzayrīb, Ramtha, Mafriq, Zarqā', Balqā', Qaṭrāna, Ḥasā, ʿAnaza, and Maʿān. The length of the road to Maʿān is 103 hours, as already indicated.

Damascus, sometimes called al-Sha'm [or al-Shām] was the capital of Syria before Islam, since its foundation. It remained the capital of Islam for some centuries,[1] and was titled [*19*] the Noble One. Special books singled out its advantages. It suffices to refer to

1. An exaggeration; it was the capital of the empire solely under the Umayyads, for less than a century (661–750 C.E.).

the traditions, monuments, and information about Damascus, which al-Ḥāfiẓ Ibn ʿAsākir collected in his history book,[2] as did others. I [myself] composed the following poem about it:

> Damascus is a Garden of Eden,
> Flowers surround it.
> Don't you notice how there flow
> Rivers underneath it?

Then I composed yet another poem:

> Damascus was haughty in coquetry
> Above the whole desert,
> With its Umayyad Mosque
> And its Paradise-like rivers!

The abundance in Damascus is obvious and its boons are evident. Only envious, reprehensible, spiteful, sordid, hostile, or criminal persons find fault with it, as well as anti-social types who disobey Allah and His Messenger. Damascus is the stronghold of Muslims and the fort (*kahf* [cave]) of their religion. Whoever wants additional information about this, let him read our book, *The Praiseworthiness of the Time in the Predilection of our Great Messenger for the Text of the Koran.*[3]

The start of the first railway station was made at the Damascus gate now known as the Gate of Allah, formerly called the Gate of Egypt [or Cairo]. Between this gate and Dhū'l-Nūn there is the station where the procession of the pilgrimage comes to rest and the cover of the maḥmil [also *maḥmal*] is replaced. That place is named al-'Asālī, for the great Shaykh Aḥmad al-'Asālī'l-Khalwatī (may Allah have mercy on him, and may his memory be beneficial to us). In that open space there is a small memorial shrine for a saint and a raised outdoor stone bench. [*20*] The distance from the Gate of Allah to this place is ten minutes. A Muslim hospice (*takiyya*) and station are on the east of the road. Facing the road, on its west side, is a village called al-Qadam al-Sharīf (the Noble Foot), thus named after a stone in which there is an imprint of the Prophet's foot (——). This is a mark which he had left there while honoring Syria with his

2. Author of a famous *Chronicle of Damascus* (d. 1176 C.E.).
3. *Ḥamīdiyyat al-zamān bi-afḍaliyyat rasūlinā'l-aʿẓam bi-naṣṣ al-Qur'ān.* The term *Ḥamīdiyyat al-zamān* seems an intentional pun, referring also to the period of Sultan Abdul-Hamid II.

visit, prior to the date he started to prophesy, and reached Boṣrà; then the stone was transferred to al-Qadam's mosque and is there now [see *EI*].

Between al-ʿAsālī and ʿAqabat al-Shujūn, also known as ʿAqabat al-Kiswa, there are two bridges. One of them is over a little stream of al-Maza Canal; the other is above water from al-Bārida Spring. These lands are wonderful to behold; they form a countryside seen from the road. When the road ends its upward climb towards ʿAqabat al-Shujūn, it starts to descend to the lands of al-Kiswa. It crosses on a bridge over al-Aʿwaj, a famous large river. At the side of the western bridge there is the village of Kiswa on an elevation, then the road rises slightly to a plain from which Dhū'l-Nūn is observable. Nowadays there is a military camp in Dhū'l-Nūn, situated on the eastern side of the road; nearby a brook runs to al-Aʿwaj River. Between them and Katība, to the east of the road, is the village of Ghabāghib, in which a spring of warm water gushes; and the village of Ṣanamayn, to the west of the road and Katība. The latter is a village to the east of the road, having a flowing spring, too. On the road's western side, between Katība and Muzayrīb, are the villages of Shaykh Miskīn, in which there is a great torrent, and Ṭafs. Muzayrīb, also on the western side of the road, has springs and a river named Bajta [?], whose water is bad, and in which there are many fish; whoever partakes of them is struck with fever. Ramtha, where there are cisterns for rain water, again is on the road's west. A rivulet flows in Mafriq. Zarqā' has a fort and a large river, [both] west of the road. In Balqā' [*21*] there is a fort and a rain water reservoir, also west of the road. Qaṭrāna has a fort and a cistern for rain water, east of the road. Two and a half hours before Ḥasā there is a slope towards ʿAnaza, in which there is a fort and water collected from rainfall, on the road's west. This road divides the lands of Ḥawrān into halves. Near this are the lands of Jaydūr [?], Lijjā, Jawlān, and Ghawr Bayān. Here the road is about two hours east of the Ottoman administrative center (*mutaṣarrifiyya*) of the Ḥawrān. An equal distance from the road's sides there is some waste land, as well as much empty land, whose soil is as fertile as that of Ḥawrān; furthermore, some of it is better. It has the capacity for growing all sorts of grains, watermelons, cucumbers and grapes, as well as fruit trees and others, particularly the mulberry tree, whose leaves feed the silkworm, and the clove of garlic. These two—mulberry and clove of garlic—if planted there, would multiply in our country. The same is true of the white beet, from which sugar is produced. In some of the neighboring lands, such as Ghawr Bayān, it would be appropriate to plant sugar cane, coffee, tea, and the like; our country spends a great share of its wealth to import these things from India, Japan, and elsewhere. Ghawr Bayān is a place with a warm climate, similar to Hejaz, suitable for planting trees and plants requiring hot land [climate]. It requires care in planting and sowing; the farming of bees and the like may suit it, too.

The Syrian pilgrimage caravan reaches Muzayrīb on 7 or 8 Shawwal. Then, there is a large market there for trading, to which anyone who so desires comes. [*22*] Merchants put up their tents in this market, as do the traders in the Syrian caravan. The latter carry special wares for this market, as well as for others along the way, and sell them there. The people of Ḥawrān, Jaydūr, Lijjā, and Salṭ, as well as Arabs [Bedouins] near these places, up to a distance of three or four days, come [to this market]. They bring camels, wool, and other things with them; they buy from the merchants, and sell what they have brought along to them. In this market one may find whatever one desires, whether edibles, clothes, or other merchandise. This market functions for 18 days. On 25 Shawwal the Syrian caravan leaves Muzayrīb. During these [market] days the Banū Ṣakhr and Wuld ʿAlī [local Bedouin tribes] arrive to take the loads, which they put on the backs of their camels; they [also] bring fodder for the animals and merchandise for the caravan, as will be detailed later. When the Syrian caravan leaves Muzayrīb, the merchants and others leave [too], returning to their places. All this occurs on the Syrian caravan's way [to Medina], but on its return it stops [here] for only a few hours to rest. Most of the pilgrims who ride camels or horses, as well as those whose relatives welcome them in Zarqā', leave the caravan there and proceed to Syria. Therefore the pilgrims do not tarry in Muzayrīb [on their return way] for more than several hours, to let the camels rest; then the caravan continues towards Syria.

There is a distance of six hours between Ghawr Bayān and Muzayrīb. He who goes to the former from the latter passes near Irbid. The lands of the Ghawr (valley [of the Jordan River]) adjoin the Dead Sea (Buḥayrat Lūṭ [Lake of Lot]), the Lake of Tiberias (Birkat Ṭabariyya), the grounds of Jericho, in the district of Jerusalem, and Zarqā', possessed of an immense spring, from which a large river with good water comes forth. Several of the officers of the Syrian caravan carry drinking water [*23*] from it [all the way] to Medina. The soil here is very fertile. After that there are ups and downs in the land, called Qallābāt (changeable [land of]) Zarqā', to be covered in four hours.

Maʿān had been the center of a mutasarrifiyya subject to Syria, before the [administrative] center was moved to Karak. Maʿān is a large town, divided in two by the road on which the pilgrimage passes, the main road for anyone crossing these parts. Its residents have a greenish color. They grow grapes, figs, pomegranates, and other trees. Olive trees grow there [too]. Their number would have increased had the people paid attention to cultivating them in a spirit receptive to civilization, settlement, and progress. The center of Maʿān is commercial. The Syrian caravan stays there for a day, called the Day of Ṭarrāq. During that day a large market is held for trading. Since the fruit of its trees and the produce of its soil remain there [often unsold (a sign of abundance?)], when the passing of the Syrian caravan occurs, or the time of the ripening of fruit arrives, they sell everything they have. Maʿān is near Hebron (may Allah have mercy on Abraham[4]). Its lands [however] extend to Gaza and reach al-ʿArīsh. It is in Maʿān that the pilgrims write letters to their relatives, in which they inform them how they are and what they need, and they send them by post. This is the first mail of the pilgrimage caravan to reach Syria, and it is called the Courier of Maʿān.

Near it is famous Karak,[5] now the center of the mutasarrifiyya formerly in Maʿān. This is one of the best-fortified Muslim strongholds. [It is] on top of a mountain, around which is a large valley with baths, gardens, water, and various trees. One may reach Karak by only one road. The tomb of our Sayyid Jaʿfar al-Ṭayyār (——) is near its access gate. Water is hauled to Karak from the outside. After Karak the countryside is fertile land, most of which [*24*] is vacant. By settling people on this land and caring for it, the wealth of the country and the revenues of the rulers would increase. Its situation is secure, in particular after the construction of the railway reaches it, if Allah (—) so wishes.

ROAD STATIONS OF THE SECOND TYPE

This relates to ʿAqaba, Mudawwara, Dhāt Ḥajj, Qāʿ, Tabūk, Ẓahr al-Mughr, Akhḍar, Janā'in al-Qāḍī, Muʿaẓẓam, Tabrīka, and

4. Buried in Hebron; venerated by Muslims, Jews, and Christians.
5. Not so near! Karak is about 75 miles north of Maʿān.

Madā'in. One covers the distance between all these places and forts in 137 hours. All are suitable for farming and planting trees. Several have wells; some of the lands are sandy. Both the Bedouins and the Syrians do not live there at all, contrary to the villages in Hejaz.

'Aqaba is named Syrian 'Aqaba (*'Aqaba al-Shāmiyya*) to distinguish it from 'Aqaba near the northeastern shore of the Red Sea Gulf [Gulf of 'Aqaba (or Eilat)] which is on the other side of the Bath of Pharaoh in the Gulf of Suez. Syrian 'Aqaba is one half of a degree latitude [north] of it and has a fort, to the west of the road, and a cistern of rain water.[6] When the traveler going to Hejaz crosses it, he will look down on a depression which, on descending into it, he may pass in half an hour. This is why it was named 'Aqaba (steep incline[7]). ([Footnote] It is rather important that the railway line be extended from Ma'ān to Western 'Aqaba on the above-mentioned shore of the [Red] Sea, and from there to Tabūk—for the various advantages of tying it up with the sea. Then this railway line will be connected to the Red Sea, and the use of the Gulf of Suez and the passage through Egypt by land may be avoided. Thus, commerce would increase and it would become possible to employ Ottoman merchant and naval ships, thanks to this connection, renouncing the use of others.)

Mudawwara is where the sand begins. It has a fort and a spring of water, west of the road. Dhāt al-Ḥajj has a fort and a spring of water, on the east of the road; its earth is composed of sand too. Qā' is on the plain, having no fort or water. Tabūk, however, is fertile and suitable for agricultural progress; it has a fort on the right of the road, as well as a flowing spring. A garden wall in it is ascribed [*25*] to the Prophet (——). In this place one finds grapes, palm dates, and other fruit; its soil is fertile. It is said that the Dwellers in the Woods lived here,[8] to whom Allah (—) sent Shu'ayb [Jethro] (may he rest in peace) as a prophet. Shu'ayb was not one of them, but came from Midyan, which is quite close. Tabūk was once settled and populated, but now lies mostly in ruins, having no inhabitants, or extremely few. This is due to its remoteness from both Damascus and Medina, and the absence of soldiers to guard it from attacks by Bedouins or savages [highway-men?]. Pilgrims are accustomed to writing letters to their relatives

6. 'Aqaba al-Shāmiyya is actually almost 45 miles directly east of 'Aqaba on the gulf.
7. One of the meanings of *'aqaba.*
8. K 15: 78, 26: 176, 38: 14, 50: 14. Believed to refer to the land of Midian.

about their return, and dispatching them there with the fifth mail, called the Jūkhadār Courier, their last post [while on pilgrimage].

Ẓahr al-Mughr is on the plain, with no water, fort, or town [to speak of]. On the way, an hour and a half before arriving at Akhḍar, there is the descent to the station. Akhḍar has a fort, west of the road, a well, and a cistern of rain water. Janā'in al-Qāḍī is on the plain, without fort or cistern, except a depression for rain water. Muʿaẓẓam has a fort and a cistern for rain water. Ẓahr al-Ḥamrā' has a fort and a cistern of rain water, also on the west of the road. Tabrīka is a station between two mountains, west and east, without a fort or water. The caravan continuously proceeds among mountains, until it comes to the last one, in Hejaz, ending with a pass between two mountains, about 20 cubits [around 45 ft.] or less [in width], so that it looks almost like a door. When the pilgrims reach it, they cross it to a sandy plain, in which their feet sink, as do the legs of the riding animals, completely. Therefore, the pilgrims encourage the camels to hurry, beating drums and rebuking them in the highest tones. Some people think they beat drums so the camels would not hear the moaning [*26*] (yearning for its mother) of the young weaned camel belonging to Ṣāliḥ,[9] lest the camels kneel and refuse to get up. The truth of the matter is that this custom is inherited *ab antiquo*, lest the camels kneel wearily on the sand, into which they are sinking, and plunge there up to their bellies. The march is feasible only with great effort. When the camels hear the chant of their drivers, the shouting and drum beating, and get struck on every side, they jump with fright and advance. When they reach this pass between the two mountains on their return, it is the custom of the pilgrims to successively recite the Fatiha in their highest voice—until the [whole] caravan has passed—praying for the spirit of those locked behind this door, meaning the pilgrims who had died between this place and Tabrīka on their way or on their return journey. [Returning] pilgrims, upon reaching this place, consider that they are entering Syria and that any disease there may be in the caravan would disappear, with Allah's permission, due to the change of climate.

From this place to Madā'in there is a distance of three hours of [riding on] sand, through which the winds play, moving it from side to side. When a sandstorm surprises the pilgrims they suffer indescribable hardship. The same applies to [their] camels which, in addition to [difficult] going, cannot keep their eyes open. This

9. A prophet (K 7: 73 ff., 11: 61 ff., 26: 142 ff., 27: 45 ff.).

station was named Tabrīka, because the camels kneel (*tabruku*) when they get to its sand. Another version has it that Ṣāliḥ's camel knelt there. (Allah knows more.)

Madā'in is [really] the Madā'in Ṣāliḥ alluded to in the Koran as "You hew houses in the mountains, skilfully." [K 26: 149] This is a large town, carved in stone, wonderful of form; it contains masterful paintings and sturdy sculpture. It is vacant now, with no inhabitants. It is seen on the east of the road of the pilgrimage [*27*] to Mecca. It is not transformed, as many simple folk imagine; Madā'in Lūṭ, the towns of Lot [Sodom and Gomorra], were transformed, not Madā'in Ṣāliḥ.

When the people of Ṣāliḥ wounded the female camel,[10] Allah (—) annihilated them by an outcry. This is how it happened. The Thamūdians, the people of Ṣāliḥ, were long-lived. They were wont to build homes of clay, resulting in their falling down and burying their owners alive. Therefore, they carved houses in their mountains. They asked our Sayyid Ṣāliḥ (may Allah rest his soul) to show them a miracle, to prove that he was a messenger of Allah to them. Then Ṣāliḥ prayed to his Master, Who provided them with the female camel. The miracle was that one day she gave enough milk to enable them to dispense with drinking any water; she herself drank all the water that day, leaving none for them; she left them all the water the second day, so they did not take any of her milk. Allah (—) revealed to Ṣāliḥ they were going to wound the female camel. Ṣāliḥ informed them that he who was going to do it would be a youth with dark blue eyes and fair red hair, who was to be born among them. So they patrolled the village, and whenever they saw a woman in labor, they looked at her baby; if it was a boy, they examined his features, but if it was a girl, they left her alone. Then one day the police found a youth with these features and wanted to take him along. His paternal and maternal grandfathers [however] were [both] from the aristocracy of Thamūd and prevented this. The youth was the worst of the born. His body grew in a day as another's would in a week. Then eight men, who were causing mischief on the earth and benefiting no one, met and demanded that the two grandfathers of the youth make him their leader—due to his standing and the aristocratic character of his grandfathers in relation to them. Then they numbered nine [and] are mentioned in the Koran, "And there were in the town nine, a band

10. According to pre-islamic legends; obviously a terrible misdeed by Bedouin standards.

[*28*] which was causing mischief in the land and benefiting no one." [K 27: 48] Our Sayyid Ṣāliḥ was spending the nights in his place of prayer, not sleeping in the village. When morning came he would go to them, preach, and remind them; and in the evening he would return to his place of prayer. Hence they wanted to doublecross him. So they went to the place where Ṣāliḥ was accustomed to drink. Eight of them hid and said [to one another], When he draws near us, let us kill him, then proceed to his people and contrive a plot against them. Then Allah commanded the earth, and it stood smooth and firm. So they gathered and went to the female camel, while she was standing at her trough. The miserable one said to one of them, Go to it and wound it. So he went to her, but this was too much for him and he desisted. So he sent another, and the same happened. Everyone he sent considered this too much of a feat. Until he [himself] approached her, stretched out and hit her in the two hamstrings; she then fell and lay down. One of the men saw Ṣāliḥ and told him, Go to the female camel, since she was wounded. So he came. Then they came to him, apologizing, O Prophet of Allah! Only a certain person wounded her, there is no sin whatsoever on us. He replied, Search and find her young; if you find it, maybe Allah would lift the punishment off you. So they went out to search it. [However] when the young camel saw its mother reeling, it went to a low mountain named al-Qāra and climbed it. The men went [there] to take it, [but] Allah commanded the mountain and it rose [so high] into the sky that even the birds could not reach its top. Ṣāliḥ [meanwhile] entered the village; when the young camel saw him, it wept; it turned its face and frothed [at the mouth] and cried in rage three times. Then Ṣāliḥ told his people, For every frothing of this camel, [your own] camels will froth [and perish]. Go and enjoy yourselves at home for three days. This is a promise which is not trumped up. But the proof of punishment is that on the first day your faces will turn yellow, on the second red, and on the third black. Indeed, when they got up on the first day, lo, their faces [*29*] were as if daubed by nature; when they got up on the second day, lo, their faces were as if dyed in blood; when they got up on the third day, lo, their faces were black as if coated with tar. Then they all shouted together, Has not punishment caught up with you? When they got up on the fourth day, a cry from the sky reached them and cut out their hearts from their bodies, so that they became corpses in their [own] homes.

Therefore, this Madā'in [Ṣāliḥ] was not transformed, as people who do not know the truth believe. The station of the Syrian caravan is not [right] by it, but rather located near the fort before it, in the direction of Syria. At the station there is a well from which the Syrian caravan drinks. It rests there for a day. It is there that the pilgrims write letters to their relatives on their outbound journey, and they send these with the second mail, which is called the Courier of Madā'in. On its return trip the caravan meets with a convoy of supplies there, as will be detailed further on. A large market is set up [then], which the Bedouins attend; there they sell butter, [fresh] dates, pressed dates, sheep, camels, and fodder for the riding animals.

The people of ʿUlā [El Olla[11]] come there, too. This is a village to the southwest, about six hours away from Madā'in. It is inhabited and grows sweet and bitter lemons, as well as citrons of various kinds, [but] not oranges; it has numerous palm dates, grapes, and other trees and fruits. It has running water. Its people are of dark complexion, inclined to farming and learning [about it]; they are accustomed to leave their place and go to Syria, where they engage in agriculture. Most of those who go to Syria are [about] fifteen years of age, and join the Syrian caravan. When they arrive in Syria they work in agriculture there, some of them possibly engaging in other pursuits. When one of them finds work and saves up some money, he remains in Syria, if he so wishes, and marries. If he wants [*30*] to return to his own village, he buys Syrian manufactured clothes for himself and others, to bring as presents for his relatives and friends. He then takes along the rest of his money and returns home, joining the Syrian caravan. His relatives welcome him, greet him, and extol his merits. He then buys a plot of land, which he plants and farms, and makes into a garden. He may marry; or he may use all his funds for buying land and wait until he gets a return before marrying on the basis of his income.

The people of ʿUlā bring appropriate produce to the Syrian pilgrimage caravan, such as lemons and citrons, which they sell, and with the money they buy whatever they need. They take such crops that they can carry to Medina and sell them there; however, due to the distance, they do not get much revenue [from this]. Consequently, they do not go to Medina solely for trading but, contrariwise, for visiting [the tomb of] the Prophet (——). They take along that part of their produce which would not impede their visit; so that it would be subordinate to their journey, not its [main] aim. Some people, unfamiliar with the facts, assume that the fruit

11. *TS:* 660.

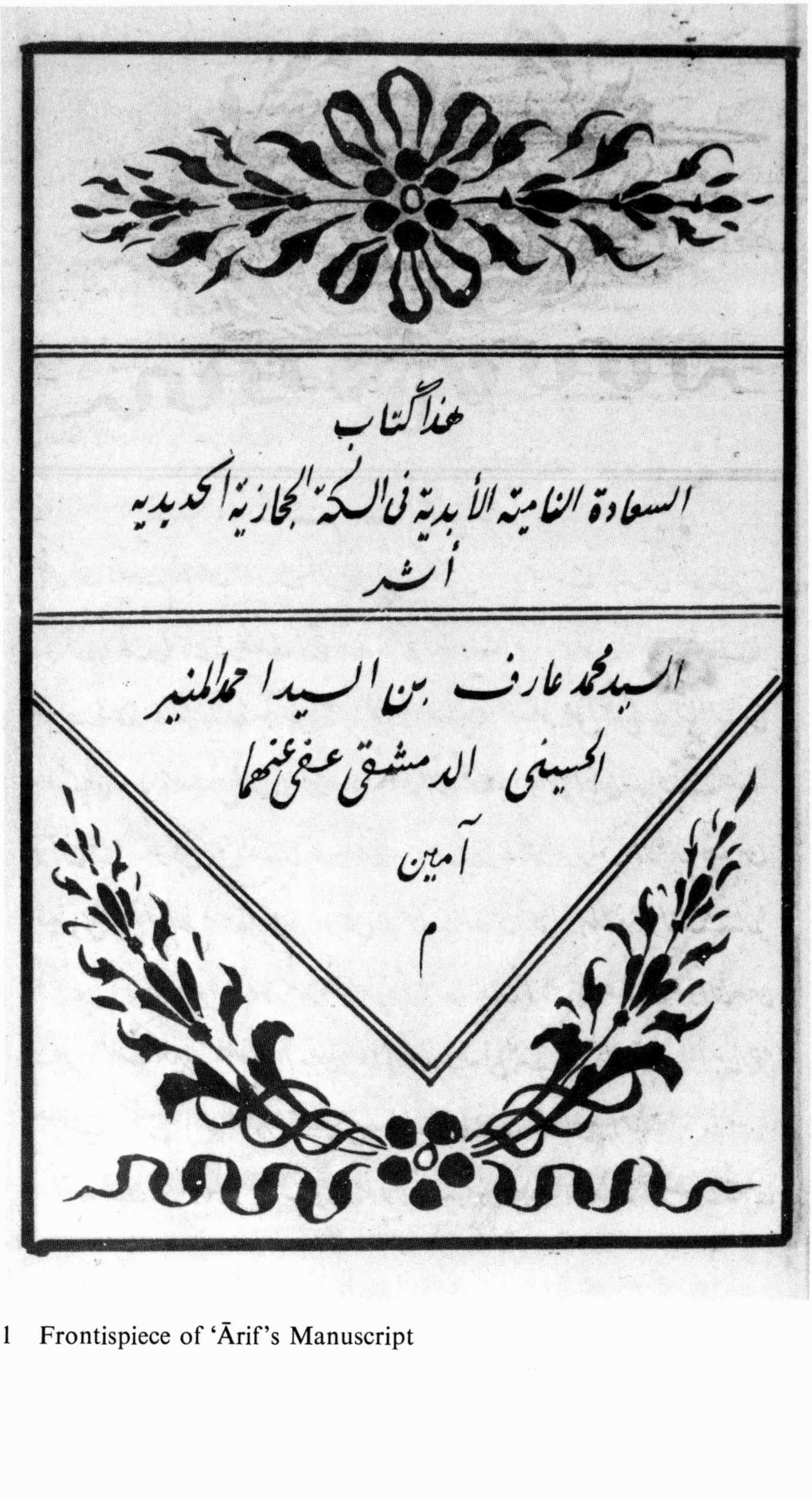
هذا كتاب
السعادة النامية الأبدية في السكة الحجازية الحديدية
أنشد
السيد محمد عارف بن السيد احمد المنير
الحسيني الدمشقي عفي عنهما
آمين
م

1 Frontispiece of ʻĀrif's Manuscript

بسم الله الرحمن الرحيم
نحمدك اللهم يا من مهدت السبل للسالكين   وقومت الطريق للمهتدين
ونسألك يا من فرضت الحج والعمرة وندبت الزيارة   وشرعت
الصناعة والزراعة والتجارة   أن تصلي وتسلم على من سن لنا الشرع
المبين   وأسس السياسة وأحكم الأحكام والقوانين   حجتك القوية
البالغة   ومحجتك القويمة الدامغة   سيدنا محمد الرؤوف الرحيم خير من
هدى الى صراط مستقيم   وعلى أصحابه الذين فتحوا البلاد واستسلموا
العباد   ورتبوا الأمور الدولية   وأحكموا النظامات المرعية   والتابعين
لهم السالكين سبلهم آمين   أما بعد فيقول السيد محمد عارف   ابن المرحوم
السيد الشيخ أحمد المنير الحسيني إمام الشافعية في الشام المحمية   لما من
الله تعالى على عبده   سيدنا ومولانا أمير المؤمنين   خليفة الرسول الأمين

2 The Beginning of ‘Ārif’s Manuscript

(٥٥)

يضربون المرافع وينشدون الأناشيد البدائع ويصلون على النبي صلى الله عليه وسلم
ويحملون التجاميل ومن تجاميلهم قولهم

عبد الحميد سلطاننا عبد الحميد يا عزنا
عبد الحميد مليكنا عبد الحميد خير الملوك

وقولهم

عبد الحميد يا امام يا إمام كل الإسلام
الله ينصرك دوام بالنبي خير الأنام

وقولهم

عبد الحميد لا نهتم أنت سلطان الكرم
كل الناس لك خدم أنت سلطان الأمم

يتصلون في تلك الأثناء الى المابين الهمايوني على تلك الحال ومعهم جمالان غير محملين فيدخلون المابين الهمايوني وتكون تلك المعينة السابقة وغيرها مكملة بانتظار حضورهم جالسين في الغرف العالية المشرفة عليهم وغيرها ينظرون اليهم ويصطف المؤذنون يصلون على النبي صلى الله عليه وسلم الصلاة الابراهيمية ويكبرون تكبير العيد برواية ابن عباس رضي الله تعالى عنه ثم يخرجون المحمل الذي في الخيمة يضعونه على جمل والموسيقى تصدح والعكافة تحمل التجاميل المتقدمة وغيرها والبعض يلعب بالسيف والترس وتلك الفسحة الواسعة غاصة بالموحدين الصادقين والسنتهم رطبة بالدعاء

3 Page 55 of ‘Ārif’s Manuscript

4 Relief Convoy with Water for the Syrian Pilgrimage Caravan (Early 20th Century)

5 Fort of Dhāt al-Ḥajj, a Station on the Syrian Pilgrimage Route

6 Fort of the Tabūk Oasis, a Station on the Syrian Pilgrimage Route

7 Mudawwara, a Station on the Syrian Pilgrimage Route Converted into a Station of the Hejaz Railway

8 Constructing the Hejaz Railway in Southern Transjordan

9 Turkish Soldiers Building and Guarding the Hejaz Railway

10 Railway Track through the Rocks near Der‘ā

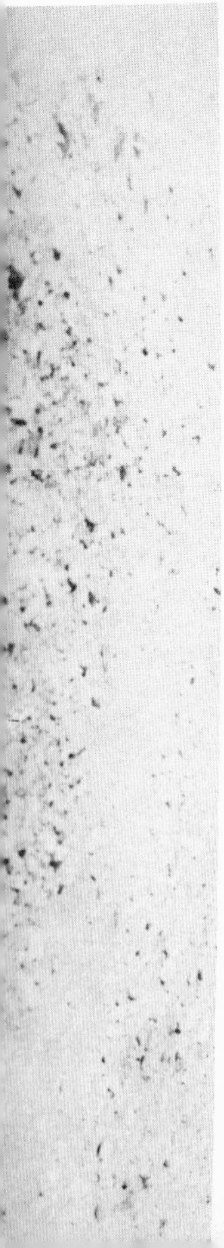

11 Bridge on the Hejaz Railway near Der'ā

12 Hejaz Railway Prayer Car

13 Pilgrims Using the Hejaz Railway Before Completion, c. 1906

14 Pilgrims Using the Hejaz Railway Before Completion, c. 1906

15 The Pilgrimage Road Crossing the Mountains near ‘Aqaba (author’s photo)

and vegetables the people of ʿUlā bring along originate in Madā'in. The inhabitants of ʿUlā follow the Malikite School. Probity, faith and piety rule them; their morals have not been corrupted. They are serious, diligent, zealous, industrious, and receptive to learning [new methods in] farming, manufacture, progress, and civilization.

ROAD STATIONS OF THE THIRD TYPE

This relates to Badā'iʿ, Zumurrud, Jadīd, Barrāqa, Hadiyya, Iṣṭabl ʿAntar, and Ābār Nāṣif. The distance between these stations to Medina is covered in 102 hours. Badā'iʿ is on the plain, with no fort, village, or water. Zumurrud is a fort on the east of the road; it has a well. So does Jadīd, which is a fort on the east of the road, with a cistern of rain water. Barrāqa is a station which has neither a fort nor [*31*] water. Hadiyya is a fort on the east of the road; it is enough to dig a little in its soil and water gushes out, but it is nonpotable. After Hadiyya, near enough, there is a hill of sand which the traveler may climb, and then descend into a depression which can be covered in about half an hour. Iṣṭabl ʿAntar, which is an ancient building on a mountain peak, on the right of the road, is seen from afar. The station has been named after it; it has neither a fort nor water, and the ground is level. Ābār Nāṣīf[12] is a station in which there are several wells, but no fort or village; these wells are to the northeast of the road. Midway between this place and Medina a descent of about two hours starts. Most of the lands of these stations are fertile, despite their being sandy. Wood thickets are numerous, and the Bedouins pitch tents in their vicinity, moving from one place to another and from one desert to another, according to the change of time and season, the suitability of these spots, roadwise and travelwise, and other requirements, such as torrential streams or wells.

Since it is populated, the first type [of road station] has less desert vegetation, compared to the others. In the other two types, however, there are large long and wide thickets on the side of the road, from which travelers cut wood, and do not have to carry it along for more than two stages.[13] These thickets grow and maintain themselves without anyone's caring for them. Their water comes from rain and dew. They can suffice for both the land of the Two Shrines [Hejaz] and Syria, if tended in the same manner like agriculture and given

12. Also called Biyār Nāṣīf herein; both mean wells of Nāṣīf (a man's name).
13. Presumably because more wood is easily accessible farther on.

the proper care. Most trees in these woods are in thickets. If [properly] attended to, they would grow and increase; the government, inhabitants, and country would get revenues and [other] advantages from them. By means of [*32*] the railway, abundant benefits would accrue from these woods. Leaving them as they are is bound to destroy them and their advantages, for trees that are cut are a total loss, unless others grow in their stead, remote from the reach of beasts of burden. All this despite the fact that these lands are suitable for the increase of these woods and that additional trees may be planted, such as oaks; possibly, several fruit trees which can subsist on rain water, for example, grapes, figs, and olives, would fare well there. All this can be easily achieved with Allah's help (—) when the construction of this railway is completed.

FROM MEDINA TO MECCA

Let us now discuss some of the villages [on the road] from Medina to Mecca and detail some of their conditions, even those that are tiny and include two or three houses only.

These are Bīr Darwīsh, inhabited by the Rādda tribe[14]; Bīr 'Abbās, inhabited by the tribe of Riḥala; Wāsiṭa, inhabited by the Ḥawāzim; Badr, inhabited by the Ṣubḥ; Mastūra, inhabited by the Zubayd. Badr is the place where Allah (—) led His Messenger (——) and his Companions (——) to victory and revealed to them the following passage, "Allah led you to victory in Badr, while you were lowly." [K 3: 123] The resting place of the martyrs fallen in [the Battle of] Badr [624 C.E.], the noble, the Companions [of Muhammad], the glorious, is in Badr. When one mentions their name in prayer, Allah (—) grants one's wish. The greatest of Messengers [Muhammad] (——) had pardoned all their earlier and later sins. There is no doubt whatsoever that they continue to exist in their graves until the day when Allah (—) resurrects them. All who have visited them are agreed that the perfume of their graves is sweeter than the fragrant smell of musk. The inhabitants of Badr and the vicinity repeatedly [*33*] heard on Friday and Monday nights, in the hours of the first two watches, the sound of war drums at their tombs (——). Everyone there, young and old, knows that. People would follow the sound; when they stood at the gate of the graveyard, they would hear it; when they entered

14. Not in Kaḥḥāla. Same as Raddāda [see: 7]?

and approached the graves, it would stop; when they went out a little way off from the graves, they would hear it again. All this is certain and verified by the inhabitants of those glorious lands, even by those of Medina and Mecca. Arabs from the ends of the earth come to visit these graves and at the site vow to contribute to charity; they glorify the dead and take utmost care of their tombs. May Allah (—) benefit us, thanks to them!

Other villages are Bīr Māshī, inhabited by the Ṣawā'id; Jabal Ghā'ir, by the Tarājima; Bīr Ḥufāt, by the Lahaba; and 'Ayn Tabra and Bīr Mubayrīk by the Jahm. Still others are Ṣamt, sometimes called Ṣamt Maghribī or Mirbāṭ, inhabited by the Banū 'Awf; Rayyān, by the Banū 'Amr; Abū Ḍibā', by the Jahm; and 'Aqaba, sometimes called Bīr Riḍwān. Others are Qaḍīma, inhabited by the 'Usūm; 'Aṣāliyya and 'Asfān, by the Bashshar [Bešser[15]]; and Wādī Fāṭima,[16] by the Ḥusaynī Sharīfs, descendants of our Sayyid Ḥusayn (——). On the west side of Wādī Fāṭima is a large valley, named al-Maḍīq (mountain pass),[17] inhabited by the Ḥusaynī Sharīfs too, as well as by a part of the 'Utayba tribe. It resembles Wādī Fāṭima in agriculture, planting and trees of all kinds.

Others are Sawāriqiyya, inhabited by Ḥusaynī Sharīfs, descendants of our Sayyid Ḥusayn (——). [*34*] Rābigh has already been discussed. It is the largest of these places. Caravans of all types go there. On its west side are plains, named Baqaliyya, the distance between them being about one and a half hours. Juḥfa is in the area to the east, about an hour away.

To conclude, Ḥudayda, Ṣafrā', and Badr are on the Sultan's road; Rayyān and Abū Ḍibā', on the Branch road. In each one there are flowing rivers and in the other villages there are springs and wells. Palm dates, lemons, bananas, pomegranates, grapes, figs, and others, grow plentifully. There one can find honey, white and fragrant. Wādī Fāṭima and Wādī Laymūn are the most abundant in water. Pumpkins, eggplants, Jew's mallows, purslane, and other vegetables and grains grow in both. They are brought over to Mecca, particularly melons, which are tended at all seasons, as well as cucumbers and gherkins. The sowing of vegetables and other plants there does not follow any set date, as the soil is irrigated by river water. Thus planting may be done at any time. [As to] the soil, dependent on rain water, if there is rainfall and it is soaked,

15. *BBW:* 598; Kaḥḥāla (1: 81) prefers Bishr.
16. See *PNP* 2: 260.
17. See *PNP* 2: 147.

men sow whatever they wish. All the above [products] are farmed in these villages. However, since the crops are not [easily] disposed of—due to their being so remote from Mecca or Medina—the inhabitants take their farming lightly, not working more than they need to. They sell fresh dates, melons, samn, milk, and similar foods, which they have [and can spare], to the caravans passing there. They make and sell palm-leaf fans and leather-covered pillows to the caravans. The people in these villages [*35*] are extremely savage, looking for every opportunity to steal from the caravans. The road in those lands is not safe. The sharif or emir of Mecca guarantees the [security of] convoys and caravans, and on his part, sends one of his men to accompany them, so that the villagers fear his prowess. The railway would bring security to these roads, would populate them, and would introduce the inhabitants to civilization, progress, and industry; it would restrain the recklessness of some of them towards their fellowmen and the raids of all of them on others.

4. *Definitions*

The *rakb*, plural *rukūb* (like *badr* [full moon], plural *budūr*), is a caravan of a group that gathers together to ride on dromedaries, horses, and donkeys, without any borne sedans or other encumbrances. Syrians use this term to refer to the Syrian pilgrimage caravan. [The *rakb* is faster than the *qāfila*.][1]

The *qāfila*, plural *qawāfil* (like *sā'ima* [grazing livestock], plural *sawā'im*), is a caravan of a group that gathers together to ride on camels with loads and sedans. The people of Mecca and Medina use these definitions. The Syrians however apply the term *rakb* [chiefly] to denote the caravan that proceeds from Syria on pilgrimage.[2]

The *hajīn*, plural *hujun*, is a dromedary trained for riding, not for carrying loads; it has great stamina for speed on the march.

The *rahwān*, plural *rahāwīn*, is an Arabian horse specially trained in a riding trot.

1. *MLPNC:* 42.
2. *PNP* (2: 50) interprets *rakb* in the same manner.

The *birdhawn* [plural *barādhīn*] is a non-Arabian horse [mainly a work horse].

The *miḥaffa* [plural *miḥaffāt*] is a litter.

The *shuqdhuf*, plural *shaqādhif*, is a sedan carried on the back of a camel. It is a litter divided into two parts; a man may ride in each part.

The *shibriyya* [cot[3]], plural *shabārī*, is a litter with a partition between its parts, and its shafts are supported on two camels or mules, one behind the other. A man marches on each of its four sides and a fifth man leads the animal in front. The Syrians also use the terms *khashab* and *maḥāra* [for this kind of litter]. In earlier days only the custodian of the purse (*amīn al-ṣurra*) and the superintendent of the pilgrimage (*muḥāfiẓ al-ḥajj*) rode in such a litter [*36*] on two mules; now its usage is unrestricted.

The *maḥmil* [or *maḥmal*] is [a portable shrine] shaped like a little quadrangular house with a kind of cupola firmly raised in its center. In every corner there is something resembling the tip of a flagpole [ball finial] and another one in its center—all these tips being of silver. The [ceremonial] haircloth cover for the maḥmil, adorned with silverwork, is sent by the Ottoman government from Istanbul to Damascus. Whenever the cover wears out, it is replaced by a new one.

3. *PNP* 1: 244.

5. *The Procession of the Syrian Pilgrimage Caravan Through Damascus*

In the past the Syrian pilgrimage caravan has had considerable importance. This was due to the fact that an imperial irade would arrive, appointing one of the greatest dignitaries in Istanbul as amin al-ṣurra (custodian of the purse) on behalf of the sultan. This was established by the late Ottoman Sultan Selim I, as gifts for the people of Damascus [or Syria?], Jerusalem, and the Two Shrines. On 15 Sha'ban several scholars, imams, khaṭībs, and some of the officials in the department of waqfs, proceed to the anteroom of the imperial palace in Istanbul. The amin al-ṣurra presents himself before His Majesty the sultan, the Victorious, the Commander of the Faithful. A group of the pilgrimage officers also have specially arrived from Syria to accompany the amin al-ṣurra to the anteroom. As is customary, they gather there, then set out together in a large procession (to be described later) and go to Scutari. It was here that the march of the ṣurra used to start when it proceeded to Damascus by land via Anatolia. They remain there until [*37*] mid-Ramadan. Then they request permission of the sultan to depart. When the imperial irade arrives, nowadays they travel by sea to Beirut, and thence to Damascus.[1] If the amin al-ṣurra must attend to any such affairs in Beirut as cashing a bill of exchange, he would remain there to settle them; if not, he would proceed directly to Damascus. The wali of Syria, in his administrative council, would have already started to provide for the needs of the pilgrimage to Hejaz: establishing fees and prices for transportation, litters, sedans, seats, and palfreys; appointing muqawwims, those entitled to rent camels and tents to the pilgrims, or bring them water; selecting one of them to be in charge of carrying the maḥmil, the ṣurra, the amin al-ṣurra, the jūkhadār, and other officials of the pilgrimage, such as the superintendent. This muqawwim is called the chief camel-master (*bāsh muqawwim*). This is done with the knowledge [and consent] of the superintendent of the pilgrimage who takes it from and returns it to Damascus. Formerly, the superintendent of the pilgrimage used to be the wali of the vilayet of Syria. One of the duties ascribed to him was to accompany the Syrian pilgrimage to Mecca to supervise it, going and returning, in the same manner that the wali of Tripoli in Syria [now in Lebanon] used to lead the relief convoy (*jurdī*) to meet the Syrian pilgrimage with supplies, as will be detailed later. Two or three days after the amin al-ṣurra arrives [in Damascus] he starts distributing their due to those deserving the charity of the ṣurra, whether in cash, grain, clothes, slippers, shoes, snuff, or other things, according to the written instructions in the ledger he received from the department of waqfs in Istanbul. Then a representative [*38*] of those deserving the ṣurra comes to Damascus from Jerusalem. He brings along legal proof of his being the representative entitled to obtain the charity allotted for the Jerusalemites. Then the Syrian and other pilgrims busy themselves to acquire provisions, clothes, riding animals, fodder, water skins, tents, and the like, that they need. The superintendent of the pilgrimage starts buying what he and his retinue would need in the way of provisions, ammunition, and equipment. He also supplies information to the surgeon-physician the government has appointed to accompany the pilgrimage, to doctor and cure the pilgrims free of cost and to supply them with free medicine. The physician prepares for this and buys whatever medicine and drugs he may need for the pilgrims on the road, so that he may be ready to set out. The pilgrims call him the dispenser of medicine (*al-shāfī* [?] or healer [possibly surgeon (*al-niṭāsī*)]).

1. This change from travel by land to sea dates from 1866; see *PSVSI:* 69.

The pilgrims arrive in Damascus from all sides: Persians, Daghestanis, Turks, and others. They continue to come and get ready until 13 Shawwal. On that day they fetch the olive oil manufactured in Syria, [a present] which they take to the Two Shrines from the village of Kafr Sūsa or other parts of Syria. This is a memorable day, on which people make gay, leave their work, and adorn the camels which are to carry the oil. A large drum is carried on a camel whose two riders beat the drum. [Other] drums and wind instruments [resembling the oboe] are played, preceding this camel. Young and old assemble, carrying long sticks, flourishing swords, shields and sticks, lighting bonfires, singing poems, and reciting prayers for the Chosen Prophet, such as the following:

Let us pray!
  We pray for thee, O Muhammad!
We pray to the kibla from here!
  We pray for thee, our Prophet!
We pray!

They walk before the camels in this manner, from the Gate of [*39*] al-Sarīja to the Gate of al-Jābiya in Damascus, and then into the city proper, up to the market that divides Damascus into southern and northern sections, adjacent to the Market of Chaqmaq, which joins another market extending up the Gate of the Posts and facing the entrance of the revered Umayyad Mosque at its west. Then they proceed to the New Market, pass by the door of the department of war, and continue to the entrance of Government House, which serves as a depot for some of the things pertaining to the pilgrimage.

All the above occurs in the forenoon. When the call to the noon prayer is sounded, the muezzins of the Umayyad Mosque pray—their number being seventy five—followed by muezzins who are not employed there and imitate their example. Afterwards, they all go to the house where beeswax candles are poured, to be taken and lit in the shrines of Medina and Mecca. They enter this house, and the story of the Prophet's birth is retold. Those present are offered sweet pistachios and sugar-coated almonds, so-called dragées (*mulabbas*), along with syrup-water. The military band of the nizam troops comes to that house with its musical instruments. Then people wrap the candles in expensive shawls and respectfully carry them on their shoulders, praising Allah. The military band marches in front, playing delightful tunes; they are followed by the muezzins who recite Abraham's prayer (*al-ṣalāt al-Ibrāhīmiyya*), extol Allah's greatness, proclaim that there is no god but Allah, and sing poems praising the Prophet, with lusty voices and beautiful melodies; then come men carrying on their heads glass bottles filled with local scented rose water and flowers of the Syrian bitter orange; the whole crowd is flanked on all sides by the nizam troops and the gendarmerie with their standard weapons. [*40*] Everyone carries on in this manner up to the depot for the things pertaining to the pilgrimage. All this while the population assembles in the markets, roads and shops, feasting and delighted, praying for the Prophet (——) and wishing the present Ottoman caliphate [sultanate] to continue to reign for many nights and days.

Next day (14 [Shawwal]), the muezzins pray at noon in the Umayyad Mosque, then proceed to army headquarters, where the sanjak (standard or flag) of the pilgrimage is kept. The troops and the gendarmerie assemble there and carry the standard pole and cloth. The military band plays delightful tunes. The muezzins begin to pray, proclaim that there is no god but Allah, and extol His greatness. Several civil and military flags are raised. Men march, carrying censers, several of aloeswood; others carry bottles of orange-blossom and rose water. When the cloth of the standard emerges through the gate of the Military House, a cannon in the fort announces its exit. All that time the markets, streets, shops, and roofs swarm with crowds of all groups and communities. People accompany the standard in the New Market, which faces the gate of the Military House, to the eastern gate of the fort, through which they enter. When the standard enters the fort a cannon fires to announce its arrival. Then everyone proceeds to the mosque in the center of the fort. In this mosque lies the tomb of Abū'l-Dardā' (——), a respected Companion of Muhammad. Those who have not yet prayed perform the noon prayer there. This is termed blessing [Muhammad's name] at noon. Then they drape the cloth of the standard on its pole and carry it, surrounded by military and other insignia. [*41*] They proceed in the same order they entered the fort, until they reach the gate through which they came in. Then a cannon fires to announce the standard is leaving. Afterwards, they march from the fort's northern side, on al-Manākhiliyya (sieve?) to [the Bazar of] the Saddlers, then up to the Mosque of al-Sanjaqdār (standard-bearer), which they enter. When the standard arrives, another cannon is fired from the fort. Upon this, the men enter [the mosque] for the afternoon prayer, while the soldiers, officers, gendarmerie, and civilians look on. When they have completed the prayer and the standard is taken out of the mosque, another cannon shoots, and all accompany the standard. Meanwhile, the road is swamped with people, as are the shops, houses, and other places. Every time a group [accompanying the standard] passes nearby, the crowds get up to honor them and pray for the Prophet (——) until the procession reaches the offices of the [Ottoman] military commander. When the standard passes in through the gate of this house, another cannon salutes it. The people stand in the courtyard of the house. The military commander, the wali, the qadi, the mufti, the ulema who are there, the representative of the naqīb al-Ashrāf, ranking military officers and civil officials, the notables of the city, and others, descend from the highest quarters to the lowest, into the courtyard, and accompany the standard up. When the gathering comes to order and the standard is set in the designated place, parts of the Koran are distributed to those present, who recite the end of the Koran and more [from its beginning], in honor of the Prophet (——). Then they recite the story of the Prophet's birth. Afterwards they are offered dragées and depart. Following the evening meal a similar gathering meets again to recite from the Koran the story of the Prophet's birth, and prayers, but this is a special gathering [of important people].

Next day (15 Shawwal), the ulema, bemedaled notables, ranking military officers, and high officials come in their official uniforms [*42*] to the department of war. Invitations for this occasion had been sent to them by the office of the wali, setting the appointed time after sun[rise?]. The troops had already gone out and stood on the road through which the maḥmil and the military bands were going to pass, from the department of war to the Gate of Allah. Cannons are transported to the outside of this gate, tents are pitched, and chairs are set up in them, at the side of the Mosque of Aḥmad al-'Asālī'l-Khalwatī (the blessed). So the cannons are emplaced near the gate and the people gather in that open space by the thousands, on their feet, in carriages, or riding. They stand in rows on the sides of the road, in shops, houses, mosques, and on roofs. Others march in groups on the road itself, waiting for the arrival of the maḥmil.

When the set hour arrives, the maḥmil is adorned with a cover made of green silk embroidered with intertwined gold and silver. Six large tips of silver are installed on the maḥmil in the department of war, where it is placed on a camel designated for this purpose.

This camel has been fed on fodder for a whole year, as the maḥmil is heavy and only a strong youthful camel can carry it. Then the camel kneels for the maḥmil to be loaded on its back. The muezzins and the students of the military schools stand up to pray for the Prophet (——) to proclaim that there is no god but Allah and that Allah is great, and to perfume with incense of aloewood and ambergris.

As soon as the maḥmil is dressed up, and the camel lifts it, a previously nominated person rides near it. He is the caretaker of the maḥmil (*maḥmiljī*), who gets special appointments from the government for this job. Another man rides on another camel, carrying the standard. Then the military commander, the wali, the qadi, the mufti, the dignitaries among the ulema, high ranking officers and officials, the superintendent of the pilgrimage, and the amin al-ṣurra ride their horses and stand in line according to their rank.

[*43*] The military band sets forth first. It is followed by the cavalry which paces to guard the caravan; then a unit of mounted gendarmerie, then the sedans of the amin al-ṣurra and the superintendent of the pilgrimage, then the ranking dignitaries—two by two—and the amin al-ṣurra himself, bringing up the rear and bidding farewell to the crowd. All wear their official uniforms with their medals. Then comes the representative of the naqīb al-Ashrāf, wearing a green[2] turban, while a few others wear green jubbas. The accouterments of the naqīb's mare and its reins are green; his servants also wear green turbans and green jubbas. The muezzins surround the maḥmil, most of them in front of it, then come the students of the military schools on its four sides, praying for the Prophet (——), proclaiming that Allah is great and that there is no god but Allah. They are preceded by the Mawlawī Dervishes, followers of [the mystic Persian poet] Jalāl al-Dīn al-Rūmī (——), in two long rows—with their shaykh riding in front—praising Allah's name. The camel with the standard paces behind the maḥmil. Sometimes the representative of the naqīb al-Ashrāf has a difference of opinion with the shaykh of the Mawlawī Dervishes concerning precedence, each desiring the other to precede him. Then the ʿAkīl [Bedouin escort tribe] march behind the maḥmil and the standard, carrying one or more flags and drums, which they play; they chant in their own style in groups answering one another while they ride male and female camels.

2. Distinctive color for the Ashrāf, descendants of the family of Muhammad.

All that time the caravan is advancing at a leisurely pace in this order. When the maḥmil sets out from the gate of the department of war, twenty-one cannons in the fort salute it. The caravan proceeds thus, with an officer called the head of protocol (*teshrīfatjī*) in its midst. He watches over everyone, holding a written paper that lists the names of the riders and their ranks. If one of these rides either before or after his appropriate place, he makes him return to it. When the maḥmil reaches the small mosque built over the tomb (*zāwiya*) of Saʿd al-Dīn al-Jibāwī [*44*] (may Allah (—) hallow his secret[3]) in Upper Square (al-Maydān al-Fawqānī), it is taken near the mosque's window, whose shaykh awaits the procession there. He holds in his hand a large mouthful of almonds and sugar, which he feeds to the maḥmil's camel. The common people snatch these sweets from the mouth of the camel and munch them, [wishing] to be blessed thereby; they are unaware that these sweets have been defiled by the camel's mouth, which renders food impure by chewing it. Afterwards, they all proceed unhurriedly and leave through the Gate of Egypt [or Cairo]. All the way from the offices of the military commander up to this place, people as numerous as a plague of locusts line the road. When the maḥmil passes before the soldiers lined up along the road to welcome it, they raise their hands, acclaim it, and play music to greet it. Whenever the procession reaches men who are seated [dignitaries who did not have to stand?], everyone stands up and prays for the Prophet (——). Then they touch the maḥmil and rub their faces with their hands, as a sign of blessing. Many weep from their desire to join the pilgrimage and visit the [Two] Shrines. Some people give a handkerchief to a student of a religious school, or to someone else, for him to rub it on the maḥmil and return it to them, as a sign of blessing. When the maḥmil reaches the tents [mentioned above], those who have outstripped it greet it there—the military commander, the wali, and others. This is because the real leader of this procession is the amin al-ṣurra. When they make the camels kneel down the artillery hurries to fire a twenty-one gun salute to announce the procession has arrived at the station. They place the maḥmil in front of the tents. Then the ulema, ranking officers, and others present, drink coffee, syrup, or tea. They all return home, after having prayed for the Commander of the Faithful, the pilgrimage, the military expeditions, and the travelers. Then they take off the maḥmil's silk curtain, embroidered with gold and silver, and adorned

3. Customary formula after mentioning the name of a deceased holy man.

with its six silver tips. This is stored in [special] chests, another green curtain is placed over the maḥmil, and the cloth of the standard is also placed in a chest.

[*45*] After a brief while the maḥmil proceeds from al-'Asālī to the station of Dhū'l-Nūn, then to Muzayrīb. The soldiers, cannons, military band, superintendent of the pilgrimage, amin al-ṣurra, and the 'Akīl return to Damascus. The maḥmil remains in Muzayrīb, along with soldiers appointed to guard the caravan during its travels, all waiting for the pilgrims, the superintendent, and the amin al-ṣurra. Meanwhile, pilgrims from Persia and elsewhere, latecomers all, arrive in Damascus and bargain with those appointed to rent beasts of burden. On 22 [Shawwal] the pilgrims, local people and foreigners, start on their trip to Muzayrīb. It is a memorable day when the borne chairs, litters, and loads leave, but less so than the day of festivities for the maḥmil. Then the superintendent and the amin al-ṣurra proceed to Muzayrīb. The Bedouins of Banū Ṣakhr and Wuld 'Alī come, carrying supplies, fodder, and the like, all of which is called the load (*al-ḥamla*), as has been mentioned. The Bedouin shaykhs, whom the Ottoman government has favored with money and certain commodities—via the kīlār—attend and take these gifts.

Large crowds gather in Muzayrīb, as already mentioned. These three days of the candles, the standard, and the maḥmil—and the day the pilgrimage caravan sets forth—are memorable days in Damascus and its vicinity. Crowds from all the neighboring villages and even nearby towns, such as Beirut, Sidon, Homs, and Hamah, flock to Damascus. Crowds are present in Damascus to witness these days; afterwards, they return to their homes. On 28 or 29 [Shawwal] the caravan leaves Muzayrīb for Ramtha.

All this was so in earlier times. Nowadays, on 3 Shawwal there are the festivities of the candles, while as a whole those of the oil have been canceled, despite the importance formerly attached to them. On 4 [Shawwal] [*46*] there are the festivities of the standard, according to previous custom. On the fifth the crowds and troops rejoice with the maḥmil; but the military commander, the wali, the qadi, and the mufti do not ride horses at the procession's head; rather, before the procession they ride to the station in their carriages wearing their official uniforms, both on the caravan's going and on its return. They proceed to the tents at the above-mentioned station of 'Asālī and greet the amin al-ṣurra; the superintendent of the pilgrimage, however, has arrived earlier and then he returns to the station [after the greetings?]. They sit awhile, then leave in their carriages before the procession. In the same fashion [nowadays] most of the dignitaries do not ride in the procession at all. Some of them imitate the military commander and the wali, and also ride in carriages. This is a result of personal grudges and individual ambitions, which cannot be listed in detail here.

The departure of the pilgrimage from Damascus on 5 Shawwal is performed only according to an imperial irade from our master, the Commander of the Faithful, the caliph of the trustworthy Prophet (——), the sultan, son of Sultan al-Ghāzī (Victorious Conqueror) ʿAbdul Hamid Khan, son of the late Sultan al-Ghāzī ʿAbdul Majid Khan. The sultan writes the irade in his own name, to obtain the blessing of all believers for His Majesty, that the divine solicitude continue to be bestowed on him and that godly protection continue to preserve him. In this way the pilgrimage caravan sets forth from Muzayrīb on 25 [Shawwal]. This irade is the very essence of sagacity.

The pilgrims used to endure crowding and discomfort on the road to an excessive extent, due to their having been delayed in Damascus until the 15th and in Muzayrīb until the 28th or 29th. In consequence, they had to proceed energetically, night and day, so that they might show up in Mecca for the pilgrimage days [rites]. Nowadays, however, they have an additional ten days, during five of which [*47*] they remain in Muzayrīb to attend to their affairs; and another five on the road. This is thanks to the minute attention of His Majesty [the sultan] and his care for the interests of his subjects [by having the arrangements start earlier, thus] enabling them to reach Mecca two or three days before the pilgrimage days in a wholly leisurely fashion.

Afterwards the maḥmil remains covered with the same green cloth up to the arrival of the caravan in Medina. When it reaches Ābār [Wells of] ʿUthmān (——), that is, two hours before Medina, tents are pitched and the caravan is welcomed there by the officials of Medina, its ulema and leaders. The cloth cover is removed from the maḥmil, which is then draped with its green silk cover, embroidered with gold and silver, and its six silver tips are placed above. A long procession is formed by the inhabitants of Medina, the amin al-ṣurra and the superintendent of the Syrian pilgrimage. It enters Medina by the Syrian Gate and proceeds until it reaches Bāb al-Salām. The superintendent of the pilgrimage, wearing a white turban, holds the reins of the camel carrying the maḥmil.

Afterwards, people unload the maḥmil from its camel, bring it into the shrine and place it facing Bāb al-Salām there, opposite the Purified Room. As to the standard, they place it inside the noble Purified Room, until the day the caravan proceeds on its journey, when people take it out in a long procession to the station. There they remove the ceremonial cover and drape it with the green cloth, until they arrive in Mecca. They descend there to the station of Shaykh Maḥmūd, which the inhabitants of Mecca call Shuhadā' (martyrs).

On Yawm al-Su'ūd, the day the maḥmil ascends into Mecca, it is draped with its embroidered silk cover. Along with the standard, it is taken in a long, festive procession to [Mount] Arafat. They are brought back after sunset on the Night of the Immolation [10 Dhu'l-Hijja]. A part of this way passes [through the valley of] Minà, imitating the maḥmil from Egypt in the process. Indeed, the Egyptian maḥmil [advances] on the left side of the Syrian one. The cannons in both the Syrian and the Egyptian caravans fire from Arafat until they reach Minà. The maḥmil remains there in its [ceremonial] cover [*48*] until the second of the three days following the Day of Immolation. They return to Mecca in this manner. When they bring it to the gate of the shrine of Mecca known as Bāb al-Nabī or Gate of the Prophet (——), they take it down from the back of the camel. Then they bring the maḥmil into the shrine, facing the above-mentioned gate, under the stoa. They drape it with the green cloth, its usual accouterment on the road. It remains there until the day of its setting forth; this differs from Medina, where it lay in state draped by its embroidered silk cover, with its silver tips, and the standard.

A long procession accompanies the maḥmil [from Mecca] to the station of Shaykh Maḥmūd, draped by its green cloth all the way to Medina. It is welcomed [in Shaykh Maḥmūd] and everyone comes to the station at the Syrian Gate, where the maḥmil and the standard are draped with their embroidered silk covers and brought to Medina, as in the outbound journey. When the caravan finally reaches the station of ʿAsālī, outside Damascus, festivities are organized as on its outbound journey. However, they now take only one day at the station of ʿAsālī. People accompany it to the department of war, then carry the standard in a large ceremony, complete with military music and muezzins, up to the Umayyad Mosque. There they all stand facing the mausoleum of our Sayyid Yaḥyà [John the Baptist] (may he rest in peace), reciting the Fatiha prayer, while the muezzins pray for the Prophet (——). Then they proceed to the shrine of al-Ḥusayn (——), where his noble head lies in a cupolated memorial built over it. They leave it [standard or maḥmil?] and depart. People visit it for three days. Then they remove its cover, fold it, and take it to the depot of the pilgrimage caravan.

When the custom of bringing the ṣurra by land was changed, [*49*] the number of pilgrims decreased, and overland trade between Scutari and Damascus suffered. Earlier, the Syrian pilgrimage caravan would include about fifty borne chairs and litters and a proportionate number of riders and pedestrians. Now, however, barely one or two borne chairs may be found; perhaps not even one rider would travel with it idly, both ways [but most go along on business or for lucrative appointments]. Earlier, a great crowd would walk before the caravan; called the pious ones (*ṣalaḥa*), they would sometimes outnumber the caravan at that time. The 'Akīl were a group of eastern Bedouins from the Najd, living in the Maydān quarter of Damascus, which the authorities would appoint to convoy the caravan. They would follow it—rescuing those who got separated from the caravan, directing those who lost their way, picking up whatever fell down and returning it to its owner—oppose any Bedouins who attacked the caravan, and fight them. This was their job in former times and this was what they were expected to do. Now, however, we do not know [if this continues].[4] The people of Syria in particular show considerable interest in the pilgrimage and visiting [the tomb of] the Prophet (——). Even youngsters, who are barely thirteen years of age, run away from their families and go on foot to perform the pilgrimage. Some Syrians go on pilgrimage thirty or forty times, or more. Some join the Syrian pilgrimage caravan solely to visit [the Prophet's tomb]; when they reach the soil of Medina, they remain there until the caravan returns [from Mecca] and then go back with it, or wait for the [next] caravan. My paternal uncle Muḥammad al-Munīr (——) did this, studied a book by the Qāḍī 'Iyāḍ there "in the pure garden," and then returned.

[Appended note] Information. Al-Ḥajjāj al-Thaqafī[5] was the first person for whom maḥmils were arranged, with pilgrims to ride with them.

4. A roundabout way of implying that the 'Akīl did not perform their duty conscientiously any more.

5. Al-Ḥajjāj Ibn Yūsuf al-Thaqafī, famous late 7th century C.E. Umayyad governor in the eastern provinces of the empire.

[50] # 6. The Ṣurra Procession in Istanbul and Related Matters

Know that the first to arrange and establish the imperial ṣurra was the late Sultan Selim I al-Ghāzī (may Allah (—) rest him in peace, with His mercy and grace), as already mentioned. From that time to the present, the Ottoman sultans have kept it up (may Allah (—) perpetuate their reign to the end of time).

At the beginning of the year an irade of His Imperial Majesty, the greatest caliph, is issued, appointing the amin al-ṣurra from among the [important] men of Istanbul. He is actually an official representing His Majesty, our master the sultan, in transmitting the stipends of the imperial ṣurra to their recipients, according to the lists the department of waqfs furnishes, copied from the records kept in the department. When he is appointed, the leader of the drivers of the pilgrimage caravan (*'akkāms*) and the Syrian drivers take red, green, and white flags, and hang them on the wall of his house, above the door, to make it known that the owner of the house is the amin al-ṣurra for the year. These flags remain there until he proceeds to Scutari. Then the müjdeci—the man who takes all the letters and the deposits-in-trust from the imperial anteroom to the Two Shrines, both ways, as well as from [private] people, besides those arranged for, and paid by the government—is appointed, as also are the quftānjī and the mubashshir, all of whom will be discussed later. Afterwards, the department of waqfs begins to prepare the stipends —in money, clothes, and the like—for the ṣurra.

The drivers who have come from Damascus with the former amin al-ṣurra, upon his return, now gather. [*51*] They beat on drums which, in their own terminology, they call *marāfi'*. Two of them carry an object resembling an oblong box (which they [themselves] make) shrouded in a green cover, and in whose corners flags are inserted. They also carry a little standard [while] chanting and praying for the Prophet (——). They call the chanting *tajmīla*, plural *tajāmīl* (adornment). They make the rounds of the streets of Istanbul and all the quarters of the straits and the gulf—street by street and market by market. Every time they reach the house of an important person, a known merchant, or a government official, they put that box-like object in front of the house and stand [there], chanting and blessing its owner. The latter then sends them some money or if he and his men are absent, the women throw them some money wrapped in a handkerchief through a window [and thus do not reveal themselves to strange men]. In this manner they proceed farther and farther from house to house. Meanwhile, the middle of the month of Shaʿban draws near. On 14 Shaʿban they gather at their [usual] residence above one of Istanbul's forts. They put on their long jubbas and carry drums and several small flags. They also have a maḥmil similar to the Syrian one, on which they place a green cover embroidered with yellow silk, which they call a *thawb* (cover). It is carried on a mule or a camel. [Simultaneously] the litter of the amin al-ṣurra, which will be taken to Damascus for him to ride in during the pilgrimage, is [loaded] on two mules, and the leader of the drivers rides a mare, followed by his crowd, who chant tajāmīl, beat marāfiʿ and flourish sticks, swords, and shields. In this manner they proceed to the gate of the commander-in-chief (*ser ʿasker*), and the leader enters the courtyard of his palace. All the while they flourish their swords, shields, [*52*] and sticks, beat marāfiʿ, and chant tajāmīl. The commander-in-chief orders remuneration to be given to their leader. Afterwards, they proceed to the department of finance, then to the department of waqfs, then to the Sublime Porte, where their leader enters the anteroom. The grand vizir, the ministers of finance and waqfs, as well as other [dignitaries], award him some remuneration. Then they go from the Sublime Porte directly to the New Bridge, Galata, and Tophane [quarters], then to the Mosque of Dolma Bahçe. There they take down the quasi-maḥmil and the litter. They enter the mosque, where they are served dinner from the [adjacent] kitchens [of the palace] of the sultan. They spend the night there.

Meanwhile the department of waqfs has already completed writing the registers, prepared the money requested, and placed everything in boxes. On that very day it sends these [things], loaded on mules and nags, to the anteroom [of the imperial palace]. They put red curtains on the above-mentioned boxes and then place them in a tent pitched there. (This year [1900] the boxes numbered 58, carried on the backs of 29 beasts of burden, two on each.) On the very same day two large pavilions are pitched in the anteroom, facing the women's quarters of the palace. They are furnished with two large rugs and with chairs covered with expensive silk, and are decorated with many-varied adornments. Candles are lit in both pavilions and perfumes released—all this indicating high respect and concern. Near these two pavilions are the offices of the agha of Dār al-Saʿāda.

Afterwards there comes out of the anteroom an object [the maḥmil] resembling an octagonal dome, from whose angles there protrude [*53*] sticks about two-thirds of a cubit long [about 18 in.], and adorned by a costly curtain; it is placed in one of the two pavilions. Later, half an hour after sunset [or sunset prayer], the following personages gather in the anteroom: His Majesty the sultan's first and second imams, the supervisor of the anteroom, the mābeyinjī (court chamberlain), the bāsh kātib (chief clerk), some of the distinguished ulema, khaṭibs, and imams of the mosques, and the muezzins of the anteroom. The two imams of the sultan, an alim designated by the ulema, and memorizers of the Koran from among the muezzins possessed of melodious voices (who cause discriminating people to marvel) enter a room specially set apart for them. They sit down and an alim recites a verse from the Koran, interprets it, tells an oral tradition [in the matter] and explains it, and then ends with a special prayer appropriate for the occasion. It is, indeed, the custom of the ulema of Istanbul to pray on every festive occasion in a suitable manner; this is a good custom. Afterwards, when all this is completed, the first imam [of the sultan] starts reciting several verses from the Koran, then one of the memorizers of the Koran recites ten verses from the beginning of the Chapter of the Cow [K. ch. 2] and then is silent. After this the first imam prays for [or blesses] our sultan, the greatest. Then they get presents, prepared for them according to an annual custom, and the two imams and the alim leave the room. The others proceed to the pavilion with the maḥmil. There the imams, khaṭībs, and the other muezzins have already gathered. They sit down with them and one starts reciting the Chapter of Victory [K. ch. 48]. When he completes reciting the first verse, the rest of the memorizers of the Koran halt with him, and someone else recites the second verse, and so forth; everyone recites one verse until the end of the chapter. Perfumes are released. Later, one of those present offers a special prayer, then sugared water and sweets are served all around. In the other pavilion [meanwhile] the agha of the sultan's palace is seated [*54*] with people connected with the imperial anteroom. When the recital from the Koran and the prayers end in the first pavilion, the assistant of the agha of the sultan's palace comes in, together with a scribe carrying a register which lists all the gifts to be distributed that night and the names of those who are to receive them. Everybody gets a present, takes it, blesses His Majesty the Commander of the Faithful, and departs. Only one group remains in the pavilion, reciting the Koran and blessing the memory of the Prophet (——); and perfumes are released, until morning. Then the group leaves the pavilion, which remains empty. Later, women from the imperial harem arrive, bringing along silk fabrics embroidered with gold and silver, as well as valuable embroidered kerchiefs and other things, which they hang over the maḥmil. They recite the Fatiha, bless the memory of the Prophet, and offer the reward due them as a gift to his pure, noble soul. As soon as they leave, high dignitaries of the state arrive: the shaykh al-Islām and the grand vizir [side by side], and others. They enter a room specially set aside for them. Then the ulema, memorizers of the Koran, imams, khaṭībs, and muezzins return and recite the Chapter of Victory, verse by verse, within earshot of His Majesty, the Commander of the Faithful (may Allah (—) encompass him with His protection). Afterwards, one of them prays, as on the preceding night. Then the ever-victorious soldiers parade with military music. The military band lines up in an open space in front of the two pavilions. Then they chant greetings to the sultan. The leader of the drivers and his people carry the maḥmil and the litter of the amin al-ṣurra, and raise the standards they have brought along. The whole crowd moves from Dolma Bahçe directly to the imperial anteroom, headed by the leader of the drivers, who is riding, while everyone else follows him in the manner of the previous day, [55] beating on drums, singing wondrous songs, blessing the memory of the Prophet (——), and making up tajāmīl, such as the following:

> ʿAbdul Hamid is our sultan,
> ʿAbdul Hamid is our glory,
> ʿAbdul Hamid is our king,
> ʿAbdul Hamid is the best of kings!

or

> ʿAbdul Hamid, O imam,
> O the imam of all Islam,
> May Allah let you always triumph
> With the Prophet—best of humans!

or

> ʿAbdul Hamid, don't worry,
> You are the sultan of noble nature,
> All people are your servants,
> You are the sultan of the nations![1]

Thus they arrive, in the meantime, at the imperial anteroom, accompanied by two camels free of load. The people then enter the imperial anteroom. The previous group and other persons are expecting their arrival, sitting in the upper rooms and others overlooking them [the new arrivals], and gazing at them. The muezzins line up, while praying Abraham's prayer in memory of the Prophet (——), praising the greatness of Allah, and retelling the story of Ibn ʿAbbās (——). Then they bring out the maḥmil from the pavilion and place it on the back of a camel. The military band chants, the drivers make up tajāmīl or sing old ones, and some people fence with swords and shields. The large place overflows with sincere Muslims; their tongues are wet with blessings [56] for His Majesty, the Commander of the Faithful. Then the amin al-ṣurra follows, with customary etiquette. An imperial irade arrives, ordering him to take a letter from the sultan to the emir of Mecca. He receives it, descends from his place [in honor of the sultan's missive], and gives it to his assistant responsible for administering such matters, called his *kikhya* (steward). The muezzins, as beforehand, praise Allah's greatness and bless the memory of the Prophet (——). The military band plays. The people in the imperial anteroom stand up—the aghas, the imams, the khaṭībs, and the soldiers. The agha of the

1. Or: You are the sultan of all communities [Muslim and others?].

sultan's palace, holding batons, conducts the affairs in this great gathering and grand spectacle, and orders what should and should not be done.

Then there ride groups of soldiers, khaṭībs and imams, and the amin al-ṣurra and his assistant, carrying the sultan's above-mentioned letter, several officials of the department of waqfs, and the inspector of waqfs, in their official uniforms and Ottoman decorations. The soldiers march first in the procession in two parallel rows. Between them are the imams and khaṭībs, then the officials of the department of waqfs, then the assistant of the amin al-ṣurra, carrying the sultan's letter in his hand, lifting it opposite his chest. Afterwards there come the amin al-ṣurra, the inspector of waqfs, the former's litter, and the maḥmil, crowned by the fabrics hung on it in the imperial anteroom; indeed, the curtains of the maḥmil are hardly seen because of the many things hung on it that morning. Then comes the imitation Syrian maḥmil. All this is surrounded by muezzins, praising Allah, proclaiming His greatness and praying—from the imperial anteroom to their arrival at the Beshikṭāsh Iskele (pier), where a steamship has been waiting to convey everybody to Scutari.[2] When the maḥmil enters the ship, twenty-one cannons salute from the seaside. Then the ship takes the people to Scutari. When the maḥmil is brought out there, another twenty-one cannon salute is given to proclaim its arrival. [*57*] The mutasarrif of Scutari, his lieutenant and other government officials, and local dignitaries, along with crowds of people, have been awaiting its arrival there. The government officials in Scutari join the procession and march up to Government House. There they bring down the maḥmil, the imitation maḥmil, and the amin al-ṣurra's litter, and stay for a while at Government House. Then they depart and return the [imitation] maḥmil to the imperial anteroom in an unofficial manner; the imitation maḥmil remains in Istanbul until the following year, while the litter of the amin al-ṣurra stays in Scutari until he sets forth and takes it with him. The drivers also remain in Scutari. The amin al-ṣurra returns to his home to complete his work [in preparation for the pilgrimage], as does also the müjdeci. The latter takes charge of the letters and money-trusts from the imperial anteroom and the residents of Istanbul to the people of the Two Shrines; these moneys are exclusive of those in the appointed ṣurra. The quftānjī receives a jubba as a gift for the sharif of

2. Pierre Loti (*Aziyadé* [Paris n.d.]: 75–76) gives a shorter description of this ceremony, c. 1876.

Mecca. In the middle of Ramadan the amin al-ṣurra presents a petition to His Majesty the sultan, asking for permission to set forth [on pilgrimage]. Then an imperial irade is granted and a steamship is prepared for them by the relevant Ottoman department, in which they sail to Beirut, which they reach [in about a week] early in the last decade of Ramadan. From Beirut they all proceed to Damascus except the quftānjī, and thence with the Syrian pilgrimage to Hejaz.

THE DUTIES OF THE AMIN AL-ṢURRA

The amin al-ṣurra receives 500,000 piasters for expenses. Of this sum, he earmarks 50,000 for the expenses of the caravan taking him to Beirut. Then he gets the imperial ṣurra, from the treasury of the waqfs. The müjdeci goes with him. When they arrive in Beirut, if the amin has a [*58*] draft on the treasury, he stays awhile to cash it; if not, he proceeds forthwith to Damascus. There he distributes the allocations to those listed in the register he carries with him. Every recipient signs under his name. If one of these has died [meanwhile], his children—or someone else—get it in his stead. Nowadays the council of administration for Syria prepares the directions [for disbursing these funds]. Formerly, this depended solely on the decision of the amin al-ṣurra. Everything is recorded [nowadays?] in the directions determined in the provincial council of administration. An official comes from Jerusalem, bringing along a power-of-attorney (certified by the sharʿī court [there]) from those who are to receive allocations. He obtains their allocations, as detailed in the pertinent register. The amin al-ṣurra gives this official the register he received from the department of waqfs, together with the allocated funds. The official takes them and proceeds to Jerusalem, where he distributes the allocations to the recipients, according to the register. Each recipient signs under his name. Then the official sends the register back to Damascus, and the amin al-ṣurra gets it upon his return [from Hejaz].

When the amin al-ṣurra arrives at the Madā'in station, a representative of the Ibn al-Rashīd tribe comes to receive the gift of His Majesty, the sultan, the greatest caliph, the Commander of the Faithful, ʿAbdul Hamid Khan, the sultan of this era. This amounts to 30,000 piasters for himself [the chief of the tribe] and another 6,000 for his retinue, together with a mantle embroidered with silver for himself and thirty mantles for his retinue. For all this the amin obtains receipts, as is customary. After having entered Medina, blessed the Prophet and prayed for him, he hands over the register pertinent to the residents of Medina, along with the allocated funds, to the keeper of the shrine of the Prophet, who [*59*] distributes the funds. Everyone who gets them signs in the register under his name. The register is held for the return of the amin al-ṣurra, who then takes it with him.

The same procedure is followed in Mecca. The amin hands the register and the funds he has brought to the keeper of the shrine in Mecca. Before he leaves Mecca he gets the register back and returns with the Syrian caravan to Damascus. There might still be found, as in earlier times, among the agents of the amin al-ṣurra, some who would pay extra money out of their own pocket—additional to the allocated funds—to the ulema, sharifs, and venerable elders (*mashā'ikh*). They would put this in a purse, tie it up and present it to them, endeavoring in this manner to impress their hearts and obtain the beneficence of their prayers, for the sake of the Commander of the Faithful, the Ottoman government, and themselves. Some of these [however] do not attend to such charity, but rather go [on pilgrimage] for gain from their status as agents [of the amin al-ṣurra]. (Anyway, praise to the One who changes [everything] and does not change [Himself]; He is the One who remains forever, while everything else perishes!)

Then the amin al-ṣurra takes a steamship to Istanbul, where he kisses the feet of the greatest caliph and presents him with a bottle of Zamzam water [famous well near Mecca] and with dates from Medina (blessed be its Resident [Muhammad], his Family and Companions). The sultan accepts both and thanks Allah (—) for His grace to His Majesty (the sultan). When the amin al-ṣurra reaches his own home, his gate is painted green; the same is done for the gate of every pilgrim, to announce that he has performed the pilgrimage and to express joy for his safe return.

THE MÜJDECI AND HIS DUTIES

The müjdeci is the person who takes the letters, donations, and gifts, from the imperial anteroom and the inhabitants of Istanbul to the official attendants, litigants, those to be visited [in Hejaz], and some of the residents [*60*] of Medina (on whose elevated site he prays and blesses the Prophet, his noble Family and great Companions), as well as to some of the pilgrim guides (*muṭawwif*), guards of the Zamzam Well, and residents of Mecca. He himself is but a "chief coffeemaker" (*kahwajī pasha*) in one of the palaces of the sultan's family. It has been the custom to place those allocations in leather pouches, on each of which the name of its owner is inscribed, with the name of the intended recipient—attendant, litigant, resident of Mecca, pilgrim guide, Zamzam guard, and others. The recipient's name is written on one side of the pouch, the sender's on the other. The müjdeci hands over pouch and letter. The people of Mecca come forth and take their trust [funds] and letters from him after the pilgrims' visit to [Mount] Arafat. Then they return the pouches to him, with presents they have selected and liked; the Zamzam guards send Zamzam water with him, too. The residents of Medina who received their trusts and letters [when the outbound pilgrimage caravan stopped there] await the return of the müjdeci from Mecca. They place gifts in the leather pouches, as they wish, everyone on his own account or as a return present for that sent to him, such as rosaries, signet rings, perfumes, and the like, together with heaps of Medina dates, splendid and abundant. These they hand over with letters for the owners of the pouches.

The müjdeci had received these pouches and letters in Istanbul, via the department of waqfs, according to a register in which they were recorded. The owners are given a numbered piece of paper, listing the date of receipt. When he returns to Istanbul the müjdeci delivers the letters and gifts he has brought, through the department of waqfs also, [*61*] according to the documents he has brought. (The number of pouches sent through him this year [1900] from Istanbul to Medina was 870, to Mecca 560, and an equal number of letters for the recipients.)

THE DUTIES OF THE QUFṬĀNJĪ AND THE MUBASHSHIR

The qufṭānjī is appointed annually to carry the jubba or cloak dispatched on behalf of His Majesty (the sultan) to the sharif of Mecca, and to hand over several objects to the people in the Two Shrines. He goes directly from Istanbul to Jedda by sea. After the pilgrimage he proceeds to Medina, together with the representatives dispatched by the sharif of Mecca. He proceeds from Mecca to Yanbuʿ; the expenses of this stretch are covered by the emir of Mecca, independently of the remuneration he gets from the Ottoman government.

The mubashshir accompanies the amin al-ṣurra to Damascus, then to Medina. One day before the arrival of the ṣurra, he heralds the event. The same is repeated in Mecca. When the caravan proceeds to Syria, he precedes the amin al-ṣurra to Istanbul, heralding his arrival [there].

THE JURDĪ, WHICH JOINS THE SYRIAN PILGRIMAGE CARAVAN

The jurdī is a [relief] convoy, organized by the Ottoman government (may Allah (—) support it) to care for the comfort of the pilgrims' manner of living and from fear of their being hard-pressed by what may occur to them. In past times the commander of this convoy used to be the wali of Tripoli in Syria, who would come to Damascus, take over the lead of this convoy, and guard the caravan. Now, however, this job falls to whomever the government nominates; generally, this is [*62*] with the knowledge of the superintendent of the pilgrimage. He is accompanied by a lieutenant and 100 mounted gendarmes, a cannon, and sufficient equipment [or stores]. People send food, clothes, and other necessities to their relatives and acquaintances among the pilgrims. Fodder for the riding animals may be sent too, when needed. Local people attend that [relief] convoy. The convoy accepts consignments for delivery from these people. Each consignment is labeled "In trust, for so-and-so, the son of so-and-so." The senders pay the fee for those who carry the consignments in advance. It was [formerly] the custom to set out from Damascus on the third day of ayyām al-tashrīq [13 Dhu'l-Hijja]. Now, however, they tarry awhile. When they set forth, cannons from the fortress of Damascus salute to announce their departure. They encamp in Muzayrīb. Many Syrian merchants join this convoy. A market is held, to which people, Druses and Arabs, come from Ḥawrān, Jaydūr, Jawlān, and Salṭ, a numerous crowd. This, however, is not comparable [in size] to the market held in the pilgrimage caravan. Then the convoy proceeds from there and generally meets the pilgrimage caravan in Madā'in. There the pilgrims get letters and presents from their relatives. The following day is an impressive, memorable one, on which they rejoice immensely concerning the news they have received from their own families. The pilgrims exchange some of their gifts among themselves, and start eating and drinking [feasting]. If anyone among the pilgrims died [meanwhile], they auction away the gifts intended for him. After the arrival of the convoy, many pilgrims suffer from diarrhea, generally due to extremely bad water in Madā'in and to eating the sweets they received, particularly [*63*] maʿmūl, gharība, and baqlāwa—things made of dough, dairy fats, sugar, and pistachios or almonds, or fruit dipped in sugar trickle or extract, apricots and apricot jelly, pistachios or almonds—dried or roasted with salt—and the like. All these cause diarrhea, often followed by dysentery. Many continue to suffer from this [back] in Syria, and many die of it. It is, therefore, most appropriate to abstain from eating these things, or to taste but a little, and anyway, not to mix them with fat foods and the like. The convoy then mixes with the pilgrimage caravan and returns with it to Damascus. The pilgrims start writing letters to their relatives in Damascus or elsewhere. When the caravan reaches Tabūk, the jūkhadār leaves the caravan, after having received its letters, and directs his steps to Damascus.

7. The Mail Service of the Syrian Pilgrimage Caravan

The postman (*barīd*) is the person taking letters from one place to the other; now they call him the *bōstajī* and the sending of letters is called *bōsta*, while the place for its administration is named the *bōsta-khāne* (post office). The Syrian pilgrimage caravan has five postmen. This has been arranged from early times to serve the need of pilgrims and their relatives, as we shall explain, Allah (—) so willing.

The first mail goes from Maʿān, and is called *kattāb Maʿān* or *najjāb* (courier of) *Maʿān*. [*64*] This is so because, when the pilgrims reach Maʿān with the caravan and stay there for a day (as we have already related), they busy themselves with writing letters to their folks, informing them of their situation and what they need to let them know, which they forgot to do [before departure], such as the interests of [their] commerce and farming, and allay their worry about their condition and health. This is so, because most of those who performed the pilgrimage in past times had never traveled before. The pilgrimage is difficult, due to the great distance as well as the exposure to heat and cold, and the weariness of moving and encamping. Therefore, the relatives of the pilgrims are concerned. Hence, when the letters from Maʿān arrive and the pilgrims mention their rest and safe arrival there, whatever irritation and anxiety their relatives may have felt diminishes. Because of this, when the courier reaches Damascus, a cannon from the fort salutes him. He proceeds [forthwith] to the wali of Syria. He gets his due there, then presents the letters he has brought to one of the top officials concerned, from whom he gets a sum of drachmas. The official who has received the letters, and paid the courier, proceeds to a place at Darwīsha in Damascus, where he distributes the letters to the addressees [gathered there to collect them], except the known wealthy, to whom he delivers them [by hand]. No letter is delivered to its addressee without a release (*fikāk*), a sum of drachmas which he demands. If the addressee does not agree, the official does not hand him the letter, and so forth.

The second mail is the post of Madā'in. When the caravan reaches that station and stays [*65*] there for a day, the pilgrims write letters to their relatives. The postman or courier takes the letters and returns to Damascus. Upon his arrival, two cannons fire a salute from the fort to announce it. Then [everything] is repeated as with the first post [from Maʿān]. When the people hear the two cannons, they say, "The courier of Madā'in has arrived!" They rush to pick up the letters. The advantage of these letters is that during their journey the pilgrims have learnt what they need for the return trip. They tell their relatives, accordingly, to send their needs to them with the [relief] convoy, as the courier from Madā'in arrives [in Damascus] a day or two before it leaves. He may arrive after the convoy's departure [however] and then there is no opportunity to send the pilgrims what they have requested with the convoy.

The third mail is the post of Medina, known as the Courier of Medina. The letters for this courier are written in Medina. In them the pilgrims tell about their arrival and welcome in Medina, their visit to the tomb of Muhammad (——), beseeching his intercession on their behalf and that of their beloved ones. Then they describe their condition, health, and what they encountered on the way and in Medina—high or low prices, heat and cold—and what they require done in their absence, and so forth. When the post reaches Damascus, three cannons fire a salute from the fort to announce it has arrived. Then [everything] is done as with the first post. On every side people outrun one another. This [same] postman may return with letters from Damascus to the pilgrims and catch up with them in Medina. This has a good effect on the pilgrims, [*66*] as he brings them news of their families for the first time since their departure.

The fourth mail is the post of Minà, where the pilgrims write their letters after the stone-throwing [ceremonies] and the sacrifices [in Mecca]. This is a very important post, for when infectious diseases befall pilgrims (may Allah (—) prevent it), they generally do so in Minà. Therefore, the pilgrims inform their relatives what they have encountered in Mecca—the festivities, the praying and rites of pilgrimage, on what day the ritual of Arafat was held, and similar matters—to make their relatives glad about their having achieved them. The courier takes the letters and leaves the caravan on the third day of the tashrīq. When he enters Damascus, four cannons offer a salute from the fort, so that people hurry to receive the letters and read them. Some of the recipients laugh, while others weep (praise to Him who makes [people] laugh and weep).

The fifth mail is the post of Tabūk. This is the last mail [on the pilgrimage]. The courier is known in Damascus and its surroundings as the Post of the Jūkhadār. This courier takes the letters from the pilgrims and leaves the Syrian caravan at Tabūk. A number of pilgrims readily accompanies him. They all ride dromedaries, as does the jūkhadār himself, who came from Istanbul with the amin al-ṣurra, this being his main job. The group [to accompany him] makes the rounds among the pilgrims as soon as they get to Arafat, requesting their letters to their families; sometimes they may start doing this even earlier. Everyone in this group obtains a heap of letters, as many as he can get [for the remuneration he expects to receive]. They proceed together from Tabūk until they all arrive in Zarqā'. [Then] some of them precede the others [*67*] to Damascus. The jūkhadār proceeds to Kiswa, where he spends the night at the home of the local headman. The latter obtains several letters from him [in lieu of payment for accommodations?], leaves the jūkhadār at his home, rides to Damascus, and informs the wali of his arrival. The wali gives the headman of Kiswa a suit of clothes (*kiswa*), as appointed.[1] This practice has been abolished. [Nowadays] the wali sends a troup of mounted gendarmerie to meet the jūkhadār. The latter reaches Damascus, in any case, seven days before the return of the pilgrimage caravan. He [ceremoniously] enters the city through the Gate of Allah in a procession with his group and

1. A pun?

the riders and officers sent to welcome him. In past times it was customary to bring a long dry log, kindled at one end, and to carry it, burning, before him, with a large mob all around. A man in the mob would shout, at the highest pitch of his voice, "May Allah burn the log!" Others would reply, together, "May Allah curse the renegades [or heretics]!" The reason for this was every year renegades would spread rumors about the pilgrimage—that it was completely lost, or had contracted an infectious disease, or had drowned, or the like. Then, when the pilgrimage returned safely, they would be confronted with this. This practice has been abolished. Then the jūkhadār proceeds directly with the procession to the seat of the Ottoman government, the department of war, and the sharʿī court, where he visits the qadi and the naqīb al-Ashrāf; then to the house of the mufti. He gets remuneration from them such as cloaks and the like. A salute of five cannons from the fort heralds his arrival. Those who have accompanied him then disperse with their letters to the houses of the addressees.

They precede [the return of the pilgrimage caravan] by a day or two. The relatives of the pilgrims suffer general distress and total spoliation, for these messengers do not deliver a letter to its addressee unless they take all he possesses, if they can. They quarrel among themselves [*68*] about dividing [the spoils], until the matter ends with everyone getting a suit of clothes, made of cloth or silk, or a gold coin [Turkish pound] or two, depending on each messenger's skill and resourcefulness.

When a death occurs in the pilgrimage caravan (may Allah prevent it), it is a disaster. Then you see the families of the pilgrims wandering in the markets and streets, following the letter carriers. The latter, riding their dromedaries, go from quarter to quarter and from village to village. Furthermore, they take [all their] letters and travel to distant towns, such as Homs, for a single letter whose addressee is well-known for his wealth. In such a case they are real plunderers: they deliver a letter only after having taken from the addressee over and above their expectations. A poor man, however, may enquire about a letter [he is expecting] and be told it is [now] in such a village. He follows it and is informed it has gone to such [another] village. In this manner this continues until he manages to meet the letter carrier. When they do meet, the problem is not solved except by a gathering of people who urge the letter carrier [to part with it]; the addressee has to pay the price agreed upon after [all] the haggling to get his letter. The greatest misfortune in all this matter is that some of the letters for the relatives of the pilgrims are sent by others than their related pilgrim, for the latter may have died meanwhile. So the family learns [first] of his death, then of a letter from him! So they strive, day and night, to get it. After hardship and much effort, and then the payment of the fine [letter carrier's fee], they get the letter, [only] to learn that it is from somebody else and that their relative is dead. Then the family's misfortune is [even] greater and it seeks refuge in Allah (—).

The considerable importance of the Post of the Jūkhadār lies in its being the last mail, bringing recent information about the conditions of the pilgrims. Nowadays its significance has decreased, because His Majesty, [*69*] the sultan (may Allah (—) protect him and lead him to victory), has granted a favor to all the pilgrims by having a telegraph line installed between Damascus and Mecca. Thanks to this, there is no further need for branch [postal] stations on the road. The pilgrim may inform his family or they may inform him or enquire about him, in any place on the road having a telegraph branch. May Allah (—) reward our master and sultan, the caliph, with the best of rewards. Amen!

CEREMONIES CELEBRATING THE RETURN OF THE PILGRIMAGE CARAVAN

According to the contents of these letters, people [in Damascus] base their preparations for arranging festivities [for the return of the Syrian pilgrimage caravan], or organizing mourning ceremonies. Women may be seen in various houses, some of them shouting with joy (their cries are named *zalāghīṭ*), others groaning and shrieking with grief (their shrieks are named *walāwīl*); some laugh, others weep. The families of the pilgrims and their friends, all hoping for their return alive and sound, start making [new] clothes for them and sending them to their homes, preparing sweets and sending gifts—such as sheep, samn and rice—everything suited to the relationship—and the importance of the pilgrim. The female relatives of the pilgrim and his friends assemble at his home and rejoice there, day and night. Three days before the return of the pilgrims, expensive sweet foods, meats, and the like, are prepared for the so-called *mulāqāt* (encounter). People gather and proceed to welcome the pilgrims, each according to his importance and situation; [some persons] meeting them may go as far as Zarqā'. When they meet a pilgrim there, they greet him, visit with him, and take out some food they have prepared for him. Then they all eat and ride together, letting him ride one of their own animals, while one of them may ride in his stead in the caravan; [thus] they precede the caravan. If they meet him riding in the caravan, on the road, they ask him to dismount, dismount themselves, sit down, [*70*] greet him, spread out a repast, to which they also invite their friends among the other pilgrims and friends of their relative the pilgrim. They eat and rest briefly. Afterwards, they mount, rejoin the caravan, and return home to Damascus.

All this was so before the existence of the railway [from Damascus] to Muzayrīb [owned by a French company]. Now, however, after its construction, the families of the pilgrims [may] proceed by train to greet their relatives, and bring them back by train [too]. Some individuals may [still] ride from Muzayrīb, going in one stretch from Muzayrīb or Damascus to Zarqā'. They accompany their relative the pilgrim, riding to the railway station, whence they all proceed directly to Damascus [by train]. Insofar as non-Damascenes are concerned, they also arrive from their own towns, such as Hamah or Beirut, and stay as honored guests with their friends, residents of Damascus, with no difference whatsoever between them [all being honored alike]. Sometimes their hosts accompany them [to greet their pilgrim relatives]. When the pilgrims arrive in Damascus, they find people waiting for them; those who know them and those who do not greet them alike, blessing and asking forgiveness from the Prophet (——), who said, "O Allah, forgive [the sins] of the pilgrim and of whomsoever the pilgrim blesses [or prays for]." Sometimes the pilgrim cannot meet his [secluded] womenfolk before midnight, due to the multitude of those gathered to greet him. (This is an unseemly custom which ought to be changed so that people would not come to greet the traveler until the second day of his arrival.) This practice [now] goes on for three days and nights. The custom is that all Muslims present at the pilgrim's home at breakfast and dinner time take their meals there. If a Muslim is an important person, he is served with sweets, of which he partakes. Sometimes [*71*] sweets are offered to all the Muslims [present], and anybody who refuses would be pressed to help himself. Nowadays, however, people content themselves with serving coffee, or some serve Zamzam water instead, while others add dates. The Muslim [guest] eats a date and drinks a cup of Zamzam water. This is, indeed, a praiseworthy custom. When the three days following the arrival of the pilgrim are over, women come to greet other women—

women pilgrims, if any—or for well-wishing only [in other cases]. The women arrange for gay festivities with songs and music, according to their social status. This continues for seven days and nights. During those days men do not enter the house where these women are [and feast]; not even the pilgrim himself, unless he has quarters located at the outermost point away from the harem, called *barrānī* (exterior) by the Syrians, *selamlık* by other Turks,[2] and *maḥall al-istiqbāl* in Arabic.

As for those whose pilgrim has died [on the way], after verifying the news their joy turns into mourning. They invite memorizers of the Koran for three days, from noon to sunset. Some add memorizers after dinner; this continues for three nights until they finish reciting the complete Koran (*khatma*). On the last night they invite many people to recite the formulas, "Allah, be His name exalted" and "There is no god but Allah," 70,000 times, in order to rescue the deceased from the fire [of eternal punishment], as has been handed down in the matter by the good sufis (mystics) (may Allah (—) let us profit from them. Amen!). They bless the Prophet (——), give alms, and distribute food [to the needy] for the spirit of the dead one.

You note that the readiness of the pilgrims to send letters with the Post of the Jūkhadār varies and wavers. Many pilgrims, who know [*72*] the manner of those who carry the letters and what suffering they cause to their families, slip their letters within those of others. Or they mention the names of their friends, saying: So-and-so greets you and his family; he is, thanks to Allah, in the best of health; do inform his family of this. Thus they do away with some of the bother and find out the truth.

AUTHOR'S RECOMMENDATION

In 1303/1885–86 I wrote a memorandum on this matter and sent it to the wali of Syria. Its subject was to benefit the treasury, to increase the revenue of the state and the well-being of the inhabitants, and to have the procedures conform to the rules and basic laws of the Ottoman state. [The main suggestion was] to set a leather box in the jūkhadār's tent—all the way from Madā'in, where the

2. Characteristically, ʿĀrif regards the Syrians as *Turks*, obviously in allegiance to the Ottoman Empire.

pilgrims start writing letters to their relatives, to Tabūk, where the jūkhadār leaves the pilgrimage caravan. Letters would be dropped into this box which the jūkhadār, upon arriving in Damascus, would hand over to the [local] postal administration. The latter would open the box, sort the letters, and hold them. Whenever the recipient of a letter came to ask for it, the clerk would stick a stamped postal slip on it. He would get from the addressee the postage dues, according to the letter's weight. The postal administration would then hand over to the jūkhadār [copies of] the stamped postal slips before he left, so that he would be acting as an agent for the postal administration [and could redeem them for payment?]. However, my suggestion was not acted upon. People still suffer hardship in finding the letters addressed to them and in haggling with the letter carriers.

[*73*] AUTHOR'S COMMENT

We have already mentioned that the amin al-ṣurra returns to Damascus by land with the Syrian pilgrimage caravan. However, in recent years most pilgrims return by sea from Jedda, as they see no need for continuing all the way with the caravan. In the same manner, there is no further need for the müjdeci or the quftānjī. The jubba is sent [by sea?] to the emir [*sic*] of Mecca, along with the funds of the ṣurra. The mubashshir also is rendered useless by the telegraphic service. Indeed, it would be desirable that the Ottoman government (may Allah (—) support it) should economize and dispatch the funds of the ṣurra to Damascus by check. It might also send pouches with money and letters by steamer. Thus, it could save on the needless expenses it incurs annually for the amin al-ṣurra, the müjdeci, the quftānjī, and the mubashshir. The government might consider also the funds of the pilgrimage spent on the kīlār, which could be trimmed, too. The superintendent of the pilgrimage ought to do with travel expenses, as established for state officials, similar to the allocations granted to those traveling to another place, such as the kharjirāh. The government ought to be satisfied with the officer accompanying the jurdī, instead of [its own] superintendent. This fits in with the other instances [relating to the pilgrimage] of substituting a superintendent for the wali of Damascus, the superintendent of the jurdī for the wali of Tripoli, applying postal regulations to the letters of the pilgrims instead of the [actual] system for sending the mail, and dispensing with the quftānjī and mubashshir, as we have mentioned. All this would bring about savings for the Ottoman government and comfort the people, preserving them from sizable inroads on their funds. If this is not [possible], [*74*] let the superintendent's expenses conform to regulations, particularly when he travels by sea from Istanbul to Syria, and returns from Jedda by sea too.

8. *The Medina and Mecca Caravans*

THE CARAVANS FROM MEDINA TO MECCA

These caravans go from Medina to Mecca to perform the two pilgrimages—major (*ḥajj*) and minor (*'umra*). We have already explained that there are no shuqdhuf, maḥāra, shibriyya, takht, or similar accouterments [on these occasions]. Rather, the caravans are composed of dromedaries, nags, and donkeys. There are five such caravans per year, at most. There may be fewer, proportionate to the number of pilgrims from the people of Medina. The five caravans are called as follows: 'Abbās Efendi, al-Khiyārī, Shaykh Muḥammad al-Dāghistānī, Shaykh Muḥammad Ḥawwāla, Aghas of the Shrine in Medina. In the past year [only] four caravans went out.

During the early part of the sacred month of Dhu'l-Hijja these caravans leave Medina, one after the other. Anybody who cannot participate in them, on account of his being too weak to support the hardship of riding dromedaries or other animals, may ride in a litter along with the Syrian caravan when it leaves Medina. These caravans reach Mecca on the seventh day after leaving Medina.

They spend the night of al-Tarwiya (moistening) in Mecca and the night of Arafat in Minà. They return from Mecca to Medina on the nineteenth day; they reach Mecca in groups [*75*] on 26, 27, and 28 Dhu'l-Hijja. The inhabitants of Medina welcome them in Bi̅r 'Urwa with food, drink, fruit, and merrymaking. They accompany them back to Medina, greet them, and wish them [another] pilgrimage and well-being. There are various poems which the people of Medina recite as they ride to and from [Mecca]. For instance, they recite the following on their way to Mecca:

O my God, pave for us the way easily.
—We are directing our steps to the Shrine.
We shall walk around the ancient House.
—Then all of us will join the Interceder [Muhammad].
My eye has denied sleep,
—As if sleep had not been created.
Whoever reproaches me, cease reproaching.
—Whoever likes sleep will not love [Allah].
He changed the sleep into interdiction
—And made my head the abode of grey hair.
Oh, the dweller of those tents,
—Would that we meet in Minà!

On their return from Mecca, they recite:

My farewell to Ṭi̅ba [Mecca],
—My farewell to the Shrine.
My farewell to him whom
—Allah has specially honored!

One person recites, and the others reply in ringing voices and wondrous melodies.

The Medinese are distinguished by their purity, friendliness, morals, nobleness, gentleness of appearance, and sincerity of heart. [*76*] They like anybody who settles among them and hold no rancor in their breasts. Allah (—) praised them in the Koran and they were blessed by the Prophet (——). We have the following account in Muslim [a compiler of hadiths], on the authority of Abū Hurayra (may Allah (—) grant him peace), "The Prophet (——) said: O Allah, Abraham was Thy slave, companion and prophet; I am Thy slave and prophet. Abraham blessed Mecca; I call on Thee to bless Medina, just as Abraham called on Thee to bless Mecca." The following is in al-Ṭabarānī's *al-Awsaṭ*, on the authority of 'Alī Ibn Abī Ṭālib (may Allah (—) grant him peace), "The Prophet (——) said, O Allah, Abraham, Thy slave and companion called on Thee to bless the Meccans; I, Muhammad, am Thy slave and messenger, and call on Thee to bless the Medinese in all their deeds, just as Thou hast blessed the Meccans. Double the blessing!" In another oral tradition he asked [Allah] to bless their fruit, too. And in another—"O Allah, I have consecrated the two rocky fields [black volcanic grounds in Medina], just as Mecca was made sacred by Abraham's request." The Medinese obtained the vicinity of the compassionate Prophet and his Family and Companions—with the worthiest prayer and perfect blessing.[1] We congratulate the Medinese for what they got and may they enjoy it!

All together, these caravans include 1,000 dromedaries, 500 donkeys, and 150 nags. A tenth of these dromedaries belong to their riders, while the rest are rented. Most of the nags [however] belong to their riders, the number of rented ones being small. Indeed, when the Syrian caravan arrives, the Medinese buy nags [from the pilgrims] and use them for riding in their own pilgrimage [to Mecca]. Upon returning to Medina, he who does not need the nag, sells it; while he who can use it, [*77*] keeps it. The sale of these nags, after the return from Mecca, may bring in a profit; if a loss is incurred, it does not amount to more than the cost of renting a beast-of-burden for the pilgrimage [from Medina to Mecca]. Insofar as donkeys are concerned, all of them are rented.

THE CARAVANS FROM MECCA TO MEDINA

Thirteen caravans set forth from Mecca to Medina in order to visit the [tomb of the] Prophet (——). The first caravan sets forth from Mecca to Medina on the first day of the sacred month of Rajab to attend the visit of [the tomb of] Ḥamza, Master of the Martyrs, the uncle of the Prophet (——). This caravan does not tarry in Medina for more than one week; then it returns home to Mecca. Between 1,000 and 3,000 camels assemble in this caravan.

The second leaves Mecca for Medina on 5 Dhu'l-Qa'da. It is made up of from 1,500 to 2,000 camels. The third leaves on the

1. A reference to the fact that Muhammad and many of his Companions are buried in Medina, while according to Muslim legend, Abraham laid the Ka'ba stone in Mecca.

following day, that is 8 [*sic*] Dhu'l-Qa'da, and so forth for the first eight caravans, including altogether 20,000 camels.

The ninth caravan leaves Mecca on 7 Dhu'l-Hijja, followed by four caravans—one each [succeeding] day. All these set forth from Mecca before the Syrian, Egyptian, and Baghdad caravans leave it.

When the [Mecca] caravans have reached Medina and visited it, [*78*] and attended the Feast of 'Āshūrā', they leave before the Syrian, Egyptian, and Baghdad caravans arrive there. If they were late and the time of the arrival of the said [foreign] caravans approached, the local administration would order the heads of the [Mecca] caravans to get out of Medina; consequently, they would leave quicker than a wink to return to Mecca.

The [last] five caravans together are made up of 4,000 to 7,000 camels, according to the number of their riders. All in all, the [thirteen Mecca caravans] amount to 27,000 camels at most; they may add up to less.

On their way to Medina, the Meccans have their [own] songs, poems, and religious verses, which they recite on their outbound trip as well as on their homecoming journey. These are nearly the same as those we have quoted when referring to the Medinese caravans. The pilgrim may consider the Meccans uncouth and harsh; however, this is not so. Indeed, some of the residents of Mecca, who are no strangers [there], are overwhelmed by the majesty [of the place], while they frequent the House [Ka'ba] and worship assiduously. They are esteemed people, pious and observant. Some of them have regard for beauty, humor, and social relations; they are those who occupy themselves with worldly matters and livelihood. As to those who have malicious traits and the like, they are not native sons, but newcomers. Hence, one should beware of talking [disparagingly] of the Meccans, for they are the neighbors of the House of Allah; and a neighbor absorbs [some of] the sanctity of the neighborhood. Muhammad (——) said, "When I was with Gabriel [the archangel] he commanded me to take care of the neighbor, until I thought he would make him my heir!"

[79]

9. The Pilgrims and Merchants Who Come to Mecca

The people who come by sea to Jedda, and then to Mecca, as well as those who come by land from the south, east and north of Mecca, from the lands around, from Yanbu' to Medina, from Egypt and Syria—all these are pilgrims and merchants. Those who come via Jedda are Muslims from India, China, Indochina [?] (Shīn), Java,[1] Yemen, Takrūr [in the Sudan], Zanzibar [Negroes], Crete, Morocco, and Yemenites near the shore, as well as Egyptians, Turks, and people from the shores of the Mediterranean. None of these would be affected by the [eventual] existence of the Hejaz–Syria Railway.

Those who are going to increase in numbers are the people who live in Syria or pass through: the inhabitants of inland Syria, of Aleppo and Baghdad, the Persians, Kurds and Bukharans, as well as others who reside near the railways to Baghdad and Birejik, which are expected to connect with the Hejaz–Syria Railway. Their numerical growth will be endless, so that it cannot even be

1. In Mecca *Java* was used not only for pilgrims originating from this island but from the whole East Indian archipelago; see *MLPNC:* v, 215 ff.

evaluated now. This growth will add to the wealth of Hejaz; one cannot even imagine now the gains which would accrue from the increase in pilgrims, visitors, and merchants. The people of Hejaz would become rich, indeed notably wealthy.

Let us now mention some figures about the pilgrims, visitors [and merchants] who leave Mecca to visit and trade [in Medina]. There are many estimates. Those who exaggerate report a million or even more; others put it at 700,000, 500,000, or 200,000. All these are nothing but conjecture and speculation, impossible [*80*] to substantiate, for one cannot count all the people who come from the surroundings of Mecca or the extensive lands adjoining Hejaz. However, one may approximately count those arriving in the Syrian, Egyptian, and Baghdad caravans. It is related that the Prophet (——) said, "Allah has promised this House [Ka'ba] that 500,000 people would visit it annually; if the number happened to be smaller, He would make it up with [His] angels." Indeed on the Day of Resurrection, the Ka'ba will be called upon, like a bride at her wedding, with all the pilgrims who grasp its curtains milling around it—until the Ka'ba enters Paradise and they enter with it.

One has to look at the evidence. We maintain that whoever goes to Arafat and witnesses this noble occasion would be impressed, indeed overwhelmed. However, he would be unable to determine whether the crowd numbers more than 200,000 or less. He cannot know [exactly], as it is impossible to count those coming by land from all parts. But this seems very close to the correct figure. There is no point in wasting [further] effort in this matter, since it is impossible to get at the exact truth.

However, it seems worthwhile to investigate the numbers of those arriving at Jedda by sea. Indeed, my assumption in writing this book was based on the premise that they are counted; the conclusion would be based on knowing these figures. They are those who have to hire camels from the Bedouins of Hejaz. If we surmise that the [total] number of pilgrims reaches 250,000, then those coming via Jedda are twenty thousand, the rest arriving by land. This is no biased surmise concerning those coming by sea via Jedda [for] there is a way of counting those arriving via Jedda [from] the registers of those passing [through]. Anyone consulting these registers, for a ten-year span [*81*] or more, finds out that they do not reach this figure [of 20,000 annually] at any time. The cause lies in the dangers of crossing the sea, and in the annoyances and restrictions imposed by the health regulations [such as quarantines].[2]

As to those coming by land and staying in Mecca and its surroundings, they are practically all pilgrims. In Mecca itself, there are more than 100,000 people, of which a quarter, certainly, are never absent [25,000 residents]. Let us assume that those who are pilgrims there number 75,000; another 100,000 from Wādī Fāṭima, Wādī Laymūn, Maḍīq, Ṭā'if and its surroundings, the Bedouins in the deserts and in the area adjoining Mecca and Medina, up to the Yemen, and from the Yemen itself; another 55,000—those arriving in the Baghdad caravan from the Najd, in the Syrian caravan from Yanbu', in the Egyptian caravan, and the Bedouins roaming the area between Medina and Syria. The sum total would be 250,000.

Actually, there are numerous pilgrims from Mecca and its neighborhood, due to their desire for reward [in Paradise] and their fear of shame. Indeed, anybody in those neighboring parts who can perform the pilgrimage, and does not do so, is considered vile by his people; his refraining is taken as a sign of his avarice and vileness. This is in addition to the general desire of Muslims to perform the pilgrimage; they would wish to repeat it every year, if they could, due to their desire for reward. The oral tradition, indeed, says that the pilgrimage absolves the Muslim of all his sins and that he comes out of the pilgrimage as pure as a newborn baby. Another tradition has it that whoever performs the pilgrimage once, has done his religious duty; twice, has put his God in his debt; thrice, Allah (—) will prevent his hair and flesh from burning [in after-life]. Otherwise said, you never see any Muslim but he desires to perform the pilgrimage every year, and in particular to visit the tomb of the Master of the created [Muhammad] and to pray for him, his Family, and his Companions, and wish them peace. [*82*] This is indicated and confirmed by the multitude of poor pilgrims, to whom Allah (—) has not made the pilgrimage mandatory, due to their [financial] inability to perform it. Despite their wretched condition, they go on pilgrimage, walking barefoot, naked and bareheaded, begging for bread and water. These are numerous, coming from all places, chiefly from the area between the Two Shrines and Takrūr. Their womenfolk carry their babies over one shoulder in a leather sack resembling a gourd, attached to the end

2. Cf. Firmin Duguet, *Le Pèlerinage de la Mecque au Point de Vue Religieux, Social et Sanitaire* (Paris 1932), esp. pt. 2.

of a stick; and their belongings and water container over the other [shoulder]. When people do not donate bread or water, they die of hunger or thirst. On account of this, our Ottoman government (may Allah (—) strengthen it), among all its arrangements relating to the Syrian caravan, has [also] set aside special funds for poor pilgrims to be expended for food, drink, riding, night lodgings, and other needs, [all] at the government's expense. Likewise, the government has earmarked certain sums to cover carrying water to places known to be waterless. This is called *ifāza*; it is intended for the needy—to save them from perishing of thirst—out of pity for them.

In recent years, for instance last year, it was rumored that a simoon (sand storm) killed a certain number of pilgrims on the road; this happens mostly [on the road] between the Two Shrines. The dead are only from among the poor who cannot obtain water. Those who ride horses, while on the pilgrimage road, do not provide for water to be carried for the poor (*ifāza*). It may happen that the caravans do not find water at certain stations. The poor, however, are thirsty and hurry to the stations to drink; they do not find water there and consequently die of thirst. Sometimes they die [even] before they can reach the station. If it were true, as it is rumored, that the death of these poor is due [*83*] to the simoon, then the rich should also have died. But we have not heard of any rich man dying in a simoon along with those poor who could not obtain water. Whoever searches for the truth of the matter knows that the death of these poor, unfortunate people was of thirst, not of the simoon. Had they obtained water, as the rich did, the simoon alone would not have overcome them, and they would still be among those whose eyes see. They suffer all the above and other troubles: the fatigue of marching, the blight of dozing or sleeping in the open air without cover or bed, the hardship of hunger and thirst, the humiliation of begging, the bitterness of refusal, the endurance of consuming heat and cold. Nonetheless, time after time you may see them going on pilgrimage and visiting [the Prophet's tomb].

This and similar instances serve as proof that on the pilgrimage the aim of Muslims is to please Allah (—), and in visiting the tomb of the Prophet (——), to ask for his intercession [before Allah]. It is related in the oral tradition, on the authority of Ibn 'Umar [son of Caliph 'Umar I?] (——), who said, "Whoever visits my tomb, my intercession on his behalf is certain." Another tradition relates, on the authority of Ibn 'Abbās ['Abd Allah Ibn 'Abbās

Ibn ‘Abd al-Muṭallib?] (——), that [Muhammad] said, “Whoever performs the pilgrimage to Mecca, then continues and visits my [tomb] mosque [in Medina], I shall credit him with two blessed pilgrimages!”

The poor, who witness how others like themselves die in those lands, do not hesitate, nevertheless, to go to the Prophet’s tomb under these conditions. They are not afraid of death [and gather courage] from an oral tradition. This is attributed to Ḥāṭib Ibn Ḥārith (——), who quotes the Prophet (——) as saying, “Whoever visits me after my death, this is as if he had visited me during my life. Whoever dies in one of the Two Shrines will be one of those believers who will be resurrected on the Day of Judgment.”

In this context, it is suitable that we mention a matter at which the ignorant wonder and [*84*] the hearts of the wise grieve. Certain influential persons on pilgrimage take water along from Istanbul to Damascus, and thence to Mecca, going and returning. Likewise, they take pure water to Medina, and thence to Mecca, and the same on their way back to Damascus. All this while the poor are dying of thirst. However, those persons are not moved by either pity or humaneness to get them water at the expense of the state (may Allah (—) preserve it and protect it, up to the Day of Judgment. Amen!) and for the glory of the Master of the Prophets (blessings on them).

To sum up: despite what people say that the pilgrims are very numerous, those coming [annually] via Jedda do not number more than 30,000. If there are more, this would be exceptional and should not serve as a basis for any conclusion.

10. The Correct Rationale for the Pilgrimage and the Visit to the Prophet's Tomb

Know that there is no command or interdiction in the religion of Islam without a rationale. However, a part of the rationale is evident, while another is hidden. It is the practice of Allah (—) to reveal some of the reasons and to conceal others. For He is the First and the Last, the Revealer and the Concealer, while He [alone] is omniscient. He has concealed some of the rationale, so as to increase faith. Allah (—) said in the Koran: "*Alif. Lām. Mīm.* This is the Scripture whereof there is no doubt, a guidance unto those who ward off [evil], who believe in the unseen, and establish worship, and spend of that We have bestowed upon them. And who believe in that which is revealed unto thee [Muhammad], and that which was revealed before thee, and are certain of the Hereafter. These depend on guidance from their Lord. These are the successful." [K. 2: 1–5]

Now, if everything had been evident, or if man believed [*85*] [only] in what his reasoning showed him, but would not have believed in what his reasoning would have concealed from him—then he would not have believed in what his reasoning showed him either. So, since the Prophet received the Koran from Allah, people would have believed in him only if its reasoning was evident! After all, both the believer in Allah (—) and the nonbeliever accept that whose reason is obvious; consequently, there would be no difference between the believer in Allah (—) and the nonbeliever! Hence, [only] he who believes in the Koran and in the Messenger of Allah, in matters whose reason is concealed, is one who truly believes in Allah (—). Do you not see that Allah (—) praised those who believe in the concealed? He has commended those as being on the righteous path versus their God, the successful ones.

Doubtlessly, the pilgrimage is a pillar of Islam; according to the consensus of Muslims, one who denies this is considered an atheist. Of course, this important pillar has an evident reason, since it is required of everyone who can perform it, be he far from or near [the Two Shrines]. Nothing [else] in Islam resembles it at all, as Allah (—) has not required anybody to travel to a distant place, any more than he is required to hear the call to the Friday prayer. [For] when a Muslim goes out of his village before sunrise on Friday to a place where he does not hear the call to prayer, he is not required to undergo undue hardship to come to prayer. This refers to the Friday prayer, to which people do not have to come [from afar]. The pilgrimage, on the contrary, is binding on anyone who can perform it, even if he were living in a country at the North Pole, for instance. Consequently, one must strive to perform the pilgrimage from far or near.

This obligation, of course, requires a reason, or rather, a number of reasons. Is this reason evident or concealed? Healthy logic immediately requires that it is [*86*] evident, even though some actions of the pilgrimage, such as the stone throwing, have a hidden rationale. That the reason is evident finds support in the words of Allah (—) in his Book, "And proclaim unto mankind the pilgrimage. They will come unto thee on foot and on every lean camel; they will come from every deep ravine. That they may witness things that are of benefit to them and mention the name of Allah." [K. 22: 27–28] So Allah (—) proclaimed the advantages Muslims can find in the pilgrimage. This is the most valid rationale. Then He continued, saying, "Mention the name of Allah." [K. 22: 34] Then He said, referring to the pilgrimage and its exposition, "When you press on in the multitude from Arafat, remember Allah by the sacred monument. Remember Him as He has guided you."

[K. 2: 198] And later, "Then hasten onward from the place whence the multitude hastens onward, and ask forgiveness of Allah. Lo! Allah is forgiving, merciful. And when ye have completed your devotions, then remember Allah as ye remember your fathers or with a more lively remembrance." [K. 2: 199–200] Then, "Remember Allah through the appointed days. Then whoso hastens [his departure] by two days, it is no sin for him, and whoso delays, it is no sin for him; that is for him who wards off [evil]. Be careful of your duty to Allah, and know that unto Him ye will be gathered." [K. 2: 203]

It is known that remembering Allah (—) in this world leads to the greatest reward in the next world. Allah (—) said, "Lo! Men who surrender unto Allah and women who surrender, and men who believe and women who believe, and men who obey and women who obey, and men who speak the truth and women who speak the truth, and men who persevere and women who persevere [in righteousness], and men who are humble and women who are humble, and men who give alms and women who give alms, and men who fast and women who fast, and men who guard their modesty and women who guard their modesty, and men who remember Allah much and women who remember—Allah has prepared for them forgiveness and a vast reward." [K. 33: 35] He also said, "Worship preserves from lewdness and iniquity, but verily remembrance of Allah is more important." [K. 29: 45] Allah (—) has commanded that His name be mentioned in the Koran in more than one place, namely, [*87*] "Remember the name of thy Lord at morn and evening." [K. 76: 25] And also, "Remember the name of thy Lord and devote thyself with a complete devotion." [K. 73: 8] These references to remembering the name of Allah and to the great future reward for it are not discussed here alone, but are frequently mentioned in [other] books.

The advantages of the pilgrimage, as mentioned in the Koran, are obscure, indefinite, and stated in a general way—not clear, definite, and detailed enough to convey classification and amplification. This is why their wording is mostly in the plural. They are not limited to any one area, but relate to matters of both this world and the next. Some of the advantages of the pilgrimage, which relate to the next world, may be found in what al-Bazzār and others have handed down about the Prophet (——) who said, "The pilgrim intercedes for four hundred of his relatives and is sinless as on the day his mother gave birth to him." Many keepers of the oral tradition, as well as others, have related that the Prophet (——) said, "Between one 'umra and another, all sins are redeemed; while the reward for the blessed pilgrimage is nothing but Paradise!" He also said, "Funds expended for the pilgrimage are like those expended for alms; every drachma is worth sevenhundredfold!"

Among the benefits of the pilgrimage for this world are the following: Muslims get in touch with each other and get better acquainted with conditions, news, and affairs from near and far; they conclude agreements and assist one another in their worldly and religious matters; they cooperate, reciprocally, until they become as one. If Allah so wills it, this mutual assistance in worldly and religious matters will bring about good results. In our article, "The Sultan's Greatest Feats," and in this book, we have listed this appropriately. You may refer to both of them, if you so desire.

[*88*] Another benefit is sufficiency. There is an oral tradition that the Prophet (——) said, "If you perform the pilgrimage, you get enough to spare; if you travel, you keep healthy."

Yet another benefit is the establishing of commerce. When pilgrims meet, they are accustomed to ask after commercial matters. Then they make deals and form companies. Sometimes, they exchange wares with one another, they get acquainted with the ways of sending merchandise and enlarging their business from land to land, as well as with the manner of engaging in business. Men ask around about persons with whom they would like to trade or enter into a partnership. After all, people may understand and explain so much more by talking face-to-face than by corresponding from afar.

Yet another benefit lies in instituting industry and broadening its scope. When pilgrims leave their countries, they take along samples of their home industries: woven stuffs, clothes, and the like. This they do perforce, either for their own use on the trip or for business to make some profit, or as gifts for the residents of the Two Shrines or people on the road in the lands they are going to cross. When the people of Hejaz or the pilgrims whom they meet in the Two Shrines, or the inhabitants of the lands through which they travel, see these products and like them, they learn about these industries. Sometimes they invite a person, who came along knowing such a craft, to stay with them—either to practice this industry or to instruct them in it. Likewise, during their travels when pilgrims themselves notice certain valuable industries which may suit their own countries and sell well there, they learn them, or invite those skilled in them to come to their homelands. In this way an industry spreads in their country, where formerly it had been absent. This is a proven fact.

Then another benefit is the expansion of agriculture. This happens through the pilgrims' taking along [*89*] certain grains, vegetables, and fruits from their own countries to the lands they will be crossing on their pilgrimage to Hejaz. If these vegetables, grains, or fruits please the inhabitants who do not have them, they request them. When they get them, they sow them—and they become common there. Contrariwise, pilgrims take along what [agricultural produce] they like that they find in the lands they cross between their homeland and Mecca, going and returning. In addition, the pilgrimage encourages the progress of agriculture in Hejaz itself. The pilgrims require foodstuffs for themselves and fodder for their riding animals. This necessitates developments in agriculture, oriented towards food and fodder in Hejaz, or an increase in commerce in the case of what is not grown there, but rather imported from elsewhere.

In addition to everything we have mentioned about the causes of wealth, the pilgrimage itself brings about wealth, irrespective of these causes. This is like marriage, being a means of livelihood, as confirmed by oral tradition. The Prophet (——) said, "Seek livelihood through marriage." Likewise, travel brings about health. In what we have mentioned about the establishment and growth of commerce, industry, and agriculture, you will have seen an indication that pilgrimages bring about wealth. This is also attested by oral tradition. Allah (—) has not ordered him who can to perform the pilgrimage without due cause. On the contrary, doubtlessly there is a rationale, or furthermore, many evident reasons. Some of them are:

First, the pilgrimage requires expenditure; if he who cannot perform it had been commanded to do it, this would have meant an unfeasible imposition. However, Allah (—) said, "Allah tasks not a soul beyond its scope." [K. 2: 286] Secondly, the person who cannot perform the pilgrimage is in no position to gain spiritual benefit, either directly or through somebody else. Since he is preoccupied with his misery and poverty, his chief concern is to make a living, or to cure the disease which weighs him down and get rid of it. Furthermore [*90*] that person cannot get any spiritual benefit at all through contemplation. It has been reported, in the name of the great Imam Muḥammad Ibn Idrīs al-Shāfi'ī[1] (——), as one of

1. A founder of a major school of legal interpretation in early Islam.

his wise sayings, "Had you been required to travel to me, you would not have had time to study the subject." Another report has it that the fear of travel and the hardship and difficulty in passing the road impose ruin. Allah (—) has already said, "Be not cast by your own hands to ruin." [K. 2: 195] Indeed, Allah (—) does not wish the ruin of his servants.

Generally speaking the pilgrimage holds immense advantages for people; these cannot be evaluated or defined. It is a general exhibition [or fair] for Muslims. Allah (—) made it mandatory once in his lifetime for whoever can afford it. If one who can perform the pilgrimage dies without doing so, this is held against him until one of his heirs or someone else performs it in his name. It is customary to repeat the pilgrimage in order to increase the worldly benefit. Likewise, it is customary to visit the tomb of the Prophet (——). There are worldly benefits in this visit, such as a gathering of Muslims from every deep valley, just as during the pilgrimage—proportionate to the size of the gathering.

Some of the other benefits concerning the next world have already been listed above, in oral traditions, and in other sources, as detailed in books. We have also mentioned them in our article, "The Sultan's Greatest Feats," namely, that Muslims have four types of religious gatherings, some more general than others. The most all-embracing is the pilgrimage; general ones are the prayers of the Two Feasts and of Friday noon; the least general is group prayer. We enlarged upon this theme in our article.

The importance of such gatherings, in previous times and in our own, is known. The Arabs held a large fair in Mecca, the 'Ukkāẓ Market, which they would attend, coming from all parts [or occupations]. This fair became famous. Nowadays Europeans, too, have shown considerable interest in general gatherings. In order to arrange them, they have organized [*91*] fairs [or exhibitions] in the capitals of their states. This is mostly a means for general gatherings. However, the reader of my words and the listener to them will certainly notice that there is a basic difference between the general gathering of the Muslims—that is, the pilgrimage—and the gathering of Europeans in their fairs. Attending the general gatherings of Muslims is a religious obligation, enjoined on every Muslim who can manage to get there. Therefore, these gatherings are constituted on religious precepts, which Allah (—) ordained as Muslim law. In such gatherings Muslims are solely busy with matters of religion. When they have fulfilled their religious obligations, they pass to their worldly affairs; legally, the religious matters are the most important.

Some of the religious matters are the basis of the world. Indeed, religion cannot exist without a sense of community and esprit de corps, both of which are consistent with worldly affairs. One is enjoined to busy oneself with religious matters; likewise, however, one should treat of worldly affairs too, for they are the basis of religion. People should not pay attention to what the heedless and ignorant say; namely, that Islamic religious law, the shari'a, commands one to renounce this world *in toto*. This view most certainly contradicts religion. One should not pay any attention to people who behave, according to this view, to get money under false pretenses through negligence, sloth, indolence, hypocrisy, hearsay, or misrepresentation. This is prohibited by religious law. Such people are like those of whom Allah (—) said, "And Allah coins a similitude: Two men, one of them dumb, having control of nothing, and he is a burden on his owner; whithersoever he directs him to go, he brings no good." [K. 16: 76] Is this not like those who leave a job, profitable to religion and to the world, and live in indolence, delusion, and begging, pretending righteousness, asceticism, and modesty? Are these not like the rumormongers in war, whose matter will be dealt with later—and then the talk will be about them. How many times have these [*92*] "advisers" deceived a believer, and impoverished a rich person, leaving him in temptation, after he had been steadfast in his faith? How do they dare to deny this? Allah has ordered one to ready one's strength, permitted buying and selling, forbade interest, praised commerce and labeled its profits as virtue, associated it with the jihad (holy war) and even mentioned it first, saying, "While others travel in the land in search of Allah's bounty and others still are fighting for the cause of Allah." [K. 73: 20] Allah (—) also said, "Lo! The bounty is in Allah's hand." [K. 3: 73, 57: 29] He attributed unto Himself the instruction of David's trade, saying (—), "And We taught him [King David] the art of making garments [of mail] to protect you in your daring." [K. 21: 80] And He attributed unto Himself (may He be glorious and pure) sowing, too, as He said, "Have you seen that which ye cultivate? Is it ye who foster it, or are We the Fosterer? If We willed, verily We could make it chaff, then would ye cease not to exclaim: Lo! We are laden with debt! Nay, but we are deprived!" [K. 56: 63–67]

All this requires assiduity, wealth, and economy. Allah taught

Adam a thousand trades and told him to instruct his descendants in these trades, so that they should not eat on the basis of their religion alone. Consequently, Adam was a ploughman, Idrīs a tailor, Noah and Zaccariah carpenters, Abraham and Lot farmers, Ṣāliḥ a merchant, Shu'ayb [Jethro] and Jonah shepherds, David a shieldmaker, Jesus a weaver—or as some say a dyer—while our Prophet, ere he started to prophesy, was a merchant and tended sheep (may Allah (—) bless them all). Likewise, the Prophet's Companions (——). 'Umar Ibn al-Khaṭṭāb took turns with several Companions in attending the presence of the Prophet (——), since he would work one day and attend another. [Caliph] 'Uthmān Ibn 'Affān, the Commander of the Faithful, was a merchant. 'Abd al-Raḥmān Ibn 'Awf was wealthy; 80,000 dinars from the estate he left were settled on one of his four wives. Each of the four wives of al-Zubayr Ibn 'Awwām inherited [*93*] 1,200,000 [dinars] from his estate. All this did not harm the religiousness of these people and did not distract them from the prophecy and the companionship [of Muhammad].

This neglect [of worldly affairs] does not imply reliance on Allah, as several people say, and thus lie about Allah (—). The teacher of righteousness, our Prophet (——), asked a Companion who had entered the mosque, leaving his female camel untied at the door, about both of them. The Companion answered that he was relying on Allah (—) and therefore left it untied. Upon this, the Prophet (——) said, "Tie her, and rely on Allah!" Then he knew that reliance on Allah does not succeed without pursuing some activity; indeed, pursuing an activity does not contradict reliance on Allah.

Assiduity, economy, and wealth are not contradictory to righteousness, piousness, and religiousness. Economy is intended to allow expenditure for the people, that is, almsgiving. Allah (—) praised almsgiving in more than one passage of the Koran, saying (—), "Those who spend their wealth for the cause of Allah and afterwards make not reproach and injury to follow that which they have spent; their reward is with their Lord, and there shall no fear come upon them, neither shall they grieve." [K. 2: 262]

In *The Book of Stringed Pearls* (*al-Durr al-Manthūr*) [by Jalāl al-Dīn al-Suyūṭī] there is an oral tradition attributed to Ayyūb [a Companion] (——), "A man gazed at the Prophet (——) from the top of a hillock. People said [to the Prophet], How strong this man is. Would that he would use his strength [to fight] for Allah! The Prophet (——) replied, Is he who kills the only one [who fights] for Allah? Then the Prophet added, Whoever sets forth to seek somethings lawful for himself or his family that they have had to forego, he is for Allah; whoever sets forth to seek the excessive, he is for Satan." In the collections of oral traditions compiled by al-Bukhārī and Muslim,[2] one reads that the Prophet (——) said, "There is no expenditure [mainly almsgiving] which you intend for Allah, but it is credited to you; this refers even to what you spend on your wife." Another oral tradition has it that he said, "What you feed yourself or your servant is considered almsgiving."

There are many such oral traditions, all of them indicating that it is desirable to earn lawfully [*94*] and to spend funds on oneself and one's relatives. All this is in the category of almsgiving; and no tradition forbidding almsgiving has reached us! On the contrary, it is not allowed to prohibit it. Furthermore, it is interdicted to forbid it. When necessary, commerce, agriculture, and industry are farḍ kifāya. When the inhabitants of a village neglect it, despite their needs, they sin. He who practices the farḍ kifāya relieves the sin of him who does not, and so is rewarded for it. Never have we grasped in the Muslim religious law that somebody was rewarded for the action which he demanded to abrogate![3]

It is not wrong to say that people are guilty of neglecting to learn several trades for which there is general need. These are now imported, but it is necessary to study them and introduce them into our country, so that we can manage without depending on others. Then our wealth would stay with us, our strength and finances would not decline, our lands would not remain neglected or our men and animals unemployed—while we are waiting for imports! In our day a decline has set in: men are leaving their work in a rush to seek a livelihood by throwing themselves on foreign commerce. This has brought many people to straits and penury. Moreover, this is unlawful, according to religious law, for in this way the country's wealth decreases, its strength declines, and poverty dominates the [sultan's] subjects. Would that the ablest of our merchants would note it!

One may deduce from this that reliance on Allah comes instead of assiduity and renders it superfluous. This seems to be implied in an oral tradition saying, "If you were to rely on Allah, He would

2. The two most famous early compilations of hadiths.
3. That is, in no religion would one ask for the abrogation of actions for which he is rewarded. A *farḍ kifāya* is a command imperative upon all Muslims, but if one person in eight or ten performs it, it is as if all had done so.

feed you just as He feeds the birds, who get up in the morning on empty stomachs and return in the evening with full ones." However, this tradition does not actually support such a view! In another oral tradition the Prophet (——) enjoined assiduity, saying, "In the morning thou shalt go and in the evening come back [that is, thou shalt work hard]—this is the utmost of what one may say concerning assiduity." Yet another tradition says, "The above *if* is a hypothetical particle in an unreal condition."[4] For, if the Prophet's Companions [*95*] (——) were unable to achieve such reliance on Allah without assiduity, how can this be maintained by such people whose situation is known and need not be elaborated?

Allah (—) ordered [Muslims] to go to the ends of the earth in order to find a livelihood, saying, "He it is Who has made the earth subservient unto you, so walk in the paths thereof and eat of His providence." [K. 67: 15] Some people have interpreted this as a permission, not a command. However [this is not so], for whoever needs money to spend on himself and his relatives, and has no opening [for an income], must work for it; and if he works, but cannot earn it, he must borrow money and spend it on himself and his relatives, so that they should not die of hunger. Hence, even borrowing is one of all the ways of striving for a livelihood. This has been so ordered in oral tradition, with reference to the need of borrowing for expenses.

Yet another passage in the Koran has it that Allah (—) said, "Whoever keeps his duty to Allah, Allah will appoint a way out for him, and will provide for him from whence he has no expectation." [K. 65: 2–3] He did not say, "Whoever relies on Allah."[5] Keeping one's duty to Allah (—) [piety] is profitable in all matters. When a servant reveres his Master [Allah], in whose hands are his life, livelihood, death, and revival, He makes his livelihood easy; that is, He prepares for him an opening [livelihood] he is not counting on. Allah (—), according to His will and desire, gives him livelihood from it. All this [however] is in a manner that the servant should not count on livelihood descending upon him from Heaven or unexpectedly, while he remains a parasite on other people. Allah (—) has not ordered the latter and does not want it for His servants, the believers.[6] Those who do not keep their duty to Him

4. This refers to a famous syntactic rule, quoted here in another context.
5. 'Ārif seems rather careless here, for verse 3 continues, "And whoever puts his trust in Allah, He will suffice him."
6. That is, Allah helps Muslims in getting a livelihood, but He does not want them to count on Him, but rather to work assiduously for it.

and refrain from remembering His name are hard put to make a living in this world. Allah (—) said, "He who turns away from remembrance of Me, his will be a narrow life." [K. 20: 124]

One ought not to take seriously the argument that Allah (—) allows livelihood to infidels, their heresy notwithstanding; for infidels are not called upon to keep their duty to Allah or to remember His name orally. The fact that [*96*] some Muslims make a good living, despite their not keeping their duty to Allah or remembering His name, may be explained as follows: either they are believers in secret, or they are infidels [allowed by Allah to make a good living]. Allah (—) said, "Think they that in the wealth and sons wherewith We provide them, We hasten unto them with good things? Nay, but they perceive not." [K. 23: 55–56] Or some of them are believers and this [livelihood] leads them on, step by step [to the true revelation], as He said, "Step by step We lead them on from whence they know not. I give them rein, [for] lo! My scheme is strong." [K. 7: 182–83] The reward of them all is in the next world.

There is no doubt whatsoever that livelihood is in the hands of Allah; He (—) said, "Allah is gracious unto His slaves. He provides for whom He will. And He is the Strong, the Mighty." [K. 42: 19] Also, "We have apportioned among them their livelihood in the life of the world." [K. 43: 32] If Islam had ordained reliance on Allah and [consequent] neglect of work, certainly the Lawgiver would have mentioned both matters [in the above passage]! [This would have been registered] for the Prophets [*sic*] and Companions (——) were writing down the words of Muhammad (——) and ceaselessly keeping him company, so as to receive from him the religion and the laws. Consequently, this is the best proof for what we said, namely, that nobody is allowed to leave his work and livelihood, not even for the sake of learning [or scholarship].

Hence, the claim made by the idle—that reliance on Allah (—) alone suffices, without a need to work—has no evidence in the religious law. However, work alone, without relying on Allah (—) —when one thinks that he can make a living, or that his work can provide him with a livelihood, without relying on Allah (—)— is undiluted atheism, or rather, heresy. The worthlessness of such an opinion is evident through its carrier's not being able to make a living, try as hard as he would. All the matter is in the hands of Allah (—).

Anyway, those who claim that reliance on Allah obviates the need for work, press for it eagerly, more than flies on garbage or dogs on a cow's carcass. No sooner do they hear of a fee to be obtained from teaching, leading the prayer, or preaching, that they compete for it. No sooner do they get word of an inalienable charitable endowment (*waqf*), that they quarrel about it. Or of [*97*] a hospice for the invalid or needy (*takiyya*), or a will concerning an orphan, or a management (*naẓāra*) entrusted in waqf, that they race one another for it. Whenever they see a judge, they surround him; whenever they see a chance to cheat the treasury of funds, they take advantage of it. These, indeed, are the followers of Satan; and they are going to be the losers. Why do they isolate themselves and why do they refrain from earning a living—all the while practising idleness and begging, on one hand, and pretending to be pure, on the other? This is like the following [popular] verses:

> Oh, you who speak evil of Salmà,[7]
>   You remind me of the fox
> Desirous of a bunch [of grapes], but when
>   He saw the bunch, got scared.
> He said, "It is sour," when
>   He saw he would not get it.

Nevertheless, I do not deny that reliance on Allah is welcome, and that there is a basis in religious law for the adoration of Allah and striving on His behalf, along with asceticism and begging. This however applies to those whose regard [for holy matters] has prevented them from providing the necessities for themselves and their relatives, who are satisfied with their misery and straitened circumstances, and who do need to throw something on the ground and beg of people. So much so, that he who ignores their situation would think them wealthy—due to their managing with very little and their souls not craving much. They are the modest ones, who do not ask others for favors or fawn upon them. They have pinned their hopes on Allah and held His strongest link. In consequence, Allah has enabled them to do without everything but Him. Their hearts have no place for worldly considerations; the uppermost and lowermost ranks of this world seem equal to them (——). These are the followers of Allah and they are going to be the winners [as against the followers of Satan, the losers].

7. A girl's name. This poem apparently was inspired by the fable of the fox and grapes, attributed to Aesop and later rendered famous by La Fontaine.

The treasury of the Muslims (*bayt māl*) is solely for the interests of Muslims. Indeed, the righteous ancestors, [*98*] shaykhs, sufis, and the like, were accustomed to maintaining themselves by working, without having recourse to either the Muslim treasury or handouts; they would not seek funds from a will or philanthropy. On the contrary, the majority would refuse gifts, unless pressed hard to accept them. All the more, these righteous ancestors would not ask anything from any person, or meddle by word or deed, or dress differently from other people—so as to be recognized and remembered. These, indeed, are a model for us to imitate. Whoever desires to know of them in more detail and to delve into this, should read the books of *The Generations of Sufism* (*Ṭabaqāt al-Ṣūfiyya*) [by Abū ʻAbd al-Raḥmān al-Sulamī] (——).

The Railway is the main reason for our mentioning all these matters here. Allah is the One who makes it easy and to Him we hope to return [or "with Him is a more excellent abode"]. [K. 3: 14]

11. *The Railway's Advantages for Muslims in General*

We have already mentioned the benefits of the pilgrimage [to Mecca] and the visit [to Medina]. The main purpose is a gathering during the pilgrimage, which is the most general meeting of Muslims. If this is so, the more all-embracing the gathering is, the more useful it is going to be. There is no doubt that the pilgrims do not originate solely from Mecca and its environs or from the residents of the Two Shrines, or from the Bedouins, or from specific areas, or from one community rather than another. On the contrary, they come from all Muslim communities, from all countries on earth.

If this is so, any facility which can be provided for them is a matter recommended by religious law and humaneness. These lands are remote from the caliph [Ottoman sultan], in whose hands lie their rule, protection, enforcement of security, and comfort. Their inhabitants owe him obedience in every matter (commanded or forbidden), in accordance with the Koran and the sunna of Allah's Prophet (——) whose substitute the caliph is. Therefore, shortening the distance [*99*] between them and him is one of the most important political matters in the world. Doubtlessly, in our days the railway is the best means of communication, as well as the safest and speediest. The construction of this Hejaz Railway is one of the most necessary measures—from the point of view of religious law, and for reasons of expediency and humaneness. The advantages to be derived from it cannot [even] be evaluated or defined.

One should not maintain that steamships render the railway unnecessary. I maintain that whoever wishes to travel to Medina by sea—whether via Yanbu' or Jedda—has to undergo considerable hardship. For between Yanbu' and Medina there is a distance of six days in an almost uninhabited and unsafe savage desert. He who wishes to travel from Yanbu' to Medina has to join a caravan. Caravans cannot be found all the time, nor do they have appointed dates. In addition, traveling with a caravan is not devoid of great danger too. Between Jedda [46 miles from Mecca] and Medina there is a distance of twelve days. We have already listed the days on which caravans leave Mecca for Medina. Should the traveler not chance on these days, he would be unable to join a caravan. Furthermore, there is considerable hardship in riding with the caravans. All this, in brief, adds up to the great dangers of the sea voyage, the storms, and the impossibility of traveling at any [unscheduled] time, for known reasons.

There are advantages to the Damascus–Mecca Railway which are not found in the steamships and ought not to be overlooked at this time. We have already stated that these advantages are numerous. To discuss them in detail would require a large tome, for which this book has no space. However, although everything cannot be included, the subject should not be ignored. It is appropriate to list several of the advantages [*100*] here, so they will not be missing from our book. They are as follows:

1. An increase in the number of pilgrims, visitors, and merchants. The extension of this railway line from Damascus to Mecca would raise the number of pilgrims manifold. If the present number of pilgrims from Damascus is, for example, one thousand, it would certainly be twenty or thirty thousand after the construction of this railway, particularly if the fare is low. This would also apply to other pilgrims from the environs of Damascus, as well as to those traveling from Homs, Hamah, and Aleppo, via Damascus. Doubtlessly, their numbers would grow by the same ratio or more. All this, assuming that the Anatolian Railway, which reaches nowadays

from Scutari to Konya, would not be linked with the above Syrian Railway. If it is linked with the railway line planned to connect Birejik and Baghdad, as well as with the line to be extended from Damascus to Baghdad through the savage desert, crossing Palmyra, then one cannot estimate the increase in the number of travelers at all! Whoever remembers the large size of the Syrian pilgrimage caravan—as we have mentioned—will grasp how the number of pilgrims would grow then. Proportionately to the increase in the numbers of pilgrims, visitors, and merchants, the hoped-for benefits from the pilgrimage—those we have listed above and others—would multiply, too.

2. When necessary the Ottoman government would be able to send required supplies [or reinforcements] and equipment to the areas [served by the railway] at any time it so wished. Then, these would get there in the shortest time, so that hostile acts by savage Bedouins would be prevented. Consequently, these lands, their inhabitants, and the pilgrims would attain complete security.

[*101*] 3. We have already said that all the area in Hejaz between Medina and Mecca is appropriate for growing grains, vegetables, watermelons, cucumbers, gherkins, and the like, and for planting various fruit trees, such as the vine, date palm, pomegranate, fig, walnut, banana, quince, lemon, and citron of all kinds. Of these [nowadays] only what grows in Wādī Fāṭima and Wādī Laymūn is taken over to Mecca. The rest remains in its place, as it would spoil during the long time required for transportation. Even dates and the like, which do not spoil in transportation, are [brought to Mecca only] from nearby, not from afar. Even so, the prices these fruits fetch do not cover the expenses. Due to this, people have confined themselves to planting what suffices them [alone], while now they are not fully using the available water. If the railway line were extended to reach their lands or their vicinity, transportation would be easy, and consequently the produce would not spoil. Also, perforce, the transportation charges by rail would be lower than by camel. As a result, the inhabitants would profit and increase their farming, planting, and commerce. The same would apply to the vicinity of Medina. This advantage, again, cannot be rightly estimated at the present time, as it is liable to improvement and growth. Types of that produce may be transported to Damascus and its neighborhood, so that its usefulness [or profit] would double. We may say that these areas could then manage without importing grains from Egypt and other distant countries. At present, when

their arrival is delayed, their prices rise; if the situation gets serious, famine may set in; this happens, mostly in Medina, due to its distance from the seashore and the risks of travel.

[*102*] 4. The Bedouins of Hejaz now have no industries—as is the case even in Mecca and Medina. They get most of their woven cloth and other things from the merchants of the Syrian caravans when these pass there. The Bedouins near Mecca and Medina, or those who go there, buy them [in these two cities]. Most imports, however, come from Syria; it is very unusual to find any products from elsewhere. The same applies to all the belongings of the Bedouins, their furniture and [other] household effects. All this they buy at exorbitant prices. Some of the merchants in the Two Shrines have no regard for Allah (—) in their business, hence they deal in the most debased articles, those quick to disintegrate. They sell them, however, at handsome prices, and after a short while they are worn out. Most of the people in the Two Shrines are poor. Later, the buyer stands before the Ka'ba or at the threshold of the tomb of the Prophet (——). Be the buyer man or woman, old or young, he curses the seller; Allah (—) avenges him and brings evident and hidden troubles [on the seller], and he loses because of his fraud and his taking the money of that poor buyer in a forbidden way. The arrows of trouble hit him. Sometimes, Allah (—) postpones his chastisement to the Day of Judgment. Those Bedouins sell their own products at very low prices—such as sheepskins, cowhides, camelskins, and wool, as well as a few products from which they make no profit, such as laban [sour milk or yogurt], firewood, and goat hair. When the railway is constructed in those parts and completed—if Allah (—) wills it—it would be easy to institute bureaus for industry and farming among the Bedouins. At first these could be specialized in the matters of the area, then could become general in scope. When the Bedouins learn how to deal with their products, profit from them, and introduce what they require themselves—tanning skins, [*103*] cotton, wool, and hair weaving, carpentry, smithcraft, making cheese and samn—then, indeed, they could live in luxury and wealth; they could refrain from buying imported articles, and from raiding one another, as well as those who cross their lands.

5. The railway would facilitate the search for minerals [or metals] in these deserts and wastelands, which have remained unexplored until now, their treasures hidden. When the construction of this railway is completed, it will be easy to travel in these countries,

to dig in the earth and sand, and to pierce the stones; consequently, hidden coal and minerals would be discovered, and the secrets entrusted there would be unveiled. As a result these countries would experience a second period of prosperity. Their sun and moon would shine brightly, and these countries would enjoy affluence and wealth, in full contentment and luxury.

6. Furthering civilization in the population; spreading learning and knowledge among them, as well as security of life, property, and children; acquiring better morals [or finer customs]; and leading a comfortable life. The Ottoman state would establish primary and secondary schools to teach religious sciences, desirable morals [or manners], housekeeping, and economy. The people would enjoy the pleasures of knowledge, and escape the noose of ignorance, squalor, and indolence. They would clean their clothes and meeting places, restore their homes and vary their foods, rest themselves, and lead a life of ease.

7. The Ottoman government (may Allah (—) grant it victory over its enemies and continued glory and prosperity) will employ inhabitants who are suitable in matters related to this railway. [*104*] It would pay them a salary, from the proceeds of the railway. If these employees serve correctly and reliably, their services in the railway would be permanent, not temporary or forbidden [illegal].

8. The inhabitants would sell the train passengers various foods, drinks, and other things—all of which would in no way be sold except through the railway. Examples are bread, meat, eggs, laban, and refreshing water. None of these are [now] taken for sale in Mecca or Medina. Here is a source for large profit, tied up with the passengers.

9. The number of livestock would increase due to the railway, since—as we maintain—agriculture would develop and become general. When agriculture prospers, pasture land and fodder for the animals will be found. Hence, agriculture will increase and develop [further]. The people of the Two Shrines are in great need of an increase in the number of livestock, particularly sheep and cattle, for laban, samn, and meat, which they have not ceased eating at any time. Let not the pilgrims be misled by the sizable number of sheep brought [for sacrifice] in the season of Arafat.[1] Most of those

1. In 1893 more than 120,000 sheep were sacrificed at Arafat during the pilgrimage; cf. J. C. Gervais-Courtellemont, *Mon Voyage à la Mecque* (Paris 1896): 227, based on A. Proust, *L'Orientation Nouvelle de la Politique Sanitaire.*

originate in Najd. Very few, comparatively, originate in the environs of Mecca. The Bedouins of Hejaz, however, bring all their sheep then, for it has been verified that anybody who fails to bring his sheep to the season of Arafat will become very sick or undergo some great calamity; they are ready to give them all up, without exception, even for the lowest price. Only [special] care for raising sheep would fill the need of the Two Shrines for an increase in their number. This, in turn, would be achieved only by enlarging the scope of agriculture in those countries. This is further indicated by the fact that an okka [about $2\frac{3}{4}$ lbs.] of samn is maintaining its price at no less than half a mejidi, sometimes rising [*105*] to a mejidi [about 20 piasters]—as it is imported. When imports do not arrive, the price goes up. Laban follows the same rules as samn. An okka sells in Mecca for four piasters, sometimes rising to more than six. Whoever was honored [has visited] in that wide land would know the truth of our statements. Perhaps, with the increase in livestock and samn production, it would be sent to other places which import samn, such as Jedda. This may turn out to be big business in these parts.

All the above is in addition to the advantage which the Bedouins would derive from renting their camels for the trip from Mecca to Arafat when the railway is completed. We are going to devote a special discussion to this below, if Allah (—) so wills it. This is the most important of all the advantages, insofar as the Hejaz Bedouins are concerned.

12. *The Railway's Advantages for the Bedouins of Syria*

We have already explained that there are many completely ruined and deserted villages on the road from Damascus to Maʿān. The very existence of the Damascus–Medina Railway would mean the restoration of that area and the construction of new villages, along the railway. In this manner, wealth and riches would be the lot of all the inhabitants, particularly of the Bedouins in the vicinity, indeed of others too, in that extensive, huge wasteland, which is fertile [however]. In case these Bedouins do not become civilized, but remain in their present nomad state—as their wealth consists in sheep, goats, camels, and cattle—even then they would profit. When an opening is found for their wool, samn, and lambs, the Bedouins would increase their efforts in this direction: consequently, they would increase in scope. Likewise, if the Bedouins turn to buying and raising goats, there are important advantages to this, in addition to laban and its profits, [*106*] such as [the sale of] goat hair, kids, and skins—all very valuable. Whoever considers the large area of Damascus, and its consumption of sheep and samn, knows that the

Damascenes are badly in need of these products. However, lands suitable for raising sheep are remote from Damascus. This imposes heavy expenses for transportation. Also, the Bedouins do not see any great advantage to be derived nowadays from these products. They are afraid other Bedouins might raid them. Consequently, they limit production to their own needs. Dealers in sheep and samn who reach the Bedouins buy okkas of samn at ridiculously low prices. Sometimes the farmers of Syrian villages go to the Bedouins, taking along their fruit; then they exchange an okka of apples, pears, grapes, or honey for an okka of samn. Hence the Bedouins do not see much profit in raising sheep; in addition, they fear raids by other tribes. Nearby land suitable for sheep raising is very expensive, so that people may spend more on the sheep than gain thereby.

The samn brought by these Bedouins to Damascus is called southern samn. Generally, that coming from the vicinity of Balqā' is the best, purest, most perfumed, and tastiest of all the kinds of samn, including those brought from Homs, Hamah, or al-Dayr (the last is called iron samn). The Damascenes prefer Balqā' samn, valuing it above all the other kinds. It is [however] in limited supply. Most of the samn [used] throughout Syria comes from the areas just indicated. In Damascus itself there is very little; it is brought over from abroad and from nearby towns, such as Beirut and Tripoli. The same is true of Istanbul, lately. As it has to be brought from afar, the prices of samn have risen in Damascus, Aleppo, and elsewhere. Earlier, an okka of samn cost seven piasters in Damascus, but nowadays it is no less than thirteen. [*107*] In Istanbul those who go for Syrian samn are the people of good taste, about one out of fifty. The others prefer the samn of Switzerland or samn made with inferior grease (*çerviş*); they maintain that the favorable perfume of these two is superior to that of the Syrian samn, which also upsets the stomach. All these claims are nothing but the expression of their spoilt taste and smell! Indeed, fifteen days after I first arrived in Istanbul, I was offered rice prepared in Swiss samn. When I took it, its smell was like that of a cadaver; I had to hold my nose and could not eat it. That was the first night of Ramadan and I had to do without suḥūr. Furthermore, one should note the source of Swiss samn. It is not samn [at all], but only the fat and lard of slaughtered or dead animals, put into skins of large animals, such as cows, and sent to Istanbul. Mice and rats frequently multiply there. This type of samn is very cheap when the supply increases, mainly when diseases are rampant among large animals. Actually, I have heard from the greatest physicians in Istanbul that this samn is wholly polluted and noxious; hence whoever does not know this samn ought to beware. Now, if the people of Istanbul had preferred to eat Syrian samn instead of all other kinds, it would have risen in price so much that in Damascus only the luxury-minded wealthy could have afforded it, while all the others would have missed it. Praise to Allah for this! This land [Syria], although fertile, does not get enough samn.

Just as Syria needs samn, it needs sheep. Its sheep originate in distant places, like Erzerum. Sheep cover the way in three or four months, and many die during the trip. They may die of the glanders (*rōja*), which kills them all [when it strikes] to the very last one. Some die from the terrible cold. [*108*] Nevertheless, the merchants make a good profit, sending some of the sheep to Cairo [or Egypt], Istanbul, and other places.

When some of the Bedouins living in Syria—who are numerous as locusts and whose number only Allah (—) can count—become civilized and concentrate on raising sheep, leaving agriculture aside, they would gain from the sheep, their wool, samn and skins, as well as from goats and cattle, manifold more than they make now, even a hundred times as much. Then Syria could do without the samn of Homs, Aleppo and al-Dayr, iron samn, and others; without the sheep of Erzerum, and the like. Then it would be self-sufficient, having a surplus of sheep, samn, wool, goat hair, and skins. It would not need to import any of these. Commerce and industry will grow in Syria, because these Bedouins—if they so prefer—would spend their money on acquiring commodities, clothes, and the like, from Damascus, perforce. Just like Damascus, Istanbul too would do without imported samn, particularly without the above-mentioned noxious, evil-smelling kind, brought in the skins of large animals, mixed with the fat of animals, about which nobody knows whether they were edible, whether they were slaughtered or choked, sick or healthy. This is something which should cause pure souls and sane persons to avoid it and flee from it, not even taking into account [*109*] its smell—an indication of its nature. Only a person who has lost his senses of smell and taste would approach and eat it!

Trustworthy persons have repeatedly told me that in winter dogs are accustomed to visit the samn stores [of Istanbul]. When bitches find an empty samn container of the type described, they bear puppies there. The store owner comes and sees this, but lets the bitch stay and raise its puppies there—pitying her in the cold weather. This may happen, also, in the salesroom. So he leaves the bitch in one corner and sells in the other. One wonders how anybody, claiming refinement and good taste, would eat this samn; or how anyone, claiming some knowledge of hygiene and its basic rules, would allow his family to partake of it! This is an amazing thing! However, if southern samn is produced in larger quantities in Syria, it is going to be more than enough for the needs of its inhabitants; it would even suffice for neighboring lands. Its price would fall then and be more economical than the imported samn. Indeed, it might be sent at low prices to Istanbul, which consequently could renounce its present imports of samn. As a result, the wealth of the Ottoman state would be preserved.

All the above is in addition to what the [Ottoman] department of education is going to do for those countries [through which the railway will be constructed]. It will help their inhabitants with funds; send them graduates of agricultural schools; pave the road for them to get the money they need for agricultural and trade schools; teach them [*110*] farming and trades; sow the grains they need, such as wheat, barley, sorghum, pearl millet, lentils, chick-peas, beans, flax, cotton; plant mulberry trees and grow silkworms; introduce many varieties of fruit trees: citrons, lemon, apple, quince, walnut, almond, grape, and fig; also plant other trees (not bearing fruit), needed for construction, like white poplar and willow; instruct them in weaving, tailoring, tanning, smithcraft, carpentry, pottery, and other very necessary trades; and discover and exploit minerals. When the government does all this, then, indeed, these lands would be reconstructed and populated [even] more than in former times, and their inhabitants would become rich, possessing considerable wealth. Security would reign and civilization would be widespread. They would reach high standing and wear strings of pearls. After all, they are distinguished by acumen, eloquence, zeal, and excellence; they are interested in civilization, learning, progress, and a livelihood; and they are not prone to deception, stupidity, and distrust. The railway alone could bring about repopulation and civilization; the spread of agriculture, industry and commerce; better roads and safer travel. Therefore, we ask Allah (—) to pave the road for the success of the Muslim community (*al-umma al-Muḥammadiyya*) and the good fortune of the Ottoman sultanate!

13. Construction of the Railway Considered as Preparation of Force

Perceptive persons, well-versed in matters of truth, in [all] their details, and proficient in the religious sciences, are aware that a state must have every place close to its capital. Thus communications, defense, transportation and necessary movements would be facilitated in case of need.

The Two Shrines [*111*] are the two centers of Islamic practice and the two poles of the Muslim axis. All Muslims of the Hanifite School converge there. Both are the recourse for the Islamic community (*al-umma al-Islāmiyya*) and the place to which the glances of all Muslims aspire and all feet crowd. Their ruler is the greatest caliph of Allah's Prophet (——). Watching over the Two Shrines and everything connected with or near both of them is a most necessary matter. However, watching over them is feasible only if it is possible, in case of need, to get there quickly and promptly, without delay and tarrying. Preparedness for this means getting the forces ready. Allah (—) said in the Koran, "Make ready for them all thou canst of [armed] force and of horses tethered, that thereby ye may dismay the enemy of Allah and your enemy, and others beside them whom ye may know not. Allah knows them. Whatsoever ye spend in the way of Allah, it will be repaid to you in full, and ye will not be wronged." [K. 8: 60] These lands are distant from one another, particularly from the site of the rulers, who may command or forbid, whose duty it is to care for their interests, laws, policy, defense, protection and safeguarding—whenever their rights are affected or the situation requires this.

That is one of the most important matters. Due to this, travel by sea has increased, surpassing in numbers travel by land. Whoever can get to his destination by sea, avoids the land route completely—because of the distance. It is not necessary to mention [however] that a sea voyage runs into great perils, like heavy storms, malfunctioning of the steamer's engines, fire hazard on board ship, contrary winds, encountering [*112*] foes during the voyage, restrictions of passage imposed by several states [quarantine regulations?], and so forth. This is known and does not require further mention.

The means of communication by land are speedier than those by sea, less dangerous, and more advantageous. Let us assume that one state attacks another, or that a revolt breaks out somewhere, which the government's [local] armed forces are insufficient to quell or that the subjects clash with one another. Then it is necessary to inform the authorities [speedily], so that they may send supplies and forces to prevent hostile actions and quell revolts. Otherwise, the situation may become critical and momentous, the land be ruined, and Muslims perish. This is all the more so in case some enemy attacks an extensive area. Then, if the means for rapid transportation and communication are missing, the enemy may be firmly established before the defending forces arrive; nay, before the very news arrives, if the telegraphic service is not there or is broken—as often happens just in [such] incidents. After all, the first thing insurgents or enemies do is to cut telegraph lines or destroy them to prevent the news from reaching [the authorities].

All this considered, the construction of the railway would be one of the greatest feats for preparing force, as stipulated for Muslims in the Koran; furthermore, the very greatest of such feats for our times. Allah (—) unequivocably ordered us in this matter in the Koran, "Make ready for them all thou canst." [K. 8: 60] The construction is important in this respect—hauling weapons, cannons, gunpowder, cartridges, horses, and the like, indiscriminately. Even more, its construction is to be preferred to other means [of war], [*113*] since the use of other armed forces is conditional on its existence in many places. If the weapons are prepared and the soldiers readily organized, but there is no way for them to reach the required spot, soldiers and weapons are as if non-existent, due to the impossibility of using them. On the contrary, if the means of communication—such as the railway—are available, and the soldiers get there, their arrival and presence bring many advantages, even if they do not have sufficient weapons or are disorganized [as was not infrequently the case in the Ottoman army then]. This is well known and does not need elaboration.

The railway on land is more advantageous than the steamship at sea, as the railway may be used at any time, while the steamship is liable to be beset by difficulties impossible to avoid, such as storms. Sometimes the situation results in the ship's perishing with all its contents—sinking, destroyed by fire, or overcome [by the enemy]. Although it is liable to dangers too, the railway is never wholly destroyed. Compared to the steamship, the danger in the railway is one percent. Even if it is in grave danger in the deserts and wastelands, these areas can be developed, civilized, and populated; then the dangers would disappear. The railway will populate the country, introduce civilization into it, increase crops and harvests, since it is certain to facilitate communications and to create centers of commerce, resulting from [this] means of transportation, such as the Hejaz–Syria Railway. It is also valuable as [*114*] a main preparation of force against enemies.

The above-mentioned Koranic verse explicitly makes mandatory the preparation of force, without specifications. It is, rather, an order for a general type of readiness of all sorts, according to circumstances of time and place. This includes shooting [firearms], forts, steamships, cannons, torpedoes [?], dynamite, railways, and the like. Indeed, preparation ought to be made before the need arises. The above verse warns against delaying until the time of need; on the contrary, it enjoins preparation before the need arises. Evidently, if the matter is set right [only] in time of need, it is of little or no avail, for the conditions are adverse then. Obstacles would hinder preparations [at the time of need], such as the lack of money or [other] essentials, missed opportunities, and similar impediments.

When we do not prepare before the time of need, we are guilty of disobeying the explicit command of Allah in His Book, as revealed by His Prophet. We believed in Him and swore to abide by the contents of the Book. We shall keep our obligation in this matter solely by preparing the force necessary to encounter our enemies before it is needed. In that verse special mention was made of "horses tethered" [K. 8: 60], due to the immense importance [of preparation] in war and its increasing effect in time of need. Horses must be broken in and trained. No man can ride animals which have not been exercised for riding; consequently, the command [of Allah] about tethering them. This command is supported by numerous oral traditions relative to tethering horses. It has been related in an oral tradition [*115*] attributed to Abū Hurayra (——), who reported that the Prophet (——) said, "The good is pinned to the forelocks of the horses until the Day of Judgment. There are three types of horses: of reward, burden, and protection. As for horses of protection, [they belong to] whoever treats them respectfully and kindly, not forgetting all their various needs in difficult or easy conditions. Horses of reward—whoever rides them for Allah, anything they do will carry a reward, even mentioning their dung or urine—run they but a course or two in the valley, this is credited to the rider's balance. Horses of burden—whoever rides them to show off before others, everything they do will be considered a burden, even mentioning their dung or urine—run they but a course or two in the valley, this is debited in the rider's balance." This [also] has been related by Ibn Abī Shayba, Muslim, al-Bayhaqī, and others. Al-Ṭabarānī and al-Ajurrī have related, on the authority of Abū Kabsha (——), "The good is pinned to the forelocks of horses until the Day of Judgment. Their owners are [enjoined] to see after them. Whoever spends on them is like the one who stretches [out] his hand and gives alms." There are numerous oral traditions concerning horses. In ancient and recent times the learned [or ulema] have devoted special books to horses and the relative merits of their tethers, as well as the various types of horses and everything concerned with them. You may refer to these books, if you wish.

Since archery, just as riding horses, was considered indispensable in any situation during peace or war, the Prophet (——) specifically ordered it to be engaged in. In this connection Muslim has related the following oral tradition on the authority of ʿAqaba Ibn ʿĀmir, "I heard the Prophet (——) saying, The Byzantines are going to attack you, [but] Allah will protect you; let no one fail to delight in mentioning His name!" The same source reports, in a long oral tradition, "I heard the Prophet saying, [*116*] Whoever learnt to shoot and then neglected it, is no more one of us; he has renounced his obedience [to Allah]." Evidently, horse riding and shooting are indispensable for both war or an encounter with the enemy, in any time or place, in any situation or ratio of forces.

Aḥmad [Ibn Ḥanbal], Muslim, Abū Da'ūd, Ibn Māja, and others, have related, on the authority of 'Āmir al-Juhanī (——), who quoted the Prophet (——) as saying from the minbar, "Make ready for them all thou canst of [armed] force. [K. 8: 60] Force means shooting, force means shooting, force means shooting." This the Prophet repeated three times, implying that the most important part of force is shooting, not that the force is limited to shooting. This compares, indeed, with the saying of the Prophet (——), "The pilgrimage was to Arafat." What he implied was that the major part of the pilgrimage was to Arafat, although the pilgrimage has four parts—the intention to go, standing in Arafat, circumambulation of the Kaʿba, and running seven times between Ṣafā and Marwa. This text specifying horse riding and shooting is wondrous, indeed.

Like the above books about horses, people (——) composed books about shooting, because of their absorbing interest in it. These books ought to be studied continuously until everyone is proficient in them. Shooting is not confined to arrows, as in earlier days; the intent is most general—as explained in the second oral tradition, above, and other sources. The [Prophet's] injunction about shooting includes shooting with arrows, bullets, rifles, cannons, catapults, and so forth. This injunction is all-embracing.

On the authority of Saʿd Ibn Abī Waqqāṣ, the Prophet (——) said, "Study shooting, as it is the best of your games." On the authority of al-Bayhaqī, who got it from Ibn ʿUmar (——), the Prophet (——) said, "Teach your sons to swim and shoot; instruct women to spin." Ibn Manda related, on the authority of Bakr Ibn ʿAbd Allah Ibn al-Rabīʿ al-Anṣārī (——), "The Caliph ʿUmar Ibn al-Khaṭṭāb [*117*] (——) wrote, Teach your sons to swim and ride horses." As for shooting, the Prophet (——) made the instruction of children in shooting compulsory upon their fathers.

There is an oral tradition, on the authority of Abū Rāfiʿ (——), that the Prophet said, "A father has the obligation to teach his son to write, swim, and shoot." This is retold by Abū'l-Dunyā and al-Bayhaqī. Another source adds, "to give him a good name." Yet another adds, "to marry him off when the son reaches maturity." To sum up: riding, shooting, and swimming are matters of concern, by religious law. The oral traditions about this are many, indeed countless.

The construction of the railway is the strongest preparation of force in our times. Only a person who has a hidden design in his heart would remain aloof or spread rumors about it. However, Allah will bring out what they have been concealing and then those wrongdoers will know how grievously they will be upset.

14. Expenditure on Railway Construction Means Rebuilding the Two Shrines

In the Koran Allah (—) urged the rebuilding of mosques. He maintained that believers should do this. When they had done it, He would reward them with [divine] guidance. Allah said, "He only shall tend Allah's sanctuaries who believes in Allah and the Last Day and observes proper worship and pays the poor-due and fears none save Allah. For such [only] is it possible that they can be of the rightly guided." [K. 9: 18] This is stated positively and definitely.

Rebuilding mosques is feasible by constructing them anew or repairing them; or making them suitable for worshipping and reinstating the marks of religion there. Either of these purposes applies to the rebuilding of mosques. A verse in the Koran sanctions them all; oral traditions urge this too. [*118*] In [the collections of] al-Bukhārī and Muslim there is a tradition on the authority of Caliph 'Uthmān Ibn 'Affān (——), "I have heard the Prophet (——) saying, Whoever builds a mosque for Allah, desiring to honor Allah (—) Allah will build for him a home in Paradise." Again al-Bukhārī and Muslim relate, this time on the authority of Abū

Hurayra (——), that the Prophet (——) said, "Whoever walks back and forth to the mosque—for him Allah has prepared guest houses in Paradise, every time that he walked back and forth."

Al-Tirmidhī relates, on the authority of Abū Sa'īd al-Khudrī (——), that the Prophet (——) said, "When you see a man who is accustomed to visiting mosques, you may testify in his favor as to his faith, as Allah asserted, He shall tend Allah's sanctuaries who believes in Allah and the Last Day." [K. 9: 18] Al-Tirmidhī has à good oral tradition (*ḥadīth ḥasan*), saying, "We saw several of our ancestors, who used to stay in the mosque, without leaving it, except for some [pressing] need." My father (——) was one of them. He resided within the Umayyad Mosque in Damascus, during his whole life, not leaving it except for some [pressing] need. He used to pray there, as a first imam. He would sit on a bench in that mosque, facing the grave of Sayyid Yaḥyà (may he rest in peace), in the northern end of the mosque. So much so that the bench came to be called after my father. From it my father would teach religious sciences, particularly Muslim jurisprudence and oral tradition. He would give legal responsa (*fatwà*) to enquiries from far away. Often, he would interpret dreams. He was so well-versed in the jurisprudence of the Shafiite School, that he was nicknamed the Little Shāfi'ī. He would not let up reciting the Koran, mentioning Allah's name, praying for the Prophet (——), teaching religious science, or giving legal responsa—always quiet, not fooling around. He remained in these good conditions [*119*] until he died (——).

There is no doubt whatsoever that rebuilding the two sacred mosques—the one in Mecca and the one of the Prophet (——) [in Medina]—will be achieved, thanks to the construction of the railway, progressing day by day. Rebuilding, in this case, may equally apply to repairing and constructing, or to mentioning Allah's name, prayer, and teaching there. Those who are instrumental in initiating and constructing the railway may be sure of the reward [reserved] for those who rebuild the two sacred mosques—of both types of rebuilding—without losing any of the reward for rebuilders. In this context the Prophet (——) said, "Whoever establishes something good, his reward is certain; whoever has done this, his reward is kept [for him] until the Day of Judgment." Those who speak up for the construction of this railway, or assist its construction with funds or by themselves, are equal to those who rebuild the two sacred mosques with prayer, mention of Allah's name, and so forth, or with funds. Both types will get their full reward. Whosoever offers himself [to assist] in the construction of the Hejaz–Syria Railway is as one who rebuilds the two sacred mosques.

You have already noted what reward Allah (—) has prepared for him who rebuilds any mosque. How much more so for him who rebuilds the two sacred mosques! Surely, the good deed is multiplied, by comparison. Now, prayer in the mosque in Mecca is counted a hundred thousand times more, and in the mosque of Medina, a thousand times more. This refers to the mosque in which the Prophet himself (——) prayed, in his time, not to the parts added since. This conforms with what the imam Aḥmad [Ibn Ḥanbal] related in his *Musnad* and al-Bayhaqī in his collection of oral traditions, and others besides these two, on the authority of 'Abd Allah Ibn al-Zubayr (——), that the Prophet (——) said, "A prayer in my mosque is preferable to a thousand in another, [*120*] with the exception of the sacred mosque [in Mecca], where a prayer is preferable to a hundred in my mosque." Indeed, Mecca was preferable to Medina. This is based on the views of al-Shāfi'ī, Abū Ḥanīfa, and Aḥmad [Ibn Ḥanbal][1] (——), as well as those agreeing with them. However, according to Mālik [Ibn Anas][2] (——), Medina is superior. This is a renowned conflict of views.

In the same manner that good deeds multiply [in value], so do evil ones. So much so, that if one plans something evil in his mind outside the Two Shrines, this is not held against him—but not so in Mecca. Allah (—) said, "Whoever seeks wrongful partiality therein, him We shall cause to taste a painful doom." [K. 22: 25] One finds in the book *al-Durr al-Manthūr* that Ibn Abī Shayba, 'Abd Ibn Ḥamīd, and Ibn al-Mundhir relate, on the authority of Mujāhid, that the Prophet said, "The multiplication of evil deeds in Mecca is equal [in value] to the multiplication of the good ones." And by the reporting of 'Akrama, he said, "Allah does not punish any Muslim who thinks of sinning, except when he plans evil in the Ancient House [Ka'ba, and by extension, all of Mecca]; then Allah punishes him swiftly." According to a report by Abū'l-Ḥajjāj, the Prophet said, "Let the man, who plans to sin in Mecca know that Allah (—) will write it down against him as a sin [actually committed]." According to Ibn Mas'ūd, the Prophet, commenting on the above Koranic verse, "Whoever seeks wrongful partiality therein, him We shall cause to taste a painful doom," said, "Whoever plans a transgression

1. Founders of three of the four major schools of law interpretation in early Islam.
2. Founder of the fourth school, who lived and taught in Medina (see above).

and does not carry it out, if he plans it anywhere except in Mecca, this is not written down against him, until he actually performs it. Whoever plans a transgression in Mecca [however], Allah does not let him die before meting out to him a painful punishment in this world."

How blessed, then, is the person whom Allah (—) lets have the good fortune to assist in the construction of this railway, in order to rebuild the Two Shrines, in both of which good deeds are counted as manifold. That person will then get the same reward as one who rebuilds [the shrines]. Allah is the One who grants success, says the truth, and leads on the righteous path.

15. *Other Benefits the Hejaz Railway Will Afford Muslims*

CONSTRUCTION OF THE RAILWAY EQUALS ALMS-GIVING, AND THE REWARD THEREOF

[*121*] From the preceding it is now proven that constructing this railway means preparing force against enemies and rebuilding the mosques, as is strictly enjoined and urged in the Koran. Awakening interest in it and assisting it financially equal almsgiving for the cause of Allah.

The term "for the cause of Allah" (—) applies to the holy war (*jihād*), as Allah said, "Those who believe and have left their homes and striven with their wealth and their lives in Allah's way." [K. 9: 20] It also applies to various sorts of righteousness enjoined on Muslims, such as almsgiving, as Allah said, "The alms are only for the poor and the needy, and those who collect them, and those whose hearts are to be reconciled, and to free the captives and the debtors, and for the cause of Allah, and for the wayfarer; a duty imposed by Allah." [K. 9: 60] Or as the Prophet (——) said, "We, the relatives of Muhammad, are not allowed to benefit from the alms." As Allah (—) said, "The likeness of those who spend their wealth in Allah's way is as the likeness of a grain which grows seven ears, in every ear a hundred grains. Allah gives increase manifold to whom He will. Allah is All-Embracing, All-Knowing." [K. 2: 261] And He also said, "Those who spend their wealth for the cause of Allah and afterward make not reproach and injury to follow that which they have spent, their reward is with their Lord, and there shall be no fear come upon them, neither shall they grieve." [K. 2: 262]

Doubtlessly, assisting a believer with money is a sort of righteousness—giving alms for the cause of Allah. Consequently, the construction of the Hejaz Railway is for the cause of Allah in both meanings: that of the holy war, for it means preparing force against enemies; and almsgiving, for this is one of the sorts of righteousness and doing good—to rebuild the mosques in the Two Shrines, assist those who come riding [*122*] to worship, visit [the tomb of the Prophet], walk around [the Ka'ba], perform the 'umra and the pilgrimage, raise the standard of Islam, and help Muslims on a reciprocal basis. All these are some of the greatest ways of spending for the cause of Allah. However, one who spends here is also a warrior in the holy war, as the railway also prepares force against the enemy. This is explicitly stated in the Koran as follows, "Those who strive with their wealth and their lives for the cause of Allah [*passim*]." Also, "Allah has bestowed on those who strive a great reward above the sedentary." [K. 4: 95] Hence the man who spends money for the jihad is called a *mujāhid* (soldier in the holy war).

Consequently, the jihad is performed either in person or by funds. The first is preferable to the second; the most desirable is both together. It is related in *al-Durr al-Manthūr*, on the authority of a number of Companions, that the Prophet (——) said, "Whoever sends money in the course of Allah and remains at home, every drachma he has sent is worth seven hundred. Whoever fights in the course of Allah and in addition participates with money, every drachma he has given will be worth seven hundred thousand on the Day of Judgment." Then the Prophet recited the following verse, "The likeness of those who spend their wealth in Allah's way is as the likeness of a grain [which grows seven ears, in every ear a hundred grains]." [K. 2: 261] Here Allah (—) has put the money first, the soul second. The reason is, first, that the soul usually is avaricious in matters of money; and second, that many people are not capable of going to fight in a jihad. Also, a jihad is dependent on money in order to prepare forces; rather, it is unfeasible without money, particularly in these times. It is customary that men would soldier for a fee with a state whose subjects they are not, as is evident and well-known. Nowadays money makes soldiers superfluous, for it is possible to hire men with money, while it is impossible to get men without money.

As a result, a state has to be permanently wealthy, with well-filled coffers. This is the best preparation for a state, since money [*123*] means readiness. When a state is rich, it is prepared very well indeed, for one can get everything with money. With money at his disposal, man can do everything, with the permission of Allah (—). A state is in an even better position in this respect, for basically nothing impedes a state so much as the need [of money] or the lack of justice; for indeed, money and justice are the cornerstone of every state. Allah (—) mentioned money first [as noted above] out of concern for those who cannot participate in the jihad personally—so that their reward would not be less than that of the fighters themselves. It is related on the authority of Zayd Ibn Thābit (——), in the name of the Prophet (——), "Whoever equips a warrior in the course of Allah (—) gets the same reward as the warrior; whoever appoints a warrior in his family and financially takes care of the family, gets the same reward." The compilers of the Six Books of Oral Traditions relate that the Prophet (——) said, "Whoever equipped a warrior in the course of Allah, it is as if he fought himself; whoever appoints a warrior in his family at his own expense, it is as if he fought himself." Furthermore, if a man is a coward who desires to participate in the jihad; while another is brave, but has no equipment; and the coward equips the brave and spends on the upkeep of the brave's family, taking care of their needs; and the brave goes to fight—the coward who stays home gets a larger reward than if he had gone to fight himself, particularly as he would have shaken the army by his fear and cowardice. Very probably, he ought to do this. [Send somebody else in his stead, and care for that warrior's family.] Similar to him is the intelligent and economical man who desires to participate in the jihad but is poor and unable to go; another man is rich and able to go; however, the poor one is better suited for this purpose than the other. If the rich man equips the poor man, he will get a larger reward than he would have obtained, had he gone to the jihad personally and at his own expense. There are many other examples. The [divine] injunctions in this sense, Allah's urging expenditures in His course and His assurances of rewarding the fighters [*124*] more than the sedentary, are too numerous in the Koran and the oral traditions to list here. Allah (—)

said, "He has bestowed on those who strive a great reward above the sedentary. Degrees of rank [come] from Him, and forgiveness and mercy. Allah is ever forgiving, Merciful." [K. 4: 95–96] He also said, "Those who believe, and have left their homes and striven with their wealth and their lives in Allah's way are of much greater worth in Allah's sight. These are they who are triumphant. Their Lord gives them good tidings of mercy from Him, and acceptance, and gardens where enduring pleasures will be theirs; there they will abide forever. Lo! with Allah there is immense reward." [K. 9: 20–22] Also, "And whatsoever ye spend [for good], He replaces it." [K. 24: 39] Then, "Who is it that will lend unto Allah a goodly loan [without interest or gain], so that He may give it increase manifold" [K. 2: 245, 57: 11] (and then forgive his sins). Or, "The likeness of those who spend their wealth in Allah's way is as the likeness of a grain which grows seven ears, in every ear a hundred grains. Allah gives increase manifold to whom He will." [K. 2: 261] And, "Those who spend their wealth for the cause of Allah and afterward make not reproach and injury to follow that which they have spent; their reward is with their Lord, and there shall no fear come upon them, neither shall they grieve." [K. 2: 262]

The Prophet (——) said, "Expenditure for the cause of Allah will be increased sevenhundredfold." This is related by al-Bukhārī in his *History*. Al-Ṭabaranī relates, on the authority of Mu'ādh Ibn Jabal, that the Prophet (——) said, "How fortunate is the man who has mentioned Allah's name many times, as his contribution to the jihad. Indeed, every such word counts as seventy thousand good deeds; and every [such] good deed would be rewarded tenfold or more." He was then asked, "Oh, Messenger of Allah, and what about expenditures [in the course of Allah]?" Muhammad replied, "Even a very tiny amount counts!" 'Abd al-Raḥmān added, "Thereupon I asked Mu'ādh, Would such expenditure be rewarded sevenhundredfold? He answered, Your understanding is little. This reward applies to those who stay at home, without going to war. However, when they go to war and in addition spend money [for the course of Allah], then Allah keeps for them hidden treasures, of which His servants have no inkling. Those are the troops of Allah, [*125*] and they are victorious." Oral traditions and Koranic verses elaborating on this matter are numerous. Whoever desires [to read] more, let him refer to them. Had not the mention of further instances sidetracked us from the purpose in writing this book, we would have cited more—from what was left out—for our purpose.

CONSTRUCTION OF THE RAILWAY ASSISTS BELIEVERS, AND THE REWARD THEREFOR

We have already briefly discussed mutual assistance [among Muslims], in our article "The Sultan's Greatest Feats." Let us here elaborate on this with supporting arguments, if Allah (—) so wills it.

The construction of this railway will assist believers in performing the pilgrimage, 'umra, and visit to the tomb of the Prophet (——). It will also help commerce, industry, and agriculture; it will civilize the savages, enrich the poor, satiate the hungry, enrich the country, and bring [many] Muslims to life. We have already explained this and more, so the rest is already known. When the construction of this railway is completed, with the help of Allah (—), all those who are [now] unable to perform the pilgrimage, or to sustain the hardship and crowding on the road, would be able to perform it, visit the Prophet's tomb, buy and sell, and achieve what they desire to do in those lands, with the greatest ease and comfort. Hence, they should support the construction of the railway, personally, financially, or by giving a favorable opinion.

Both the Koran and the oral traditions explicitly enjoin Muslims to arouse others and assist them in a good cause. Allah (—) said, "Help one another unto righteousness and pious duty. Help not one another unto sin and transgression" [K. 5: 2] (and unto disobeying the Messenger of Allah). Al-Bukhārī, Muslim, and al-Tirmidhī relate that the Prophet (——) [*126*] said, "Whoever aids his brother in need, Allah aids him." Muslim relates that the Prophet (——) said, "Whoever relieves a believer of a worldly worry, has relieved Allah of a worry in the Day of Judgment. Whoever makes it easy for a man in straitened circumstances, Allah will make it easy for him in this world and the next. Allah assists His servant whenever His servant aids his brother. Whoever walks on a road in which he seeks knowledge, Allah will facilitate his road to Paradise. Whenever a group of people met in some House of Allah to recite the Koran and instruct one another in it, the presence of Allah descended on them, His mercy enveloped them, and the angels surrounded them. Allah will keep a record of them. However, He would not hasten to ascribe the deeds of the man who tarries." Al-Tirmidhī relates in his book *al-Ṣaḥīḥ* that the Prophet (——) said, "Whoever relieves a believer of a worldly worry, has relieved Allah of a worry in the Day of Judgment. Whoever protects [or covers the faults of] a Muslim, Allah protects him in this world and the next. Allah assists His servant, whenever His servant assists his brother."

Anyone who requires more information in this matter may read our book, *The Nearest Waterskin for Relieving Worries.* Now, the construction of this railway means assistance to the believers, our brethren, in fulfilling the duties of pilgrimage, ʻumra, visit to the Prophet's tomb, commerce, and the like. Allah will assist him who assists in its construction—all the years that it would function. The railway would provide believers a relief from the hardship of riding or walking, hunger or thirst, fear, and so on. Undoubtedly, Allah (—) will relieve those who bring about its construction, participate in it, and assist it, from the worries of the Day of Judgment.

THE RAILWAY ASSISTS BELIEVERS AND PROVIDES ADVANTAGES IN THIS WORLD, AND REWARDS IN THE HEREAFTER

Know that the construction of this railway will facilitate mutual contacts between Muslims. [*127*] Doubtlessly, all believers are brethren, according to an explicitly clear text in the Koran, namely, "The believers are naught else than brothers." [K. 49: 10] Belief in Allah (—) and His Prophet (——) forms the only bond that unites them in view and word, that makes them agree and assist one another. Nobody can deny the advantages and good consequences of mutual assistance and common agreement—particularly in regard to the one and only caliph and emir, as specified in the Islamic religion.

Allah (—) said, through the intermediary of Moses (may he rest in peace), "Appoint for me a henchman from my folk. Aaron, my brother. Confirm my strength with him. And let him share my task." [K. 20: 29–32] Also, "We will strengthen thine arm with thy brother." [K. 27: 35] Al-Bukhārī related in his *Ṣaḥīḥ* that the Prophet (——) said, "One believer is unto the other like a building, one part of which bolsters the other. Then he tightened his fingers." Muslim also quoted this in his own *Ṣaḥīḥ*, but did not mention the Prophet's tightening his fingers. Another tradition, related by Muslim, has it that the Prophet (——) said, "The believers, in their mutual good terms, love and affection, are like the [human] body. If any member of the body complains, the others respond with sleeplessness and fever." It is related, on the authority of Ibn Dā'ūd, that the Prophet (——) said, "It is the duty of the believers to feel grief for one another, just as the body feels pain for the head."

The best means for believers to discover one another's situation and get each other's news in remote, extensive countries, is by pilgrimage. There are many advantages to the pilgrimage—religious and political. Several of them have been mentioned. This is not the place to list the rest, as they are well-known to anybody having some acquaintance with the religious sciences [*128*] and the secrets of the Koran. We have adduced a sample [of them] in our article, "The Sultan's Greatest Feats."

Altogether there lies in the mutual assistance and cooperation of the believers a hidden secret, which is obvious and the mainstay of religion and temporal power. [Only] by cooperation will the believers escape from the evil designs of their enemies. Cooperation, both open and secret, making them as one limb, will give them a strong stance against any hostile injury to their religion, temporal power, or their [own] persons. This will bring them the signal advantage which is obtainable only through cooperation. Cooperation as enjoined by religious law will be carried out only by unity of view and word. This, in turn, will be accomplished solely by rallying around a single imam or emir and by obeying his commands and bans, just as the Muslim religious law orders. It is truly imperative that all Muslims will be under authority of one imam—the caliph[1] of the Prophet (——).

Ibn Māja relates, on the authority of 'Arafja al-Ashja'ī, that the Prophet (——) said, "Whoever comes and sets all of you against one man, intends to break your stick and bring discord among you; so kill him! If all Muslims together will follow one man, nobody could withstand them." This is indeed obligatory for the continued existence of the Muslim community. This explanation suffices here, for the matter is well known to anyone who is unbiased, objective, and uncontaminated, for a span of ground is too narrow to walk on [one should see matters as they are and not distort them?]. Allah is the One who brings success and to Him our fate leads us.

[*129*] By cooperation you will find all good;
By disunity you will get evil and failure.
Hence, discard self-love, isolated;
By cooperation, everything planned is done!

1. The reigning Ottoman Sultan Abdul-Hamid II, proponent of the panislamic theory just summarized.

In addition to this, cooperation brings uncounted worldly advantages, and likewise, endless rewards in the next world. Since the construction of this railway is a means for cooperation, as we have explained, its outcome will bring success in this world and the next for those who carry it out, or assist it with money, in person, and by their views, or arouse others in its favor. Allah (—) is the One who leads to success.

EVERY BELIEVER IS ENJOINED TO OBEY THE CALIPH IN ASSISTING THE CONSTRUCTION OF THIS RAILWAY; ANY OPPOSITION OR STAYING BEHIND IS FORBIDDEN

> Obedience to the Sultan is mandatory;
> This is enjoined by the Koran and oral tradition.
> Any Muslim who contradicts this
> Is, surely, a wicked hypocrite!

We have shown above that the construction of this railway means preparing force, as clearly enjoined in the Koran. This is an obligatory command [for Muslims]. Also, it would assist the hoped for cooperation, ordered by religious law; the performance of the pilgrimage, ‘umra, and visit to the Prophet's tomb; rebuilding of the two sacred mosques; enlarging the scope of commerce, industry, and agriculture; facilitating the penetration of civilization among savage communities; making terrorized roads safe, and difficult ones easy; populating the country; adding happiness to the servants [of Allah]; and other matters which form part of Islam, this religion which incorporates justice, virtue, purity, and cleanliness.

There can be no doubt that the pilgrimage is a pillar [*130*] on which Islam has been built. The Prophet (——) said, "Islam was built on five [pillars]: the profession of faith with the formula, There is no God but Allah, and Muhammad is the Messenger of Allah; praying; almsgiving; pilgrimage; and the fast of Ramadan." The obligation of performing them has been specified in the Koran and tradition. Religion considers them mandatory duties, so there is no need to list proofs for this, which abound. For example, Allah (—) said, "Pilgrimage to the House is a duty unto Allah for mankind, for him who can find a way thither." [K. 3: 97] We have already listed the merits of pilgrimage, mutual assistance, cooperation, and spending in the course of Allah, so there is no reason to repeat them. Our comments make additional ones superfluous; those interested will consider them sufficient.

He who assists the construction of the railway, from the point of view that it is a preparation of force, [is justified] by Allah's words, "Make ready for them all thou canst of [armed] force and of horses tethered, that thereby ye may dismay the enemy of Allah and your enemy." [K. 8: 60] Also, "O ye who believe! Obey Allah and the Messenger when He calls you to that which quickens you, and know that Allah comes in between the man and his own heart, and that He it is unto Whom ye will be gathered." [K. 8: 24] Ibn Isḥāq and Ibn Abī Ḥātim have selected the Koranic quote, "To that which quickens you" [in this context], "That is, to the war in which Allah gave you glory after [your] ignoring, strengthened you after [your] weakness, and defended you from your enemy after he had vanquished you."

It is certain that the preparation of force comes into the same category as war [itself], for this is the means for war; and that responding to a call for war by those responsible is as binding as responding to [such] a call by Allah and the Prophet, had they called. Insofar as it [the railway?] is a way for rebuilding the two sacred mosques, as Allah worded it, "He only shall tend Allah's sanctuaries who believes in Allah and the Last Day, and observes proper worship and pays the poor-due, and fears none save Allah. For such [only] is it possible that they can be of the rightly guided." [K. 9: 18] [*131*] This evident statement, that "they can be of the rightly guided," is applied to those who cause the two sacred shrines to be rebuilt, for only believers would rebuild them. This is evidenced by Allah's words, "It is not for idolaters to tend Allah's sanctuaries, bearing witness against themselves of disbelief. As for such, their works are vain and in the fire they will abide." [K. 9: 17] This verse indicates that nonbelievers should be prevented from constructing the railway. That is the cause of the two mosques' not having been rebuilt. The Koran has [thus] not attested to their belief. Insofar as the railway involves an expenditure in the course of Allah, He said, "And the likeness of those who spend their wealth in search of Allah's pleasure, and for the strengthening of their souls, is as the likeness of a garden on a height. The rainstorm smites it and it brings forth its fruit twofold. And if the rainstorm smite it not, then the shower." [K. 2: 265] And for its helping the believers to [increased] purity and piousness, the following Koranic quote is applicable, "Help ye one another unto righteousness and pious duty," [K. 5: 2] As for its reward coming from Allah, His words, "Who is it that will lend unto Allah a goodly loan, so that He may give it increase manifold." [K. 2: 245, 57: 11] As for rumormongering about the railway's being a prevention of doing good, a "Hinderer of the good, transgressor, malefactor" [K. 68: 12], many such verses can be brought in support of the railway's construction and of its opponents' having to be warded off, such as, "Lo! Those who disbelieve spend their wealth in order that they may debar [men] from the way of Allah. They will spend it, then it will become an anguish for them, then they will be conquered." [K. 8: 36] As for the compliance with its construction's being obedience to Allah, His Prophet and the caliph, the following applies, "O ye who believe! Obey Allah, and obey the Messenger and those of you who are in authority." [K. 4: 59] As to the commands for obeying the Caliph in [all] his orders or prohibitions, this is a matter which Islam enjoins absolutely; [*132*] Muslims are agreed thereupon. There are explicit proofs, which cannot be interpreted otherwise, for instance Allah's words, "O ye who believe! Obey Allah, and obey the Messenger and those of you who are in authority" [K. 4: 59] or "Whoso obeys the Messenger obeys Allah" [K. 4: 80]. The Prophet (——) said, "Whosoever obeys me, obeys Allah; whosoever disobeys me, disobeys Allah. Whoever obeys the ruler, obeys me; whoever disobeys the ruler, disobeys me." And also his saying, "Obedience to the ruler (*imām*) is mandatory on the male Muslim, so long as he does not order him to disobey Allah; should he so order, then one owes the ruler no obedience." Oral traditions abound prohibiting disobedience [of the ruler]. For example, the Prophet (——) said, "Do not inquire about three types: a man who has left his crowd, disobeyed his imam, and died in disobedience; a female slave and a male slave who ran away from their master and then died; and a woman, whose husband is absent but left her sufficient livelihood, who plays up her charms. Do not inquire about them" [they are not worthy of your attention]. Or his saying, "Whoever dissents from his ruler, dies like a pagan." And in another old tradition, "Whoever leaves his [own] crowd, even for one span, dies like a pagan" [before the revelation of Islam].

Those who want to get at the truth have no doubt that in the above Koranic verse, "O ye who believe! Obey Allah, and obey the Messenger and those of you who are in authority," He referred to the greatest imam [the Ottoman sultan] and his officials, not to the ulema, as some commentators would have it. In the book *al-Durr al-Manthūr*, the meaning of "those in authority" is discussed. Ibn Jarīr [al-Ṭabarī] explains, on the authority of Ibn Zayn, "They are the rulers [sultans]."[2] The Prophet (——) is reported to have said then, "Obedience means obedience. In obedience [one shows] creditable performance." He added, "Had Allah so wished it, he would have given the right of command to the prophets." [*133*] He meant that Allah gave the right of command to the rulers and the prophets jointly. Have you not noticed that, when they passed the death penalty over Yaḥyà Ibn Zachariah [John the Baptist] (may both rest in peace)? This is even clearer from what Allah (—) said in the matter of the story of David, "Their Prophet said unto them: Lo! Allah has raised up Saul to be a king for you." [K. 2: 247] This refers to a king, not a prophet. This, however, occurred among bygone peoples. There was no king with our Prophet (——), as the Prophet chose worship [of Allah] instead. His was the rule, and the righteous caliphs inherited it from him, not the ulema. Perhaps the saying of the Prophet (——), "The ulema of my community are like the prophets of the sons of Israel," indicates this (as it may indicate other matters, too). This is because the ulema are trained to pass judgment, not to give orders or execute [policies]. To command and forbid is a matter for the imam, not to give legal opinions.

The Koranic expression, "those in authority," evidently refers to the imam and his officials, not the ulema. This is seen in the end of that verse, "And if ye have a dispute concerning any matter, refer it to Allah and the Messenger." [K. 4: 59] This is the very best, interpretationwise. [See] Allah's (—) words, "But nay, by thy Lord, they will not believe [in truth] until they make thee judge of what is in dispute between them and find within themselves no dislike of that which thou decidest, and submit with full submission." [K. 4: 65] This indicates that in the former verse the term, "those in authority," referred to the imam, not to the ulema. For the words, "If ye have a dispute concerning any matter, refer it to Allah and the Messenger," combined with the verse, "But nay, by thy Lord, they will not believe [in truth] until they make thee judge of what is in dispute between them and find within themselves no dislike of that which thou decidest," evidently refer to ruling and judging. "Refer it to Allah and the Messenger" applies to judging and ruling. The Prophet (——) used to judge and rule according to the religious law that had been revealed to him. Therefore, the ulema are not

2. Thus doubly applicable in 'Ārif's view.

the rulers, but the imam, who is the caliph of the Prophet (——). [*134*] Consequently, he and his officials are "those in authority," mentioned in the above Koranic verse; they are those whom all Muslims are enjoined to obey.

Indeed, obedience to the imam—the caliph of the Prophet (——)—is mandatory, in the same category with obedience to Allah and the Prophet. When the ulema are "those in authority," they should be obeyed, not because they are ulema, but because they are in authority. This resembles the case of religious judges (*qāḍīs*) or people in similar positions [of authority]. When an alim pronounces a decision (*fatwà*) in a matter pertaining to religious law, the person to whom his fatwà applies has to obey it—because it is the decision of Allah (—), not because it is an order from the alim. This differs from a command issued by those in authority, which should be obeyed only when it does not contradict religious law. In the latter case, everyone is bound to obey the command, since the person who issues it may well be an authorized agent [for Allah]. Consequently, when the imam issues a command, it is mandatory. This is, indeed, the difference between his command and another's.

After having finished writing the above, I found that Allah's people, the Sufis (may Allah (—) let us benefit through them) have interpreted in the same way the intent of the term, "those in authority," as mentioned in the Koran, to refer to the imam and his officials. The great Shaykh [Ibn 'Arabī], who composed the book *Meccan Revelations* (*al-Futūḥāt al-Makiyya*), wrote as follows in its 336th section, "When people began quarreling, Allah appointed rulers to whom they could have recourse whenever they were in a dispute, so that these rulers could decide and resolve the quarrel. He also appointed one imam, to whom all could have recourse, evidently to strengthen religion. Allah ordered His servants not to contradict him. Should anybody oppose him and contradict him, Allah has ordered us to call him, execute him, and uproot him, since it is known that [such] contradiction would lead to wickedness." Allah said, "If there were therein gods besides Allah, then verily both [the heavens and the earth] had been disordered." [K. 21: 22] This verse merits a closer look, as it includes meanings that could dispel doubt.

The above book added the following, based on the Koran and tradition, "Allah (—) has commanded us not to move even one hand [finger] away from obedience to him." Then, "The law laid down by the imam is most suitable to be obeyed." [*135*] Allah said, "O ye who believe! Obey Allah and obey the Messenger and those of you who are in authority." [K. 4: 59] The above book comments, "Those in authority are the leaders, caliphs, and rulers. Their rule is allowed only in such matters in which there is no [legal or religious] restriction. Both the mandatory and the forbidden are part of the obedience due to Allah and to His Prophet. So the imams may require obedience only in such matters that are permitted. Otherwise, there is no reward or responsibility involved. When the imam, officially appointed and to whom you have sworn obedience, commands you in a matter that is permitted [legally], it is mandatory that you should obey him in this, and forbidden to disobey him. To put it clearly: what is permitted [legally] is also mandatory [in this case]. The man who obeys such orders gets the same reward as in carrying out mandatory injunctions [of Islam]. So the rule of permissibility is lifted from such a matter—by order of him [the caliph (hence the Ottoman sultan)] to whom you have sworn allegiance. Consequently, do ponder this."

The outcome of the above is that obedience to the imam, the caliph of the Prophet (——) is mandatory, as it is part of the general obedience to Allah and the Prophet. I intend to write a separate treatise on this matter, if Allah (—) wills it. The matter applies, particularly, to this railway—for obeying Allah and the Prophet in the matter of the railway's construction is greater than [merely] obeying the caliph's order about the railway. This is, indeed, one of the orders issued by the Lawgiver [Allah], which He made mandatory and urged [us] to obey them. So, obeying the caliph in the construction of the railway and its completion is a mandatory duty on every Muslim, according to his ability, financially or personally, or both together, as the religious law enjoins him to do. Allah (—) is the One who leads on the right course.

16. *How the Construction of the Hejaz Railway Will Affect the Hiring of Camels*

THE PILGRIMS' NEED FOR CAMELS BETWEEN YANBU' AND MEDINA, AND IN THE ASCENT TO ARAFAT, AFTER THE RAILWAY'S CONSTRUCTION

The camels which the Bedouins of Hejaz rent out of Yanbu' for the trip to Medina to visitors of the Prophet's tomb, merchants, and pilgrims, [*136*] will increase manifold in number after the prolongation of the railway line [to Hejaz]. The reason is that the inhabitants of those parts, who pass by Yanbu' on their way to Jedda, now do one of the following: they go out to Yanbu' and rent their camels to the caravans that proceed to Medina, some of them [do business] with the caravans proceeding from Medina to Mecca, or with the Syrian caravan; when the pilgrims proceed to Mecca, they return to their own countries via Jedda, without returning again to Medina and then to Yanbu'. Or they go directly to Jedda, thence to Mecca; and later, with the caravans that proceed from Mecca to Medina or with the Syrian caravan, to Yanbu', whence the pilgrims return home. All these visitors visit [Medina] just once, either before the pilgrimage [to Mecca] or after it, as it is possible for them. They do not visit [Medina] twice, due to the hardship of the way and the danger of riding in the caravans.

However, when the railway is there, due to the resulting comfort and security of the way, they will all proceed to Yanbu‘, and thence to Medina. Afterwards, they will ride the train to Mecca, return to Medina, and thence from Yanbu‘ to their own countries. Consequently, the Bedouins of Hejaz who own [camels rented to] caravans will make a double profit for the road from Yanbu‘ to Medina, compared to what they were making earlier.[1] To this one should add the fact that [those] pilgrims [who now only visit Mecca] will certainly visit [Medina too]—in the comfort of the railway and the safety of the road from Yanbu‘.

Now for the journey from Jedda. We have already said that at most some 20,000 people travel to Mecca via Jedda [annually]. These will continue to travel from Jedda to Mecca without any change, even after the construction of the railway [which would not go to Jedda]. The same is true for the stretch from Mecca to Arafat. Consequently, the Bedouins of Hejaz will not be losing any profit they are making from renting out their camels now, before the existence of the railway. On the contrary, their profits will increase, due to the railway's providing comfort [*137*] and security for the trip between the Two Shrines. The number of those coming on pilgrimage via Jedda will increase [too], as they will desire to visit [Medina] and enjoy the comfort and security of the railway [from Mecca to Medina]. Our discussion here treats [mainly] about the situation of this visit [to Medina from Mecca].

In the preceding pages we have assumed that the number of those who travel now from Jedda to Mecca reaches 20,000 [per year] at most. No doubt, the desire of Muslims to visit the tomb of the Prophet (——) will increase when comfort and road security are provided. As this desire will increase, so will the number of pilgrims visiting Medina. When the number of pilgrims increases, so will the commercial and other advantages for the inhabitants of the Two Shrines. We have already mentioned that [nowadays] those who come to Mecca by land, no matter from what direction, do not need to hire any camels to travel to Arafat or Medina, since they have brought along their [own] riding animals. [Nowadays] only those who arrive by sea have to hire camels. However, when the railway is constructed, whoever comes for the pilgrimage—by

1. According to this calculation, the pilgrims will use this road twice.

land or sea—inhabiting the area from Medina northwards, up to the North Pole—would have to hire camels from the Hejaz Bedouins, in order to climb Mount Arafat. Let us now size up the profit from renting out camels in the above-mentioned situation. So we say:

No more than 5,000 people come nowadays in the Syrian caravan through the Syrian lands and neighboring areas [every year].[2] However, when the railway is constructed and completed—by Allah's will and the caliph's continued activity—the number of pilgrims will naturally increase manifold; 300,000 is a low estimate, so is 500,000 too, relative to the naturally ingrained desire in the hearts of Muslims to perform the pilgrimage and to visit the Prophet's tomb. The following factors prevent them [from coming in such large numbers now]: [*138*] the long distance; the hardship and dangers of the road; added expense; the need for a long absence from their work and homeland; the troubles they experience in the health quarantine—particularly at Ṭūr—and the consequent humiliation, high costs, lack of required things, added hardship, and the like, as we have already mentioned. When the railway is completed, however, all these factors will no longer be relevant. All Muslims will come for the pilgrimage and the visit to the Prophet's tomb, until none will stay away. This will be the case even more so, if the railway fare is inexpensive. Crowds will come from the farthest areas of Syria, Aleppo, Mosul, Anatolia, Rumelia, Persia, Kurdistan, Bukhara, as well as from all northern parts, even from the land of the Swahilis [or the littoral?]—if Allah (—) wills it. Indeed, thanks to Allah, the Muslims are numerous and strong of faith. [No longer] would most be hindered from performing the pilgrimage and the visit to the Prophet's tomb, and die as transgressors, not fulfilling this mandatory duty while they could—but for the conditions we have mentioned. What strengthens our argument is the fact that, of those who perform the pilgrimage, many return to their countries without visiting the Prophet's tomb, despite their burning desire to do so. They forbear to visit the Prophet's tomb only because they know of the hardships involved in the trip from Mecca to Medina. Therefore, after having reached Mecca, they return to their countries without visiting the Prophet's tomb in Medina.

If we assume that the pilgrims using the railway will number

2. This estimate is supported by contemporary sources.

at least 300,000,[3] and that half of them will walk to Arafat, this half would need camels to carry their belongings, food, drink, tents, furnishings, and the like. Let us assume that [*139*] one camel would suffice for every three pilgrims; then they would need 50,000 camels to transport their belongings. If we assume that the other 150,000 pilgrims who do not walk to Arafat will ride, then every two such pilgrims would require one camel for riding and another for carrying their loads; thus they would need 150,000 camels. If we add these to the above 50,000, the total is 200,000 camels. This does not take into account the camels needed by those coming via Jedda, for it is not within this calculation, as their profit for the Bedouins after the completion of the railway will be the same as beforehand. So let us not prolong the argument by including them.

Then, when the railway is completed there is not the least doubt that the Egyptian pilgrims will not travel from their country on riding animals, but would ride a train to the littoral, and thence take a steamer to Jedda. Their number would increase manifold, compared to today's. They will travel on the railway [in Arabia], substituting it instead of riding on animals. So one might add the riding animals which our brethren, the Egyptian pilgrims, will require to haul their belongings, tents, and furnishings from Jedda to Mecca, or from Yanbu' to Medina, and from Mecca to Arafat. From Medina they would travel on the railway. If we assume that our Egyptian brethren would require 10,000 camels too, this brings the total to 210,000 camels. Again, this does not apply to the [other] pilgrims traveling via Jedda, which we do not include in this number, as we have already explained, since their number would neither increase nor decrease.

When the railway is completed and joined to the Birejik line and then to the Damascus line, this would affect the pilgrimage from Baghdad [too]. Nobody would come [from Baghdad] on riding animals. [*140*] The increase cannot be evaluated [because it is expected to be immense]. Let us, however, limit ourselves to what we have already discussed.

We still have to take into account the camels which those visiting the Prophet's tomb ride on from Yanbu' to Medina, and

3. Such expectations for large crowds were indeed widely held at the time, as expressed in *Thamarāt al-Funūn* (Beirut) in 1900 (reported and ridiculed by H. Slemann in *Revue de l'Orient Chrétien* 5 [1900]: 527–29). Actually, according to C. E. Bonin in *Annales de Géographie* 18 (1909): 431–32, in 1906/7 there were 281,000 pilgrims, of whom 173,000 came by land; of these, 4,000 to 5,000 used the still incomplete railway. In 1907/8 some 15,000 used the railway.

vice versa, return on their backs from Medina to Yanbu‘. We have already said that after the railway's construction their number would double. We have not, however, discussed the caravans [using this route], as they have no appointed schedules, but rather, proceed according to need. Sometimes they are few, at others numerous. Let us assume that nowadays the number of the camels in these caravans is 1,500. Add to this double that number, after the completion of the railway, or another 3,000. Together, this makes 4,500 each way, or a total of 9,000—an increase of 6,000. If this number is added to the others, above, this makes a grand total of 216,000 camels [*sic* for 219,000].

FIGURING THE REVENUE FROM RENTING CAMELS AND RIDING ANIMALS TO THE CARAVANS BEFORE THE RAILWAY CONSTRUCTION

We have explained above that nowadays—before the railway is there—the camel revenues from caravans and convoys reach 560,300 mejidis. Of these, 540,000 mejidis are paid for hiring camels for the caravans, and the remaining 20,300 are paid for hiring [other] riding animals for the caravans.

The expenditure [involved] is 505,652.5 mejidis. Of these, 364,500 mejidis are paid out as taxes for the caravans, 98,052.5 for current expenses, [*141*] 40,500 for the price of the camels who die on the road, and 2,600 for the expenses of the caravans.

When the expenditure and taxes are deducted from the revenue, there remains a sum of 54,647.5 mejidis. This is the total profit [at present] for the Hejaz Bedouins from the pilgrims, visitors to the Prophet's tomb and merchants. I have not turned my attention here to the profits of the caravans from Yanbu‘ to Medina, and have not included in it the revenues before the construction of the railway. On the contrary, I have excluded it, mentioning only the [expected] increase, if Allah (—) so wishes it.

The Rent for the Above Camels, the Expenses, and the Total

We have already said that, thanks to the railway, the number of pilgrims would rise manifold, if Allah (—) so wills it. This can be doubted only by the emotionally unbalanced, brainless, or sick-of-heart—those whose ears Allah has sealed and whose eyes He has covered. Hence, the rise in pilgrim numbers will perforce bring about an increase in camels; a rise in demand must raise prices—so that the price for hiring camels would be higher than at present.

Nowadays it costs from 5 to 10 mejidis, or more, to hire one camel for a round trip from Mecca to Arafat. That is, if unrelated to the Syrian caravan. However, when it is a part of the Syrian caravan, the camel owners never rent off a camel except along with a tent and all its prerequisites. This they term a *ta'rīfa* ([special] tariff) and it comes to 25 mejidis. Let us, however, not take this into account. Assuming the price for hiring one camel to be 10 mejidis, the total hiring price [*142*] of 210,000 camels comes to 2,100,000 mejidis. If we assume that the price for hiring a camel from Yanbu' to Medina is at present 15 mejidis, this will rise to at least 20 after the construction of the railway, due to the multitude of those arriving to visit the Prophet's tomb. Multiplying this by the number of camels, we find that the profit would be 135,000 mejidis, thanks to the railway—this after subtracting the hiring price of 3,000 camels at the rate of 15 mejidis each, that is, before the construction of the railway. When this sum is added to the hiring price of the camels to Arafat, the grand total is 1,235,000 mejidis. If we figure out an average expenditure of 3 piasters per day per camel, and reckon on an eleven-day round trip to Medina, then multiply the 3 piasters expended by eleven days, and the result by the number of camels, the total expense for that period comes to 10,421 mejidis. As to the expense on the camels taking pilgrims to Mount Arafat, hardly any is involved—anyway not worth mentioning. Let us calculate it, however, at a rate similar to that of the camels rented off for the trip to Medina. This comes to 193,684 mejidis. We shall compare this sum with what is earned at present from renting off camels; then subtract [the expenses] from it and compare the balance.

THE REVENUE FROM RENTING CAMELS AND THEIR EXPENSES WHEN THE RAILWAY IS COMPLETED

We have already mentioned that the revenue from renting off camels to Arafat will reach 2,100,000 [*143*] mejidis, while the increased revenue from renting off camels for the stretch between Medina and Yanbu' will amount to 135,000 mejidis. So the total would be 2,235,000 mejidis. As for the expenses, they also will rise, as compared to the present: for Medina they should amount to 193,684 mejidis, and for the stretch from Yanbu‘ to Medina, 10,421. The total of these expenses would amount to 204,105 mejidis. When we subtract the expenses from the revenue, the net revenue would be 2,030,895 mejidis.

THE PRESENT PROFIT AND EXPENSES OF THE HEJAZ BEDOUINS FROM THE RENTING OF CAMELS

We have maintained above that a maximum of 27,000 camels gather in Mecca to take the pilgrims and others to Medina in caravans. Possibly, the figure is considerably lower; generally it is. However, let us assume that this figure is constant and that hiring a camel for a round trip from Mecca to Medina costs 30 mejidis, when the supply of camels is low and those who visit the Prophet's tomb are numerous. Let us also ignore the fact that many [who visit the Prophet's tomb], if not most, do not return to Mecca but continue instead from Medina to their own countries, via Damascus or Yanbu‘. Therefore, in most years the number of camels does not reach that figure, or even half of it. When we reckon the hiring price for each camel at 20 mejidis [*144*] and multiply this by 27,000 camels, the total is 540,000 mejidis. As to what the Bedouins gain from the caravans of Medina, we have already mentioned that the town has 1,000 dromedaries, 150 nags, and 500 donkeys. Also, we have explained that with few exceptions most nags belong to their riders, as does a tenth of the dromedaries.

The hiring price for a dromedary is between 5 and 20 mejidis for the round trip from Medina to Mecca; for a nag, from 20 to 30; for a donkey, from 5 to 15. Assuming that the dromedaries ridden for pilgrimage [to Mecca] by the Medinese amount to 800 per year, and that the hiring price for each is always 15 silver mejidis, the total hiring price for the dromedaries amounts to 12,000 mejidis. When we assume that there are 120 nags per year, and that each hires for 25 mejidis, the total hiring price for nags amounts to 3,500 [*sic* for 3,000]. When we assume that there are 400 donkeys per year, and that each hires for 12 mejidis, their total hiring price amounts to 4,800 mejidis. Consequently, the total hiring price for [these] caravans is 20,300 [19,800] mejidis per year.

As to their expenses, know that the camels of the Meccan caravans entail more expenses than others, as these include taxes.

There are expenses and taxes not applicable [however] to the [other] caravans, which are exempt from taxes. The taxes for the [Meccan] caravans are as follows:

An ancient tax on every single camel	5 mejidis
[*145*] To the *dīwān*, here referring to the local council	1
To the *muṭawwif* (host for the *ṭawāf*)	3
To the *rahniyya* (pledge?), who guarantees the pilgrim's security before the emir of Mecca . .	1
To the *muqawwim*, who supervises the camel owners	2
For the *khurj* (saddle bags)	1

Or a total of 13½ [*sic* for 13]. When multiplied by the number of camels, the total is 364,500 [351,000] mejidis.

As to the expenses, let us assume that every single one of the caravan's camels requires 3 piasters per day. The time required for the round trip is 23 days, so the total expense per camel would amount to 69 piasters. This includes the wages of those who service them. When multiplied by the number of camels, this comes to 1,863,000 piasters, or 98,052 mejidis and a fraction.[4] To this one should add Bedouin losses from the death of camels—due to the trip, the load, sitting down, getting up, mismanagement, fatigue, and hardship, or falling down, fractures, and diseases. This is unavoidable and frequently witnessed. Perhaps 10 percent die on the road, besides those which [*146*] contract diseases on the way and then die after returning home. The latter are numerous; their owners frequently slaughter and eat them, as they despair of their recovery. Let us assume that 10 percent of the camels die on the road or back home, due to the trip. The loss would be 2,700 camels [per year]. Let us take a lower figure, half of that, say 5 percent or 1,350 camels. If we price each camel at 30 mejidis as a minimum, although some are worth 50 or more, the total value of the [dead] camels amounts to 40,500 mejidis. These expenses, however, are only a part of the expenses of the caravans. If we estimate them at 10 percent—including fodder, death of camels, and hiring prices—their total expenses amount to [only] 2,600 mejidis.

4. At the exchange rate then current of 19 piasters per mejidi, 98,052.63. A mejidi was a white coin bearing the emblem of Sultan Abdul Mejid, but no denomination in figures, so that its value varied according to its content and price fluctuations, as did the Ottoman gold pound.

Let not someone say that one should not subtract all these expenses from the revenues, as they would be spent anyway. We maintain that the Bedouins of Hejaz, like other Bedouins, lead their camels, cattle, and sheep to pasture in the desert, [thus] spending nothing on them. However, when other Bedouins rent them off, they require fodder, since they are unable to graze, because they are taken up with their loads while marching, and with their rest while sitting down. Consequently, the camels are unable to graze [during the trip]; furthermore, they can hardly get up, so tired they are. This is particularly so, since they are unaccustomed to [long] marches and [heavy] loads. As a result, the camels are so overcome by fatigue that they cannot move. Even if it is assumed that they manage to graze, it is insufficient; on the contrary, they need fodder to supplement it to be able to carry their loads. It is a well-known and witnessed matter that the hungry cannot [*147*] work and carry loads. This applies to humans, too. So, perforce, the camels' owners have to treat them gently.

One should not say, either, that their death is inevitable. True, all deadlines are in the hand of Allah (—). Allah (—) has set an appointed time for every one; and every appointed time is noted down. However, Allah (—) has based all matters on their evident causes. When it is the will of Allah (—) to originate a thing based on a cause, He first originates that cause, along with the outcome, and ties it up; then He executes His decision in the matter. He has commanded us to regard everything in the light of what is evident. All this is determined and well known; there is no need to discuss this at length.

Therefore, it is correct that the value of the camels which die on the road should be added to the Bedouins' expenses, and the total subtracted from their gross revenue—as we have computed it. However, what the Bedouins are earning at present from renting off their camels to Arafat should not be considered, for this will remain unchanged after the construction of the railway, as the pilgrims who come by sea via Jedda now will remain the same [in number]. Should their number increase, revenues would rise, not decline. It is not necessary to mention this [when discussing expenses].

THE RENTING OF CAMELS FOR THE CLIMB TO ARAFAT AND RETURN AFTER THE RAILWAY CONSTRUCTION

The period required for hiring camels in order to climb to Mount Arafat, spend there the three required days (*ayyām al-tashrīq*), and return to Mecca, does not exceed five or six days, for those who stay over in Minà for the third of these days, such as the Shafiite Sayyids. This type of hire involves no hardship on either camels or people. The pilgrims leave Mecca on the Day of Moistening, which falls on the 8th day of the sacred month of Dhu'l-Hijja, proceed to Minà and pass the night there—as was the custom of the Prophet (——), the Shafiite Sayyids, [*148*] and those who agree with their practice. On 9 Dhu'l-Hijja, the day of the ascent [to Arafat], the pilgrims proceed toward Arafat and perform the noon prayer at the Numra Mosque. Then they come to Arafat [itself] in the afternoon, as was the custom [of the Prophet]. Alternatively, they leave Mecca on the Day of Moistening, proceed to Arafat, and spend the night there. This is contrary to the custom, but the present practice of the majority of the pilgrims, from their wish to ensure their being at Arafat without fail on the 9th [of the month]. As a precautionary measure, they stay in Arafat on the 8th and 9th as they fear lest they mistake the 10th, the Day of Immolation, for the 9th and get to Arafat on the 10th [only]. Thanks to this precaution, they are sure to be in Arafat on the 9th without fail. Anyway, on that evening after sunset, the eve of 10 Dhu'l-Hijja, they rush together to Minà. Some, however, follow the custom [of Muhammad] and spend the night in Muzdalifa, where they gather stones for the [forthcoming] stone casting ceremony. At sunrise every Muslim proceeds to Al-Mash'ar al-Ḥarām [a shrine there], mentions Allah (—) in a forceful way, then goes to Minà—as the Prophet (——) used to do—for the ṭawāf al-ifāḍa [ritual circumambulation of "dispersing"].

All this differs from the Mecca–Medina round trip, whose period for hiring riding animals is no less than 23 days. Animals rented for Arafat do not require the expense needed when renting them for the trip to Medina, for after the pilgrims reach Arafat, their owners may lead them to pasture. If they need fodder for a night or two, this is a matter which does not count. This renting is devoid of expenses.

Some of the pilgrims hurry from Arafat after sunset and proceed directly to Minà. They may or may not pick up stones from Muzdalifa. They spend the night at Minà. In the morning on 10 Dhu'l-Hijja they all stone the Rock of 'Aqaba—this is called the First Stoning. Then they clip their hair or shave it off, perform the first taḥallul (rite of ceasing to be a pilgrim), put on their own clothes, and feast the Day of Immolation. Afterwards, some of them proceed [*149*] to Mecca, for the ṭawāf al-ifāḍa, persevere in the rites, and perform the second taḥallul. Then they return to Minà and spend three nights there, according to the custom [of the Prophet], or two nights, as most do at present. Then they load their belongings, tents, and whatever else they may have, and return to Mecca. Those who have not yet done so, perform the ṭawāf and the second taḥallul. The owners of the camels take them back. At most, the camels will have marched six hours from Mecca to Minà, and another six back. Perhaps they have added another two or three hours on the Day of Immolation on their way to Mecca and their return to Minà. Accordingly, we have mentioned the expense involved and have deducted it from their revenue—as you would know.

17. *Profits to the Bedouins Before and After the Construction of the Hejaz Railway*

THE PROFIT TO THE SYRIAN BEDOUINS FROM THE PILGRIMAGE BEFORE THE CONSTRUCTION OF THE RAILWAY

We have already mentioned that the tribes of Banū Ṣakhr and Wuld 'Alī, [all] Syrian Bedouins, carry loads for the government from Muzayrīb to Ma'ān. These amount to 200 [camel-]loads of supplies. Their fee is 4 mejidis [per load]; their total fee for bringing these supplies from Muzayrīb to Ma'ān is 800 mejidis. In addition, they carry 200 loads for the merchants, but this is at the rate of 3 mejidis [per load], amounting to a total fee of 600 mejidis. The authorities leave half their loads in Ma'ān. The tribe of Banū 'Aṭiyya takes [the other] 300 loads belonging to the government and the merchants from Ma'ān to Mu'aẓẓam. This fee is 4 mejidis [per load], or a total of 1,200 mejidis. Then the tribes of Labīda, Abū [Banū] Shāma, and Ḥarābsha carry 400 loads [increased through trading?] from Mu'aẓẓam to Jadīd. Their fee is 4 mejidis [per load], making a total of [*150*] 2,600 [*sic* for 1,600] mejidis. The authorities leave a part [in storage] at Jadīd for the return trip. The Banū Ṣakhr and [other] riders in the caravan carry along the rest of the loads. Sometimes the Aḥrāsh carry this from 'Aqaba to Medina. Among these loads there are the water bags, named ifāza, sent over by the authorities; these are to donate water to the poor, the military, and others, in those places where one knows by experience there is no water. Altogether, the Bedouins of Syria earn 4,000 [*sic*] mejidis from the fees for [carrying loads on] their camels in the Syrian caravan from Damascus to Medina. They make absolutely no other profit, unless the caravan chances to pass by their homes or near them. Then, if it is spring time, they sell [the caravan] laban, samn, and young sheep; but they sell these in small quantities, which do not merit consideration.

THE PROFIT TO THE SYRIAN BEDOUINS FROM THE PILGRIMAGE AFTER THE COMPLETION OF THE RAILWAY

Know that we have already mentioned some of the advantages which would ensue from the completion of this railway. For the Bedouins of Syria the greatest advantages are [1] their land would be improved for farming, [2] the planting of trees, and [3] a growing population. Due to the increase in the number of travelers and the railway's bringing the area closer to both Damascus and the Two Shrines, their wares would find ready markets, so that the people of Hejaz could do without imports from Egypt and Najd, and those of Syria without imports from Erzerum and northern parts. This would apply to sheep, samn, and other products, as detailed above. These advantages cannot even be estimated; they are incomparable! We shall confine ourselves [to what has already been said]. But [let us stress that] the prolongation of the railway line into the land of the Syrian Bedouins affords them yet another means to get rich. This is the employment opportunities on the railway. They can make a good living out of servicing the railway, provided they work sincerely and trustworthily. This would bring them more than they have been [*151*] earning from the backs of their camels—many times more, indeed. What we have said here, in addition to the above, ought to suffice in convincing the intelligent and attentive.

COMPARISON OF THE PROFITS TO THE HEJAZ BEDOUINS FROM CAMEL FEES BEFORE AND AFTER THE RAILWAY CONSTRUCTION

We are now going to discuss more particularly [the profits to] the Hejaz, not the Syrian, Bedouins, although both are connected to this road, before and after the construction of the railway, and both are going to reap advantages. This is so because, as already said, the reason for composing this book was to refute the rumors and whispers, implying that the Hejaz Bedouins would be the main losers on account of this railway, as they would [allegedly] be unable then to rent off their camels. We shall not discuss the Syrian Bedouins in this context, that is, comparing their situation before and after the construction of the railway—as we have already shown that the profits of the Syrian Bedouins from renting off their camels to the Syrian caravans are minimal and could be disregarded, when related with the profits of the Hejaz Bedouins thereof. To this one may add all the benefits that would accrue to the Bedouins, manifold compared to the situation before the railway's existence, if Allah (—) wills it.

The net income [of the Hejaz Bedouins], after the completion of the railway, would be 2,030,895 mejidis. Their net income today, before the railway is there, also after expenses, amounts to 54,647.5 mejidis. When we subtract the present income from the future one, the increase [in net income] would be [*152*] 1,976,247.5 mejidis. Assuming that an Ottoman gold pound is worth 102.5 piasters, this means that the increase in profit would amount to 366,328.75 Ottoman gold pounds. Or, assuming that a mejidi equals 19 piasters, the increase in profit would amount to 37,548,706.5 piasters! This is the profit which the people of Hejaz are going to make then from renting off their camels, if Allah (may His name be exalted) so wills it. This is besides the other advantages that we have listed.

Praise to Allah, first and last, and may Allah bless our Prophet Muhammad, his Family and his Companions.

The end.

Glossary

All terms are English or Arabic, unless otherwise indicated. Numbers in brackets refer to pages of the manuscript; they are not exhaustive.

agha (*aghā*)—an official; used in Mecca as "eunuch attendant in the mosque." See *MLPNC*: 20. [*74*]

— **of Dār al-Sa'āda** (lord of the Abode of Happiness)—an official heading the palace eunuchs in Istanbul. [*52*]

'Akīl—a Bedouin tribe, usually appointed to guard the Syrian pilgrimage caravan. [*43*, *49*]

'akkāms—camel drivers of the pilgrimage caravan, who were also runners and servants. See H. Kazem Zadeh, "Relation d'un Pèlerinage à la Mecque en 1910–1911," *Revue du Monde Musulman*, 19 (1912): 146. [*50*]

Alif. Lām. Mīm.—letters beginning the second chapter of the Koran; Muslim and other commentators cannot agree as to their meaning. [*84*]

alim (*'ālim*)—a Muslim learned in religious law.

amin (*amīn*)—an official.

— **al-ṣurra**—custodian of the purse, the Ottoman official in charge of disbursing stipends from the imperial treasury during a pilgrimage. [*35*, *57*]

amir (*amīr*), *see* emir.

ayyām al-tashrīq—the three days following 10 Dhu'l-Hijja. [*66*]

baqlāwa—a type of sweet. [*63*]

barīd—mail, mail carrier; also, a length measure of about 12 miles. [*9*, *63*]

barrānī—same as *selamlık.*

bāsh muqawwim (Turkish)—chief camel master in charge of the *muqawwims.* [*37*]

birdhawn—a non-Arabian horse, mainly a work horse. [*35*]

bōsta—the post, mail. [*63*]

bōstajī (Turkish)—a postman. [*63*]

bōsta-khāne—a post office. [*63*]

çerviş (Turkish)—inferior cooking fat, from *charbīsh* (Persian)—grease (the metathesis is quite regular); still employed as *qrīsha* in colloquial Damascene Arabic. [*107*]

Companions (*ṣaḥāba*)—Muhammad's Muslim supporters early in his career.

cubit (*dhirā'*)—about 27 inches in Syria; the Istanbul cubit is half an inch less. [*25*]

Dhu'l-Hijja (*Dhū'l-Ḥijja*)—twelfth month of the Muslim year.

Dhu'l-Qa'da (*Dhū'l-Qa'da*)—eleventh month of the Muslim year.

emir (*amīr*)—a nobleman.

— **of Mecca**, *see* sharif.

farḍ kifāya—a command imperative upon all Muslims; but if one person in eight or ten performs it, it is as if all had done so. [*94*]

Fatiha (*Fātiḥa*)—the opening chapter of the Koran, which also serves as the customary prayer. [*26*]

fatwà, *see* mufti.

fikāk—a "release," the sum paid by the recipient of a letter to its carrier. [*64*]

gharība—a type of sweet. [*63*]

ghazi (*ghāzī*)—a combatant (for Islam); an honorific title of the Ottoman sultan. [*2*, *46*]

hadith (*ḥadīth*)—a Muslim oral tradition.

— **ḥasan**—a good oral tradition, less respected than a strong one (*ḥadīth ṣaḥīḥ*), but necessary for establishing points of law. See *EI*. [*118*]

hajīn—a dromedary. [*35*]

hajj (*ḥajj*)—the major pilgrimage to Mecca, enjoined on all Muslims [*74*]

ḥamla—the load carried on pilgrimage. [*45*]

Hanafites—one of four schools of law in orthodox Islam, following the interpretation of al-Nu'mān Ibn Thābit Abū Ḥanīfa. [*120*]

Hanbalites—one of four schools of law in orthodox Islam, following the interpretation of Aḥmad Ibn Ḥanbal. [*119*]

Ḥasans (*or* **Sharifs**)—descendants of Ḥasan; Ḥusayns (*or* Sayyids) are descendants of Ḥusayn; both tribes claim relationship to Muhammad's family. See *MLPNC*: 9. [*7*]

Hegira, Hejira (*Hijra*)—Muhammad's move from Mecca to Medina, 622 C.E., from which Muslims count their calendar.

Ḥusayns, *see* Ḥasans.

ifāza (for *ifāda*)—"overflow," water officially provided for the poor pilgrims. [*82*]

ihram (*iḥrām*)—a rite in which pilgrims don seamless sheets and cease shaving or combing their hair. [*15*]

imam (*imām*)—a leader of the prayer; by extension, a Muslim leader.

irade (*irāde*) (Turkish)—a decree of the sultan. [*2*]

iskele (Turkish)—a pier *or* wharf. [*56*]

isnad (*isnād*)—the line of authorities handing down a hadith.

Java—a term used in Mecca for the whole East Indian archipelago as well as Java. See *MLPNC*: v, 215 ff. [*79*]

jihad (*jihād*)—a Muslim "holy war." [*121*]

jubba (*jubba*)—a long outer robe, slit in front. [*43*]

jūkhadār (Turkish)—the last mail courier during a pilgrimage, probably so called from the broadcloth (*jūkh*) he wore; also, a type of Ottoman palace servant. [*25*, *63*]

Jumada I (*Jumādà al-Ūlà*)—fifth month of the Muslim year.

Jumada II (*Jumādà al-Ākhira*)—sixth month of the Muslim year.

jurdī (also **jardī**)—a fast-moving provision convoy, sent to relieve a returning pilgrimage caravan, generally at Madā'in Ṣāliḥ. [*6*, *61*]

kahwajī pasha—a chief coffeemaker, an important job in the imperial household. [*60*]

kattāb (also **najjāb**)—the mail (post). [*63*]

Khalwatī—the Khalwatiyya was one of the most widespread sufi orders in the Ottoman Empire, whose shaykhs had considerable spiritual prestige. [*19*, *42*]

kharjirāh (Turkish)—travel expenses for official business. [*73*]

khashab, see *shibriyya*.

khaṭīb—the holder of the sermon after the Friday prayer. [*36*]

khurj—saddle bags. [*145*]

kibla *or* **qibla** (*qibla*)—the direction of the Ka'ba stone in Mecca. [*38*]

kikhya—a steward *or* assistant. [*56*]

kīlār—originally, an official responsible for the sultan's pantry; on a pilgrimage caravan, he was attached to the staff of the *amīn al-ṣurra* and was responsible for provisions. See *PSVSI*: 74. [*45*]

Koran (*Qur'ān*)—the sacred book of Islam.

laban—sour milk. [*102*]

mābeyinjī—a court chamberlain (Istanbul). [*53*]

maḥall al-istiqbāl—a reception hall, generally reserved for men. [*71*]

maḥāra, see *shibriyya*.

mahmil (or **maḥmal**)—a richly adorned litter, carried on pilgrimage by a camel; a kind of shrine. [*19*, *36*]

mahmilji (or **mahmaljī**)—a specially appointed caretaker of the *maḥmil*, who rides near it. [*42*]

Malikites—one of four schools of law in orthodox Islam, following the interpretation of Mālik Ibn Anas. [*120*]

ma'mūl—a sweet made of fat, cinnamon, and nuts. [*63*]

marāfi'—drums used by camel drivers. [*51*]

mashā'ikh—elders. [*59*]

mejidi (*majīdī*)—a Turkish coin on which no denomination appeared; in 1900 its market value in Syria fluctuated between 19 and 20 piasters.

miḥaffa—a litter. [*35*]

minbar (*minbar*)—a pulpit in a mosque. [*116*]

Miṣr—name for both Egypt and Cairo.

mubashshir—"a bringer of good tidings," a pilgrimage official. [*50*, *61*]

muezzin (*mu'adhdhin*)—a person who calls Muslims to prayer. [*43*]

mufti (*muftī*)—a Muslim jurist entitled to issue an opinion (*fatwà*) in Islamic law and kindred subjects. [*41*]

muḥāfiẓ al-ḥajj—the superintendent of a pilgrimage, the Ottoman official in charge of all its arrangements. [*35*]

Muhammad (*Muḥammad*)—the Prophet of Islam (?–632 C.E.).

Muharram (*Muḥarram*)—first month of the Muslim year.

mujāhid—a soldier in a jihad. [*122*]

müjdeci (Turkish)—pilgrimage official in charge of certain financial allocations. [*60*]

mulabbas—a sweet resembling dragées. [*39*]

muqawwim—a camel owner entitled to rent camels to pilgrims. [*37*]

mutasarrif (*mutaṣarrif*)—official in charge of a *mutaṣarrifiyya*. [*57*]

mutaṣarrifiyya (Turkish *mutasarrıflık*)—an Ottoman administrative center. [*21*]

muṭawwif—a guide who hosts a pilgrim in Mecca and guides him in the *ṭawāf*; at the end of the 19th century these guides formed a closely knit administration. [*60*]

najjāb—same as *kattāb.*

naqīb al-Ashrāf—the head of the descendants of Muhammad; his office carried a special standing among the aristocracy, civil administration, and ulema. [*41*]

niṭāsī—a surgeon. [*38*]

nizam (*niẓām*)—levies recruited under a system instituted by Sultan Selim III early in the 19th century. [*39*]

parasang—a length measure, about three miles. [*9*]

pasha (*pasha*)—an honorific title, frequently granted to high officials.

qaḍi (*qāḍī*)—a Muslim religious judge. [*41*]

qāfila—a caravan. [*35*]

qibla, *see* kibla.

quftānji—an official appointed to ride with a pilgrimage caravan to deliver a cloak (*quftān*), the gift from the sultan to the sharif of Mecca. [*50*]

Rabi I (*Rabī' al-Awwal*)—third month of the Muslim year.

Rabi II (*Rabī' al-Thānī*)—fourth month of the Muslim year.

rahwān—an Arabian horse. [*35*]

Rajab (*Rajab*)—seventh month of the Muslim year.

rakb—a caravan. [*35*]

— **Baghdādī**—Baghdad pilgrimage caravan, popular name for the Iraqi pilgrimage caravan.

— **Miṣrī**—Egyptian pilgrimage caravan.

— **Shāmī**—Syrian pilgrimage caravan.

Ramadan (*Ramaḍān*)—ninth month of the Muslim year.

Safar (*Ṣafar*)—second month of the Muslim year.

ṣalaḥa—pious ones; those who would accompany a pilgrimage caravan part of the way as a good deed. [*49*]

al-ṣalāt al-Ibrāhīmiyya—Abraham's prayer; a blessing Muslims recite at the end of their prayer, asking Allah to bless Muhammad and his family, as he has blessed Abraham and his family. [*39*]

samn—clarified butter. [*34*, *106–9*]

sanjak (*sanjaq*) (Turkish)—a flag *or* standard. [*40*]

sanjaqdār (Turkish)—a standard bearer. [*41*]

sayyid (*sayyid*)—a holy man; *see also* Ḥasans.

selamlık (Turkish)—that part of a house reserved for men. [*71*].

ser 'asker (Persian)—a commander-in-chief. [*51*]

Sha'ban (*Sha'bān*)—eighth month of the Muslim year.

Shafiites—one of four schools of law in orthodox Islam, following the interpretation of Muḥammad Ibn Idrīs al-Shāfi'ī. [*1*]

al-Sha'm (*or* **al-Shām**)—name for both Damascus and Syria. [*18*]

shar'i (*shar'ī*) **court**—a court which rules by the shari'a. [*58*]

shari'a (*sharī'a*)—Islamic religious law. [*91*]

sharif, sherif (*sharīf*)—a nobleman; *see also* Ḥasans.

— **of Mecca**—a descendant of Muhammad serving as a high Ottoman official in Mecca. [*61*]

Shawwal (*Shawwāl*)—tenth month of the Muslim year.

shaykh, sheik (*shaykh*)—a chief *or* headman.

— **al-Islām**—the chief Muslim dignitary; he lived in Istanbul and had great political power, sometimes equaling that of the grand vizir. See H. A. R. Gibb and H. Bowen, *Islamic Society and the West* (London 1962), 1, pt. 2: 86 and *passim.* [*54*]

shibriyya—a cot; a two-part litter carried on the backs of two camels or mules. Named by the Syrians *khashab* or *maḥāra.* [*35*]

shuqdhuf—a two-part sedan carried on the back of a camel. [*35*]

sikka—railway, railroad.

— **al-Ḥijāziyya al-Shāmiyya**—the Hejaz Railway.

sufi (*ṣūfī*)—an ascetic mystic. [*71*]

suḥūr—the last meal before daybreak, allowed before the daily fast throughout the month of Ramadan. [*107*]

ṣundūq al-manāfi'—the official fund for public works. [*2*]

sunna (*sunna*)—the practice of Muhammad, held as a model for all orthodox Muslims. [*98*]

ṣurra, *see* amin.

taḥallul—the rite of ceasing to be a pilgrim. [*148*]

tajmīla—an adornment; a chant of camel drivers. [*51*]

takht—a wooden palanquin. [*74*]

takiyya—a Muslim hospice. [*20*]

tarwiya, see *Yawm*.

tashrīq, see *ayyām*.

ṭawāf—the ritual circumambulation of the Ka'ba during pilgrimage.

— **al-ifāḍa**—the ritual circumambulation of dispersing. See G. E. von Grunebaum, *Muhammadan Festivals*: 32. [*149*]

teshrīfatjī—the head of protocol, an official designated to supervise the Damascus procession of the Syrian pilgrimage caravan. [*43*]

thawb—a cover (of the *maḥmil*). [*51*]

Two Feasts—'Īd al-aḍḥà *and* 'Īd al-fiṭr. [*90*]

Two Shrines—Mecca *and* Medina. [*2*]

ulema (*'ulamā'*)—plural of alim.

al-umma al-Islāmiyya, al-umma al-Muḥammadiyya—the Islamic community. [*110–11*]

'umra—the minor pilgrimage, recommended to all Muslims. [*74*]

vilayet (*wilāya*) (*vilâyet*) (Turkish)—Ottoman province. [*37*]

walāwīl—shrieks of grief. [*69*]

wali (*wālī*)—the governor of an Ottoman province. [*37*]

waqf (*waqf*)—a charitable endowment whose proceeds go to pious deeds. [*36*]

Yawm al-Naḥr—"Day of Immolation," 10 Dhu'l-Hijja. [*47*]

— **al-Su'ūd**—"Ascension Day," the day the *maḥmil* ascends into Mecca. [*47*]

— **al-Tarwiya**—"Day of Moistening"; in Mecca, the night preceding 8 Dhu'l-Hijja. *See* von Grunebaum, *Muhammadan Festivals*: 35. [*74*]

zalāghīṭ—shouts of joy. [*69*]

zāwiya—a small mosque built over the tomb of a revered Muslim holy man. [*43*]

ziyāra—the visit to Muhammad's tomb in Medina.

(١) بسم الله الرحمن الرحيم

نحمدك اللّهم يا من مهدت السبل للسالكين وقومت الطريق للمهتدين ونسألك يا من فرضت الحج والعمرة وندبت الزيارة وشرعت الصناعة والزراعة والتجارة أن تصلى وتسلم على من سن لنا الشرع المبين وأسس السياسة وأحكم الأحكام والقوانين حجتك القوية البالغة ومحجتك القويمة الدامغة سيدنا محمد الرؤف الرحيم خير من هدى إلى صراط مستقيم وعلى اصحابه الذين فتحوا البلاد واستسلموا العباد ورتبوا الأمور الدولية وأحكموا النظامات المرعية والتابعين لهم السالكين سبلهم أمين اما بعد فيقول السيد محمد عارف ابن المرحوم السيد الشيخ أحمد المنير الحسيني امام الشافعية في الشام المحمية لما منّ الله تعالى على عبده سيدنا ومولانا أمير المؤمنين خليفة الرسول الأمين (٢) من نفتخر بوجوده ونرتع في ظل عدله وجوده السلطان ابن السلطان الغازى عبد الحميد خان ابن مولانا السلطان ساكن الجنان عبد المجيد خان لا زال مبتهجاً به الزمان مسعداً بطلعته النيران مزيناً به عرش الخلافة الإسلامية مفتخراً بآثار جلالته الأمة العثمانية بتوفيقه لانشاء السكة الحديدية الحجازية الشامية ذات المنافع الجلية اعماراً للبلاد واحياء للعباد وخدمة للحرمين الشريفين وتسهيلا لقاصدي الزيارتين وتوسيعاً لدائرة التجارة الرابحة وتأسيساً لخطة الزراعة الراجحة وحفظاً للموازنة السياسية في البلاد المتسعة الشاسعة العربية وتبرع خلد الله تعالى ملكه للترتيب الأول بخمسين ألف ذهب عثماني من جيبه الخاص وتقرر دفع مائة ألف أيضاً من صندوق المنافع وطبعت أوراق بمليون كذلك ولات حين مناص وحصلت الارادة السنية بالمباشرة بها وأسست الجمعيات الخيرية للنظر في أمرها وتسابقت الاسلام في كل جهة للإعانة على انشائها بالأنفس والأموال ورآى المرجفون اولو الغايات ان ذلك حاصل ان شا الله تعالى في كل الأحوال اشاعوا لاغراضهم الذاتية ان انشاءها حرام بالنصوص القرآنية وانه لا يجوز الحج إلا مشياً على الأقدام أو ركوباً على الانعام والدواب تقولا من عند أنفسهم وافتراء على أصح كتاب وكنت حضرت في أثناء

تلك الاشاعة الشنيعة والفرية الظاهرة المريعة (٣) إلى الاستانة العلية عاصمة الخلافة الإسلامية ومقر السلطنة العثمانية حفظها الله تعالى من كيد الأعداء وكل بلية وذلك يوم الأربعاء السادس والعشرين من شهر ربيع الآخر من سنة ثمان عشرة وثلاثمائة وألف عربية الموافق الثامن من شهر آب سنة ست عشر وثلاثمائة مالية هجرية .

ونظمت مقالة بديعة السان[1] أهنى بها جلالته أيد الله تعالى بالعدل والاحسان والأمن خلافته وقد نشرتها جريدة المعلومات العربية التي تطبع في الاستانة العلية وتعرضت فيها لأن أعظم مآثره السنية بل مآثر سلاطين الأمة المحمدية في تلك البلاد البهية انما هو هذه السكة الحديدية الحجازية الشامية ورددت عليهم قولهم وقبحت فعلهم وسلوكهم وأبنت للناس غرضهم وفسادهم وفجورهم على قدر ما احتمله المقام من الأدلة بأفصح كلام وأثبت ان انشاءها في هذا الزمان من أهم الواجبات والزم الأسباب الموصلات ومن إعداد القوة المستطاعة ومن أعظم القربات لله تعالى والطاعة المأمورين بهما في القرآن الكريم نصاً صريحاً لا يحتمل التأويل لغير معناه ولا يحتاج للتفهيم لوضوح معناه ثم بعد ذلك بأيام شاع على افواه بعض الخواص والعوام جملة اعتراضات وايرادات منها وهو أهمها أن عرب البادية الحجازية وبعض سكان مكة المكرمة والمدينة المنورة لا يساعدون على انشائها بل يعاكسون ولا يسكتون عليه بل يعارضون (٤) لما سول لهم أصحاب الغايات ووسوس إليهم ذوو الافتراءآت من ان هذه السكة تضر بتجاراتهم وتسيء معيشتهم لكون كسبهم محدوداً بنقل الحجاج والزوار والتجار على دوابهم في تلك الأقطار وان هذه السكة تكون سبباً لتعطيل دوابهم فتنمحق ارباحهم ويصبحون فقراء معدمين فتسحق ارواحهم وسنوردها كلها في آخر هذا الكتاب مع ردها بأحسن جواب عند أولى الالباب ولما كان من يسمع يخل ويحسن السبك قد ينفى الزغل وكان التوحش في هؤلاء البدو فاشياً والجهل فيهم نامياً غاشياً ويوشك ارتياعهم لهذا الافساد ويخشى انقيادهم للمين والفساد ويحذر من اصغاء غيرهم من المسلمين لهذا الاغراء والغش

[1] Read اللسان or الشأن

المبين وكنت على ثقة من محبة الجميع الدولة العلية العثمانية ودعائهم لها في البكرة والعشية كما هو الواجب على كل فرد من أفراد الأمة المحمدية وانهم إذا فهموا حقيقة الحال لا يعيرون آذانهم سمعاً لما يتحقق عندهم من حسن المآل حركتني الحمية الإسلامية وأخذت بمجامعي الشهامة العربية وجذبتني محبتي الخالصة لأخواني المؤمنين واستفزتني خدمتي الصادقة لجلالة سلطان المسلمين نصحاً لأولئك البدو المتوحشين وايقاظاً لمن يمكن أن يغش من باقي المسلمين وكفحاً وكبحاً لأولى الأغراض المشؤمين فألفت هذه الرسالة بل الكتاب على أجنحة العجالة حب الايجاب مجيباً فيها عن تلك الاعتراضات الواهيات والايرادات الواهنات ومبيناً فيها محاسن هذه السكة ونفعها للبلاد من اعداد (٥) القوة بها وتوطيد الأمن وتسهيل السبيل في تلك البلاد وجوانبها وناشراً عظيم منة جلالة مولانا بها على العباد سيما الأقطار الحجازية وأهلها مع بيان شأنها وفضلها رغماً عن انف كل معاند وموسوس وحاسد بإعمار المسجدين العظيمين والحرمين الشريفين وتزييد عماراتهم وتوسيع نطاق تجاراتهم وزراعاتهم ودخول المدنية فيهم وانتشار المعارف في نواحيهم وتخليصهم من أنياب مغتاليهم ومخالب الظالمين المنشبة في تراقيهم فيعيشون بذلك أحراراً مرفهين أغنياء منعمين في عيش رغد رضي وبال مرتاح هني .

وسميتها السعادة النامية الأبدية بالسكة الحديدية وأرجو الله تعالى الكريم ان يجعلها مصدراً للنفع العميم ثم رفعتها من المقالة المنوه عنها إلى سدة الخلافة الإسلامية العظمى راجياً لهما القبول عنده فانه غاية المأمول وأكبر نعماً .

في الكلام على البدو الذين لهم تعلق بهذه السكة

أعلم أن البدو الذين تتعلق بهم هذه السكة من باب دمشق الشام المعروف أولا بباب مصر والآن ببوابة الله إلى مكة المكرمة قسمان بدو الحجاز وبدو الشام .

القسم الأول بدو الحجاز

المراد بهم البدو المقيمون في صحراء وقرى الحجاز ما بين مكة المكرمة والمدينة المنورة وما حولهما وسكان القرى منهم وان كانوا قرويين الا انهم لما كانوا من قبائل البدو المقيمين في الصحراء المذكورة ومشاركيهم في الطبائع والخصال ومستحكماً (٦) فيهم التوحش مثلهم بل اشد منهم توحشاً وجهالة اطلقنا عليهم اسم البدو وأدخلناهم فيهم وجعلناهم في حكمهم من كل وجه وان كان بينهما فرق جزئي واما البدو القاطنون في شمال المدينة المنورة قريباً منها وان كانوا من بدو الحجاز الا انهم لما كانت صوالحهم وصوالح بدو الشام واحدة بانشاء هذه السكة الحقناهم بهم وذلك لان البدو القاطنين في شمال المدينة المنورة من جهة الشام لا يؤجرون جمالهم لركب الحج الشامي الا ان كان للركب الشامي لزوم للاستئجار منهم لتحميل اموال التجارة في الذهاب دون الإياب لا لركوب الحجاج لا لتحميل الذخيرة اللازمة من طرف الحكومة لأن الركب الشامي يأخذ معه من الشام ما يلزمه من الدواب للركوب والتحميل وإذا احتاج للتأجير يستأجر من بدو الشام لايصال الذخيرة إلى المواضع التي تودع فيها حسب العادة وكذلك التجار يستأجرون من بدو الشام لأحمالهم إلى المدينة المنورة وفي الرجوع تكون الذخائر حاضرة في القلاع وغيرها من المواضع المعدة للإيداع فيها ويرد إليهم من الشام مع ركب الجردة ما يحتاجون إليه من المداين للشام حسب العادة واللّزوم وأما التجار فلا يحتاجون إلى الاستئجار أصلا لأن تجارتهم إذا لم تنفق كلها وكسد منها شيء سواء في الطريق أو الحرمين إما ان يبقوه في مكة ان كان مما يناسب أهلها أو في المدينة إن كان من تجارة المدينة على سبيل الأمانة والوديعة إلى العام القابل أو يوكلون من يأتمنونه (٧) يبيعه من عملائهم أو يتخلف التاجر نفسه عن السفر فيبيعه فلا يكون لهم في ايجار الجمال للركب الشامي او لغيره حظ مثل باقي بدو الحجاز ولذا جعلنا حكمهم حكم بدو الشام لا بدو الحجاز .

في بيان قبائل بدو الحجاز المذكورين

ان قبائل بدو الحجاز كثيرة وليس القصد هنا استقصاءها او بيان قبائلها وشعوبها وانما القصد ذكر من لهم تعلق بالسكة هذه تتميماً للفائدة فنقول ان القبائل التي لها تعلق بالسكة كثيرة منها اصول ومنها شعوب تتشعب منها ويقال انها كلها يطلق عليها ميمون وهي الحوازم والأحامدة وجهينة ومسروح ومطير والعتبة والسريحى والحجلة والقراف والرِّحَـلَـة بكسر الراء المشددة وفتح الحاء واللام والحماديين والفضيلى والشوارب والبحيوية والدكرة والعمروية والتِـمم بكسر التاء وأولاد محمد والسهلى واللهيبي والصاعدى والزبيدى وبنو عمرو وابن موقد وعوف وجهم والردادة والتراجمة واللهبة وبنو أيوب وصبح وزبيد وقريش وبـلِـيّ بكسر الباء واللاّم وهذيل والعسوم والعصالية وقبيلتا السادة الأشراف الحسنية والحسينية وهاتان القبيلتان ليستا معدودتين من هذه القبائل ولا متشعبتين منها فهما أشرفهم نسباً وأفخرهم حسباً وانما ذكرناهما هنا لأن لهما تعلقاً بهذه السكة فذكرناهما معهم لهذه المناسبة ولكونهما الآن مثلهم في الطبائع والمشارب .

(٨) القسم الثاني بدو الشام الذين لهم تعلق بهذه الطريق

إن بدو الشام كثيرون وقبائل متعددون وشعوب لا يكادون يحصرون وبيوت مجتمعون ومتفرقون وحدودهم من الشام إلى المداين ومنها إلى المدينة عرب الحجاز ولكن نذكرهم هنا بالنظر لكون صالحهم وصالح عرب الشام واحداً كما مر ولما كان لا فائدة في استقصائهم هنا ولا نتيجة له بالنظر للمقصود من وضع هذه الرسالة اقتصرنا على ذكر من لهم تعلق بطريق الحج وهم عنزة وولد على وبنو صخر واللبيدة والفقرا والشرارات والحريشة والسعادين والأحراش وعطية وبنو شامة ومطير وجهينة وهاتان القبيلتان من بدو الحجاز الا أنهما كما قدمنا لكونهما يقطنان شمالي المدينة ولكون صالحهما وصالح بدو الشام واحداً

ذكرناهما معهم وهاتان القبيلتان اعداء لبعضهما ومستحكم فيهما التوحش والجهالة والتعدي والنهب والسلب وشن الغارات وقد تهاجمان المدينة فتحاصر من اجلهما شهراً أو شهرين أو أكثر وتعلو فيها الأسعار ويقع فيها الخوف ولا يقدر أحد على الخروج منها ولو لمرقد سيدنا حمزة رضي الله تعالى عنه الذي يبعد عن المدينة نحو نصف ساعة وتقاسى منهما من الشدائد ما لا يحتمل وتتكبد الدولة العلية لتربيتهما من المصارف ما لا يكاد يحصر ولهذا كثيراً ما يتركان ايجار جمالهما لركب الحج الشامي فتحمله بدو الشام إلى المدينة كما سيأتي .

(٩) بيان الطريق من الشام الشريفة إلى مكة المكرمة

اعلم ان الطريق من الشام إلى مكة يمر على المدينة المنورة وهو واحد إليها لا يختلف فاذا وصل إلى المدينة تفرع منها فرعان فرع غربي يمر على رابغ وله اربعة فروع إليها ومن رابغ إلى مكة واحد وفرع شرقي لا يمر على رابغ وهو واحد .

في بيان الطريق من الشام الشريفة إلى المدينة المنورة

اعلم ان الطريق من دمشق الشام إلى المدينة المنورة واحد كما اسلفنا وطوله بالساعات ثلاث ماية واثنان واربعون ساعة ومراحله ثمان وعشرون مرحلة ونصف مرحلة على سير الجمال المعتاد وكل مرحلة اثنتا عشرة ساعة وطوله بالأميال أربعة وثمانون ميلا وستمائة ميل وبالفرسخ ثمانية وعشرون فرسخاً ومائتا فرسخ وبالبرد سبعة وخمسون بريداً والميل نصف ساعة والفرسخ ثلاثة أميال والبريد أربعة فراسخ وعدد محطات هذا الطريق باعتبار سير ركب الحج الشامي الآن واحد وثلاثون وكذا مراحله وهي متفاوتة المقدار بحسب الساعات كما يعلم مما يأتي .

المرحلة الأولى	من الشام	إلى ذي النون	وهي أربع ساعات
المرحلة الثانية	من ذي النون	إلى الكتيبة	وهي عشر ساعات
المرحلة الثالثة	من الكتيبة	إلى مزيريب	وهي ثمان ساعات

(١٠) المرحلة الرابعة	من مزيريب	إلى الرمثة	وهي أربع ساعات
المرحلة الخامسة	من الرمثة	إلى المفرق	وهي اثنتا عشرة ساعة
المرحلة السادسة	من المفرق	إلى الزرقاء	وهي ثمان ساعات
المرحلة السابعة	من الزرقاء	إلى البلقاء	وهي خمس عشرة ساعة
المرحلة الثامنة	من البلقاء	إلى القطرانة	وهي اثنتا عشرة ساعة
المرحلة التاسعة	من القطرانة	إلى الحسا	وهي اثنتا عشرة ساعة
المرحلة العاشرة	من الحسا	إلى عنزة	وهي عشر ساعات
المرحلة الحادية عشر	من عنزة	إلى معان	وهي ثمان ساعات
المرحلة الثانية عشر	من معان	إلى العقبة	وهي ثمان ساعات
المرحلة الثالثة عشر	من العقبة	إلى المدورة	وهي أربع عشرة ساعة
المرحلة الرابعة عشر	من المدورة	إلى ذات حج	وهي عشر ساعات
المرحلة الخامسة عشر	من ذات حج	إلى القاع	وهي خمس عشرة ساعة
المرحلة السادسة عشر	من القاع	إلى تبوك	وهي سبع ساعات
المرحلة السابعة عشر	من تبوك	إلى ظهر المغر	وهي عشر ساعات
المرحلة الثامنة عشر	من ظهر المغر	إلى الأخضر	وهي ثمان ساعات
المرحلة التاسعة عشر	من الأخضر	إلى جناين القاضي	وهي عشر ساعات
المرحلة العشرون	من جناين القاضي	إلى المعظم	وهي عشر ساعات
(١١) المرحلة الحادية والعشرون	من المعظم	إلى ظهر الحمراء	وهي خمس عشرة ساعة
المرحلة الثانية والعشرون	من ظهر الحمراء	إلى تبريكة	وهي اربع عشرة ساعة
المرحلة الثالثة والعشرون	من تبريكة	إلى المدائن	وهي ست ساعات
المرحلة الرابعة والعشرون	من المدائن	إلى البدايع	وهي عشر ساعات
المرحلة الخامسة والعشرون	من البدائع	إلى الزمرد	وهي ست عشرة ساعة
المرحلة السادسة والعشرون	من الزمرد	إلى الجديد	وهي ثمان ساعات
المرحلة السابعة والعشرون	من الجديد	إلى البراقة	وهي أربع عشرة ساعة
المرحلة الثامنة والعشرون	من البراقة	إلى هدية	وهي ست ساعات
المرحلة التاسعة والعشرون	من هدية	إلى اصطبل عنتر	وهي ثماني عشرة ساعة
المرحلة الثلاثون	من اصطبل عنتر	إلى بيار ناصيف	وهي عشر ساعات
المرحلة الحادية والثلاثون	من بيار ناصيف	إلى المدينة المنورة	وهي عشرون ساعة

فجملتها ثلاث مائة واثنتان وثلاثون ساعة واحدى وثلاثون مرحلة واحدى وثلاثون محطة .

في بيان الطريق من المدينة المنورة إلى مكة المكرمة

وهو طريقان طريق غربي يمر على رابغ وله اربعة فروع إليها وطريق شرقي لا يمر عليها ولا يتفرع .

الطريق الأول الغربي

(١٢) إن هذا الطريق الغربي الذي يمر على رابغ له من المدينة إلى رابغ أربعة فروع تنتهي بطريق واحد عند رابغ الفرع الأول يقال له السلطاني والفرع الثاني يقال له الغائر والفرع الثالث يقال له الفرعي والفرع الرابع يقال له عند أهل الحجاز الملف وعند أهل الشام واسطة .

الفرع الأول السلطاني

وهو الأول من جهة البحر فالبحر في جهته الغربية وفي جهته الشرقية طريق الغائر وطوله من المدينة إلى رابغ خمس وسبعون ساعة ومراحله ست وربع على سير الجمال المعتاد وعدد مراحله باعتبار سير الركب الشامي سبع ومحطاته كذلك .

المرحلة الأولى	من المدينة	إلى بيار علي	وهي ثلاث ساعات
المرحلة الثانية	من بيار علي	إلى الشهداء	وهي اثنتا عشرة ساعة
المرحلة الثالثة	من الشهداء	إلى الجديدة	وهي عشر ساعات
المرحلة الرابعة	من الجديدة	إلى الصفراء	وهي عشر ساعات
المرحلة الخامسة	من الصفراء	إلى بدر	وهي ثمان ساعات
المرحلة السادسة	من بدر	إلى المستورة	وهي عشرون ساعة
المرحلة السابعة	من المستورة	إلى رابغ	وهي اثنتا عشرة ساعة

وفي بيار علي جملة آبار وفي الشهداء بير يقال له بير عباس (١٣) وهذا الطريق أسهل الطرق كلها وأعمرها وأقل طولا منها كلها الا الغائر والملف وسيأتي انه لا يمكن سلوكه الا بصعوبة ولذا لا يسلكه الركب الشامي أصلا لتعذر سلوك المحفات منه .

الفرع الثاني الغائر

وهو ما بين السلطاني والفرعي فالسلطاني من جهته الغربية والفرعي من جهته الشرقية ولا يعرف طوله تحديداً لأن الطول الذي نذكره في غيره انما قدره الذين يسيرون مع الركب الشامي واما ركوب المدينة وقوافل مكة فلاختلاف سيرها وكونه على غير نظم لم يقدروه ولكن

نذكر المواقع التي فيه وهي بيار علي وبير الماشي وجبل الغائر وبير الحفاة وعين التبرة وبير المبيريك وهذا الطريق أقصر منها كلها وقدر بعض أهل الحرمين الذين سلكوا منه مراراً أنه ينقص عن جميعها بثمانية عشر ساعة فيكون على هذا طوله من المدينة إلى رابغ أربعة وأربعين ساعة تقريباً.

الفرع الثالث الفرعي

وهو واقع في جهة الغائر الشرقية وجهة الملف الغربية وطوله من المدينة إلى رابغ ثمانية وسبعون ساعة ومراحله ست ونصف باعتبار سير الجمال المعتاد وعدد محطاته باعتبار سير الركب الشامي الآن سبع مراحل ومحطاته سبع أيضاً .

(١٤) المرحلة الأولى	من المدينة المنورة	إلى بيار علي	وهي ثلاث ساعات
المرحلة الثانية	من بيار علي	إلى بير الماشي	وهي عشر ساعات
المرحلة الثالثة	من بير الماشي	إلى الصمت	وهي ست عشرة ساعة
المرحلة الرابعة	من الصمت	إلى الريان	وهي أربع عشرة ساعة
المرحلة الخامسة	من الريان	إلى أبي الضباع	وهي عشر ساعات
المرحلة السادسة	من أبي الضباع	إلى العقبة	وهي خمس عشرة ساعة
المرحلة السابعة	من العقبة	إلى رابغ	وهي عشر ساعات

وهذا الطريق بعد السلطاني في الحسن والسهولة الا انه يزيد عنه ثلاث ساعات .

الفرع الرابع الملف

ويعرف بهذا الإسم عند أهل الحجاز وأما الشاميون فيسمونه الواسطة وهو بين الفرعي والطريق الشرقي فيكون في شرقي الفرعي وغربي الشرقي وطوله من المدينة المنورة إلى رابغ اثنتان وستون ساعة ومراحله خمس وسدس على سير الجمال المعتاد وأما على سير الركب الشامي فمراحله ست ومحطاته كذلك .

المرحلة الأولى	من المدينة المنورة	إلى بير عروة	وهي ساعة واحدة
المرحلة الثانية	من بير عروة	إلى شعب الحج	وهي خمس عشرة ساعة
(١٥) المرحلة الثالثة	من شعب الحج	إلى بير خلص	وهي اثنتا عشرة ساعة
المرحلة الرابعة	من بير خلص	إلى بير الحصان	وهي أربع عشرة ساعة
المرحلة الخامسة	من بير الحصان	إلى بير الشيخ	وهي ثمان ساعات
المرحلة السادسة	من بير الشيخ	إلى رابغ	وهي اثنتي عشرة ساعة

وتنتهي هذه الفروع الأربعة برابغ ورابغ هذه بلدة عظيمة بالنسبة لتلك القرى المجاورة لها تبعد عن البحر إلى جهته الشرقية نحو ساعة ونصف وميتها البقلية ومناخ رابغ ردىء جداً ويسامت رابغ من جهتها الشرقية الجحفة بينهما نحو ساعة وهي ميقات إحرام أهل المدينة ومن يمر عليها عند الإمام أبي حنيفة رحمه الله تعالى ومن قال بقوله وعند غيره من خارج المدينة المنورة وهواؤها أردى من هواء رابغ وقد دعا رسول الله صلى الله عليه وآله وصحبه وسلم لما نزل المدينة وكانت فيها الحمى ان تنتقل حماها إلى الجحفة هذه فاستجاب الله تعالى دعاءه ونجت المدينة من الحمى وصارت إلى الجحفة من ذلك الوقت وطاب هواء المدينة وقد أشار صلى الله تعالى عليه وآله وصحبه وسلم إلى طيبة هوائها بتسميتها طيبة وطابة ثم تتصل هذه الفروع الأربعة بطريق واحد إلى مكة المكرمة في الطريق من رابغ إلى مكة وهو الجامع لهذه الفروع أما طوله من رابغ إليها فثمان وأربعون ساعة ومراحله أربع بالسير المعتاد على الجمال وأما على سير الركب الشامي فمراحله أربع (١٦) وكذا محطاته.

المرحلة الأولى	من رابغ	إلى القضيمة	وهي أربع عشرة ساعة
المرحلة الثانية	من القضيمة	إلى عسفان	وهي أربع عشرة ساعة
المرحلة الثالثة	من عسفان	إلى وادي فاطمة	وهي أربع عشرة ساعة
المرحلة الرابعة	من وادي فاطمة	إلى مكة المكرمة	وهي ست ساعات

وفي عسفان بئر التفلة وهو البئر الذي كان ماؤه ملحاً اجاجاً فتفل فيه سيدنا رسول الله صلى تعالى عليه وآله وصحبه وسلم فأصبح عذباً فراتاً سائغاً للشاربين وهذا من معجزاته الظاهرة الباهرة.

في الطريق الثاني من المدينة المنورة إلى مكة المكرمة

ويقال له الشرقي وهو الذي لا يمر على رابغ وموقعه في جهة ملف الشرقية وأهل المدينة لا يسلكونه في ذهابهم مع الركوب إلى مكة للحج ولا في رجوعهم وأما الركب الشامي فيسلكه كثيراً وطوله من المدينة

إلى مكة مائة وأربعون ساعة ومراحله احدى عشرة مرحلة وثلثان على سير الجمال المعتاد وأما على سير الركب الشامي فمراحله اثنتا عشرة مرحلة وكذا محطاته .

المرحلة الأولى	من المدينة المنورة	إلى العريض	وهي ساعتان
المرحلة الثانية	من العريض	إلى الخنق	وهي عشر ساعات
المرحلة الثالثة	من الخنق	إلى الغراب	وهي اثنتا عشرة ساعة
(١٧) المرحلة الرابعة	من الغراب	إلى بيار الحجر	وهي اثنتا عشرة ساعة
المرحلة الخامسة	من بيار الحجر	إلى الملاحة	وهي اثنتا عشرة ساعة
المرحلة السادسة	من الملاحة	إلى صفينة	وهي اثنتا عشرة ساعة
المرحلة السابعة	من صفينة	إلى الجبلتين	وهي اثنتا عشرة ساعة
المرحلة الثامنة	من الجبلتين	إلى بير حادبة	وهي اثنتا عشرة ساعة
المرحلة التاسعة	من بير حادبة	إلى زبيدة	وهي اثنتا عشرة ساعة
المرحلة العاشرة	من زبيدة	إلى المحروقة	وهي اثنتا عشرة ساعة
المرحلة الحادية عشر	من المحروقة	إلى وادي الليمون	وهي أربع عشرة ساعة
المرحلة الثانية عشر	من وادي الليمون	إلى مكة المكرمة	وهي ثمان عشرة ساعة

في بيان طول هذه الطرق مجموعة وعدد محطاتها من المدينة إلى مكة باعتبار سير الركب الشامي

السلطاني	طوله مائة وثلاث وعشرون ساعة	ومحطاته عشر
الغائر	طوله على ما تقدم اثنتان وتسعون ساعة	ومحطاته عشر
الفرعي	طوله مائة وست وعشرون ساعة	ومحطاته عشر
الملف	طوله مائة وعشر ساعات	ومحطاته تسع
الشرقي	طوله مائة وأربعون ساعة	ومحطاته احدى عشرة

في بيان طول الطريق من الشام إلى مكة باعتبار هذه الطرق

(١٨) من الطريق السلطاني	طوله أربعمائة وخمس وخمسون ساعة	ومحطاته احدى وأربعون
من الطريق الغائر	طوله أربعمائة وأربع وعشرون ساعة	ومحطاته احدى وأربعون
من الطريق الفرعي	طوله أربعمائة وثمان وخمسون ساعة	ومحطاته احدى وأربعون
من الطريق الملف	طوله أربعمائة واثنتان وأربعون ساعة	ومحطاته أربعون
من الطريق الشرقي	طوله أربعمائة واثنتان وسبعون ساعة	ومحطاته اثنتان وأربعون

في خريطة هذا الطريق الجغرافية

في بيان الكلام على ما في هذا الطريق من المحطات

ينقسم الكلام على المحطات التي في طريق الحجاز الآن قسمين قسم من الشام إلى المدينة وقسم من المدينة إلى مكة .

القسم الأول من الشام إلى المدينة

وهي ثلاثة أنواع .

النوع الأول

الكلام على دمشق وذي النون والكتيبة ومزيريب والرّمثة والمفرق والزرقاء والبلقاء والقطرانة والحسا وعنزة ومعان ان طول هذه البلاد مائة ساعة وثلاث ساعات كما تقدم اما دمشق الشام وتعرف بالشام فكانت عاصمة تلك البلاد قبل الإسلام منذ انشئت وبقيت عاصمة الإسلام مدة من القرون ووصفت (١٩) بالشريفة وافرد في محاسنها مؤلفات مخصوصة ويكفي ما نقله الحافظ بن عساكر في تاريخه بما ورد فيها من الأحاديث والآثار والأخبار وغيره وقلت فيها شعر .

الشام جنة عدن حفت بها الأزهار
أما ترى كيف تجري من تحتها الأنهار

وقلت أيضاً غيره .

دمشق تاهت دلالا على جميع البرية
بجامع أموي وأنهر كوثرية

البركة فيها ظاهرة والخيرات بها باهرة لا يذمها الا حسود ذميم أو ذو ضغينة لئيم أو معتد أثيم مخالف للجماعة شق لله ورسوله عصا الطاعة فانها معقل المسلمين وكهف هذا الدين ومن أراد زيادة على هذا فعليه بكتابنا حميدية الزمان بأفضلية رسولنا الأعظم بنص القرآن وقد أسس للمحطة الأولى للسكة الحديدية عند باب الشام المعروف الآن ببوابة الله وسابقاً بباب مصر وبين هذا الباب وبين ذي النون المحطة التي يستقر فيها موكب الحج ويبدل فيها ثوب المحمل ويقال لها العسالي تجاه سيدي الولي الكبير الشيخ أحمد العسالي الخلوتي رضي الله تعالى عنه

ونفعنا به وفي تلك الساحة قبة صغيرة ومصطبة مرتفعة (٢٠) ومن باب الشام إليها عشر دقائق وهذه التكية والمحطة في شرقي الطريق وفي حذائه من جهته الغربية بلد يقال لها القدم الشريف سميت باسم حجر فيه أثر قدم النبي صلى الله تعالى عليه وآله وصحبه وسلم أثر فيه حينما شرف الشام قبل البعثة ووصل إلى بصرى ثم نقل إلى مسجدها وهو الآن فيها ومن العسالي إلى عقبة الشجون المعروفة بعقبة الكسوة جسران احدهما على جدول من قناة المزة وثانيهما على ماء من عين الباردة وهذه الأراضي بديعة المنظر على جوانبها بلاد ترى من الطريق فاذا انتهى من الصعود على عقبة الشجون نزل إلى أرض الكسوة فيمر على جسر على نهر الأعوج وهو نهر عظيم مشهور وفي جانب الجسر الغربي قرية الكسوة على رتبة عالية ثم يصعد قليلا إلى سهل ترى منه ذو النون وذو النون الآن فيها موقع لمعسكر مظفر في شرق الطريق وعنده جدول ماء من نهر الأعوج وبينهما وبين كتيبة قرية غباغب في شرق الطريق فيها عين ماء حار وقرية الصنمين وهي في غربيه أيضاً والكتيبة وهي قرية في جانب الطريق الشرقي فيها عين جارية أيضاً وبينها وبين مزيريب قرية شيخ مسكين في الجانب الغربي وفيها سيل عظيم ثم طفس في الغربي أيضاً ومزيريب قرية في غربيه أيضاً وفيها عيون ونهر يقال له البجته[2] ماؤه رديء وفيه سمك كثير من يأكل منه يصب بالحمى والرمثة في الغرب أيضاً وفيها صهاريج لماء المطر والمفرق ويوجد فيها مسيل ماء والزرقاء وفيها قلعة ونهر عظيم في غرب الطريق والبلقاء وفيها (٢١) قلعة وحوض مطر في الغرب أيضاً والقطرانة وفيها قلعة وبركة من المطر في شرق الطريق والحسا وفيها قلعة وبئر وبركة مطر في شرق الطريق وقبل الحسا بساعتين ونصف انحدار إلى عنزة وعنزة فيها قلعة وماء من جمع المطر في الجهة الغربية ويقطع هذا الطريق أراضي حوران نصفين وبالقرب منه أراضي وبلاد الجيدور واللجا والجولان وغوربيان ويبعد عن مركز متصرفية حوران نحو ساعتين إلى الشرقة وعلى امتداد هذا النوع من هذا الطريق إلى

[2] Uncertain reading

جوانبه بلاد خربة وبلاد خالية كثيرة وأراضيه منبتة تشبه أراضي حوران بل في بعضها ما هو أحسن منها وفيها قابلية لزرع جميع أنواع الحبوب والبطيخ والقثاء والعنب وغرس للأشجار المثمرة وغير المثمرة سيما شجر التوت الذي يطعم ورقه الدود الحرير والفص فانهما إذا زرعا فيها يكثر هذان النوعان في بلادنا وكذلك الطائفة الشوندرية التي يخرج منها السكر وفي بعض البلاد والأراضي القريبة منه مثل غوربيان تصلح زراعة قصب السكر وشجر البن والشاي وأمثالها مما تخسر بلادنا القسم العظيم من ثروتها بجلبه من الخارج كالهند وجابونيا وغيرهما فان غوربيان قطر حار يشبه أقطار الحجاز يصلح لغرس الأشجار وغيرها المحتاجة إلى الأراضي الحارة ويحتاج إلى الالتفات إليه بالغرس والزرع ولربما يصح فيه غرس النخيل وما شاكله ومزيريب يأتيها ركب حج شامي يوم السابع من شهر شوال أو الثامن ويصير فيها سوق عظيم للتجارة يأتيه من شاء (٢٢) تجار مخصوصون ينصبون فيها الخيام وكذلك تجار الركب الشامي فانهم يأخذون أموالا مخصوصة لهذا السوق وأمثاله في الطريق فيبيعونها فيه ويأتي من أهالي حوران والجيدور واللجا والجولان والسلط والعرب القريبة لها على مسافة ثلاثة أيام وأربعة ويحضرون معهم الجمال والصوف وغيرهما فيشترون من التجار ويبيعون ما يأتون به ويوجد في هذا السوق جميع ما يرغب فيه من مأكولات وملبوسات وغيرها ويبقى هذا السوق ثمانية عشر يوماً وفي اليوم الخامس والعشرين من شوال يقوم الركب الشامي من مزيريب وفي اثناء هذه الأيام يأتي بنو صخر وولد علي يأخذون الحملة يحملونها على جمالهم ويحملون للركب علف الدواب وأموال التجارة وغيرها كما سيأتي بيانه فإذا رحل الركب الشامي من مزيريب قفل الناس التجار وغيرهم راجعين إلى بلادهم هذا في الذهاب أما في الرجوع فلا يقر الركب الشامي فيها إلا ساعات للاستراحة وأكثر الحجاج الذين يركبون الهجن والخيل والذين يستقبلهم أهلهم في الزرقاء يفارقون الركب منها ويحضرون للشام فلا يقيم الحجاج في مزيريب إلا ساعات لإراحة

الجمال ثم يذهب إلى الشام وبين غوربيان ومزيريب ست ساعات يمر الذاهب إليها من مزيريب على اربد وتتصل أراضي الغور ببحيرة لوط وبركة طبريا وأراضي أريحا من أعمال القدس والزرقاء فيها عين عظيمة يجري منها نهر كبير وماؤه طيب وبعض مأموري الركب الشامي يحملون الماء (٢٣) منه لشربهم إلى المدينة المنورة وأراضيها خصبة جداً وبعدها ارتفاع وانخفاض متعدد يسمى قلابات الزرقاء طوله أربع ساعات ومعان كانت مركز متصرفية تابعة للشام قبل نقله للكرك وهي بلدة عظيمة مقسومة قسمين بينهما طريق يمر الحج فيه وهو الطريق العام لمن يسلك من تلك الجهات وأهاليها خضر اللون وعندهم العنب والتين والرمان وسائر الأشجار وتنمو بها أشجار الزيتون وتكثر لو اعتنى بزرعها فيها وقابلة للتمدن والاعمار والترقي ومركزها تجاري ويمكث الركب الشامي فيها يوماً يسمى طراقاً ويصير في ذلك اليوم سوق عظيم للتجارة وثمر أشجارها ومحصولاتها الأرضية يبقيان فيها وإذا صادف مرور الركب الشامي عليها أو ان الفاكهة يبيعون عليه ما يكون عندهم منها وهي قريبة من خليل الرحمن عليه الصلاة والسلام وتمتد أراضيها إلى غزة هاشم وتتصل بأراضي العريش وفيها يكتب الحجاج لأهاليهم مكاتيب يخبرونهم فيها عن أحوالهم وما يلزمهم ويرسلونها مع البريد وهو أول بريد يجيء الشام من ركب الحج ويسمى كتاب معان ويقرب منها الكرك الشهيرة وهي الآن مركز المتصرفية التي كانت في معان ومن أحصن معاقل المسلمين في قمة الجبل وحوله واد عظيم فيه حمام وبساتين ومياه وأشجار متنوعة ولا يتوصل إليها إلا من طريق واحد وعلى بابه مؤتة وفيها قبر سيدنا جعفر الطيار رضي الله تعالى عنه ويجلب الماء إلى الكرك من خارجها ويتبعها بلاد فيها واردات كثيرة خصبة أكثرها (٢٤) خال من السكان وفي اعمار هذه البلاد والاهتمام بأمرها تزيد ثروة البلاد وواردات الحكام ومواقعها امينة سيما بعد وصول السكة الحديدية إليها انشاء الله تعالى.

النوع الثاني

العقبة والمدورة وذات حج والقاع وتبوك وظهر المغر والأخضر وجناين القاضي والمعظم وتبريكة والمدائن وطول هذه البلاد والقلاع مائة وسبع وثلاثون ساعة وكلها قابلة للزراعة والغرس ويوجد في بعضها آبار وبعض أراضيها رملية والبدو الشاميون لا يقطنون فيها أصلا بخلاف ما يأتي من قرى الحجاز اما العقبة ويقال لها العقبة الشامية للفرق بينها وبين العقبة التي بالقرب من شاطىء خليج البحر الأحمر الشرقي الشمالي المسامتة إلى حمام فرعون من خليج السويس وتزيد عنها العقبة الشامية نصف درجة عرضاً وفيها قلعة في غرب الطريق وبركة ماء من جمع المطر فإذا جاوزها المسافر إلى جهة الحجاز أشرف على وهدة ينخفض فيها طولها نصف ساعة وسميت عقبة لذلك * والمدورة هي أول الرمل وفيها قلعة وعين ماء في غرب الطريق وذات الحج فيها قلعة وعين ماء وهي في شرق الطريق وأرضها رمل أيضاً والقاع هي سهل لا قلعة فيها ولا ماء وأما تبوك فانها خصبة قابلة للتقدم وفيها قلعة عن يمين الطريق وعين جارية وفيها حائط بستان ينسب (٢٥) للنبي صلى الله تعالى عليه وسلم ويوجد فيها العنب والنخيل وباقي الثمار وأراضيها خصبة ويقال كان فيها أصحاب الايكة الذين بعث الله تعالى لهم شعيباً عليه السلام رسولا ولم يكن منهم بل كان من مدين وهي قريبة منها وقد كانت تبوك عامرة آهلة والآن خرب كثير منها وليس فيها سكان أصلا أو قليلون جداً وذلك لبعدها عن الشام والمدينة وعدم وجود عساكر فيها تحافظها من هجوم البدو والمتوحشين عليها وفيها يكتب الحجاج لأهلهم مكاتيب في الرجوع ويرسلونها مع البريد الخامس المسمى بالجوخدار وهو آخر البرد وظهر المغر أرض سهل لا ماء فيها ولا قلعة ولا بلد وقبل الوصول منها إلى الأخضر بساعة ونصف نزول إلى المحطة والأخضر فيها قلعة في غرب الطريق فيها بئر وحوض من جمع المطر وجنائن القاضي سهل ليس فيها قلعة ولا بركة سوى غدير من المطر والمعظم فيها قلعة وبركة

* ولا بأس بأن يمد الخط من معان إلى العقبة الغربية التي على ضفة البحر المذكورة ومنها إلى تبوك لكثرة فوائده باتصالها بالبحر فيكون هذا الخط متصلا بالبحر الأحمر ومنه يستغنى عن خليج السويس والمرور بأرض مصر وتتسع التجارة ويمكن اشغال المراكب التجارية والحربية العثمانية بواسطة هذا الاتصال بحيث يستغنى عن غيرها.

من جمع المطر وظهر الحمراء فيها قلعة وبركة ماء من المطر في غرب الطريق أيضاً وتبريكة محطة بين جبلين غربي وشرقي لا قلعة فيها ولا ماء ولا يزال الركب يسير بين جبال حتى يوافي آخرهما من جهة الحجاز فينتهي بملتقى جبلين بينهما نحو عشرين ذراعاً أو أقل كاد يكون باباً والحجاج إذا وصلوا إليه خرجوا منه إلى سهل من الرمل الذي تغوص فيه الأرجل إلى الركب وقوائم الدواب إلى آخرها فيجدون للجمال ويزجرونها بأعلى أصواتهم ويضربون الطبول يزعمون أنهم يفعلون هذا كيلا تسمع الجمال أنين (٢٦) فصيل ناقة صالح عليه السلام وحنينه لأمه فتبرك ولا تقوم والصحيح ان فعل ذلك من الأقدمين لئلا تبرك الجمال من تعبها من الرمل الذي تخب فيه وتغوص إلى بطونها فلا تستطيع المشي إلا بمشقة عظيمة فإذا سمعت الحدو والصراخ وضرب الطبول وأتاها الضرب من كل جانب تجفل فتمشي ومن عادة الحجاج إذا وصلوا في الرجوع لملتقى هذين الجبلين يصرخ أناس منهم على التعاقب إلى أن ينتهي مرور الركب منه بأعلا أصواتهم الفاتحة إلى روح من أغلق عليه الباب يعنون من مات من الحجاج من هذا المحل إلى تبريكة ذهاباً واياباً ويعتبرون أنهم بوصولهم إليه دخلوا أرض الشام وإذا كان في الركب وباء أو غيره يزول باذن الله تعالى لتغير الهواء عما قبله ومن هذا الموضع إلى قرب المدائن مسافة ثلاث ساعات رمل تلعب به أيدي الرياح فتنقله من جهة إلى أخرى وإذا صادف الركب فيه هواء يتحملون منه مشاق لا توصف وكذلك الجمال والدواب حتى لا تستطيع أن تفتح أعينها فضلا عن المشي وسميت هذه المحطة تبريكة لأن الجمال تبرك إذا وصلت إلى الرمل فيها أو لما يقولون أن ناقة صالح عليه السلام بركت هناك والله تعالى أعلم والمدائن اسم لمدائن صالح المذكورة في القرآن الكريم بقوله تعالى وتنحتون من الجبال بيوتاً فارهين وهي بلاد عظيمة منحوتة من حجر بديعة الشكل فيها صنائع النقش المحكم والنحت المستحكم خالية لا ساكن فيها ترى من طريق الحج (٢٧) عن شرق الطريق في الذهاب إلى مكة وليست مقلوبة كما يتوهم كثير من العامة

فان التي قلبت مدائن لوط لا مداين صالح لأن قوم صالح لما عقروا الناقة أهلكهم الله تعالى بالصيحة وذلك ان ثمود الذين هم قوم صالح كانت أعمارهم طويلة وكانوا يبنون مساكنهم من المدر فينهدم المسكن وصاحبه حي فنحتوا الجبال واتخذوا فيها البيوت فطلبوا من سيدنا صالح عليه السلام آية تدل على أنه رسول لهم من عند الله فدعا صالح ربه فأخرج لهم الناقة فكانت آيتها أنها تكفيهم بلبنها عن الماء يوماً وتشرب في ذلك اليوم جميع الماء فلا تبقى لهم شيئاً وتتركه لهم في اليوم الثاني فلا يأخذون فيه من لبنها شيئاً فأوحى الله تعالى إلى سيدنا صالح انهم سيعقرون الناقة فأخبرهم بذلك وان الذي عقرها غلام منهم أشقر ازرق اصهب أحمر سيولد فيهم فكانوا يطوفون في القرية فإذا وجدوا امرأة تمخض نظروا ما ولدها فان كان غلاماً نظروا أوصافه وان كان جارية أعرضوا عنها فوجد الشرطة يوماً غلاماً بهذه الصفة فأرادوا أخذه وكان جداه أبو أبيه وأبو أمه من اعزاء ثمود المنعاء فمنعاهم عن أخذه فكان شر مولود وكان ينمو جسمه في اليوم ما ينموه جسم غيره في جمعة فاجتمع الثمانية الذين كانوا يفسدون في الأرض ولا يصلحون وطلبوا من جدي الغلام ان يؤمراه عليهم بمنزلته وشرف جديه فيهم فكانوا تسعة وهم المذكورون في قوله تعالى وكان في المدينة تسعة رهط (٢٨) يفسدون في الأرض ولا يصلحون وكان سيدنا صالح يبيت في مسجده ولا ينام معهم في القرية فإذا أصبح أتاهم فوعظهم وذكرهم وإذا أمسى يرجع إلى مسجده فأرادوا أن يمكروا بصالح فمشوا حتى أتوا على شرب طريق صالح فاختبأ فيه ثمانية وقالوا إذا خرج علينا قتلناه وأتينا أهله فبيتناهم فأمر الله الأرض فاستوت عليهم فاجتمعوا ومشوا إلى الناقة وهي على حوضها قائمة فقال الشقي لاحدهم أتها فاعقرها فأتاها فتعاظمه ذلك فأضرب عنه فأرسل آخر فكان مثله فكان لا يبعث رجلا إلا تعاظم أمرها حتى مشى إليها وتطاول فضرب عرقوبيها فوقعت تركض فرأى رجلا[3] منهم صالحاً فقال له أدرك الناقة فقد عقرت فأقبل وخرجوا يتلقونه ويعتذرون إليه يا نبي الله انما عقرها

[3] Read رجل

فلان انه لا ذنب لنا قال فانظروا هل تدركون فصيلها فإذا ادركتموه فعسى الله أن يرفع عنهم العذاب فخرجوا يطلبونه فلما رأى الفصيل أمه تضطرب أتى جبلا يقال له القارة قصيراً فصعده وذهبوا ليأخذوه فأوحى الله إلى الجبل فطال في السماء حتى ما تناله الطير ودخل صالح القرية فلما رآه الفصيل بكى ثم استقبل صالحاً فرغا رغوة ثم رغا أخرى ثم رغا أخرى فقال صالح لقومه لكل رغوة أبل فتمتعوا في داركم ثلاثة أيام ذلك وعد غير مكذوب إلا أن آية العذاب ان اليوم الأول تصبح وجوهكم مصفرة واليوم الثاني محمرة واليوم الثالث مسودة فلما اصبحوا اليوم الأول إذا وجوههم (٢٩) كأنها طليت بالخلوق فلما أصبحوا اليوم الثاني إذا وجوههم كأنها خضبت بالدماء فلما أصبحوا اليوم الثالث إذا وجوههم مسودة كأنها طليت بالقار فصاحوا جميعاً ألا قد حضركم العذاب فلما أصبحوا اليوم الرابع اتتهم صيحة من السماء فقطعت قلوبهم في صدورهم فأصبحوا في ديارهم جاثمين فليست هذه المدائن مقلوبة كما يعتقد فيها من لا يعلم الحقيقة وليست محطة الركب الشامي عندها بل يحط عند القلعة قبلها إلى جهة الشام والمحطة المذكورة عند القلعة وفيها بئر ماء يستقي منه الركب الشامي ويقيم عندها يوماً وفيها يكتب الحجاج لأهلهم مكاتيب في الذهاب ويرسلونه مع البريد الثاني ويسمى كتاب المدائن وفيها يلتقي الركب مع قافلة الجردة في الرجوع كما سيأتي ويصير فيه سوق عظيم يحضره البدو يبيعون السمن والتمر والعجوة والغنم والجمال والعلف للدواب ويحضره أيضاً أهل العلا وهي بلدة تبعد عن المدائن بنحو ست ساعات إلى جهة الغرب الجنوب وهي عامرة وفيها الليمون الحلو والحامض والكباد والأترج وليس فيها البرتقال وفيها النخيل بكثرة ويوجد فيها العنب وسائر الأشجار والأثمار وفيها مياه جارية وأهلها سمر اللون وفيهم استعداد للزراعة والتعلم ويتركون بلدهم ويحضرون للشام يتعاطون فيها الزراعة وأكثر من يحضر منهم إليها من أبناء الخمسة عشر يذهبون مع الركب الشامي فإذا وصلوها اشتغلوا فيها بالزراعة وقد يشتغل قليل منهم بغيرها

فإذا اشتغل الواحد منهم وجمع ما يجمعه غيره من المال ان أراد المقام في الشام أقام فيها وتزوج وان أراد (٣٠) الرجوع لبلده اشترى ملابس له وللهدية إلى أهله وأصحابه من بضاعة الشام وأخذ ما زاد معه من المال وقفل راجعاً إلى بلاده مع الركب الشامي فيتلقاه أهله بالترحاب ويسلمون عليه ويعظمونه فيشتري أرضاً يغرسها ويزرعها ويصيرها بستاناً وقد يتزوج وقد يشتري بجميع ما معه أرضاً ويصبر إلى ان يصير له ريع فيتزوج من ريعه ويحضرون من محصولاتهم لركب الحج الشامي ما يناسب كالليمون والعجوة فيبيعونه ويشترون منه ما يلزمهم وينقلون من محصولاتهم إلى المدينة المنورة ما يمكنهم حمله فيبيعونه فيها لكن لبعد المسافة لا يجمعون غلة فلذا لا يذهبون إليها لأجل التجارة فقط بل يذهبون لزيارة النبي صلى الله تعالى عليه وآله وصحبه وسلم ويأخذون معهم من محصولات بلادهم ما لا يعيقهم عن الزيارة فيكون تبعاً لهم في السفر لا قصداً وبعض من لا يعرف الحقيقة يظن ان ما يأتي به أهل العلا من الفواكه والبقول من المدائن ومذهب أهل العلا مالكي ويغلب عليهم الصلاح والأمانة والديانة لم تفسد اخلاقهم وفيهم جد واجتهاد وهمّة ونشاط وقابلية لتعلم الزراعة والصناعة والترقي والتمدن.

النوع الثالث

البدايع والزمرد والجديد والبراقة وهدية واصطبل عنتر وآبار ناصيف وهذه المحطات طولها إلى المدينة مائة وساعتان والبدائع سهل ليس فيه قلعة ولا بلد ولا ماء والزمرد قلعة في شرق الطريق فيها بئر ماء والجديد كذلك قلعة في شرق الطريق فيها حوض من ماء المطر والبراقة محطة ليس فيها قلعة ولا (٣١) ماء وهدية قلعة في شرقي الطريق يحفر في أراضيها قليلا فيخرج الماء الا أنه ردىء وبعدها بالقرب منها تل رمل يصعد المار عليه وينزل فيه في وهدة طوله نحو نصف ساعة واصطبل عنتر وهو بناء قديم في أعلا جبل عن يمين الطريق يرى من البعد وسميت المحطة به وليس فيها قلعة ولا ماء وهي أرض سهل وآبار

نصيف محطة فيها جملة آبار ليس فيها قلعة ولا بلد وهذه الآبار في جهة الطريق الشرقية الشمالية وفي منتصف الطريق بينها وبين المدينة نزول إلى جهة المدينة نحو ساعتين وأكثر أراضي هذه المحطات خصبة وإن كانت رملية وفيها غابات كثيرة وفي جوارها كثير من البدو يقيمون في الخيام ويتنقلون من منزل إلى منزل ومن مفازة إلى مفازة بحسب اختلاف الزمان وفصوله وقابلية المواقع للحط والترحال فيها على مقتضى الأحوال وفيها سيول وآبار .

ثم ان النوع الأول لما كان مأهولا بالنسبة للنوعين الآخرين كان الشجر البري فيه قليلا وأما النوعان الأخيران ففيهما غابات كبيرة طويلة عريضة يحتطب المسافر فيهما من جانبي الطريق ولا يحمل الحطب معه إلا في مرحلتين منها وهذه الغابات تنبت بنفسها وتعيش بدون ان يتعهدها أحد وشربها من ماء السماء المطر والندى وتكفي بلاد الحرمين والشام إذا تعهدت على حسب فن الزراعة وخدمت وأكثر شجر هذه الغابات الغيلان فإذا خدمت تنمو وتكثر ويتحصل منها واردات ومنافع للحكومة والأهالي والبلاد وبواسطة (٣٢) السكة الحديدية تحصل الفوائد الجمة منها لأن بقاءها على حالها الآن مميت لها ولمنافعها فالذي يقطع منها لا يعوض إلا أن ينبت بنفسه ويكون بعيداً عن وصول الدواب إليه مع ان هذه الأراضي قابلة لتزييد هذه الغابات ويمكن ان تزرع فيها أشجار آخر غيرها مثل السنديان ولربما يجيد فيها بعض الأشجار المثمرة التي تعيش بالمطر فقط كالعنب والتين والزيتون وهذا كله سهل بعونه تعالى إذا تم انشاء هذه االسكة لحديدية .

القسم الثالث من المدينة إلى مكة

ونحن الآن نتكلم على بعض القرى التي من المدينة إلى مكة ونبين بعض أحوالها ولو كانت صغيرة جداً تشتمل على بيتين أو ثلاثة .

فمنها بير درويش ويسكنه الرادة وبير عباس ويسكنه الرحلة والواسطة ويسكنها الحوارزم وبدر ويسكنها صبح والمستورة ويسكنها زبيد وبدر

هذه هي التي نصر الله تعالى فيها رسوله وصحابته صلى الله تعالى عليه وسلم وأنزل فيها عليهم ولقد نصركم الله ببدر وأنتم أذلة وفيها مرقد لشهداء بدر الكرام الصحابة الأجلاء الذين يستجيب الله تعالى بتلاوة أسمائهم الدعاء واخبر الرسول الأعظم صلى الله تعالى عليه وآله وصحبه وسلم ان الله تعالى غفر لهم ما تقدم من ذنبهم وما تأخر ولا ريب أنهم أحياء في قبورهم إلى يوم يبعثهم الله تعالى فقد أجمع من تشرف بزيارتهم ان رائحة قبورهم أطيب من المسك الاذفر وتواتر عند أهل بدر ومن جاورها (٣٣) أنه يسمع في ليلة الجمعة والاثنين بين العشائين صوت طبل الحرب عند قبورهم رضوان الله تعالى عليهم يعرف ذلك منهم الصغير والكبير حتى أنهم كانوا يأتون على صوته فإذا وقفوا على الباب سمعوه فإذا دخلوا عند القبور انقطع فإذا خرجوا وابتعدوا قليلا عنها سمعوه وهذا ثابت مقرر عند أهل تلك الاقطار المعظمة حتى في المدينة المنورة ومكة المكرمة ويأتيهم العرب من أقصى الأرض للزيارة وينذرون لله تعالى الصدقات عند قبورهم ويجلونهم ويرعونهم حق رعايتهم نفعنا الله تعالى بهم .

ومنها بير الماشي للصواعد وجبل الغائر للتراجمة وبير الحفاة للهبة وعين التبرة لجهم وبير المبيريك لجهم أيضاً .

ومنها الصمت ويقال لها صمت المغربي والمرباط أيضاً لبني عوف والريان لبني عمرو وأبو الضباع لجهم والعقبة ويقال لها بير رضوان ومنها القضيمة ويسكنها العسوم والعصالية وعسفان ويسكنها بشر ووادي فاطمة ويسكنه الأشراف الحسينية من أولاد سيدنا الحسن رضي الله تعالى عنه وفي جانب وادي فاطمة للغرب واد عظيم يقال له المضيق ويسكنه أشراف حسينية أيضاً وبعض من قبيلة عتيبة وهو مثل وادي فاطمة في الزرع والغرس والأشجار من كل نوع .

وفيها السوارقية ويسكنها أشراف حسينية من أولاد سيدنا الحسين رضي (٣٤) الله تعالى عنه وأما رابغ فقد تقدم الكلام عليها بأنها أعظم هذه الأماكن وإليها مرجع الركوب والقوافل وبجانبها أسكلة[4]

4 أسهلة Read

تسمى البقلية من جهة غربها بينها وبينها نحو ساعة ونصف ومساحتها من جهتها الشرقية الجحفة على نحو ساعة منها وبالجملة فان الحديدة والصفراء وبدر من السلطاني والريان وأبو الضباع من الفرعي في كل منها أنهر جارية وباقي هذه القرى فيها عيون وآبار ويزرع فيها النخيل والليمون والموز والرمان والعنب بكثرة والتين وغيرها ويوجد فيها عسل النحل الأبيض الطيب الرائحة وأكثرها مياهاً وادي فاطمة ووادي الليمون ويزرع فيهما القرع والباذنجان والملوخية والبقلة الحمقاء وجميع الخضر والبقول والحبوب ويؤتى بها إلى مكة المكرمة ولا سيما البطيخ فانه يزرع في كل وقت والخيار والقثاء وليس لزرع البقول فيها وما أشبهها وقت معين فانها في الأرض التي تسقى بماء الأنهار تزرع في كل وقت وفي الأرض التي تسقى بماء المطر متى نزل المطر فمتى نزل المطر ورويت الأرض يزرع الشخص منهم مهما أراد وكل هذه القرى يزرع فيها ذلك إلا أنه لما كانت محصولاتها لا تصريف لها لبعد المسافة بينها وبين مكة أو المدينة يتساهل أهلها في زرعها ولا يزيدون على قدر حاجتهم ويبيعون للركوب التي تمر بهم التمر والعجوة والبلح والبطيخ والسمن والحليب وما ماثلها مما يكون عندهم ويصنعون المراوح من ورق النخل والوسادات من الجلود ويبيعونها لهم أيضاً وأهلها (٣٥) متوحشون غاية التوحش ينتظرون الفرصة للسرقة من الركوب والقوافل والطريق في تلك الأراضي غير آمنة والشريف أمير مكة يتعهد للقوافل والركوب ويرسل من طرفه أحد الأشراف معها فيخشون بأسه والسكة الحديدية تؤمن هذه السبل وتعمرها وتدخل أهلها في المدنية والترقي والصناعة وتكف بأس بعضهم عن بعض وتعديهم كلهم عن غيرهم.

في بيان الركوب والقوافل

الركب هو ما يشتمل على الهجن والخيل والحمير ولا يكون فيه شقادف ولا محفاة وجمعه ركوب كبدر وبدور والقافلة هي ما تشتمل

على جمال وأحمال وشقادف وجمعها قوافل كسائمة وسوائم وهذا في اصطلاح أهل مكة والمدينة وفي اصطلاح أهل الشام يسمون قافلة الحج التي تخرج من الشام ركباً والهجن جمع هجين وهو نوع من الجمال مختص بالركوب دون التحميل وله قوة عظيمة في شدة السرعة في المسير والرهاوين جمع رهوان وهو البرذون الذي يطبع على مشية مخصوصة والبرذون الفرس الذي هو غير عربي والشقادف جمع شقدف وهو شيء يشبه المحفة مقسوم قسمين يحمل على ظهر الجمل يركب في كل قسم إنسان والمحفة ويقال لها عند الشاميين خشب ومحارة والشبارى جمع شبرية وهي تشبه المحفة إلا أن لها بين قسميها حاجز والتخت كالقبة الصغيرة يحمل على جملين أو بغلين أحدهما أمام الآخر ويمشي في أركانه الأربعة أربعة رجال ويسحب الجمل الذي هو قدام رجل آخر وقد كان في الزمن السابق لا يركب أحد تختاً (٣٦) على بغلين إلا أمين الصرة ومحافظ الحج وأما الآن فمطلق والمحمل قبة لها وسط عالٍ مركوزة على بيت صغير مربع على كل ركن منه كرأس العلم وفي وسطه كذلك وهذه الرؤس كلها من فضة وفي الوسط من جهة الأمام كذلك رأس من فضة وثوبه المسجى به مشغول بالفضة تشتغله الدولة العلية وترسله من الأستانة العلية إلى الشام وكلما تقادم عهد واحد بدل بغيره جديداً.

في بيان ركب الحج الشامي وموكبه في الشام

إن ركب الحج الشامي كان له في الزمن السابق أهمية وشأن عظيم وذلك أنه تحصل الارادة السنية بتعيين رجل من عظماء الاستانة أميناً للصرة السلطانية التي عينها ساكن الجنان السلطان سليم الأول من سلاطين الدولة العثمانية عطايا لأهل الشام والقدس والحرمين وفي اليوم الخامس عشر من شعبان يذهب بعض أصحاب الرتب العلمية الأئمة والخطباء وبعض موظفي نظارة الأوقاف إلى المابين الهمايوني ويتشرف أمين الصرة بالمثول لدى جلالة السلطان المنصور أمير المؤمنين وتذهب طائفة

من خدمة الحج الذين يحضرون من الشام لمرافقة أمين الصرة للمابين أيضاً ويجتمعون فيه حسب العادة ثم يخرجون بموكب عظيم وسيأتي بيانه في الكلام عليه وحده ويذهبون إلى اسكدار حيث كان مسير الصرة أولا حينما كانت تذهب للشام من البر عن طريق الأناضول ويمكثون فيها إلى منتصف (٣٧) رمضان ثم يستأذنون فإذا حصلت الإرادة السنية سافروا في البحر إلى بيروت ومنها للشام فإذا كان لأمين الصرة شغل في بيروت كحوالة أموال تأخر إلى قضائه وإلا ذهب حالا للشام ويكون والى الشام ابتدأ في مجلس إدارة الشام بتدارك اللوازم الحجازية وتعيين أجرة للحمل والشبارى والخشب والتخت والرهوان وتعيين المقومين وهم الذين يؤجرون الجمال للحجاج والخيام ويجلبون لهم الماء وتخصيص مقوم منهم لحمل المحمل والصرة وأمين الصرة والجوخدار وما يتبع ذلك من خدمة الحج كالمحافظ واتباعه وهذا المقوم يسمى باش مقوم وذلك بمعرفة محافظ الحج الذي يذهب معه من الشام ويعود معه إليها وقد كان محافظ الحج أولا والي ولاية الشام فقد كان من جملة وظائفه المعين إليها ان يذهب مع الحج الشامي إلى مكة ليحافظه ذهاباً وايابا كما أنه كان الذي يذهب بالجردة لركب الحج الشامي والي طرابلس الشام وسيأتي وبعد وصول أمين الصرة بيومين أو ثلاثة يبتدئ باعطاء أصحاب الصر مرتباتهم في الشام من أموال وجبب وثياب وخفاف ونعال ونشوق وغير ذلك على ما هو محرر في الدفتر الذي يستصحبه معه من الاستانة من نظارة الأوقاف فيها ويأتي من القدس الشريف للشام وكيل (٣٨) عن أصحاب الصر معه حجة وكالة شرعية بأخذ الصر المعين للقدسيين ويباشر الحجاج من أهل الشام وغيرهم بشراء ما يحتاجون إليه من الزاد والثياب والدواب والعلف والقرب للماء والخيام وما أشبهها ويباشر محافظ الحج بما يلزم له ولمن في معيته من الزاد والذخيرة والمهمات وكذلك الطبيب الجراح الذي عينته الحكومة للذهاب للحج ليطبب ويعالج الحجاج مجاناً ويعطيهم الأدوية فانه يتهيأ ويستحضر ما يلزمه من العلاجات والعقاقير

للحجاج في الطريق ليكون على أهبة السفر وقد عرف هذا الطبيب عند الحجاج بالساطي[5] والحجاج تتوارد للشام من سائر الجهات من العجم والداغستان والترك وغيرهم ولا يزالون يتواردون ويتأهبون ويتهيأون إلى اليوم الثالث عشر من شوال وفي ذلك اليوم يجلبون الزيت الذي يأخذونه للحرمين الشريفين من قرية كفر سوسة أو غيرها من أعمال الشام ويكون يوماً مشهوداً يحتفل به الناس ويتركون أشغالهم ويزينون الجمال التي تحمله ويحمل طبل عظيم على جمل يركبه أثنان يضربان عليه وتضرب الطبول والزمور أمامه ويجتمع الشبان والكهول ويحملون بأيديهم العصي الطوال ويلعبون بالسيوف والتروس والعصي ويشعلون المشاعل وينشدون الأشعار والصلوات على النبي المختار كقولهم صلوا نصلي صلينا عليك يا محمد صلينا من هنا القبلة عليك يا نبينا صلينا ويمشون أمام الجمال على هذه الحال من باب (٣٩) السريجة في الشام إلى باب الجابية ومنه إلى المدينة في السوق الذي يقطع دمشق قسمين جنوبياً وشمالياً إلى أن يصل إلى سوق جقمق ثم يمرون في السوق الذي يصل إلى باب البريد تجاه باب الجامع الشريف الأموي الواقع في جهته الغربية ثم يمشون في سوق الجديد على باب دار العسكرية ثم على باب دار الحكومة إلى مستودع اشياء الحج ويكون هذا كله قبل الظهر فإذا اذن الظهر وصلى مؤذنو الجامع الشريف الأموي الظهر فيه وعددهم خمسة وسبعون ويتبعهم مؤذنون غير موظفين فيه نحواً منهم ذهب جميعهم إلى الدار التي يسكب فيها الشمع العسلي الذي يوقد في الحرم الشريف المدني والحرم الشريف المكي فيدخلون الدار المذكورة وتتلى فيه قصة المولد الشريف ويوزع عليهم السكر على الفستق واللوز المسمى الملبس ويسقون ماء السكر وتأتي العساكر النظامية الموسيقية مع آلات الموسيقى إلى تلك الدار ثم يلفون الشمع بالشال الثمين وتحمله الرجال على اعناقهم بالأحترام والتعظيم وتمشي أولا الموسيقى العسكرية تصدح بالأنغام المطربة ويتبعهم المؤذنون يتلون الصلاة الابراهيمية ويكبرون ويهللون وينشدون القصائد والمدائح النبوية بالأنغام

[5] Read الشاني or النطاسي

الشهية والأصوات الحسنة الداودية ومعهم أناس يحملون على رؤسهم قناني الزجاج المملوءة ماء الورد البلدي العطر وزهر النارنج الشامي ويحف الجميع العساكر النظامية والضبطية بالأسلحة الرسمية (٤٠) يحملون ذلك على تلك الحالة إلى مستودع أشياء الحج والأهالي مجتمعة في الأسواق والطرق والدكاكين محتفلة بذلك مبتهجة به مصلية على النبي صلى الله عليه وآله وصحبه وسلم داعية لهذه الخلافة العثمانية بالدوام على ممر الليالي والأيام وفي اليوم التالي وهو اليوم الرابع عشر يصلي المؤذنون في الجامع الشريف الأموي الظهر ثم يذهبون إلى دار العسكرية حيث يكون علم الحج الشريف فيه المسمى بالسنجق والعساكر النظامية والضبطية يجتمعون فيحملون ثوب السنجق وعصاه وتصدح العساكر الموسيقيون بالأنغام المطربة ويبتدى المؤذنون بالصلاة والتهليل والتكبير وتنشر بعض أعلام عادية وعسكرية وتمشي أناس بأيديهم مباخر منها العود والند وأناس بأيديهم قماقم فيها ماء الزهر والورد فإذا خرج ثوب السنجق من باب دار العسكرية أطلق من القلعة مدفع اعلاماً بخروجه والأسواق والأزقة والدكاكين والاسطحة غاصة بالناس من كل لمة وطائفة فيمرون به في سوق الجديد المقابل باب دار العسكرية حتى ينتهوا إلى باب القلعة الشرقي ثم يدخلون منه القلعة فإذا دخل السنجق أطلق مدفع اعلاماً بذلك فيذهبون إلى الجامع الذي في وسطها وفيها قبر الصحابى الجليل سيدنا أبي الدرداء رضي الله تعالى عنه فيصلي الظهر فيه من لم يكن صلى من الناس والعامة يقولون صلوا عليه الظهر ويلبسون ثوب السنجق على العصى ويحملونه وحوله جملة من الأعلام العسكرية وغيرها منشورة (٤١) ويمشون بالهيئة التي دخلوا بها حتى يوافوا الباب الذي أتوا منه فيطلق من القلعة مدفع ايذاناً بخروجه ثم يذهبون من جهة القلعة الشمالية على المناخلية إلى السروجية إلى جامع السنجقدار فيدخلون إليه فإذا دخل السنجق أطلق مدفع آخر من القلعة فيدخل الناس لصلاة العصر وتقف العساكر والضباط والضبطية والأهالي ينتظرون فإذا صلوا العصر وأخرج السنجق من الجامع أطلق مدفع آخر

فيمشون به والطريق غاصة بالناس والدكاكين والدور وغيرها وكلما مر على ملأ منهم قاموا أجلالا وصلوا على النبي صلى الله تعالى عليه وآله وصحبه وسلم حتى يصلون إلى دائرة المشير العسكرية فإذا دخل السنجق بابها أطلق مدفع آخر فتقف الناس في صحن دار العسكرية المذكورة وينزل المشير والوالي والقاضي والمفتي ومن يوجد من العلماء وقائم مقام نقيب السادة الأشراف وأمراء العسكرية والملكية ووجوه البلدة وغيرهم من الدائرة العليا فيها إلى أسفل الدرج ويصعدون به إلى فوق فإذا استقر المجلس ووضع في المحل المعدّ له وزعت أجزاء القرآن الشريف على الحاضرين وقرأوا ختمة شريفة أو أكثر للنبي صلى الله تعالى عليه وآله وصحبه وسلم وقرأوا قصة المولد النبوي الشريف ووزع عليهم الملبس ثم ينصرفون وبعد العشاء تحصل جمعية أيضاً مثلها بقراءة القرآن والمولد والأدعية إلا أنها خاصة وفي اليوم الثاني الذي هو الخامس عشر من شوال يحضر العلماء أصحاب الرتب وأمراء العساكر وأصحاب الرتب الملكية بالألبسة الرسمية (٤٢) إلى دائرة العسكرية وتكون أرسلت لهم تذاكر من طرف الولاية بذلك في الوقت المعين لهم بعد الشمس وتكون العساكر النظامية خرجت ووقفت في الطريق التي يمر فيها المحمل والموسيقات من دائرة العسكرية إلى بوابة الله وتخرج المدافع إلى خارج البوابة المذكورة وتنتصب الخيام وتوضع فيها التخوت والكراسي بجانب مسجد سيدي أحمد العسالي الخلوتي قدس الله سرّه وتوضع المدافع بالقرب منها وتقف الناس في تلك الفسحة الوفا مؤلفة رجالا وركباناً في عربيات وعلى دواب ويمتدون صفوفاً في الطريق على الجانبين وفي الدكاكين والبيوت والمساجد وعلى الأسطحة وبعضهم يمشي أفواجاً أفواجاً في الطريق ينتظرون مجيء المحمل الشريف فإذا جاء الوقت المعين البسوا المحمل الشريف ثوباً من الحرير الأخضر الموشى بالذهب والفضة المموهة ووضعوا عليه ستة رؤس فضة عظيمة في دائرة العسكرية وحملوه على الجمل المعدّ له وهذا الجمل يعلف السنة كلها من أولها إلى آخرها لأن المحمل الشريف ثقيل لا يقدر

على حمله إلا جمل قوي فتى فيبرك الجمل ليحمل عليه ويقف المؤذنون وطلبة المكتب الاعدادي والرشدي العسكريين يصلون على النبي صلى الله تعالى عليه وآله وصحبه وسلم ويهللون ويكبرون ويبخرون بالعود والعنبر فإذا ألبس المحمل الشريف ووقف الجمل به ركب فيه رجل يعد له في الطريق يسمى المحملجي وله تعيينات مخصصة من الحكومة لذلك ويركب رجل على جمل آخر ويحمل السنجق فينزل المشير والوالي والقاضي والمفتي وأولو الرتب من العلماء والأمراء وأصحاب الرتب الملكية ومحافظ الحج وأمين الصرة ويركبون الخيل ويصطفون بحسب رتبهم ثم تخرج (٤٣) أولا موسيقى عسكرية ثم تتبعها الخيالة العسكرية التي تسافر لمحافظة الركب ثم تمشي فرقة من خيالة الضبطية ثم يمشي تحت أمين الصرة ثم تحت محافظ الحج ثم تمشي أصحاب الرتب زوجاً زوجاً وفي آخرهم أمين الصرة يسلم على الناس ويكونون كلهم بالملابس الرسمية والوسامات وبعده قائمقام نقيب السادة الأشراف وتكون عمامته خضراء وبعض النقباء يلبس جبة خضراء ويجعل جلال فرسه أخضر ويلبس خدمته عمائم وجبباً خضرا ويحيط بالمحمل الشريف المؤذنون قدامه ثم طلبة مكتب الاعدادية والرشدية العسكرية من جوانبه الأربع يصلون على النبي صلى الله تعالى عليه وآله وصحبه وسلم ويكبرون ويهللون وقدامهم المولوية مريدو طريقة سيدنا جلال الدين الرومي رضي الله تعالى عنه صفين مستطيلين وأمامهم شيخهم راكباً يذكرون اسم الجلالة ويمشي جمل السنجق وراء المحمل وقد يختصم قائمقام نقيب السادة الأشراف مع شيخ المولوية على التقدم والتأخر كل منهما يريد أن يتأخر عن صاحبه ثم يمشي وراء المحمل والسنجق العكيل يحملون علماً أو أكثر وبيدهم الطبول يضربون بها وينشدون بلغتهم ويرد بعضهم على بعض وهم راكبون الجمال والنوق ويمشي الركب الهوينا على هذا الترتيب فإذا خرج المحمل الشريف من باب دائرة العسكرية أطلق من القلعة احدى وعشرون مدفعاً وهكذا يمشون في وسطهم ضابط يسمى التشرفتجي يلاحظهم وبيده ورقة محرر فيها أسماء الراكبين ورتبهم

فإذا تقدم أحدهم عن محله أو تأخر أرجعه إلى محله فإذا وصل المحمل إلى زاوية سيدنا سعد الدين الجباوي قدس (٤٤) الله تعالى سره التي في الميدان الفوقاني أتوا بالمحمل الذي يحمله إلى قرب شباكها ويكون شيخ الزاوية المرقومة منتظر هناك في الطريق قدام الشباك المذكور وبيده لقمة كبيرة من لوز وسكر يطعمها للجمل فيختطفها العوام من فمه ويأكلونها تبركا ولا يعلمون أنها تنجست من فمه لأنه يتنجس بالاجترار ثم يمشون الهوينا الهوينا إلى أن يخرجوا من باب مصر والناس من دائرة المشيرية العسكرية إلى هناك كالجراد المنتشر فإذا مر المحمل على العساكر مصطفة لاستقباله على الطريق رفعوا أيديهم ونطقت ألسنتهم وضربوا الموسيقى بالسلام وكلما وصل على أناس قعود وقفوا وصلوا كلهم على النبي صلى الله عليه وآله وصحبه وسلم ومسحوا وجوههم بأيديهم تبركاً وكثير منهم من يبكي شوقاً للحج والزيارة وبعضهم يعطي أحد القريبين منه من طلبة المكاتب أو غيرهم منديلا يمسح له بها على المحمل ويعيدها له تبركاً أيضاً فإذا وصل إلى الخيام تلقاه الذين كانوا سابقين إليها من مشير ووالي وغيرهما لأن هذا الموكب يكون صاحبه أمين الصرة فإذا أناخوا الجمل ابتدرت العساكر المدفعية باطلاق المدافع فتطلق احدا وعشرين اعلاماً بوصوله إلى المحطة ويضعون المحمل الشريف أمام الخيام ثم يشرب العلماء والأمراء ومن حضر القهوة أو ماء السكر أو الجاي ويقفلون راجعين بعد الدعاء لأمير المؤمنين والحجاج والغزاة والمسافرين فيرفعون عن المحمل الستار الحريري الموشى بالذهب والفضة ورؤسه الستة الفضية ويخبئونها في الصناديق ويضعون عليه ستاراً آخر أخضر وكذلك السنجق يضعون ثوبه في صندوق (٤٥) وبعد هنيهة من الزمان يذهبون من العسالي إلى محطة ذي النون متوجهين إلى مزيريب ويرجع إلى البلد أيضاً العساكر والمدافع والموسيقى والمحافظ وأمين الصرة والعيكل[6] ويبقى في مزيريب المحمل الشريف والعساكر المعينة لمحافظة الركب في الطريق ينتظرون الحجاج والمحافظ وأمين الصرة وفي اثناء هذه المدة تتوارد للشام حجاج العجم وغيرهم ممن يكون

[6] Read العكيل

متأخراً ويساومون المقومين ومن الثاني والعشرين تبتدئ الحجاج والأهالي والغرباء بالسفر إلى مزيريب ويكون ليوم خروج التخوت والمحارات والشباري والأحمال يوم مشهود أيضاً ولكن دون يوم المحمل ثم يذهب المحافظ وأمين الصرة إلى مزيريب وتأتي بنو صخر وولد علي يحملون الذخيرة والعلف وغيرهما ويسمونها الحملة كما تقدم ويأتي مشايخ البدو الذين أحسنت لهم الدولة العلية بأموال وحوائج معينة من الكيلار فيأخذونها .

ويجتمع في مزيريب أمم عظيمة كما قدمنا وهذه الأيام الثلاثة يوم الشمع والسنجق والمحمل ويوم سفر ركب الحج مشهودة في دمشق وضواحيها وتقصدها الجما[7] الغفير من جميع القرى المجاورة لها وتقصد أيضاً من بعض البلاد القريبة كبيروت وصيدا وحمص وحماة فتحضر منها جماعات تشهد هذه الأيام في دمشق ثم ترجع لبلادها وفي اليوم الثامن أو التاسع والعشرين يقوم الركب من مزيريب متوجهاً للرمثة وهذا في الزمن السابق أما الآن ففي اليوم الثالث من شوال يحتفل بالشمع وأبطل الاحتفال بالزيت من أصله مع أنه كان فيه شأن عظيم وفي اليوم (٤٦) الرابع يحتفل بالسنجق على عادته الأولى وفي اليوم الخامس يحتفل بأفواج المحمل الشريف لكن لا يخرج أمامه المشير ولا الوالي ولا القاضي ولا المفتي على الخيل مع الموكب بل يركبون عربيات بالألبسة الرسمية إلى المحطة في ذهاب الركب قبل الموكب وكذا في رجوعه فيذهبون إلى الخيام في محطة العسالي المذكورة ويسلمون على أمين الصرة أما المحافظ فيكون وصل قبلهم ثم يعود للمحطة فيجلسون قليلا ثم يعودون قبل الموكب بعربياتهم وكذا أكثر أهل الرتب ولا يركبون أصلا في الموكب وبعضهم يقلد المشير والوالي ويركبون عربيات أيضاً ويفعلون مثلهم وذلك لضغائن نفسية وأغراض ذاتية ليس هنا محل بيانها وخروج الحج من الشام في خامس شوال إنما كان بارادة سنية من حضرة سيدنا ومولانا أمير المؤمنين خليفة الرسول الأمين صلى الله تعالى وسلم عليه وآله وصحبه أجمعين السلطان ابن السلطان

[7] الجمع ؟ Read

السلطان الغازي عبد الحميد خان ابن ساكن الجنان مولانا السلطان الغازي عبد المجيد خان المؤلف هذا الكتاب باسمه ليكون جالباً دعاء المؤمنين لجلالته بدوام العناية الألهية تلحظه وبقاء الوقاية الربانية تحفظه وكذا قيامه من مزيريب في الخامس والعشرين منه وكانت هذه الارادة عين الحكمة فقد كان الحجاج يتحملون من الزحمة والثقلة في الطريق من أجل تأخرهم في الشام إلى الخامس عشر وفي مزيريب إلى الثامن أو التاسع والعشرين ما لا مزيد عليه فيجدون السير ليلا ونهاراً حتى يوافوا أيام الحج في مكة أما الآن فقد زاد معهم عشرة أيام خمسة أيام (٤٧) يبقون فيها في مزيريب يقضون مصالحهم وخمسة أيام في الطريق وهذه من دقة نظر جلالته وتدبره في أمور رعيته فيمكنهم فيها أن يوافوا مكة قبل أيام الحج بيومين أو ثلاثة مع الراحة التامة في الطريق ثم أن المحمل يبقى بهذا الثوب الأخضر حتى يوافي الركب المدينة المنورة فإذا وصل إلى آبار عثمان رضي الله تعالى عنه قبلها بساعتين حيث تنصب فيها الخيام ويستقبل الركب فيها حكام المدينة وعلمائها ورؤسها ينزع عن المحمل هذا الثوب ويلبس ثوبه الحريري الأخضر الموشى بالذهب والفضة وتوضع عليه رؤسه الستة ويؤلف موكب عظيم من أهالي المدينة المنورة وأمين الصرة ومحافظ الحج الشامي ويدخلون المدينة المنورة من الباب الشامي حتى يوافوا باب السلام ومحافظ الحج يمسك زمام جمل المحمل متعمماً بعمامة بيضاء ثم ينزلونه عن الجمل ويدخلونه الحرم الشريف يضعونه تجاه باب السلام فيه مقابل الحجرة المطهرة أما السنجق فيضعونه في داخل الحجرة الشريفة المطهرة المعظمة إلى يوم السفر فيخرجونهما بموكب عظيم إلى المحطة وهناك يرفعون هذا الثوب ويضعون عليه الثوب الأخضر إلى أن يصلوا مكة فينزلون هناك في محطة الشيخ محمود وأهل مكة يسمونها الشهداء ويوم الصعود يلبسونه الثوب الحريري الموشى المذكور ويأخذونه مع السنجق بموكب محفل عظيم إلى عرفات ويعودون بهما ليلة النحر بعد الغروب منها إلى منى محاذياً لمحمل مصر في المسير فيكون المحمل المصري في جهة

المحمل الشامي اليسرى والمدافع من الركبين الشامي والمصري تطلق من عرفات حتى يوافوا منى ويبقى فيها بثوبه المذكور (٤٨) إلى ثاني أيام التشريق فيعودون به إلى مكة المكرمة على تلك الحالة فإذا وصلوا به إلى باب حرم مكة المعروف بباب النبي صلى الله تعالى عليه وآله وصحبه وسلم أنزلوه عن الجمل وأدخلوه الحرم من ذلك الباب ووضعوه في الحرم الشريف تجاه الباب المذكور تحت الرواق وألبسوه ثوبه الأخضر الذي يلبسه في الطريق وبقي هناك إلى يوم السفر بخلافه في الحرم الشريف المدني فانه يبقى فيه بكسوته الحريرية الموشاة وتوضع عليه رؤسه وكذا السنجق ويتألف موكب عظيم يمشي معه إلى محطة الشيخ محمود وتنزع كسوتهما المذكورة ويكسى كسوته الخضراء إلى المدينة فإذا تشرفوا برحابها ونزلوا المحطة في الباب الشامي كسى المحمل والسنجق كسوتيهما الحريرية الموشاة وأدخل المدينة كما في الذهاب فإذا وصل الشام وأنزل في محطة العسالي ظاهر دمشق احتفل به كالاحتفال به في الذهاب إلا أنه يكون الاحتفال يوماً واحداً في محطة العسالي ويأتون به إلى دائرة العسكرية ثم يحملون السنجق باحتفال عظيم والموسيقى العسكرية والمؤذنون إلى الجامع الشريف الأموي فيقفون به أمام ضريح سيدنا يحيى عليه السلام يقرأون الفاتحة الشريفة والمؤذنون يصلون على النبي صلى الله تعالى عليه وآله وصحبه وسلم ثم يذهبون به إلى مشهد سيدنا الحسين رضي الله تعالى عنه حيث رأسه الشريف في القبة المبنية عليه فيضعونه فيها وينصرفون وتأتي الناس لزيارته ثلاثة أيام وبعدها ينزعون عنه الكسوة ويطونها ويأخذونها مع الرأس مستورة إلى مستودع ركب الحج الشريف وفي تغيير عادة مجيء الصرة من البر (٤٩) قلّت الحجاج وعدمت التجارة من اسكدار إلى الشام براً وكان ركب الحج الشامي أولا يشتمل على نحو خمسين تختاً والمحفات والشباير بنسبتها وكذا الذين يركبون الدواب والمشاة أما الآن فقد يوجد في الركب تخت أو تختان وقد لا يوجد فيهما راكب يذهب فارغاً ويعود كذلك وقد كان يذهب مع الركب جماعة يمشون أمامه يسمون الصلحة هم أكثر

من الركب في هذا الزمان والعكيل جماعة من بدو الشرق جهة نجد يسكنون الميدان في الشام تعينهم الحكومة لمحافظة الركب فيمشون وراءه يحملون المنقطعين منه ويدلون التائهين ويرفعون ما يسقط منه فيوصلونه لأربابه ويردون من يريد التعدي على الركب من البدو ويقاتلونه هذه كانت وظيفتهم فيما سلف والمقصود منهم أما الآن فلا ندري ولأهل الشام خصوصاً اعتناء عظيم بالحج وزيارة النبي صلى الله تعالى عليه وآله وصحبه وسلم فان الولد الذي لا يجاوز عمره ثلاث عشرة سنة يفر من أهله ويذهب للحج ماشياً ومن أهل الشام من يحج ثلاثين أو أربعين أو خمسين حجة أو أكثر ومنهم من يذهب مع ركب الحج الشامي للزيارة فقط فإذا تشرف بتراب المدينة المنورة بقي فيها لرجوع الركب فيعود معه أو يبقى للقابل وقد ذهب عمي السيد محمد المنير رحمه الله تعالى لذلك وقرأ الشفاء الشريف للقاضي عياض في الروضة المطهرة وعاد بعد ذلك .

انباء

أول من صنعت له المحامل وركب فيها الحجاج الثقفي .

(٥٠) في بيان موكب الصرة في الاستانة العلية وما يتعلق بها

أعلم أنه أول من رتب الصرة الهمايونية ووضعها ساكن الجنان المغفور له السلطان سليم الأول الغازي طاب ثراه وتغمده الله تعالى برحمته ورضاه كما تقدم ومن ذلك الزمان إلى الآن حافظت عليها ملوك بني عثمان أيد الله تعالى ملكهم إلى آخر الدوران .

ففي أول السنة تصدر ارادة جلالة الخليفة الأعظم السنية بتعيين أمين للصرة من رجال الأستانة وهذا الأمين هو في الحقيقة وكيل من طرف جلالة مولانا السلطان بايصال مرتبات الصرة الهمايونية لأربابها بحسب الدفاتر التي تعطى له من نظارة الأوقاف الجليلة منقولة عن الأصل المحفوظ فيها وعند ما يعين يأتي إليه العكام باشي والعكامة الشاميون

بالرايات الملونة بالأحمر والأخضر والأبيض ويعلقونها في حائط داره فوق الباب فيعلم أن صاحب هذه الدار هو في هذه السنة أمين الصرة وتبقى هذه الرايات معلقة إلى أن يذهب إلى اسكدار ويعين أيضاً الموزدهجي وهو الذي يأخذ المكاتيب والأمانات من المابين الهمايوني والأهالي إلى الحرمين الشريفين غير المرتب من طرف الدولة ذهاباً وايابا والقفطانجي والمبشر وسيأتي الكلام عليهم كلهم ثم تبدأ نظارة الأوقاف الجليلة بتهيئة مرتبات الصرة من دراهم وملبوسات ونحوها وتجتمع العكامة التي تحضر من الشام مع أمين الصرة السابق في رجوعه (٥١) فيحملون طبولا تسمى في اصطلاحهم مرافع يضربون بها ويحمل اثنان منهم شيئاً يصنعونه مثل الصندوق مستطيلا مسجى بستار أخضر مغروزة في أركانه رايات ملونة ومعهم علم صغير يحملونه أيضاً وينشدون نشائد ويصلون على النبي صلى الله تعالى عليه وآله وصحبه وسلم يسمون هذا النشيد تجميلة وجمعها تجاميل ويطوفون في أزقة الأستانة والبلاد الثلاثة وجميع بلاد البوغاز والخليج زقاقاً زقاقاً وسوقاً سوقاً وكلما وصلوا عند دار رجل كبير او تاجر معروف أو من رجال الدولة يضعون شبه الصندوق أمام البيت ويقفون ينشدون ويضربون المرافع ويدعون لصاحب البيت فيرسل لهم دراهم أو يرسل لهم النساء ان لم يكن رجال في البيت وقد يرمين لهم الدراهم مصرورة بمنديل من الشباك وهكذا من دار إلى أخرى حتى يستقصوا فيكون قارب نصف شعبان وفي اليوم الرابع عشر منه يجتمعون في محل اقامتهم في تحتة قلعة من الأستانة ويلبسون جبباً حمراً ويحملون المرافع وبعض أعلام صغيرة وعندهم شبيه محمل الشام يضعون عليه ستاراً أخضر مطرزاً بحرير أصفر يسمونه ثوباً يحملونه على بغل أو جمل وتخت أمين الصرة الذي يأخذه معه إلى الشام ليركبه إلى الحج على بغلين ويركب العكام باشي فرساً ويمشي وراءه العكامة ينشدون التجاميل ويضربون المرافع ويلعبون بالعصي والسيف والترس ويمشون على هذه الهيئة إلى باب السرعسكر فيدخل رئيسهم عنده وهم في صحن السراي يلعبون بالسيف

والترس (٥٢) والعصي ويضربون المرافع وينشدون التجاميل فيأمر له بعوائد ثم يذهبون إلى نظارة المالية ثم إلى نظارة الأوقاف ثم إلى الباب العالي ويدخل العكام باشي إلى الصدر وناظري المالية والأوقاف وغيرهم ويعطونه العوائد ويذهبون من الباب العالي تواً إلى الجسر الجديد إلى غلطة إلى طوب خانة إلى جامع طولمة بغجة وهناك ينزلون شبه المحمل والتخت ويدخلون الجامع المذكور ويأتيهم العشاء من المطبخ السلطاني هناك للجامع ويبيتون فيه وتكون نظارة الأوقاف اتمت عملها من كتابة الدفاتر وتهيئة الدراهم المطلوبة منها ووضعتها في الصناديق فترسلها في ذلك اليوم محملة على بغال وبراذين إلى المابين فيضعون على الصناديق المذكورة ستارات حمر فيضعون تلك الصناديق في خيمة منصوبة فيه وكان عدد هذه الصناديق في هذا العام ثمانية وخمسين محملة على تسع وعشرين دابة كل اثنين منها على دابة.

ويضرب في هذا اليوم نفسه في المابين خيمتان عظيمتان تجاه دائرة الحرم وتفرشان ببساطين عظيمين وبالكراسي الحريرية الثمينة وتزينان بأنواع الزينة وتوقد فيهما الشموع ويطلق فيهما البخور إلى غير ذلك مما يدل على التعظيم والاحترام والاعتناء التام وبالقرب من هاتين الخيمتين دائرة أغا دار السعادة.

ثم يخرج من المابين شيء يشبه قبة مثمنة الأركان ناتئة من أركانها (٥٣) عصى نحو ثلثي ذراع فيوضع في احدى الخيمتين وله ستار ثمين ثم يأتي بعد المغرب بنصف ساعة إلى المابين الأمام الأول لجلالة السلطان والثاني ومشير المابين وباش مابنجي والباشكاتب وبعض أهل العلم الممتازين وخطباء وائمة المساجد ومؤذنو المابين فيدخل الامامان وعالم مخصوص من العلماء وحفظة القرآن من المؤذنين أولي الأصوات الحسنة المعجبة المعينين لذلك غرفة مخصوصة لهم فيجلسون ويبتدئ عالم ويقرأ آية من القرآن الكريم ثم يفسرها ثم يروي حديثاً ويفسره ثم يختم ذلك بدعاء مخصوص مناسب للمقام كما هي عادة علماء الاستانة أن يدعوا في كل محفل بما يناسبه وهي عادة حسنة ثم بعد إتمام ذلك

كله يبتدئ الإمام الأول بقراءة بعض آيات من القرآن المجيد ثم يقرأ أحد الحفظة عشر آيات من أول سورة البقرة ثم يسكت فيدعو الإمام الأول إلى جلالة مولانا السلطان الأعظم ثم تعطى لهم العطايا المرتبة لهم حسب العادة في كل سنة ثم يخرجون من الغرفة وينصرف الإمامان والعالم ويأتي الباقون إلى الخيمة التي فيها المحمل ويكون فيها الأئمة والخطباء مجتمعين وباقي المؤذنين فيجلسون معهم فيبدأ أحدهم بقراءة سورة الفتح فإذا أتم الآية الأولى منها حط معه باقي الحفظة ويقرأ غيره الآية الثانية التي بعدها فإذا أتمها حط معه الباقون وهكذا يقرأ كل واحد آية ويحط معه الباقي إلى أن تتم السورة والبخور يطلق ثم يدعو أحدهم بدعاء مخصوص ثم يؤتى لهم بماء السكر والحلويات فتدار عليهم ويكون في الخيمة الثانية اغا دار السعادة (٥٤) وعنده بعض الرجال المنسوبين للمابين الهمايوني فإذا تمت القراءة والدعاء في الخيمة الأولى يأتي إليها وكيل اغا دار السعادة ومعه كاتب بيده دفتر مكتوب فيه العطايا التي تعطى في تلك الليلة واسماء أصحابها فيعطي لكل واحد عطيته فيأخذها ويدعو لجلالة مولانا أمير المؤمنين ثم ينصرف إلا جماعة تبقى منهم في الخيمة تتلو القرآن الكريم وتصلي على النبي صلى الله عليه وسلم وتطلق البخور إلى الصباح ثم تخرج منها وتبقى فارغة فيأتيها البعض من دائرة الحرم الهمايوني بالأقمشة الحريرية الموشاة بالذهب والفضة والمناديل الثمينة المطرزة وغيرها ويعلقنها على المحمل ثم يقرأن الفاتحة الشريفة ويصلين على النبي صلى الله عليه وسلم ويهدين ثواب ذلك لروحه الطاهرة الشريفة ولا يفرغن منه إلا وقد حضر رجال الدولة العلية شيخ الإسلام والصدر الأعظم وغيره ويدخلون غرفة مخصصة لهم ويعود العلماء والحفاظ والأئمة والخطباء والمؤذنون ويتلون سورة الفتح الشريفة بمسمع من جلالة سيدنا أمير المؤمنين حفه الله تعالى بعنايته وحرسه بوقايته آية آية ثم يدعو أحدهم كما في الليلة الماضية ثم تأتي العساكر المنصورة المظفرة ومعهم الموسيقى العسكرية فتصطف الموسيقى حلقة تجاه الخيمتين في تلك الفسحة ويصدحون بالسلام السلطاني

ويكون عكام باشي والعكامة وجماعتهم حملوا المحمل وتخت أمين الصرة ورفعوا الرايات التي معهم وتوجهوا من جامع طلمة بغچة حيث يأتوا تواً نحو المابين وأمامهم عكام باشي راكباً وهم وراءه على حالهم السابقة في اليوم قبله (٥٥) يضربون المرافع وينشدون النشائد البدائع ويصلون على النبي صلى الله عليه وسلم ويعملون التجاميل ومن تجاميلهم قولهم.

عبد الحميد سلطاننا عبد الحميد يا عزنا
عبد الحميد مليكنا عبد الحميد خير الملوك

وقولهم

عبد الحميد يا إمام يا إمام كل الاسلام
الله ينصرك دوام بالنبي خير الأنام

وقولهم

عبد الحميد لا تهتم انت سلطان الكرم
كل الناس لك خدم أنت سلطان الأمم

فيصلون في تلك الأثناء إلى المابين الهمايوني على تلك الحال ومعهم جمالان[8] غير محملين فيدخلون المابين الهمايوني وتكون تلك الهيئة السابقة وغيرها مكملة بانتظار حضورهم جالسين في الغرف العالية المشرفة عليهم وغيرها ينظرون إليهم ويصطف المؤذنون يصلون على النبي صلى الله عليه وسلم الصلاة الابراهيمية ويكبرون تكبير العيد برواية ابن عباس رضي الله تعالى عنه ثم يخرجون المحمل الذي في الخيمة يضعونه على جمل والموسيقى تصدح والعكامة تعمل التجاميل المتقدمة وغيرها والبعض يلعب بالسيف والترس وتلك الفسحة الواسعة غاصة بالموحدين الصادقين والسنتهم رطبة بالدعاء (٥٦) لجلالة أمير المؤمنين ثم يجري أمين الصرة

[8] جملان Read

المراسيم المعتادة وتحصل الارادة السنية بتسليمه كتاباً من طرفه إلى أمير مكة المكرمة فيستلمه وينزل به فيعطيه إلى وكيله الذي يدبر أموره المعروف بكخيه والمؤذنون على حالهم يكبرون ويصلون على النبي صلى الله تعالى عليه وآله وسلم والموسيقى تصدح ورجال المابين والأغوات والأئمة والخطباء والعساكر وقوف واغا دار السعادة بيده عصى وله إدارة الأمور في ذلك المجمع العظيم والمشهد الفخيم فيأمر وينهي .

ثم يركب جماعة من العسكر والخطباء والأئمة وأمين الصرة ووكيله حاملا الكتاب السلطاني المذكور وبعض موظفي نظارة الأوقاف ومفتش الأوقاف بالألبسة الرسمية والوسامات العثمانية ويمشي أولا العساكر صفين متقابلين وفي وسطهم الأئمة والخطباء ثم موظفو الأوقاف ثم وكيل أمين الصرة حاملا الكتاب السلطاني بيده رافعه إلى حذاء صدره ثم أمين الصرة ثم مفتش الأوقاف ثم تخت أمين الصرة ثم المحمل مكللا بالأقمشة التي علقت عليه في المابين ولا ترى ستارته لكثرة ما علق عليه منها في صباح ذلك اليوم ثم شبه المحمل الشامي محاطين بالمؤذنين بالتهليل والتكبير والصلاة الابراهيمية من المابين الهمايوني إلى أن يصلوا إلى اسكلة بشكطاش ويكون فيها مركب بخاري ينتظر فينقلهم إلى اسكدار وحينما يستقر المحمل في المركب المذكور يطلق أحد وعشرون مدفعاً من البحر ثم ينطلق بهم إلى اسكدار وحينما يخرج المحمل المذكور إليها يطلق احد وعشرين مدفعاً آخر أيضاً ايذاناً بوصوله ثم (٥٧) يكون متصرف اسكدار والنائب وغيرهما من رجال الحكومة وأعيان الأهالي مع جماهير الناس منتظرين وصوله فينضم رجال الحكومة في اسكدار إلى الموكب المذكور ويسيرون حتى ينتهوا إلى دار الحكومة فيها فينزلون المحمل وشبه المحمل وتخت أمين الصرة ويجلسون في دار الحكومة قليلا ثم ينصرفون ويرجعون المحمل إلى المابين بصورة غير رسمية ويبقى شبه المحمل في الاستانة إلى السنة القابلة وتخت أمين الصرة يبقى في اسكدار إلى أن يسافر فيأخذه معه ويبقى العكامة فيها أيضاً ويرجع أمين الصرة إلى بيته ليتمم أعماله والمزدهجي كذلك يأخذ المكاتيب

ومحافظ الأموال من المابين الهمايوني ومن أهل الاستانة إلى أهل الحرمين وهذه الأموال غير الصر المعين والقفطانجي يستلم الجبة للشريف أمير مكة المكرمة وفي نصف رمضان يرفع أمين الصرة عريضة لركاب جلالة مولانا السلطان بالاستئذان للسفر فتصدر ارادته السنية ويكون هيء لهم مركب بخاري من الإدارة المخصوصة العثمانية فيركبون إلى بيروت فيصلونها في أوائل العشر الأخير من رمضان ثم منها إلى الشام عدا القفطانجي ويسافر مع الركب الشامي إلى الحجاز .

في وظيفة أمين الصرة وبيان المرتبات

إن أمين الصرة يأخذ خمسمائة ألف قرش مصارفات له ويقتطع منها خمسون ألفاً لمصارفات الركب الذي يحمله إلى بيروت ثم يستلم الصر الهمايوني من خزينة الأوقاف الجليلة ويسافر ومعه المزدهجي فإذا وصلوا إلى بيروت فان كان له على (٥٨) صندوق مالها حوالة أقام فيها حتى يأخذها وإلا فيذهب حالا للشام ويعطي أصحاب المرتبات عطاياهم بحسب الدفتر الذي معه ويختم كل صاحب عطية تحت اسمه فإذا مات أحدهم وجهت لأولاده فيأخذونها بعده أو إلى غيره ويكون التوجيه الآن بواسطة مجلس إدارة الشام وكان قبلا برأي أمين الصرة وحده ولأمور وقعت في التوجيهات ربطت بمجلس إدارة الولاية ويحضر للشام من القدس الشريف وكيل معه حجة مصدقة من المحكمة الشرعية فيها عن أصحاب المرتبات فيقبض مرتباتهم بحسب الدفتر المختص بهم ويسلم أمين الصرة إلى الوكيل المذكور الدفتر الذي يحضره معه من نظارة الأوقاف الجليلة أيضاً والمرتبات فيأخذها ويتوجه إلى القدس الشريف ويوزعها لأربابها بحسب الدفتر ويختم كل صاحب عطية تحت اسمه فيه ويرسله إلى الشام فيستلمه أمين الصرة في عودته وإذا وصل أمين الصرة إلى محطة المداين جاء وكيل عن ابن الرشيد وأخذ عطيته التي أحسن بها عليه جلالة مولانا السلطان الخليفة الأعظم أمير المؤمنين الغازي عبد الحميد خان سلطان هذا الزمان وقدرها ثلاثون ألف

قرش لذاته وستة آلاف قرش لجماعته وجبة موشاة بالفضة له وثلاثون جبة لجماعته ويأخذ منه وصولا حسب العادة فإذا تشرف بتراب المدينة المنورة على ساكنها أفضل الصلاة واتم السلام وعلى آله المطهرين وصحبه الكرام سلم الدفتر المختص بأهلها والمرتبات التي معه إلى مدير الحرم الشريف النبوي والمدير المومى إليه (٥٩) يوزعها ويختم كل من له شيء منها تحت اسمه في الدفتر ويحفظه إلى رجوع أمين الصرة فيأخذه منه وكذلك إذا تشرف برحاب مكة المكرمة فيسلم الدفتر الذي معه والمرتبات إلى مدير الحرم المكي وقبل رجوعها منها يستلم الدفتر منه ويعود مع الركب الشامي إلى الشام وقد يوجد في امناء الصرة كالزمن الأول من يدفعون من أموالهم زيادة على المرتبات للعلماء والأشراف والمشايخ يضعون ذلك في صرة ويربطونها ويدفعونها إليهم يرجون بذلك جبر قلوب المذكورين وجلب دعواتهم الخيرية لأمير المؤمنين والدولة العلية ولهم ويوجد في بعضهم من لا يلتفت لشيء من هذا بل يذهب للربح من هذه المأمورية فسبحان من يغير ولا يتغير وهو الباقي وما سواه فاني[9] ثم يسافر منها في الوابور إلى الاستانة فيتشرف بتقبيل قدم الخليفة الأعظم ويقدم له من ماء زمزم وتمر المدينة المنورة على ساكنها أفضل الصلاة وأتم السلام وعلى آله وصحابته الكرام فيأخذهما ويتبرك بهما وبحمده تعالى على تمام تلك النعمة التي انعم بها على جلالته وإذا وصل أمين الصرة لداره دهنوا بابها بالأخضر وهكذا يفعل بكل باب دار حاج ايذاناً بأنه حاج والسرور بسلامته.

في المزدهجي ووظائفه

المزدجي هو الذي يأخذ المكاتيب والعطايا والهدايا من المابين الهمايوني ومن أهالي الآستانة العلية إلى الفراشين والمدعين والمزورين وبعض أهالي (٦٠) المدينة المنورة على مشرفها أفضل صلاة وأربى سلام وتحية وعلى آله الكرام وصحبه العظام والمطوفين والزمزميين وبعض أهالي مكة المكرمة ولا يكون الا قهوجي باشا في احدى سريات أولاد

9 فان Read

السلاطين العظام وقد جرت العادة فيها بارسال تلك المرتبات ان توضع في محافظ من جلد يكتب على كل محفظة اسم صاحبها الذي يرسلها إلى فراشه أو مدعيه أو غيرهما وكذلك من أهل مكة المكرمة للمطوفين والزمزميين وغيرهم وكل محفظة لها وجهان مكتوب على احدهما اسم الفراش مثلا وعلى الآخر اسم المرسل إليه فيسلمه المزدهجي المحفظة والمكتوب فأما أهل مكة فيأتون إليه فيأخذون أماناتهم ومكاتيبهم منه بعد عرفات ويرجعون إليه المحافظ فيها من الهدايا ما ينتخبونه ويستحسنونه والزمزميون يرسلون معه من ماء زمزم أيضاً وأما أهل المدينة فيستلمون أماناتهم ومكاتيبهم وينتظرون إلى عودته من مكة فيسلمونه المحافظ ويضعون فيها من الهدايا ما يشاؤن كل بحسبه وبحسب ما أرسل إليه كالمسابح والخواتم والطيب وأمثالها ويصحبونها بمجمع من تمر المدينة العظيم البركة الفاخر ويسلمونها مع مكتوب منهم لصاحب المحفظة ويكون استلام المزدهجي المحافظ والمكاتيب المذكورة في الأستانة بواسطة نظارة الأوقاف الجليلة بموجب دفتر تقيد فيه ويعطى صاحبها ورقة تحت العدد وفيها تاريخ التسليم فإذا رجع إلى الاستانة العلية سلم ما معه من المكاتيب والهدايا بواسطتها أيضاً (٦١) بموجب السندات التي يعطيها وقد كان عدد المحافظ التي قد ارسلت معه في هذه السنة من الأستانة لأهل المدينة ثمان مائة وسبعين ولأهل مكة المكرمة خمس مائة وستين ومعهما بقدرهما مكاتيب لأصحابهما .

في وظيفة القفطانجي والمبشر

القفطانجي رجل يعين ليوصل الجبة التي ترسل من طرف جلالة مولانا السلطان إلى شريف مكة في كل سنة وايصال بعض أمتعة لأهل الحرمين الشريفين ويذهب تواً من الآستانة إلى جدة من البحر وبعد الحج يذهب إلى المدينة المنورة مع المأمورين من طرف الشريف أمير مكة ومنها إلى ينبع ومصارفه من مكة إلى ينبع من أمير مكة علاوة على ما يأخذه مرتباً له من الدولة العلية أما المبشر فيذهب مع أمين

الصرة إلى الشام ثم للمدينة وقبل دخولها بيوم يسبق فيبشر وكذلك في مكة وإذا رجع الركب للشام سبق أمين الصرة للآستانة مبشراً .

في الجردة التي تلحق ركب الحج الشامي

الجردة هي قافلة اسستها الدولة العلية أيدها الله تعالى احتياطاً لسعة أمر عيشة الحجاج وخوفاً من ضيقهم لما يجوز ان يطرأ عليهم وهذه القافلة كان أميرها في الزمن السالف والي طرابلس الشام يحضر منها للشام فيأخذ تلك القافلة ويحافظها وأما الآن فمن تنتخبه الحكومة والأكثر أن يكون (٦٢) بمعرفة محافظ الحج ويرفق بملازم ومعه مائة من الخيالة الضبطية ومعهم مدفع ومهمات تكفيهم ويرسل الناس لأهاليهم الحجاج ومعارفهم من مأكولات وملبوسات وما يحتاجون إليه وقد يرسل علف للدواب إذا كانت له حاجة ويرافق تلك القافلة أناس من الأهالي فيستلمون من الناس مرسلاتهم وعلى كل مرسل يكتب هذه أمانة فلان ابن فلان ويدفعون الأجرة سلفاً لمن يرسلونها معه وكانت العادة ان يسافروا ثالث أيام التشريق من الشام أما الآن فيتأخرون قليلا فإذا سافروا أطلقت من قلعة دمشق مدافع ايذاناً بسفرهم فيحطون في مزيريب ويخرج مع هذه القافلة من أهل الشام تجار كثيرون إليها ويصير فيها سوق تجارة يأتيه من أهل حوران والجيدور والجولان ومن السلط والدروز والعرب خلق كثير ولكن ليس كسوق ركب الحج فيها ثم يرحلون منها ويلاقون الركب المذكور في المداين غالباً وهناك يستلم الحجاج من أهاليهم المكاتيب والهدايا ويكون عندهم يوم عظيم مشهود يفرحون فيه الفرح الذي لا مزيد عليه بوصول أخبار أهاليهم إليهم ويهدي الحجاج بعضهم بعضاً من تلك الهدايا ويقبلون على الأكل والشرب ومن يكون من الحجاج ميتاً وله هدية يبيعونها بالمزاد وقد لا تباع بأجرتها ويقع بعد وصول الجردة في الحجاج مرض الاسهال غالباً لأن ماء المداين ردىء جداً وأكل الاطعمة الحلوة التي تأتيهم خصوصاً (٦٣) نحو المعمول والغريبة والبقلاوة مما يصنع

من العجين والسمن والسكر والفستق أو اللوز ونحو الفواكه المصنوعة بقطر السكر والخالصة كالمشمش والقمر الدين والفستق واللوز الخالصين والمحمصين بالملح وأمثالها فانها كلها تسبب الأسهال وكثيراً ما يعقب هذا الأسهال داء الدوسنطارية وكثير منهم من يلازمه للشام وكثير منهم من يموت به فالأولى الاجتناب عن أكله بالكلية أو يؤكل منه مقدار قليل وحده لا مع الأطعمة التي فيها دهن ونحوه ويختلط ركب الجردة بركب الحج ويرجع معه إلى الشام وتبتدئ الحجاج بكتابة المكاتيب لأهليهم سواء في الشام أو في غيرها فإذا وصل الركب إلى تبوك فارق الجوخدار الركب بعد ما يستلم المكاتيب منه متوجهاً إلى الشام .

في بيان برد ركب الحج الشريف الشامي

البرد جمع بريد وهو الذي يأخذ المكاتيب من محل إلى آخر واصطلح عليه الآن بالبوستهجي وارسالية المكاتيب تسمى بوستة ومحل ادارتها يسمى بوستة خانه فللركب الحجازي الشامي خمس برد وقد رتب من قديم الزمان لحاجة الحجاج وأهاليهم إلى ذلك كما سنبينه انشاء الله تعالى

البريد الأول من معان ويسمونه كتّاب معان أو نجّاب معان (٦٤) والكتاب بفتح أوله وتشديد ثانيه ومثله نجاب وذلك ان الحجاج إذا وصلوا مع الركب إلى معان وأقاموا فيه يوماً كما قدمنا اشتغلوا بكتابة المكاتيب إلى أهليهم يخبرونهم عن احوالهم وما لزم لهم ان يعرفوهم عنه وقد نسوه كمصالح تجارة وزراعة ويطمنونهم فيها عن راحتهم وصحتهم سيما لأن أكثر الذي[10] كانوا يحجون في الزمن السابق لم يكونوا سافروا وسفر الحج صعب لبعد الطريق وتصادف الحر والبرد والتعب من الحط والترحال إلى غير ذلك فتكون أفكار أهالي الحجاج مشغولة فإذا جاءتها مكاتيب معان وذكر الحجاج راحتهم ووصولهم إليها بالسلامة تخفض ما كان عندهم من الكدر والهم لأجلهم فيعطون هذه المكاتيب إلى المعين لذلك فإذا وصل إلى الشام أطلق له من القلعة مدفع واحد ويذهب عند والي الشام وله عوائد يأخذها ثم

[10] الذين Read

يعطي هذه المكاتيب التي معه لأحد المتصدرين لذلك ويأخذ منه بدلها مبلغاً من الدراهم والذي يأخذها منه ويدفع له الدراهم يأتي إلى محل في الدرويشة من الشام ويضع المكاتيب إلى أهلها غير اغنياء معروفين ويأتي أصحابها لأخذها فلا يسلمون مكتوباً لصاحبه إلا بفكاكه وهو مبلغ من الدراهم بقدر ما يرضيه فإذا لم يتفق معه لم يسلمه المكتوب وهكذا .

البريد الثاني بريد المداين فإذا وصل الركب إلى محطة المداين وأقام (٦٥) فيها يوماً وهو الطراق كتب الحجاج مكاتيب لأهلهم وأخذها البريد المعروف بالكتاب أو النجاب وعاد إلى دمشق ويطلق لوصوله مدفعان من القلعة ايذاناً بوصوله ويفعل كالأول فإذا سمع الناس المدفعين قالوا جاء كتاب المداين فيهرعون لأخذ المكاتيب وفائدة هذه المكاتيب ان الحجاج في مدة سفرهم هذا عرفوا ما يحتاجون إليه في الرجوع للطريق فيعرفون أهلهم ليرسلوه لهم مع الجردة لأن كتاب المدينة قد يصل قبل طلوع الجردة بيوم أو يومين وقد يصل بعدها فلا توجد فرصة لارسال ما يطلبون منهم ليرسلوه مع الجردة إليهم .

البريد الثالث بريد المدينة المنورة ويعرف بكتاب المدينة ومكاتيب هذا الكتاب تكتب في المدينة المنورة ويذكر الحجاج فيها وصولهم إليها وتشرفهم بتلك الرحاب وزيارتهم رفيع الجناب وطلبهم منه الشفاعة لهم ولمن يحبون صلى الله تعالى عليه وآله وسلم ويعرفونهم أحوالهم وصحتهم وما لاقوه في الطريق وفي المدينة من غلاء ورخص وحر وبرد وما يحتاجون إليه في بلادهم وما يلزم ان يفعلوه في غيابهم إلى غير ذلك فإذا جاء البريد الشام يطلق له ثلاثة مدافع من القلعة اعلاماً بوصوله ويفعل كالأول وتتسابق الناس لأخذ المكاتيب من كل جهة وقد يعود هذا البريد بمكاتيب من الشام إلى الحجاج فيلحقهم في المدينة المنورة ويجد الحجاج له وقعاً عظيماً (٦٦) لمجيئهم بأخبار أهلهم المنقطعة عنهم .

البريد الرابع بريد منى ويكتب الحجاج المكاتيب في منى بعد رمي

جمرة العقبة والأضحية وهذا البريد مهم جداً لأن الأمراض الوبائية إذا وقعت لا سمح الله تعالى يكون وقوعها غالباً في منى فيخبر الحجاج أهلهم بما لاقوه في مكة من الأنوار والدعاء لهم وأعمال الحج وأي يوم كان يوم عرفة إلى غير ذلك مما يسر أهلهم ببلوغهم إياه فيأخذ البريد المكاتيب ويفارق الركب في ثالث أيام التشريق فإذا دخل الشام أطلق له من القلعة أربعة مدافع وتسرع الناس لاستلام المكاتيب فيقرأونها ويضحك أناس ويبكي آخرون فسبحان من أضحك وأبكى .

البريد الخامس بريد تبوك وهو آخر البرد ويعرف في الشام وضواحيها بالجوخدار ويأخذ هذا البريد المكاتيب من الحجاج ويفارق الركب الشامي من تبوك ويصحبه من الحجاج جماعة مستعدون لذلك يركبون كلهم الهجن وكذلك الجوخدار وهذا الجوخدار يأتي من الآستانة العلية مع أمين الصرة ويوظف في هذه الوظيفة منها وهؤلاء الجماعة يدورون على الحجاج من حين نزولهم من عرفات يطلبون منهم مكاتيبهم إلى أهليهم ولربما من قبل ذلك فيأخذ كل واحد منهم جملة من المكاتيب بقدر ما يستطيع أن يحوز عليه ويخرجون كلهم من تبوك حتى يصلوا جميعاً للزرقاء فيسبق حينئذ أناس (٦٧) منهم إلى الشام ويأتي الجوخدار حتى يصل الكسوة فيبيت فيها عند شيخ البلد ويأخذ شيخ الكسوة منه مكاتيب ويتركه في بيته ويذهب للشام إلى الوالي فيبشره بمجيئه ويعطيه الوالي كسوة معينة له وقد ابطلت هذه العادة فيرسل الوالي شرذمة من الخيالة الضبطية لملاقاته ويصل الشام قبل وصول ركب الحج بسبعة أيام دائماً فيدخل من بوابة الله بموكب هو وجماعته والخيالة والضابط الذي جاء لاستقباله وقد كانت العادة في الزمن السابق أن يؤتى بخشبة يابسة طويلة تحرق من رأسها وتحمل قدامه شاعلة ومعها رعاع من الناس ينادي واحد منهم بأعلى صوته الله يحرق الخشبة فيرد عليه الباقون الله يلعن الأرفاض والسبب فيه ان الأرفاض كل سنة يشيعون على الحج أخباراً كاذبة إما أنه فقد بالكلية أو وقع فيه وباء أو غرق أو نحو ذلك فإذا جاء الحج سالماً قابلوهم بذلك وقد ابطلت

هذه العادة ثم يأتي تواً بموكبه إلى دائرة الحكومة السنية والعسكرية ثم للمحكمة الشرعية يدخل عند القاضي وكذا نقيب السادة الأشراف ثم لدار المفتي وله عليهم عوائد من جبب وغيرها ويطلق له من القلعة خمسة مدافع فينتشر الذين أتوا معه ومعهم المكاتيب إلى دور أصحابها وقد يسبقون بيوم أو يومين وحينئذ يكون لأهل الحجاج البلاء العام والسلب الطام[11] فلا يسلمون المكتوب لصاحبه إلا أن يأخذوا جميع ما يملكه لو قدروا وتقع بينهم (٦٨) المشاحنة بالمساومة إلى أن يتم الأمر بحسب ما يقدر كل منهما أن يرضي صاحبه من ثوب قماش حرير أو ذهب أو ذهبين كل بقدرته وشطارته وإذا وقع في ركب الحج موت لا سمح الله كانت الداهية الدهماء فترى أهل الحجاج جائلين في الأسواق والأزقة وراء الذين معهم المكاتيب وترى حاملي المكاتيب على هجنهم ذاهبين من حارة إلى حارة ومن قرية إلى قرية بل يأخذون معهم مكاتيب الناس ويسافرون إلى بلاد بعيدة كحمص لأجل مكتوب يكون صاحبه مشهوراً بالغناء وفي مثل هذه الحال تكون الغنيمة لهم فلا يتركون مكتوباً إلا ان يأخذوا من صاحبه فوق ما يؤملون والفقير يسأل عن مكتوبه فيقال له في قرية كذا فيتبعه فيقال ذهب إلى قرية كذا وهكذا حتى يمكنه ان يجتمع به فإذا اجتمع لا يفصل المسألة بينهما إلا اجتماع عدد من الناس يرجون حامل الكتاب فيدفع له ما تم عليه السوم ويأخذه . وأعظم بلية من كل هذا ان بعض المكاتيب لأهالي الحجاج يرسلها لهم غير حجاجهم اذ يكون قريبهم الحاج قضى نحبه ومات فيسمع أهله بموته ثم يسمعون بمجيء مكتوب منه فيجدون الليل والنهار للحصول عليه وبعد العناء والجهد ودفع الغرامة وأخذ الكتاب يجدونه من غيره وانه ميت فتتعاظم المصيبة والعياذ بالله تعالى وانما كانت الأهمية بهذا المقدار للبريد المعروف بالجوخدار المذكور لأنه آخرها وينبئ عن أحوال الحجاج الأخيرة أما الآن فلم يبق لذلك عظيم أهمية لأن جلالة (٦٩) مولانا السلطان أيده الله تعالى بالحفظ والنصر قد أحسن إلى عموم الحجاج بمد السلك البرقي من الشام إلى

[11] Read التام

مكة فلم يبق لذلك مزيد احتياج لتعدد مراكزه في الطريق فيمكن للحاج ان يخابر أهله أو يخابروه أو يستفسروا عنه من أي موقع في الطريق للسلك البرقي فجزى الله تعالى عنا سيدنا وسلطاننا الخليفة خير جزاء امين وعلى ما في تلك المكاتيب يبنون أعمالهم من الاستعداد لاقامة الأفراح أو عمل المآتم فترى النساء في البيوت بين صارخات بأصوات الفرح المعروفة بالزلاغيط وبين نائحات صارخات بألفاظ الحزن المعروفة بالولاويل هؤلاء يضحكون وهؤلاء يبكون ويبتدئ أهالي الحجاج وأصحابهم الذين يتمنون حياتهم وسلامتهم بخياطة الملبوسات لهم وارسالها لدارهم وعمل الحلويات وارسال الهدايا كالغنم والسمن والأرز وما أشبهها كل بحسبه وعلى قدر مناسبته للحاج ويجتمع الناس من أهالي الحاج وأصحابه في داره ويقيمون الأفراح ليلا ونهاراً وقبل وصول الحجاج بثلاثة أيام يهيئون الأطعمة النفيسة الحلوية وغيرها من اللحوم وأمثالها ويسمون هذه الأطعمة ملاقاة ويجتمعون ويذهبون لاستقبال الحجاج كل بحسب قدرته وحاله ونهاية ما يكون الاستقبال إلى الزرقاء فإذا اجتمعوا بالحجاج في المحطة نزلوا عنده فسلموا عليه وأخرجوا ما أعدوه له من الأكل وأكلوا وركبوا جميعاً وأركبوه دابة من دوابهم وركب منهم واحد مكانه وسبقوا الركب وان صادفوه مع الركب في الطريق أنزلوه ونزلوا وجلسوا (٧٠) وسلموا عليه ومدوا سماط الأكل ودعوا أصحابهم من الحجاج وأصحاب قريبهم الحاج وأكلوا واستراحوا قليلا ثم يركبون ويرجعون قافلين للشام هذا قبل وجود السكة الحديدية إلى مزيريب أما الآن بعد وجودها فصار أهل الحجاج يذهبون بالسكة الحديدية ويستقبلون حاجهم ويحضرونه بها وقد يذهب بعض الأفراد من مزيريب على دواب يتداركونها منها أو من الشام إلى نحو الزرقاء ويأتون به على دابة إلى محطة السكة فيركبون منها تواً إلى الشام وأما الحجاج غير الشاميين فكذلك يأتون من بلادهم كحماة وبيروت وينزلون ضيوفاً كراماً عند أصحابهم من أهل الشام لا فرق بينهم وقد يخرج معهم من نزلوا عنده فإذا وصل الحجاج للشام

وجدوا الناس بانتظارهم فيقبلون للسلام عليهم من يعرفهم ومن لا يعرفهم طلباً للدعاء لهم بالمغفرة لما ثبت عنه صلى الله تعالى عليه وآله وصحبه وسلم انه قال اللهم أغفر للحاج ولمن دعا له الحاج وقد لا يمكن الحاج ان يقابل النساء من أهله إلا بعد نصف الليل من كثرة المسلمين عليه وهذه عادة قبيحة يلزم تبديلها بأن يصطلحوا على كون السلام على المسافر في اليوم الثاني من وصوله ويمتد هذا الحال ثلاثة أيام بلياليهن ومن العوائد ان الحاج يفطر ويتعشى معه من يكون حاضراً وقتهما من المسلمين وإذا كان المسلم من خواصه يقدم له من الحلويات فيأكل وقد (٧١) تقديم الحلويات للمسلمين كلهم عاما ويعاب على الذي لا يأكل وأما الآن فقد اقتصر على سقاية القهوة وبعضهم يسقي عوضها ماء زمزم وبعضهم يضيف إليه تمراً فيأكل المسلم تمرة ويشرب فنجاناً من ماء زمزم ونعمت العادة فإذا تمت الأيام الثلاثة من وصول الحاج أقبل النساء للسلام على النساء ان كان منهن حاجات والا فللتهنئة فقط ويقمن الأفراح بالتغني والآلات كل بحسبه تتمة سبعة أيام بلياليهن ولا تدخل الرجال في تلك الأيام للدار التي فيها أولئك النساء حتى الحاج نفسه ان لم يكن عنده محل متطرف عن موضع الحرم ويسمى عند أهل الشام برانيا وعند غيرهم من الأتراك سلاملقا وفي العربية محل الاستقبال وأما الذين مات حاجهم فعندما يتحققون خبره ينقلب فرحهم عزاء فيحضرون حفظة القرآن الكريم ثلاثة أيام كل يوم من الظهر إلى المغرب وبعضهم يزيد حفظة أيضاً من بعد العشاء إلى أن يتموا الختمة الشريفة ثلاث ليال وفي آخر ليلة يجمعون أناساً كثيرين يذكرون الله تعالى ولا إله إلا الله سبعين ألفاً فداء للميت من النار لما ورد فيه عن السادة الصوفية الأخيار نفعنا الله تعالى بهم أمين ويصلون على النبي صلى الله تعالى عليه وآله وصحبه وسلم ويتصدقون ويطعمون عن روح الميت فترى استعداد أهل الحجاج لهم مختلفاً ومتوقفاً على أخذ المكاتيب مع بريد الجوخدار وكثير من الحجاج الذين لهم اطلاع على (٧٢) أحوال الذين يحضرون المكاتيب وما يقترفونه من العذاب لأهلهم يضعون مكاتيبهم في مكاتيب

بعض ويكثرون من ذكر أسماء أصحابهم فيها فيقولون فلان يسلم عليكم وعلى آله وهو ولله الحمد سالم بغاية الصحة بلغوا ذلك أهله فيستغنون عن بعض العناء ويقفون على الحقيقة .

تنبيه

كنت سنة ألف وثلاث مائة وثلاث كتبت تقريراً بهذا الخصوص وأرسلته إلى والي سورية مضمونه لأجل نفع الخزينة وتكثير واردات الدولة العلية وراحة الأهالي وتطبيق الاجراءآت على قواعد الدولة العلية وقوانينها المؤسسة وذلك بأن يوضع في خيمة الجوخدار من المدائن حيث تبتدئ الحجاج بكتابة المكاتيب لأهاليهم إلى تبوك حيث يفارق الجوخدار ركب الحج صندوق من جلد توضع فيه المكاتيب ثم يسلمه الجوخدار إذا وصل الشام إلى إدارة البرد فتفتحه وتخرج المكاتيب منه وتضعها عندها وكلما جاء صاحب مكتوب يريده تلصق الإدارة عليه ورقة البريد المدموغة وتأخذ منه قيمتها بحسب وزنه وتسلم الإدارة الجوخدار أوراق البرد التي تلصق على المكاتيب قبل سفره وهو يعامل الناس كمأمور من إدارة البرد فلم يلتفت لذلك وبقي الناس في عناء وجود المكاتيب والمساومة مع حامليها إلى الآن .

(٧٣) ملاحظة

لقد ذكرنا أن أمين الصرة الهمايونية يرجع إلى الشام عن طريق البر مع ركب الحج الشامي وفي هذه السنين الأخيرة أكثرهم يرجع عن طريق البحر إلى جدة لأنهم لم يروا لزوماً لحضورهم مع الركب وكذلك المزودهجي لا لزوم له والقفطنجي فترسل الجبة لأمير مكة مع أموال الصر والمبشر المستغنى عنه الآن بالسلك البرقي ويا حبذا لو كانت الدولة العلية ايدها الله تعالى تقتصد فترسل أموال الصرة بواسطة حوالات للشام الشريفة ومحافظ الأموال والمكاتيب أيضاً بواسطة احدى المراكب البخارية وتوفر هذه المصاريف التي تتكبدها في كل سنة لأمين الصرة

والموزده‌جي بلا ضرورة والقفطانجي والمبشر وكذلك تلتفت إلى أموال الحج المعروفة بالكيلار فتنقحها أيضاً ويكون المحافظ له مصارفات سفرية حسب نظام مأموري الدولة في مصارف الذين يسافرون منهم لجهة من الجهات المعروف بخرجراه وتكتفي بالضابط الذي مع محافظ الجردة عن محافظها كما سبق لهذا من الأمثال من تبديل والي الشام في المحافظة بمحافظ ووالي طرابلس بمحافظ الجردة ووضع مكاتيب الحجاج تحت نظام ارسال المكاتيب وعن القفطانجي وعن المبشر بما ذكرنا فيكون في هذا من التوفير على الدولة العلية وراحة الأهالي وصونهم من التعدي على أموالهم ما لا يخفى ولا يستحقر وان لم يكن (٧٤) ذلك فليكن مصرفه بحسب هذا النظام سيما وانه يذهب من الأستانة للشام من البحر ويعود إليها من جدة عن طريق البحر أيضاً.

في بيان الركوب التي تذهب من المدينة المنورة إلى مكة المكرمة

إن هذه الركوب تذهب من المدينة المنورة إلى مكة المكرمة لأداء فريضتي الحج والعمرة وقد بينا أنه لا يوجد فيها شقدف ولا محارة ولا شبرية ولا تخت ولا غيرها وانها تكون مركبة من هجن ورهاوين وحمير أكثر ما تبلغ هذه الركوب في السنة كلها خمسة وقد تكون أقل من ذلك بحسب كثرة الحجاج من أهالي المدينة المنورة وقلتهم.

والركوب الخمسة ركب الافندي عباس وركب الخيارى وركب الشيخ محمد الداغستاني وركب الشيخ محمد حوالة وركب أغوات الحرم الشريف المدني وقد خرج في السنة الماضية منها أربعة.

وتخرج هذه الركوب من المدينة المنورة في أوائل ذي الحجة الحرام متتابعة والذين لا قدرة لهم على الخروج مع الركب لضعف بنيتهم عن تحمل مشقة ركوب الهجن وغيرها يركبون المحارة أو الشبرية مع الركب الشامي حينما يمر عليهم وتصل هذه الركوب بعد خروجها من المدينة المنورة إلى مكة المكرمة يوم السابع من خروجها ويبيتون ليلة التروية في مكة وليلة عرفة في منى ويرجعون من مكة إلى المدينة يوم التاسع عشر

(٧٥) ويصلونها متفرقين يوم السادس والعشرين والسابع والعشرين والثامن والعشرين من ذي الحجة الحرام ويستقبلهم أهل المدينة في بير عروة بالمآكل والمشارب والفواكه والولائم ويرجعون معهم إلى المدينة ويسلمون عليهم ويهنئونهم بالحج والسلامة ولأهل المدينة مدائح وقصائد وموشحات نبوية ينشدونها وهم سائرون في الطريق ذهاباً وايابا كقولهم في الذهاب لمكة .

يا إلهي سهل الخير لنا قصدنا البيت الحرام
ونطوف بالبيت العتيق ثم يجمع بالمشفع شملنا

دور

انكرت عيني المنام وكأن النّوم لم يخلق
عاذلي كف الملام من أراد النوم لم يعشق
صير النوم حرام واحل الشيب في مفرقي
نازلي تلك الخيام ليت شعري في منى هل نلتقي

وقولهم في الاياب من مكة

سلامي على طيبه سلامي على الحرم
سلامي على من خصه الله بالكرم

فينشد واحد ويرد الباقي عليه بأصوات مطربة وانغام معجبة وأهل المدينة فيهم صفاء ومودة وحسن أخلاق وكرم نفوس وطلاقة وجه وسلامة قلب (٧٦) يحبون من هاجر إليهم ولا يجدون في صدورهم حاجة مما أوتوا مدحهم الله تعالى بذلك في القرآن الكريم ودعا لهم رسول الله صلى الله تعالى عليه وآله وصحبه وسلم فعن مسلم عن أبي هريرة رضي الله تعالى عنه أن رسول الله صلى الله عليه وسلم قال اللهم ان ابراهيم عبدك وخليلك ونبيك واني عبدك ونبيك وأنه دعا لمكة واني أدعوك للمدينة بمثل ما دعاك به لمكة ومثله معه وعن الطبراني

في الأوسط عن علي ابن أبي طالب رضي الله تعالى عنه قال قال رسول الله صلى الله تعالى عليه وسلم اللهم ان ابراهيم عبدك وخليلك دعاك لأهل مكة بالبركة وأنا محمد عبدك ورسولك واني ادعوك لأهل المدينة ان تبارك لهم في صاعهم ومدهم مثل ما باركت لأهل مكة واجعل مع البركة بركتين وفي حديث آخر زيادة وثمارهم وفي آخر اللهم اني حرمت ما بين لابتيها كما حرمت مكة على لسان ابراهيم وفازوا بجوار النبي الرءوف الرحيم وأهل البقيع عليه وآله وصحبه أفضل الصلاة واتم التسليم فهنيئاً لهم بما حازوه وطوبى هم بما نالوه .

وتشتمل هذه الركوب كلها على ألف هجين وخمسمائة حمار ومائة وخمسين رهواناً ويوجد العشر من هذه الهجن ملكاً لركابها والباقي بالأجرة وكذلك الرهاوين أكثرها ملك لأربابها والمؤجر منها قليل فان أهالي المدينة المنورة إذا جاءهم الركب الشامي يشترون منه الرهاوين ويحجون عليها فإذا رجعوا إلى المدينة من الحج فالذي لا يلزمه الرهوان يبيعه والذي يكون له لزوم إليه (٧٧) يبقيه عنده وقد تربح هذه الرهاوين إذا بيعت بعد الرجوع من مكة وإذا خسرت لا تخسر أكثر من اجرة دابة يحج عليها وأما الحمير فكلها بالأجرة .

في بيان القوافل التي تخرج من مكة إلى المدينة للزيارة في السنة كلها

القوافل التي تخرج من مكة إلى المدينة المنورة لزيارة النبي صلى الله تعالى عليه وآله وصحبه وسلم ثلاث عشرة قافلة .

القافلة الأولى تخرج من مكة المكرمة إلى المدينة المنورة في غرة رجب الحرام لحضور مشهد زيارة سيدنا حمزة سيد الشهداء وعم سيد الأنبياء صلى الله تعالى عليه وآله وصحبه وسلم ولا تمكث هذه القافلة في المدينة المنورة أكثر من جمعة ثم تقفل راجعة إلى مكة المكرمة ويجتمع في هذه القافلة من ألف جمل إلى ثلاثة آلاف جمل .

القافلة الثانية تخرج من مكة المكرمة إلى المدينة المنورة أيضاً في خامس ذي القعدة وتؤلف من ألف وخمسمائة جمل إلى ألفي جمل .

ويتبعها في اليوم التالي لخروجها الذي هو الثامن من ذي القعدة قافلة أخرى مثلها وهكذا إلى ان تتم القوافل سبعة متوالية فيصير جملتها ثمانية[12] قوافل تشتمل كلها على عشرين ألف جمل.

القافلة التاسعة تخرج من مكة أيضاً في اليوم السابع من ذي الحجة ويتبعها أربع قوافل مثلها متوالية كل يوم قافلة وكلها تخرج من مكة قبل خروج الركب الشامي والمصري والبغدادي منها فإذا وصلت المدينة المنورة وزارت (٧٨) وحضرت يوم عاشوراء خرجت منها قبل وصول الركب الشامي والمصري والبغدادي إليها وإذا فرض أنها تأخرت إلى أن قارب وصول الركوب المذكورة إليها تأمر الحكومة المحلية رؤساء القوافل بالجلاء عن المدينة المنورة فيخرجون منها في أسرع من طرفة عين أو لمحة نظر آيبة إلى مكة وتؤلف هذه القوافل الخمسة كلها من أربعة آلاف جمل إلى سبعة آلاف بحسب قلة الركاب وكثرتهم فيصير جملتها سبعة وعشرين ألف جمل وهذا نهاية ما يكون وما يتصور وقد تكون أقل من ذلك وهو الأكثر ولأهل مكة عندما يخرجون منها إلى المدينة نشائد وقصائد ومدائح وأبيات نبوية يترنمون بها في الطريق ذهاباً وكذلك في الرجوع من المدينة في حق البيت من قبيل الأبيات التي ذكرناها في بيان الركوب لأهل المدينة المنورة وقد يتوهم الحاج ان في أهل مكة فظاظة وجفاء وليس كذلك فان أهل مكة الذين ليسوا غرباء منهم من يغلب عليه تجلى الجلال وهم الملازمون للبيت المواظبون على العبادة فهم أهل وقار ونسك وعبادة ومنهم من يحكم عليه الجمال والمزح والأنس والملاطفة وهؤلاء الذين يشتغلون فيها بأمور الدنيا والتعيش وأما الذين يوجدون فيها من أولى الأخلاق الشرسة وما أشبههم فأولئك ليسوا من أهلها وانما هم دخيلون فيهم فليحذر من التكلم على أهل مكة فانهم جيران بيت الله وللجار حرمة الجوار وقد قال صلى الله تعالى عليه وآله وصحبه وسلم أتاني جبريل فما زال يوصيني بالجار حتى ظننت أنه سيورثه.

12 Read ثماني

(٧٩) في الكلام على الحجاج والتجار الذين يردون مكة

إن الذين يردون من البحر إلى جدة ومنها إلى مكة المكرمة ومثلهم الذين يجيئون من جنوبي وشرقي مكة وشمالها براً ومن الأقطار التي حولها ومن الينبع إلى المدينة ومن مصر ومن الشام فهؤلاء الحجاج والتجار لا غير ثم الذين يردون من جدة انما هم أهل الهند والصين والشين الاسلام والجاوى واليمن والتكرور والزنج والحريتيين والمغاربة وبعض أهل اليمن القريبين للساحل وهكذا وبعض المصريين والأتراك وسواحل البحر الأبيض وهؤلاء كلهم يبقون بعد وجود السكة الحديدية الحجازية الشامية كحالهم قبلها لا يزيدون ولا ينقصون وانما الذين يزيدون من كانوا في جهة الشام أو يمرون في طريقهم عليها كأهالي بر الشام وحلب وبغداد والعجم والكرد وبخارى وغيرهم ممن تقرب بلادهم إلى سكة بغداد وبره جيك الحديديتين المتوقع اتصالهما بخط الشام الحديدي فهؤلاء يزيدون زيادة لا منتهى لها ولا يمكن الآن أن تقدر وبهذه الزيادة تزيد ثروة البلاد الحجازية وفوائدها من الحجاج والزوار والتجار زيادة لا يتصورها العقل الآن ويصير أهاليها من الأغنياء أصحاب الثروة المعدودين فيها .

ولنذكر الآن عدد الحجاج والزوار الذين يذهبون من مكة للزيارة والتجار فنقول لقد كثرت الأقاويل في عدد الحجاج فمن مبالغ يقول يوجد مليون بل أكثر ومن قائل سبعمائة ألف ومن قائل خمسمائة ألف ومن قائل مائتا ألف وهذا كله ظن وتخمين لا يمكن (٨٠) ضبطه على وجه الحقيقة لأن الواردين من أطراف مكة وأقطار الحجاز القريبة والشاسعة لا يمكن حصرهم وأما الواردون مع الركب الشامي والمصري والبغدادي فيمكن حصرهم على وجه التقريب وقد روي أن النبي صلى الله تعالى عليه وآله وصحبه وسلم قال ان الله عز وجل قد وعد هذا البيت أن يحجه في كل سنة خمسمائة ألف فان نقصوا اكملهم عز وجل من الملائكة وان الكعبة تحشر كالعروس المزفوفة وكل من حجها يتعلق بأستارها يسعون حولها حتى تدخل الجنة فيدخلون معها

بقي علينا أن ننظر للظاهر فنقول أن من ذهب إلى عرفات وشاهد هذا الموقف الشريف يندهش ويندهل إلا أنه لا يمكنه أن يجزم بأنه أقل من مائتي ألف وأما أكثره فلا يعرف لأن الواردين من جهات البر لا يمكن حصرهم وهذا هو الأقرب للصواب ولا فائدة في أفراغ الجهد في هذه الجهة لعدم الفائدة لاستحالة الوقوف على الحقيقة لكن البحث في عدد الذين يأتون من البحر عن جدة لا يخلو عن فائدة فان الأصل في تأليف هذه الرسالة مبني على تقدير أنهم معدودون لتوقف بيان النتيجة على معرفة عددهم لأنهم هم الذين يحتاجون لاستئجار الجمال من بدو الحجاز فإذا فرضنا أن الحجاج مائتان وخمسون ألفاً كان الواردون من جدة عشرين ألفاً والباقي الواردين من البر وليس هذا باجحاف بالنسبة لمن يرد من البحر عن جدة لأن في الواردين عن جدة جهة يمكن عدهم منها وهي دفاتر قيد تذاكر المرور في جدة فمن يرجع إلى تلك الدفاتر منذ عشر (٨١) سنين أو أكثر يعلم أنهم لم يبلغوا هذا العدد أصلا وذلك لما في ركوب البحر من الأخطار وفي المحاجر الصحية من التشديد والتضييق عليهم وأما الواردون من البر فالمقيمون في مكة وحواليها قلما يوجد أحد منهم لا يذهب للحج وفي مكة وحدها ما يزيد عن مائة ألف ولا يتخلف منهم الربع قطعاً وبتاً ولنفرض أن الذين يحجون منهم خمسة وسبعون ألفاً ومن وادي فاطمة ووادي الليمون والمضيق والطائف وجهته والعرب المقيمين في الصحارى والبلاد القريبة من مكة إلى المدينة وإلى جهة اليمن ومن اليمن كذلك مائة ألف والواردين من الحج البغدادي ومن نجد ومن الحج الشامي ومن ينبع والحج المصري والعرب المنتقلين في أرض المدينة والشام خمسة وخمسون ألفاً كان الجميع مائتين وخمسين ألفاً وإنما كثر الحجاج من مكة وجوارها رغبة في الثواب ودفعاً للذل والعار فالذي يكون مستطيعاً أن يحج ولا يحج من أهالي تلك الأقطار يعد دنيئاً بين قومه وينسب للبخل وخسة النفس هذا إذا لم ننظر إلى أن المسلمين على وجه العموم يودون الحج ويرغبون فيه كل عام لو أمكنهم طلباً

للثواب فقد جاء في الحديث الشريف أنه يكفر الذنوب كلها ويخرج الحاج من الحج كيوم ولدته أمه وجاء أيضاً من حج واحدة فقد أدى فرضه ومن حج اثنتين فقد داين ربه ومن حج ثلاثة حرم الله تعالى شعره وبشره على النار أو كما قال فلا ترى مسلماً إلا يود أن يحج كل عام سيما لأجل زيارة النبي سيد الأنام عليه وآله وصحبه أفضل الصلاة وأتم السلام (٨٢) يرشدك لهذا ويؤيده لديك كثرة الحجاج الفقراء الذين لم يوجب الله تعالى عليهم الحج لعدم استطاعتهم فانهم مع حالهم البائسة يحجون مشياً على الأقدام حفاة عراة مكشوفة رؤسهم يسألون الخبز والماء وهم كثيرون من كل جهة وأكثرهم بين الحرمين التكرور والمرآة منهم تحمل على عاتقها عصى معلقاً بطرفها الواحد قرعة أو شيئاً مثلها من جلد فيها طفلها أو طفلاها وبالطرف الثاني أمتعتها وكوز مائها فإذا لم يتصدق الناس عليهم بالخبز والماء يموتون عطشاً أو جوعاً ولذا رتبت دولتنا العلية أيدها الله تعالى في جملة مرتباتها لركب الحج الشامي مصارفات مخصوصة لمن يحج من الفقراء على نفقتها للمأكل والمشرب والمركب والمبيت وما يلزم وعينت كذلك مبالغ معلومة يحمل بها الماء في الطريق في المحلات التي يعلم عدم وجود الماء فيها ويسمى ذلك افازة[13] ليعطى لهؤلاء الفقراء حفظاً لحياتهم من الموت عطشاً رحمة بهم وشفقة عليهم وما يسمع في بعض السنين كالسنة الماضية من أنه هبت ريح سموم مات بها كذا وكذا من الحجاج في الطريق وأكثر ما يقع ذلك بين الحرمين إنما يكونون من الفقراء المعدم وجود الماء من تساهل من بيدهم أمر ركوب الحج في الطريق فلا يحتاطون بتحميل الماء للفقراء المسمى بالافازة وقد يصادف أن الركوب لا تجد ماء في بعض المحطات ويكون الفقراء الذين يحجون على أقدامهم عطاشاً فيسبقون إلى المحطات ليشربوا فلا يجدون ماء فيها فيموتون عطشاً وقد يدركهم الموت قبل وصولهم المحطة ولو كان كما يشاع ان موت هؤلاء الفقراء (٨٣) من ريح سموم يشاركهم فيه الأغنياء ولكن لم نسمع ان غنياً مات به مع هؤلاء الفقراء المعدمين

[13] Read إفاضة

الماء فمن نظر إلى حقيقة الحال علم أن موت هؤلاء الفقراء والمنكودي الحظ من العطش السموم لا من الريح السموم ولو وجدوا ماء كما وجد الأغنياء لما تسلط عليهم الريح السموم وحدهم فاعتبروا بأولي الأبصار ومع هذا كله وما يقاسونه من تعب المشي وأذية النعاس ومشقة النوم تحت السماء بغير غطاء ولا وطاء ومقاساة الجوع ومكابدة العطش وذل السؤآل ومرارة الرد وتحمل الحر والبرد المهلكين تراهم يذهبون إلى الحج والزيارة المرة بعد المرة والكرة بعد الكرة وهذا وأمثاله دليل على أن قصد المسلمين بالحج رضاء الله تعالى وبزيارة النبي صلى الله تعالى عليه وآله وصحبه وسلم رجاء شفاعته ففي الحديث الشريف عن ابن عمر رضي الله تعالى عنهما عنه صلى الله تعالى عليه وآله وصحبه وسلم أنه قال من زار قبري وجبت له شفاعتي وفي حديث آخر عن ابن عباس رضي الله تعالى عنهما من حج إلى مكة ثم قصدني في مسجدي كتبت له حجتان مبرورتان ولم يرتدع الفقراء الذين يرون أمثالهم يموتون في تلك الأقطار عن الذهاب إليه على تلك الحال ولم يخشوا من الموت فيها لما جاء في الحديث الشريف عن حاطب ابن الحارث رضي الله تعالى عنه عنه عليه وآله وصحبه الصلاة والسلام من زارني بعد موتي فكأنما زارني في حياتي ومن مات في أحد الحرمين بعث من الآمنين يوم القيمة وبهذه المناسبة يحسن بنا أن نذكر شيئاً يتعجب منه الجاهل وينفطر (٨٤) قلب العاقل وذلك ان بعض أولي الأمر في الحج يأخذ الماء معه من الاستانة إلى الشام إلى مكة ذهاباً واياباً وكذلك البعض من ماء الزرقة إلى المدينة المنورة ومنها إلى مكة وكذلك في الرجوع إلى الشام والفقراء يموتون عطشاً ولا تأخذهم الرأفة ولا تحركهم الإنسانية لرحمتهم بحمل الماء إليهم على نفقة الدولة العلية صانها الله تعالى وحماها آمين بجاه سيد المرسلين عليهم الصلاة والسلام إلى يوم الدين فتلخص من هذا أن الحجاج مهما قيل بكثرتهم لا يزيد الواردون من طريق جدة عن ثلاثين ألفاً وإذا زادوا تكن زيادتهم غير معتادة فلا ينظر إليها ولا ينبني عليها حكم.

في بيان حكمة مشروعية الحج والزيارة

أعلم أنه ليس في هذا الدين القويم أمر ولا نهي بدون حكمة لكن بحكم منها ما هو جلي ومنها ما هو خفي فقد جرت عادة الله تعالى ان يظهر بعض الحكم ويخفى بعضها فهو الأول والآخر والظاهر والباطن وهو بكل شيء عليم وانما جعل بعضها خفياً لزيادة الإيمان والاعتقاد قال الله تعالى في القرآن المجيد ألم ذلك الكتاب لا ريب فيه هدى للمتقين الذين يؤمنون بالغيب ويقيمون الصلاة ومما رزقناهم ينفقون والذين يؤمنون بما أنزل إليك وما أنزل من قبلك وبالآخرة هم يوقنون أولئك على هدى من ربهم وأولئك هم المفلحون ولو كانت كلها ظاهرة أو آمن إنسان (٨٥) بما ظهرت له حكمته ولم يؤمن بما خفيت عليه حكمته لم يؤمن بما ظهرت حكمته لأنه جاء به الرسول عن الله وانما آمن به لظهور حكمته والظاهر حكمته يؤمن بحكمته المؤمن بالله تعالى وغير المؤمن به فلم يكن فرق بين المؤمن بالله تعالى وبين غيره فالمؤمن بما جاء به الكتاب والرسول عن الله بما لم تظهر حكمته هو الذي آمن بالله تعالى حقاً ألا ترى أن الله تعالى مدح الذين يؤمنون بالغيب وأثنى عليهم بأنهم هم على هدى من ربهم وانهم هم المفلحون ولا جرم أن الحج من أركان الدين التي يكفر منكر بها باجماع المسلمين ولا بد لهذا الركن العظيم من حكمة باهرة حيث وجب على المستطيع القاصي والداني ولا شيء في الإسلام يشبهه أصلا فان الله تعالى لم يكلف إنساناً بالسفر أو الذهاب لمحل بعيد أكثر من تكليف سامع الآذان لصلاة الجمعة أصلا فالمسلم إذا خرج من البلد قبل فجر الجمعة إلى محل لا يسمع منه النداء لها ولو لم يكن في السعي له كلفة عليه وكان من أهل الجمعة لا يجب عليه الرواح لها وأما الحج فيجب على المستطيع ولو في البلاد التي تحت القطب الشمالي مثلا فالحج واجب السعي إليه على المستطيع قرب أو بعد فكان هذا التكليف والايجاب لا بد له من حكمة بل حكم متعددة بلا شك ولا ريب وهل هذه الحكمة ظاهرة أو خفية الذي تقضي به العقول السليمة من أول وهلة انها فيه من حيث هو

(٨٦) ظاهرة وان كانت في بعض أعماله كرمي الجمار خفية ويؤيد كونها فيه ظاهرة قول الله تعالى في كتابه المجيد وأذّن في الناس بالحج يأتوك رجالا وعلى كل ضامر يأتين من كل فج عميق ليشهدوا منافع لهم ويذكروا اسم الله فقد صرح سبحانه وتعالى بوجود المنافع لهم في الحج وهي أكبر حكمة ثم أعقب ذلك بقوله ويذكروا اسم الله وقد قال فيه أيضاً عند ذكر الحج وبيانه فإذا أفضتم من عرفات فاذكروا الله عند المشعر الحرام واذكروه كما هداكم ثم قال ثم أفيضوا من حيث أفاض الناس واستغفروا الله ان الله غفور رحيم فإذا قضيتم مناسككم فاذكروا الله كذكركم آباءكم أو أشد ذكراً. ثم قال واذكروا الله في أيام معدودات فمن تعجل في يومين فلا إثم عليه ومن تأخر فلا إثم عليه لمن اتقى واتقوا الله واعلموا انكم إليه تحشرون وقد علم ان ذكر الله تعالى في الدنيا من أعظم المنافع في الآخرة وأكثرها ثواباً قال الله تعالى أن المسلمين والمسلمات والمؤمنين والمؤمنات والقانتين والقانتات والصادقين والصادقات والصابرين والصابرات والخاشعين والخاشعات والمتصدقين والمتصدقات والصائمين والصائمات والحافظين فروجهم والحافظات والذاكرين الله كثيراً والذاكرات أعد الله لهم مغفرة وأجراً عظيماً وقال ان الصلاة تنهى عن الفحشاء والمنكر ولذكر الله أكبر وقد أمر تعالى بذكر اسمه في القرآن الكريم في غير من موضع كقوله عز (٨٧) اسمه واذكر اسم ربك بكرة وأصيلا وقوله جل جلاله واذكر اسم ربك وتبتّل إليه تبتيلا والكلام على الذكر وما فيه من عظيم الثواب والأجر ليس هنا كله وهو في الكتب كثير شائع.

ومنافع الحج المذكورة في القرآن العظيم الشان مبهمة منكرة مجملة ليست موضحة ولا معرفة ولا مفصلة تفيد التنويع والتكثير ولذا جاءت بصيغة منتهى الجموع وهي لا تنحصر في جهة ما بل هي شائعة في الدنيوية والآخروية فمن منافعه الآخروية ما رواه البزار وغيره عن رسول الله صلى الله عليه وسلم انه قال الحاج يشفع في أربعمائة من

أهل بيته ويخرج من ذنوبه كيوم ولدته أمه وروى غير واحد من أصحاب السنن وغيرهم أن رسول الله صلى الله عليه وسلم قال العمرة إلى العمرة كفارة لما بينها والحج المبرور ليس له جزاء الا الجنة وانه قال النفقة في الحج كالنفقة في سبيل الله الدرهم بسبعمائة ضعف ومن منافعه الدنيوية اتصال المسلمين بعضهم ببعض والوقوف على أحوالهم وأخبارهم وشؤونهم على القرب والبعد واتفاق كلمتهم وتعاونهم على أمورهم الدنيوية والدينية وتعاضدهم حتى يكونوا كعضو واحد وسيأتي إن شاء الله تعالى ما في تعاضد المسلمين وتعاونهم على أمورهم الدنيوية والدينية وما فيهما من النتائج الحسنة وذكرنا في مقالتنا أعظم المآثر السلطانية وكتابنا أقرب القرب ما فيه كفاية فارجع إليهما إن شئت.

(٨٨) ومنها أيضاً الغناء ففي الحديث الشريف عنه صلى الله تعالى عليه وآله وصحبه وسلم أنه قال حجوا تستغنوا وسافروا تصحوا.

ومنها أيضاً تأسيس التجارة فالحجاج إذا تقابلوا مع بعضهم تخابروا بأمور التجارة وأسسوها وتعاقدوا عليها وربطوا الشركات وقد يتبادلون بها من الطرفين فهذا يرسل لهذا وهذا يرسل لهذا ويتعرفون طرق ارسالها وتوسيعها من بلاد إلى أخرى وكيفية تعاطيها ويختبر الإنسان أحوال من يريد أن يتجر معه أو يشاركه إذ يقدر الإنسان على الفهم والتفهيم باللسان والمواجهة ما لا يقدر عليه بالغيبة والمكاتبة.

ومنها أيضاً تأسيس الصناعة وتوسيعها فالحجاج إذا خرجوا من بلادهم يستصحبون معهم من صنائع بلادهم المنسوجات والملبوسات وغيرها بالضرورة إما لأنفسهم ليستعملوه في السفر أو للتجارة ليربحوا به أو للهدية لأهل الحرمين أو لمن في الطريق من البلاد التي يمرون عليها فإذا رآها أهل الحجاز أو الحجاج الذين يلاقونهم في الحرمين أو أهل البلاد التي في طريقهم وأعجبتهم تعلموا صنعتها ولربما أوعزوا إلى من يأتي إليهم بتلك الصنعة من أهلها بالاقامة عندهم ليشتغل بها أو يعلمها لهم وكذلك إذا رأى الحجاج أنفسهم في سفرهم من الصنائع النفيسة التي تناسب بلادهم وتروج عندهم يتعلمونها أو يجلبون لبلادهم

من يعلمهم اياها فتنتشر تلك الصنعة في بلادهم بعد أن كانت معدومة فيها وهذا واقع مشاهد .

ومنها أيضاً اتساع نطاق الزراعة وهذا إما ان يكون باستصحاب الحجاج (٨٩) معهم من حبوب وبقول وأثمار بلادهم إلى البلاد التي يدخلونها في ممرهم إلى الحج حتى اقطار الحجاز فإذا اعجبت تلك البقول أو الحبوب أو الأثمار الاهالي التي ليست عندهم طلبوها منهم فإذا استحصلوها زرعوها وتعممت بينهم وبالعكس بأن يأخذ الحجاج ما يعجبهم مما يجدونه في الأقطار التي يجلبونها من بلادهم إلى مكة ذهاباً واياباً وإما بزيادة الزراعة في الأقطار الحجازية لأجل الحجاج فان الحجاج يقتضي لهم مأكولات لأنفسهم وعلف لدوابهم وهذا يقضي بلزوم زيادة المزروعات للأكل والعلف في أقطار الحجاز أو بتوسيع التجارة إذا كان لا يزرع فيها ويستجلب من غيرها .

وكل ما ذكرناه من أسباب الغناء على ان الحج نفسه من غير نظر إلى سبب من الأسباب المذكورة يورث الغنا كما أن النكاح يكون سبباً للرزق بنص الحديث قال صلى الله تعالى عليه وسلم التمسوا الرزق بالنكاح وكما ان السفر نفسه سبب للصحة فقد بان لك مما ذكرنا من توسيع وتأسيس نطاق التجارة والصناعة والزراعة ما يثبت لك كون الحج يورث الغنا كما هو نص الحديث الشريف ولم يأمر الله تعالى به ويفترضه على المستطيع دون غيره عبثاً بل لا بد من حكمة بل حكم كثيرة باهرة .

منها ان الحاج يحتاج إلى مصارفات وغير المستطيع إذا فرض عليه الحج يكون تكليف ما في غير وسعه وقد قال الله تعالى لا يكلف الله نفساً إلا وسعها .

ومنها ان غير المستطيع ليس في وسعه أن ينفع نفسه ولا ينتفع من غيره فهو مشغول ببؤسه وفقره همه تحصيل شيء يتعيش به أو يداوي مرضه الذي أضناه ليخلص منه بل (٩٠) لا يمكن مع اشتغال الفكر ان يحصل النفع أصلا ومما نسب إلى الإمام الأعظم محمد بن ادريس

الشافعي رضي الله تعالى عنه من الحكم انه قال لو كلفت إلى برحلة ما تعلمت مسألة ومنها ان خوف الطريق ومشاقه وصعوبة مسلكه توجب التهلكة وقد قال تعالى في فرقانه الكريم ولا تلقوا بأيديكم إلى التهلكة فان الله تعالى لا يريد تهلكة عباده وبالجملة فان الحج فيه منافع عظيمة للناس لا تقدر ولا تحصر وهو المعرض العام للمسلمين وقد أوجبه الله تعالى على كل مستطيع منهم في العمر مرة واحدة وإذا مات مستطيع ولم يحج يستقر هذا الفرض في ذمته إلى أن يحج عنه من تركته أو من غيرها ويسن تكرير الحج لزيادة الفائدة الدنيوية وكذلك تسن زيارة النبي صلى الله تعالى عليه وآله وصحبه وسلم وفيها من المنافع الدنيوية من حيث اجتماع الاسلام فيها من كل فج عميق كما في الحج بحسب قلة الجماعة وكثرتهم ومن المنافع الاخروية ما قدمناه في الأحاديث وغيرها مما هو مذكور في الكتب مفصلا وذكرناه في مقالتنا أعظم المآثر السلطانية العثمانية أن للمسلمين أربع اجتماعات دينية منها أعم ومنها عمومي ومنها خصوصي .

أما الأعم فالحج وأما العمومي فصلاة العيدين والجمعة وأما الخصوصي فصلاة الجماعة وبسطنا فيها الكلام عليها .

ولا يخفى أهمية الاجتماعات في الزمن السابق وفي هذا الزمان فقد كان في مكة للعرب سوق عظيم يحضره العرب من كل جهة يسمونه سوق عكاظ وبه يضرب المثل وكذلك الأوربيون في هذا الزمن فان لهم اعتناء عظيماً بالاجتماعات العامة حتى توصلوا لأجلها (٩١) إلى ترتيب المعارض في عواصم ممالكهم كما هو الأكثر لتكون وسيلة للاجتماع العام .

ولا يذهب عن التالي لكلامي والسامع له والمصغي إليه ان بين اجتماع المسلمين العام الذي هو الحج واجتماعات الأوربيين في المعارض بونا عظيما وذلك ان الحضور في الاجتماع العام للمسلمين فرض ديني على كل مستطيع على التراخي وأنه فيه وفي غيره من باقي الاجتماعات مبني على أمور دينية شرعها الله تعالى للمسلمين وليس المسلمون فيها

مشغولين الا بما يتعلق بالدين فاذا أتموا فروضهم الدينية فيها انتقلوا منها إلى أمورهم الدنيوية فالأمور الدينية هي الأهم منهما شرعاً .

ومن الأمور الدينية ما به قوام الدنيا فان الدين لا يقوم بغير جماعة وعصبية والجماعة والعصبية تتوقف على الأمور الدنيوية فكما ان الاشتغال بالأمور الدينية واجب كذلك الاشتغال بالأمور الدنيوية التي بها قوام الدين واجب ولا يلتفت إلى قول غر جاهل ان الإعراض عن الدنيا بالكلية من الشريعة الإسلامية فانه مخالف للدين لا محالة ولا إلى من يفعل ذلك تهاملا وكسلا وبطالة أو رياء وسمعة وتمويها ليأكل أموال الناس بالباطل فان هذا ممنوع شرعاً فما هم الا كما قال الله تعالى وضرب الله مثلا رجلين أحدهما أبكم لا يقدر على شيء وهو كل على مولاه اينما يوجهه لا يأت بخير فما مثل هؤلاء الذين يتركون الشغل بما فيه نفع في الدين والدنيا ويعيشون بالخمول والتخيل والتسأل مع اظهار الصلاح والزهد والعفاف الا كمثل المرجفين في الحرب الآتي حكمهم والكلام عليهم فكم غش هؤلاء (٩٢) الناصحون مؤمنا وكم أفقروا من غنى فتركوه بعد ورعه في دينه مفتنا كيف ينهون عن ذلك وأمر الله باعداد القوة وأحل البيع وحرم الربا وأثنى على التجارة وسمى ربحها فضلا منه وقرنها مع الجهاد وقدمها عليه فقال عز من قائل وآخرون يضربون في الأرض يبتغون من فضل الله وآخرون يقاتلون في سبيل الله وقال تعالى قل ان الفضل بيد الله وأسند تعليم صناعة داود إليه فقال سبحانه وعلمناه صناعة لبوس لكم لتحصنكم من بأسكم وأسند إليه جل وتنزه الزرع أيضاً فقال افرأيتم ما تحرثون أأنتم تزرعونه ان نحن الزارعون لو نشأ جعلناه حطاما فظلتم تفكهون انا لمغرمون بل نحن محرومون وكل هذا يحتاج إلى سعي وثروة واكتساب وقد علم الله تعالى سيدنا آدم ألف صنعة وقال له علمها لبنيك كيلا يأكلوا بدينهم فكان آدم حراثا وأدريس خياطا ونوح وزكريا نجارين وابراهيم ولوط زراعين وصالح تاجراً وشعيب ويونس راعي غنم وداود يعمل الدروع وعيسى حائكا وقيل صباغا

ونبينا قبل النبوة تاجراً وراعي الغنم صلوات الله تعالى وسلامه عليهم أجمعين وكذلك الصحابة الكرام رضي الله تعالى عنهم فكان عمر بن الخطاب يتناوب مع بعض الصحابة في حضور مجلس الرسول صلى الله عليه وسلم فيشتغل يوماً ويحضر يوماً وكان سيدنا عثمان بن عفان أمير المؤمنين تاجراً وعبد الرحمن بن عوف غنيا صولحت احدى نسائه الأربع على ثمانين ألف دينار عن أرثها من تركته والزبيربن العوام كانت حصة كل واحدة من نسائه وكن (٩٣) أربعا من تركته ألف ألف ومائتي ألف ولم يضر ذلك في دينهم ولم يشغلهم عن النبوة والصحبة وليس هذا الاهمال توكلا على الله كما يزعم ويكذب فيه على الله تعالى فقد سأل معلم الخير نبينا صلى الله تعالى عليه وآله وصحبه وسلم صحابيا دخل المسجد وترك ناقته مطلقة عند باب المسجد عنهما فأخبره أنه اتكل على الله تعالى وتركها فقال له صلى الله تعالى عليه وآله وصحبه وسلم اعقلها وتوكل فعلم ان التوكل لا يكون بدون تعاطي السبب وان تعاطي السبب لا ينافي التوكل وان السعي والاكتساب والغنا لا تنافي الصلاح والعبادة والتدين مع ان الاكتساب للانفاق على الاهل انفاق في سبيل الله وصدقة وقد اثنى الله تعالى على المتصدقين في غير ما موضع من كتابه الكريم فقال سبحانه وتعالى الذين ينفقون أموالهم في سبيل الله ثم لا يتبعون ما أنفقوا منا ولا اذى لهم أجرهم عند ربهم ولا خوف عليهم ولا هم يحزنون وفي الدر المنثور عن أيوب رضي الله تعالى عنه قال أشرف على النبي صلى الله عليه وسلم رجل من رأس تل فقالوا ما أجلد هذا الرجل لو كان جلده في سبيل الله فقال النبي صلى الله عليه وسلم أوليس في سبيل الله الا من قتل ثم قال من خرج في الأرض يطلب حلالا يكف به أهله فهو في سبيل الله ومن خرج يطلب حلالا يكف به نفسه فهو في سبيل الله ومن خرج يطلب التكاثر فهو في سبيل الشيطان وعن البخاري ومسلم ان رسول الله صلى الله عليه وسلم قال انك لم تنفق نفقة تبتغي بها وجه الله الا أجرت عليها حتى ما تجعل في امرأتك وفي حديث آخر ما أطعمت نفسك فهو

لك صدقة وما أطعمت خادمك فهو لك صدقة وأمثال هذه الأحاديث كثيرة وكلها تدل على طلب (٩٤) الاكتساب من الحلال والانفاق على النفس والعيال وان ذلك كله صدقة ولم يرد النهي عن الصدقة بل ولا يجوز النهي عنها بل يحرم على أن كلا من الاتجار والزراعة والصناعة إذا عمت الحاجة إليه فرض كفاية فان تركها أهل بلدة مع الحاجة إليها أثموا فترك فرض الكفاية ليس من الدين قطعا وبتا لأن الأتيان به يسقط الأثم عمن لم يأت به فيثاب عليه ولم يعلم ان في الشرع المحمدي امرأً يثاب عليه فاعله يطلب تركه أصلا وقد قلنا ان العمل من حيث هو من سنن المرسلين عليهم الصلاة والسلام وإذا احتيج إليه كان فرض كفاية ولا يبعد ان يقال ان الناس آثمون بترك تعلم بعض الصنائع مما عمت الحاجة إليها وتجلب إلينا من الخارج فيجب تعلمها واصطناعها في بلادنا لنستغني عن الغير وتبقى ثروتنا عندنا ولا تضعف قوتنا وماليتنا ولا تبقى أراضينا مهملة ورجالنا ودوابنا معطلة ننتظر ما يأتي إلينا من الخارج وأما ما فشا في زماننا هذا من تهافت الناس على ترك العمل والهجوم على التجارة الأجنبية ليتعيشوا منها حتى أدى أمر الأهالي إلى المضايقة والاضطرار فلا يجوز شرعاً إذ به تقل ثروة البلاد وتضعف قوة العباد ويستولي الفقر على الرعية فعسى أن يتنبه حذاق تجارنا لها وما يستدل به على ان التوكل يقوم مقام السعي ويغني عنه من حديث لو أنكم تتوكلون على الله حق توكلة لرزقكم كما يرزق الطير تغدو اخماصا وتروح بطانا فلا يدل على ذلك لأمور .

منها انه صلى الله تعالى عليه وآله وصحبه وسلم أثبت السعي بقوله تغدو وتروح وهذا نهاية ما يمكنها من السعي ومنها ان لو حرف امتناع لامتناع فاذا كان الصحابة الكرام رضوان (٩٥) الله تعالى عليهم لم يمكنهم ذلك بأخباره صلى الله تعالى عليه وآله وصحبه وسلم فكيف يمكن أحداً ممن عرفت أحوالهم ولا حاجة لبيانها .

ومنها ان الله تعالى أمر بالمشي في مناكب الأرض استرزاقاً فقال

عز شأنه هو الذي جعل لكم الأرض ذلولا فامشوا في مناكبها وكلوا من رزقه وحمل بعضهم الأمر على الأباحة ليس على اطلاقه فأن من يحتاج للنفقة له أو لعياله مثلا ولا جهة له يجب عليه الاكتساب فان سعي للاكتساب ولم يمكنه وجب عليه ان يستدين وينفق على نفسه وعياله ولا يموتوا جوعاً فان الاستدانة من جملة طرق الاكتساب وقد جاء الأمر بها في الحديث الشريف عند الاحتياج إليها للنفقة .

ومنها ان الله تعالى قال ومن يتق الله يجعل له مخرجاً ويرزقه من حيث لا يحتسب ولم يقل ومن يتوكل على الله وتقوى الله تعالى نافعة في كل الأمور فاذا اتقى العبد مولاه الذي بيده حياته ورزقه وموته ونشوره ييسر له الرزق من حيث لا يحتسب أي يهيء له جهة يرزقه منها بحسب ارادته تعالى ومشيئته من حيث لا يحتسب العبد لأنه ينزل عليه من السماء أو ينفق من تحت السجادة وهو كل على الناس فان الله تعالى لم يأمر بهذا ولا يرضاه لعباده المؤمنين والذين لا يتقونه ويعرضون عن ذكره يضيق عليهم في العيشة في الدنيا قال الله تعالى ومن اعرض عن ذكري فان له معيشة ضنكا ولا يلتفت إلى أن غير المؤمنين يوسع الله تعالى عليهم العيشة مع كفرهم فأنهم غير مخاطبين بالتقوى ولا بالذكر خطاب اداء وما (٩٦) يصادفه بعض المؤمنين من سعة المعيشة مع عدم التقوى والإعراض عن ذكر الله تعالى فاما ان لا يكونوا مؤمنين باطناً فيكونوا من القسم الاول وهم الكفار وقال تعالى يحسبون انما نمدهم به من مال وبنين نسارع لهم في الخيرات بل لا يشعرون واما ان يكونوا مؤمنين فيكون استدراجاً لهم قال جل جلاله سنستدرجهم من حيث لا يعلمون وأملى لهم إن كيدي متين ويكون جزاؤهم جميعه مسوفا للآخرة ولا ريب ان الرزق بيد الله قال الله تعالى الله لطيف بعباده يرزق من يشاء وهو القوي العزيز وقال عز شأنه نحن قسمنا بينهم معيشتهم في الحياة الدنيا ولو كان الأتكال وترك العمل من الدين لأمر بهما الشارع مع ان الأنبياء والصحابة كانوا كلهم يكتبون الا اصحاب الصفة الكرام فانهم رضي الله تعالى

عنهم كانوا ملازمين رسول الله صلى الله تعالى عليه وآله وصحبه وسلم ليأخذوا عنه الدين والأحكام فهذا أكبر دليل على ما قلناه من انه لا يسمح لأحد ان يترك العمل والاكتساب لا ان يكون للاشتغال بالعلم فدعوى اهل البطالة والكسل ان الأتكال على الله تعالى وحده يكفي عن العمل لا أصل له في الشرع نعم العمل وحده بدون اتكال على الله تعالى بأن يعتقد انه يرزق نفسه او ان عمله هذا كان لرزقه بدون اتكال على الله تعالى زندقة محضة بل كفر خالص مع ظهور فساده بعدم حصوله على الرزق في كل ما يسعى به فان الأمر كله بيد الله تعالى على ان الذين يدعون ان التوكل كاف عن السعي تراهم أشد تزاحماً عليه من الذباب على القذور ومن الكلاب على ميتة البقر فلا يسمعون بمرتب لدرس أو امامة او خطابة الا تسابقوا عليه ولا بوقف لخانقاه[14] (٩٧) أو تكية أو وصاية على يتيم أو نظارة على وقف إلا تراكضوا إليه ولا يرون حاكماً إلا ويحتاطونه ولا تلوح لهم بارقة اختلاس من مال الخزينة إلا ويغتالونه أولئك حزب الشيطان إلا أن حزب الشيطان هم الخاسرون فما انزواؤهم في اماكنهم واعراضهم عن الاقدام على الاكتساب مع البطالة والتسأل وتطهيرهم أنفسهم بلسانهم إلا كما قيل.

ايها العائب سلمى   أنت عندي كثعاله
رام عنقودا فلما   ابصر العنقود هاله
قال هذا حامض لـما   رأى ان لا يناله

لكننا لا ننكر أن للتوكل اهلا وللمجاهدة والعبادة مع الزهد والتكفف عن الناس في الشرع أصلا وذلك لمن صادفتهم العناية بحصول القوت الضروري لهم ولعيالهم وبالرضى ببؤسهم وضيق حالهم لا يحتاجون للضرب في الأرض ولا يسألون الناس الحافا يحسبهم الجاهل اغنياء من التعفف يصبرون عن القليل الحقير ولا تميل نفوسهم للكثير لا يقصدون زيدا وعمرا ولا يداهنون خالدا ولا بكرا قطعوا اماهم من غير الله وتمسكوا بعروته الوثقى فأغناهم عما سواه فارغة قلوبهم من

[14] إلا خانقوه Read

الالتفات لزهرة الدنيا فاستوت عندهم درجاتها العليا والسفلى رضي الله عنهم ورضوا عنه أولئك حزب الله الا ان حزب الله هم المفلحون .

فمال بيت المسلمين انما هو لمصالح المسلمين وقد كان السلف الصالح من (٩٨) المشايخ والصوفية وأمثالهم يتعيشون من كسب ايديهم ولا يتكلون على بيت مال المسلمين ولا على ما يعطى إليهم من الناس ولا يتعرضون لوصية او صدقة بل كان أكثرهم لا يقبل هدية من غير طلب فضلا عن ان يطلب من أحد شيئاً أو يتعرض له بقول او فعل كمخالفة بعض الناس في زي اللباس ليعرف ويذكر فهم لنا قدوة ونحن لنا بهم اسوة ومن اراد تفصيل احوالهم والاطلاع عليها فعليه بكتب طبقات الصوفية رحمهم الله فالسكة الحديدية أعظم الأسباب للتوصل إلى ما ذكرناه في هذا الباب والله الميسر وإليه حسن المآب .

في بيان فوائد السكة الحديدية للمسلمين عموماً ولأهل الحرمين خصوصاً

لقد ذكرنا منافع الحج والزيارة فيما تقدم والقصد من الاجتماع في الحج الذي هو أعم اجتماع عند المسلمين فإذا كان كذلك كان الاجتماع كلما كان أعم كان أكثر نفعاً ولا ريب ان الحجاج ليسوا من أهل مكة فقط أو منها ومما حواليها من البلاد بل ولا من أهل الحرمين أو العرب أو جهة مخصوصة أو أمة مخصوصة دون أمة بل هم من جميع الأمم المسلمين في جميع أقطار الأرضين وإذا كان كما قلنا كانت التسهيلات لهم من الأمور المرغب فيها شرعاً وانسانية وحيث كانت تلك البلاد بعيدة عن الخليفه الذي بيده زمام امرها ومحافظتها وحمايتها وتوطيد الأمن والراحة فيها وعلى أهلها وجوب الطاعة له في الأمر والنهي بما يوافق كتاب الله وسنة رسوله الذي هو خليفته عنه صلى الله تعالى عليه وآله وصحبه وسلم كان تقريب المسافة (٩٩) بينهم وبينه من أهم الأمور السياسية في العالم ولا شك أن خير الأسباب الموصلة وأحسنها وآمنها وأسرعها في زماننا انما هو السكة الحديدية فكان انشاء هذه السكة الحديدية الحجازية من ألزم

الأشياء شرعاً وسياسة وانسانية والفوائد التي تنجم عنها لا تقدر ولا تحصر.

ولا يقال ان البواخر البحرية تغني عنها لأنا نقول ان من يريد الذهاب للمدينة المنورة من البحر سواء من طريق الينبع أو جدة يحتاج إلى احتمال زحمة شديدة لأن بين ينبع والمدينة مسافة ستة أيام صحراء قفرى لا ساكن فيها الا قليل وغير أمينة والذي يريد الذهاب منها إلى المدينة يحتاج ان يرافق قافلة لا توجد في كل وقت وليس لها وقت معين على أن الركوب مع القافلة لا يخلو من خطر عظيم أيضاً وبين جدة والمدينة اثنا عشر يوماً وقد ذكرنا أيام القوافل من مكة إلى المدينة فاذا لم يصادف أو أنها لا يمكن الذهاب مع ما في الركوب معها من الزحمة والمشقة وهذا كله بقطع النظر عما يكون في البحر من الأخطار العظيمة والأنواء وعدم امكان المسير فيه في كل وقت لأسباب معلومة فاذا كان في السكة الحديدية من الشام إلى مكة فوائد لا توجد في البواخر البحرية ولا يستغنى عنها في هذا الزمان .

وقد قلنا انها كثيرة فالكلام عليها مفصلة يحتاج إلى سفر كبير لا تسعه هذه الرسالة ولكن لما كان ما لا يدرك كله لا يترك كله حسن بنا ان نذكر طرفا منها (١٠٠) هنا كيلا تخلو رسالتنا هذه عنها فنقول .

الفائدة الأولى تكثير الحجاج والزوار والتجار فان مد هذا الخط الحديدي من الشام إلى مكة يزيد الحجاج إلى أضعاف مضاعفة فإذا كان عدد الحجاج الآن من نفس الشام ألفاً مثلا يكون بعد وجود هذه السكة عشرين أو ثلاثين ألفاً بلا شك ولا ريب سيما إذا كانت الأجرة رخيصة وبهذا الاعتبار يكون باقي الحجاج الذين من جوار الشام وكذلك الحجاج الذين يحضرون عن طريق الشام من جهة حمص وحماه وحلب وأمثالها فلا ريب أنهم يزيدون بهذه النسبة أو أكثر هذا إذا لم يتصل خط الأناضول المتصل الآن من اسكدار إلى قونية بخط الشام المذكور فان اتصل بالخط المصمم على وصله ببره جيك إلى بغداد وبالخط الذي اشيع مده من الشام إلى بغداد توا من الصحراء القفرى

ماراً على تدمر فلا تقدر الزيادة حينئذ أصلا لأنه من أحاط علماً بما كان عليه ركب الحج الشامي من الكثرة كما أشرنا إليه يعلم ما يبلغ إليه عدد الحجاج وقتئذ وبقدر زيادة الحجاج والزوار والتجار تزيد المنافع المقصودة من الحج المار ذكرها وغيرها .

الفائدة الثانية انه يمكن للدولة العلية وقت اللزوم أن ترسل لتلك الجهات ما تحتاج إليه من الامدادات والتجهيزات في أي وقت شاءت فيصل إليها في أقرب وقت ويمتنع بسبب ذلك تعدي العرب المتوحشين وتحصل تلك الأقطار وأهاليها والحجاج على الأمن التام .

(١٠١) الفائدة الثالثة لقد ذكرنا أن أراضي الحجاز من المدينة المنورة إلى مكة المكرمة كلها قابلة لزرع الحبوب والبقول والبطيخ والقثاء والخيار وما أشبهها ولغرس الأشجار المختلفة الأثمار كالعنب والنخيل والرمان والتين والجوز والموز والسفرجل والليمون والأترج بجميع أنواعه وما اشبهها وانه لا يؤخذ لمكة منها إلا من وادي فاطمة ووادي الليمون والباقي يبقى في أرضه لأنه يفسد بطول مدة النقل وأما التمر وما ماثله مما لا يفسد بالنقل فمن الأراضي القريبة منها لا من البعيدة ومع هذا فان اثمانها لا تفي بمصارفها ولذا اقتصروا منها على غرس ما يكفيهم والمياه الموجودة عندهم لا ينتفعون بها الآن حق الانتفاع فاذا مد الخط الحديدي من أرضهم أو في جوارهم يسهل عليهم النقل فلا تفسد المحصولات وبالضرورة تكون الأجرة أرخص من اجرة النقل على الجمال فيربحون ويزيدون حينئذ في الزرع والغرس والتجارة وكذا في جوار المدينة المنورة وهذه الفائدة لا يمكن تقديرها الآن أيضاً لأنها قابلة للتحسين والنمو مهما أمكن اذ ربما تجلب من تلك المحصولات للشام وجهاتها فتتضاعف فائدتها ويمكننا ان نقول أن هذه الأقطار حينئذ تستغني عما يجلب إليها من الحبوب من مصر وغيرها من البلاد البعيدة عنها التي إذا تأخر وصولها إليها تغلو اسعارها وإذا اشتد الأمر ينتج ذلك عندهم القحط وأكثر ما يقع ذلك في المدينة المنورة لبعدها عن البحر وخوف الطريق .

(١٠٢) الفائدة الرابعة ان بدو الحجاز لا صنائع الآن عندهم بل ولا في مكة المكرمة والمدينة المنورة ويأخذون جميع ملبوساتهم المنسوجة وغيرها من تجار الركب الشامي حينما يمرون عليهم أو من مكة أو المدينة لمن يقرب منهما أو يذهب إليهما وعلى كل فهو اما من الشام وهو الأكثر أو من غيرها وهو نادر جداً وكذا جميع امتعتهم وأثاث بيوتهم ومفروشاتهم بقيمة غبن فاحش وفي بعض تجار الحرمين من لا يراقب الله تعالى في تجارته فيتجرون في أخس الأشياء وأقربها للبلى ويبيعونها بقيمة الحسنة القوية فلا تمضي أيام قلائل الا وتبلى تلك الأشياء وأكثر أهل الحرمين فقراء فيقف ذلك المشتري تجاه البيت الحرام أو في اعتابه عليه وآله وصحبه أفضل الصلاة والسلام سواء رجلا أو امرأة كبيراً أو صغيراً ويدعو على ذلك البائع فينتقم الله تعالى منه بعدله وينزل به أنواع البلاء الظاهرة والخفية فيخسر بذلك الدين لغشه وأخذه مال ذلك المشتري الفقير بالسحت والدنيا لما يصيبه من سهام المصائب وقد يؤخر الله تعالى له بجزاء إلى يوم الجزاء ويبيع اولئك البدو محصولاتهم بثمن بخس رخيص جداً وذلك مثل جلود الغنم والبقر والأبل والصوف وبعض محصولاتهم لا ينتفعون بها أصلا مثل اللبن والحطب وشعر المعز فإذا انشئت هذه السكة في تلك الجهات وتمت بعونه تعالى ومشيئته سهل عندهم تأسيس مكاتب للصنائع والزراعة ولو مختصة بما يتعلق بتلك البلاد أولا ثم تتعمم فإذا تعلموا وعرفوا كيف يتصرفون بمحصولاتهم ويستفيدون منها ويجدون ما يحتاجون لأنفسهم عندهم مثل دباغة الجلود وحياكة (١٠٣) القطن والصوف والشعر والنجارة والحدادة وعمل الجبن والسمن لصاروا من أهل الترفه وأولي الثروة واستغنوا عما يجلب لهم من غير البلاد وشن الغارات على بعضهم ومن يمر بأرضهم.

الفائدة الخامسة انه بواسطة السكة الحديدية يسهل التفتيش على المعادن في هذه الصحارى والقفار التي لم تزل إلى الآن مجهولة وكنوزها فيها مخفية فإذا تم انشاء هذه السكة سهل الجولان في تلك الأقطار وحفر

التراب ونبش الرمال وجوب الأحجار فيظهر ما استكن فيها من الفحم والمعادن وأودع فيها من الأسرار وبذلك تصبح هذه البلاد في دور ثان من أدوار الازدهار فتضيء شمسها وينير بدرها وتمسي في بحبوحة الغناء والثروة متمتعة بالعيشة الراضية والرفاهية الباهية .

الفائدة السادسة تأسيس المدنية والحضارة فيهم وانتشار العلوم والمعارف بينهم والأمن على الأنفس والأموال والأولاد والتخلق بالأخلاق الحسنة والتعيش بالعيشة الهنية فتأسس الدولة العلية عندهم مكاتب ابتدائية ورشدية فيتعلمون العلوم الدينية والأخلاق الرضية وتدبير المنزل والاقتصاد فيتنعمون بلذاذة المعرفة ويتخلصون من ربقة الجهالة والقذارة والخمول فينظفون ثيابهم وأنديتهم ويعمرون بيوتهم وينوعون اطعمتهم ويريحون أنفسهم وينعمون بالهم .

الفائدة السابعة ان الدولة العلية أيدها الله تعالى بالنصر على أعدائها ودوام العز والاقبال لها تستخدم منهم من يليق للاستخدام في أمور هذه السكة (١٠٤) الحديدية وتعطيهم أجرة لأنفسهم من وارداتها وهذه الخدمة فيها دائمة لا مقطوعة ولا ممنوعة إذا سلكوا فيها بالصدق والأمانة .

الفائدة الثامنة أنهم يبيعون المارين عليهم في السكة مأكولات ومشروبات وغير ذلك مما لا يباع بغير واسطة السكة الحديدية أصلا مثل الخبز واللحم والبيض واللبن والماء المعلل المبرد فان هذه الأشياء لا تؤخذ إلى مكة أو المدينة لتباع وفيها ربح عظيم ولها وقع عند المسافرين.

الفائدة التاسعة ان المواشي تكثر عندهم بواسطة السكة الحديدية وذلك لأنه كما قررنا تزداد الزراعة وتعمم فاذا ازدادت الزراعة وجد المرعى والعلف للدواب فتكثر وتنمو وأهل الحرمين في احتياج عظيم لزيادة المواشي سيما الغنم والبقر لأجل اللبن والسمن واللحم التي لا يستغنون عنها في آن ما ولا يغتر الحجاج بما يرونه من كثرة الغنم التي يؤتى بها في موسم عرفة فان معظمها من نجد وما يؤتى به من نواحي مكة قليل جداً بالنسبة للنجدى على ان بدو الحجاز انما تأتي بغنمها

جميعه وذلك لما هو مجرب ومحقق عندها من ان كل انسان لم يأت بغنمه إلى موسم عرفة يقع فيه وباء وفناء عظيم حتى لا يكاد يسلم له شيء وقد يفنى جميعه عن بكرة أبيه فاحتياج الحرمين لزيادة المواشي لا يسده إلا الاعتناء بتربيتها وهذا لا يتم إلا بتوسيع نطاق الزراعة في تلك الأقطار ومما يدل عليه ان اقة السمن لا تنزل قيمتها عن نصف مجيدي وقد ترتفع (١٠٥) إلى مجيدي لأنه يجلب إليها من الخارج فإذا انقطع الوارد غلا السعر ومثل السمن اللبن فان أقته في مكة تساوي اربعة قروش لا تنقص عن ذلك وقد تزيد إلى أكثر من ستة قروش ومن تشرف بتلك الرحاب عرف حقيقة ما قلناه ولربما إذا كثرت الأنعام فيها وكثر السمن ترسل إلى غيرها من البلاد التي يجلب لها السمن من الخارج كجدة وأمثالها وتكون هذه تجارة واسعة في تلك البلاد وهذه الفوائد عدا فائدة ايجار البدو وجمالهم من مكة إلى عرفات بعد تمام السكة فان لنا عليها كلاماً مخصوصاً نذكره فيما يأتي إنشاء الله تعالى فأنه بالنسبة لبدو الحجاز أهم منها جميعها عندهم .

في بيان ما يستفيد بدو الشام من إنشاء هذه السكة

لقد بينا أن في طريق الشام منها إلى معان بلاد كثيرة وقرى خربة بالكلية وعامرة خالية ففي وجود السكة الحديدية في أراضي الشام إلى المدينة اعمار لهذه البلاد والأراضي المذكورة وانشاء بلاد أخرى غيرها على طول هذا الخط وبذلك تحصل الثروة والغنا لكافة الأهالي سيما للبدو المجاورين له بل ولغيرهم مما في تلك البرية العظيمة الواسعة المخصبة وان لم يتمدنوا وبقوا على بدويتهم الحاضرة لأن ثروة البدو بالغنم والمعز والجمال والبقر ولا ريب أنها إذا وجد مصرف لصوفها وسمنها وخرافها يزداد الاعتناء بها فتنمو وتكثر وكذلك إذا التفتت لاقتناء المعز وتربيتها فأنه بقطع النظر عن لبنها وفوائده تحصل منها (١٠٦) فوائد أخرى مهمة كالشعر والجدايا والجلود فأن لها قيمة عظيمة ومن نظر إلى أراضي الشام المخصبة ونظر إلى ما تحتاجه من

الغنم والسمن علم أنها في افتقار عظيم لهما ولكن الأراضي الصالحة لتربية الغنم بعيدة المسافة عن الشام وتحتاج إلى مصارفات للجلب منها والبدو لا يرون كبير فائدة في تربيتها الآن ويخافون من شن الغارة عليهم من بعضهم فيقتصرون على ما فيه كفايتهم وتجار الغنم والسمن الذين يذهبون إليهم يأخذون منهم اقة السمن بما لا قيمة له وقد يذهب إليهم الفلاحون من قرى الشام فيأخذون معهم من ثمار قراهم ويبادلون العرب اقة تفاح أو كمثرى أو عنب أو دبس بأقة سمن فلا يرى العرب كبير فائدة لتربية الغنم مع خوفهم الدائم من شن الغارة عليهم من غير قبايل والأراضي القريبة الصالحة لتربية الغنم غالية جداً فيصرف على الغنم منها أكثر مما تربحه على أن السمن الذي يجلب من جهة العرب المذكورين للشام ويقال له السمن القبلي والأكثر ان يكون من جوار البلقاء أحسن وأذكى وأطيب رائحة وألذ طعماً من جميع أنواع السمن سواء الوارد من حمص أو من حماة أو حلب أو الدير والمعروف بالحديدي فأهالي الشام يفضلونه على سائر أنواع السمن ويأخذونه بأكثر قيمة منها جميعها وهو قليل جداً وأكثر السمن في بلاد الشام من الجهات المذكورة فالسمن في جهات الشام قليل جداً وانما يحضر إليها من الخارج والبلاد المجاورة للشام كبيروت وطرابلس يرسل إليها السمن من تلك الجهات وكذلك الاستانة العلية في هذه المدة الأخيرة وبسبب جلبه إليها غلا سعره في الشام وحلب وتلك الجهات فقد كانت أقة السمن في الشام قبل ذلك تساوي سبعة قروش أما الآن فلا تقل عن ثلاثة (١٠٧) عشر هذا والذين يعتنون بالسمن الشامي في الاستانة هم أهل الذوق السليم وانهم بالنسبة لأهلها كنسبة واحد لخمسين أما باقيهم فيفضل سمن سويسرة والجاويريش عليه ويدعون ان رائحتهما المنتنة أطيب من رائحة السمن الشامي وأن السمن الشامي يفسد المعدة وما هذا إلا من فساد ذوقهم وشمهم ولقد صنع لي ارز بسمن سويسرة بعد مجيئي للاستانة أول مرة بخمسة عشر يوماً ولما احضر بين يدي هبت منه رائحة كرائحة الجيفة فسددت

أنفي ولم أقدر على أكله وكانت ليلة أول رمضان فصمت بغير سحور وهذا بقطع النظر عن أصل السمن المذكور فانه ليس سمناً وانما هو ادهان وشحوم حيوانات مذبوحة أو ميتة يضعونها في جلود الحيوانات الكبيرة كالبقر ويرسلونها إلى الأستانة وكثيراً يتوالد فيها الفار والجرذان ويرخص هذا السمن إذا كثر وذلك في زمان وقوع الوباء في الحيوانات الكبيرة ولقد سمعت من رؤساء الأطباء في الأستانة أنه نجس قطعا ومضر بالصحة فليحذر منه من لا يعرفه ولو اعتنى جميع أهل الأستانة بأكل السمن الشامي وتركوا غيره لغلا سعره حتى لا يتمكن من أكله في جهة الشام إلا الاغنياء المترفهون وعدمه الباقون فلله الحمد على ذلك فهذه البلاد مع كثرة الخصب فيها فقيرة من جهة السمن وكما هي فقيرة للسمن كذلك فقيرة للغنم فغنمها كله من البلاد البعيدة كارضروم ولا يصل إليها الا بعد ثلاثة أو أربعة أشهر ويتلف منه في الطريق شيء كثير وقد يتسلط عليه الموت من المرض المسمى بالروجة فيموت عن آخره وكذلك من شدة البرد والقر (١٠٨) ومع هذا فان التجار يربحون فيه ربحاً زائداً ويرسلون منه إلى مصر والاستانة وغيرهما فإذا تمدد قسم من هؤلاء البدو المقيمين في أرض الشام الذين هم كالجراد المنتشر ولا يحصى كثرتهم إلا هو تعالى والتفتوا إلى تربية الغنم وحدها بدون نظر إلى الزراعة لربحوا منها وحدها ومن صوفها وسمنها وجلودها وكذلك المعز والبقر اضعافاً مضاعفة عما تربحه الآن بل المثل مائة ولاستغنت الديار الشامية عن سمن حمص وحماه وحلب والدير والحديدي وغيرها وعن غنم أرضروم ونحوها واكتفت بما يزيد عندها من نمو الغنم وزيادة السمن والصوف والشعر والجلود عما يأتيها من الخارج ولزادت تجارة بلادها وصناعتها بذلك لأن هؤلاء البدو إذا اثروا يصرفون أموالهم في شراء الأمتعة والألبسة ونحوها من بلاد الشام بالضرورة وكما تستغني البلاد المذكورة عن السمن الذي يأتيها من الخارج تستغني الأستانة العلية عن السمن الذي يرد إليها من البلاد الأجنبية سيما المنتن المضر بالصحة القبيح الرائحة الذي ذكرنا فيما

سبق عنه انه يؤتى به في جلود الحيوانات الكبيرة مخلوطاً بشحوم الحيوانات التي لا يعلم نوعها هل هي مأكولة أو لا وهل هي مذبوحة أو مخنوقة وهل مريضة أو صحيحة إلى غير ذلك مما يدعو الدين إلى الاجتناب عنه والنفوس الذكية والطباع السليمة إلى الفرار منه بقطع النظر عن (١٠٩) رائحته المنتنة المنبئة عن حقيقته الذي لا يقبل عليه إلا من عدم الشم ولا يأكل منه إلا من فقد الذوق ولقد أخبرني جماعة متعاقبون ممن يوثق بهم أن الكلاب تذهب إلى مخازن السمن فإذا وجدت فيها من ظروف السمن المذكور واحداً مأخوذاً منه تلد فيه وذلك في أيام الشتاء فإذا جاء صاحبها ورآها تركها تربي أولادها رحمة منه بها وشفقة عليها من البرد وقد يقع ذلك في مكان البائع فيتركها في جهة ويبيع من جهة أخرى فالعجب ممن يدعى اللطافة والذوق كيف يقدم على أكله وممن يدعي علم حفظ الصحة والمحافظة على قواعده كيف يسمح به لأهله هذا شيء عجاب فإذا كثر هذا السمن القبلي في البلاد الشامية يزيد عن عوز أهل الشام ويكفي للبلاد المجاورة لها فترخص قيمته ويتوفر السمن الذي يأتيها من الخارج فيرسل جميع ذلك للأستانة العلية بقيمة رخيصة فتستغني الأستانة عما يرد إليها من البلاد الأجنبية وتبقى ثروة بلاد الدولة العلية فيها.

هذا بقطع النظر عما إذا التفتت نظارة المعارف والنافعة إلى تلك الأقطار فإذا التفتت إليها ومدت أهاليها بالأموال وأرسلت إليهم بعضاً من المخرجين من مكاتب الزراعة وسهلت لهم الطريق للحصول على ما يلزمهم للنفقات على تأسيس مكاتب زراعية وصناعية فعلمتهم (١١٠) الزراعة والصنائع فزرعوا ما تصلح أراضيهم لزرعه من الحبوب كالقمح والشعير والذرة والدخن والعدس والحمص والفول والكتان والقطن وغرسوا شجر التوت وربوا دود الحرير وأشجار الفواكه المتنوعة المتعددة مثل الكباد والليمون والتفاح والسفرجل والجوز واللوز والعنب والتين والأشجار غير المثمرة المحتاج إليها للعمارة كالحور والصفصاف وعلمتهم الحياكة والخياطة والدباغة والحدادة

والنجارة وعمل الخزف وما يحتاجون إليه من الصنائع التي تلزم لكل أحد واستكشفوا المعادن واستخرجوها لأصبحت هذه الأراضي معمورة مأهولة أكثر مما كانت قبل ولأصبح أهلها أغنياء أصحاب ثروة عظيمة وتوطد الأمن بينهم وفشا التمدن فيهم واكتسبوا المعالي وازروا باللآلي فان فيهم ذكاء وفصاحة وهمة ونجابة وقربا من التمدن والتعلم والترقي والاكتساب وبعدا عن الخيانة والبلادة والأرتياب وهذا الاعمار والتمدن والحضارة وتعميم الزراعة والصناعة والتجارة وتسهيل السبل للسالكين وتأمين الطرق للمارين لا يكون إلاّ بواسطة هذه السكة الحديدية فنسأله تعالى أن ييسر ما فيه نجاح هذه الأمة المحمدية وفلاح الدولة العلية العثمانية .

في بيان إنشاء هذه السكة من اعداد القوة المأمورين به

لا يخفى على أولى الاطلاح والمعارف على حقائق الأمور ودقائقها وذوي التضلع بالعلوم الدينية ورقائقها ان الممالك الدولية مفتقرة لأن تكون قريبة من عواصمها لتسهل المخابرة والمحافظة والنقل والحركة عند الاقتضاء وان الحرمين (١١١) الشريفين هما نقطتا الانتفاع الإسلامي وقطبا محور الدين المحمدي وعليهما اتفاق الملة الحنيفية وإليهما مرجع الأمة الإسلامية ومطمع انظار كل مسلم ومزدحم أقدام كل خلال ومحرم والحاكم عليهما هو الخليفة الأعظم لرسول رب العالمين صلى الله تعالى عليه وآله وصحبه وسلم فكانت المحافظة عليهما من أضر الضروريات وكذلك ما تعلق بهما وكان في جهتهما ولا ريب أن الحصول على ذلك لا يتأتى الا بحيث يمكن الوصول إليهما حين اللزوم على الفور والتعقيب لا على الامهال والتراخي وان المهيئ للوصول لذلك من اعداد القوة وقد امرنا الله تعالى به في القرآن المجيد قال عز من قائل واعدوا لهم ما استطعتم من قوة ومن رباط الخيل ترحبون به عدو الله وعدوكم وآخرين من دونهم لا تعلمونهم الله يعلمهم وما تنفقوا من شيء في سبيل الله يوف إليكم وأنتم لا تظلمون

فبعد البلاد بعضها عن بعض خصوصاً عن البلاد التي هي مركز من بيدهم أمرهم ونهيهم ومصالحهم وأحكامهم وسياستهم والمدافعة والذب عنهم والمحافظة عليهم وعلى حقوقهم عندما تمس حقوقهم أو يقتضي الحال ذلك وهذا من أهم المهمات ولذا كثر السفر في البحر وزاد على السفر في البر فيما يمكن الوصول إلى محل القصد منه في البحر انعدم من البر بالكلية لبعد المسافة فهذا على ما في سفر البحر من تصادف الأخطار العظيمة مثل الأنواء الشديدة وتعطل آلات البواخر البخارية وشبوب النار فيها وهبوب الرياح المعاكسة لها ومصادفة (١١٢) الأعداء في أثناء سيرها أو منع بعض الدول مرورها في ممالكها إلى غير ذلك مما هو معلوم لا يحتاج إلى ذكر فكانت سرعة أسباب الإتصالات البرية أولى من أسباب سرعة الإتصالات البحرية وأقل خطراً وأكثر فائدة فإذا فرض أن دولة هاجمت دولة أخرى أو وقعت فتنة في جهة من الجهات وليس فيها من القوة الدولية الحاكمة عليها ما يكفي لمنعها أو رد الرعية بعضها عن بعض واحتيج للمخابرة مع من بيدهم الأمر ولهم الرأي وآل الأمر إلى ارسال مهمات وقوة تمنع التعدي وتكف الفتنة لتفاقم الخطب وعظم الخلل وخربت البلاد وفنيت العباد.

وهذا بقطع النظر عن مهاجمة عدو من الأعداء جهة شاسعة من الجهات فانه إذا انعدمت الأسباب لسرعة النقل والاتصال يتمكن العدو منها قبل وصول القوة المانعة بل قبل وصول الخبر إذا كان السلك البرقي معدوماً أو معطلا كما يقع كثيراً عند وقوع الحوادث فان المهيجين والأعداء أول ما يبتدئون به قطع السلك البرقي أو تخريبه لقطع المخابرة فبهذا الاعتبار كان إنشاء السكة الحديدية من أعظم إعداد القوة المأمورين به في القرآن بل أعظمه في هذا الزمان وقد أمرنا الله تعالى به في صريح القرآن فقال واعدوا لهم ما استطعتم من قوة الآية فإذا كان إنشاء هذه السكة من هذه الجهة مثل استحضار السلاح والمدافع والبارود والفشك والخيل وأمثالها لا يكون بينها فرق بل يكون إنشاء السكة الحديدية أحق بالتقديم (١١٣) على غيرها لتوقف

استعمال باقي القوة عليها في بعض الأماكن فانه إذا كانت الأسلحة متوفرة والعساكر منظمة ولا سبيل للوصول إلى محل الايجاب واللزوم كانت العساكر والأسلحة بالنسبة لعدم امكان الانتفاع بها في حكم العدم بل لو كانت الأسباب المسهلة للوصول مثل السكة الحديدية متوفرة ووصلت العساكر له وان لم يكن معها أسلحة كافية أو كانت غير منظمة كان وصولها ووجودها في محل اللزوم لا يخلو عن فوائد فضلا عن فائدة كما هو معلوم لا يحتاج إلى بيان .

فالسكة الحديدية في البر أعظم نفعاً من البواخر البخارية في البحر لامكان الانتفاع بها في كل زمان بخلاف البواخر البحرية فقد يحول دون الانتفاع بها مصاعبات لا يمكن التخلص منها وقد تكون أخطار البحر لا يمكن دفعها كالأنواع[15] وقد يؤول الحال إلى انعدام الباخرة بما فيها غرقاً أو حرقاً أو غلبة دون السكة الحديدية فانها لا تعدم بالكلية وان كانت لا تخلو من أخطار أيضاً إلا أنها بالنسبة لخطر البواخر واحدا في المائة فكانت أهم منها سيما في الصحارى والقفار القابلة للاستغلال والتمدن والعمران وعدمت منها فانها تعمر البلاد وتؤسس فيها المدنية وتكثر المزروعات والمحصولات لتسهيلها الأسباب وتصييرها مركزاً للتجارة لتوفر أسباب النقليات فيها كما في هذه السكة الحديدية الحجازية الشامية (١١٤) ومن أعظم معدات القوة للأعداء ثم هذه الآية الكريمة من ابلغ جوامع الكلم وأجمعها وقد اشتملت على الأمر الصريح باعداد ما في الاستطاعة من القوة الأمر فيها للوجوب ولم تقيده بشيء دون شيء بل جاءت عامة لتشمل إعداد القوة بجميع أنواعها بحسب الزمان والمكان فتشمل الرمى والحصون والبواخر والمدافع والتربيل والديناميت والسكك وأمثالها ومن المعلوم ان الاعداد يكون قبل اللزوم فهذه الآية تنهى عن الاهمال إلى حين اللزوم بل تأمر بالاعداد قبله فان تدارك الأمر عند لزومه لا يفيد وان كان لا يخلو عن فائدة قد لا تساعد الظروف عليه فيحول بيننا وبينه موانع كعدم وجود الدراهم أو وجود ما يلزم أو فوات الفرصة

[15] الأنواء Read

إلى غير ذلك من الأسباب التي تعرض فإذا لم نستعد قبل اللزوم لا نخرج من ربقة إثم مخالفة أمر الله الصريح في كتابه الذي أنزل على نبيه وأمنا به وعاهدناه ان نعمل بمضمونه فلا نخرج من عهدة هذا الأمر إلا باعداد القوة اللازمة لنا لمقابلة اعدائنا قبل الاحتياج إليها وقد جاء في هذه الآية الكريمة التخصيص للأمر برباط الخيل لما فيه من عظيم الفائدة في الحروب وزيادة وقعها عند الاحتياج واللزوم ولأنها تحتاج إلى ترويض وتطبيع ولا يمكن الإنسان أن يركب ما لم يكن معتاداً مطبوعاً على الركوب ولذا كان الأمر بربباطها وايد هذا الأمر بها بخصوصها ما جاء في كثير من الأحاديث الشريفة من النص على رباطها فقد ورد في الحديث (١١٥) عن أبي هريرة رضي الله تعالى عنه قال قال رسول الله صلى الله عليه وسلم الخيل معقود في نواصيها الخير إلى يوم القيمة والخيل ثلاثة خيل اجر وخيل وزر وخيل ستر فأما الستر فمن اتخذها تعففا وتكرما وتجملا ولم ينس حق بطونها وظهورها في عسره ويسره وأما خيل الأجر فمن ارتبطها في سبيل الله فانها لا تغيب في بطونها شيئاً إلا كان له اجرا حتى ذكر أرواثها وأبوالها ولا تعدو في واد شوطا أو شوطين إلا كان له في ميزانه وأما الوزر فمن ارتبطها تبذخا على الناس فانها لا تغيب في بطونها شيئاً الا كان وزرا عليه حتى ذكر أرواثها وأبوالها ولا تعدو في واد شوطا أو شوطين الا كان عليه وزرا رواه ابن أبي شيبة ومسلم والبيهقي وأخرجه الطبراني والأجرى عن أبي كبشة رضي الله تعالى عنه قال قال رسول الله صلى الله تعالى عليه وسلم الخيل معقود في نواصيها الخير إلى يوم القيمة وأهلها معانون والمنفق عليها كالباسط يده بالصدقة والأحاديث فيها كثيرة وقد افرد العلماء في الخيل وفضل رباطها وما جاء فيها وأنواعها وما يتعلق بها اسفارا مخصوصة قديما وحديثا فارجع إليها إن شئت.

ولما كان الرمى كالفروسة لا يستغني عنه بحال من الأحوال سلما وحربا أمر به صلى الله تعالى عليه وآله وصحبه وسلم وخص عليه

بخصوصه فمن ذلك ما رواه مسلم عن عقبة بن عامر قال سمعت رسول الله صلى الله عليه وسلم يقول ستفتح عليكم الروم ويكفيكم الله فلا يعجز احدكم ان يلهو باسمه وعنه أيضاً في حديث طويل قال سمعته يقول (١١٦) من تعلم الرمى ثم تركه فليس منا وقد عصى فان الخيل والرمى لا يستغنى عنهما حرب أو مقابلة عدو وفي أي زمان ومكان كان ومهما تغيرت الأحوال والقوات وقد أخرج أحمد ومسلم وأبو داود وابن ماجة وغيرهم عن عامر الجهني رضي الله تعالى عنه قال سمعت النبي صلى الله عليه وسلم يقول وهو على المنبر واعدوا لهم ما استطعتم من قوة إلا أن القوة الرمى إلا أن القوة الرمى قالها ثلاثا يعني أن معظم القوة الرمى لا أن القوة محصورة فيه فهو على حد قوله صلى الله تعالى عليه وآله وصحبه وسلم الحج عرفة أي معظم الحج عرفة مع ان أركانه أربعة النية والوقوف بعرفة والطواف والسعي والنص على الفروسة والرمى بخصوصهما من المعجزات الباهرة وكما الفوا مؤلفات في الخيل كما اسلفنا فقد ألفوا في الرمي كذلك أسفارا لعظيم اعتنائهم فرحمهم الله تعالى فينبغي تعلمها والمداومة عليها لكل أحد حتى يكون فيهما السابق الأول. وليس الرمي مختصاً بالنبل كما كان في الزمن الأول بل المراد به الأعم كما أطلق في الحديث الثاني وغيره فالرمي بالنبل والرصاص والبندق والمدفع والمنجنيق وغيرها من كل ما يلزم داخل في الأمر بالرمي وقد جاء الأمر به مطلقاً فعن سعد بن أبي وقاص رضي الله تعالى عنهما قال تعلموا الرمي فانه خير لعبكم وعن البيهقي عن ابن عمر رضي الله تعالى عنهما قال قال رسول الله صلى الله عليه وسلم علموا ابناءكم السباحة والرمي والمرأة المغزل رواه ابن مندة عن بكر بن عبد الله بن الربيع الأنصاري رضي الله عنه وكتب سيدنا أمير المؤمنين عمر بن الخطاب (١١٧) رضي الله تعالى عنه ان علموا أولادكم السباحة والفروسية وجعل صلى الله تعالى عليه وآله وصحبه وسلم تعليم الرمي من حق الولد على والده ففي الحديث الشريف عن أبي رافع رضي الله تعالى عنه قال قال رسول

الله صلى الله عليه وسلم حق الولد على الوالد أن يعلمه الكتابة والسباحة والرماية رواه ابن أبي الدنيا والبيهقي وفي غيره وأن يحسن اسمه وفي آخر ويزوجه إذا بلغ والحاصل ان الفروسة والرمي والسباحة من الأمور المهتم بها شرعاً والواردة الأحاديث بتعلمها وتعليمها وهي كثيرة لا تكاد تحصر وانشاء هذه السكة أعظم اعداد القوة في زماننا ولا يتقاعد عنه أو يرجف فيه إلا من له غرض في قلبه يخفيه والله مخرج ما كنتم تكتمون وسيعلم الذين ظلموا أي منقلب ينقلبون .

في ان الانفاق في إنشاء هذه السكة اعمار للحرمين الشريفين وبيان اجره

إن الله تعالى حث في القرآن المجيد على عمارة المساجد وبين فيه أنه انما يعمرها المؤمنون وحقق هدايتهم إذا فعلوها فقال عز من قائل انما يعمر مساجد الله من آمن بالله واليوم الآخر وأقام الصلاة وآتى الزكاة ولم يخش إلا الله فعسى اولئك ان يكونوا من المهتدين أي قطعاً وبتاً .

وإعمار المساجد إما ان يكون ببنائها مجدداً أو اصلاحها وإما أن يكون بالاقامة فيها للعبادة واقامة شعار الدين وكل منهما يصدق عليه إعمار لها والآية الكريمة تصدق على كل منهما وقد جاء في الحديث الشريف الحث عليها أيضاً (١١٨) فعن البخاري ومسلم عن أمير المؤمنين سيدنا عثمان بن عفان رضي الله تعالى عنه قال سمعت رسول الله صلى الله عليه وسلم قال من بنى لله مسجداً يبتغي به وجه الله تعالى بنى الله له بيتاً في الجنة وعن البخاري ومسلم أيضاً عن أبي هريرة رضي الله تعالى عنه ان النبي صلى الله تعالى عليه وسلم قال من غدا إلى المسجد أو راح اعد الله له في الجنة نزلا كلما غدا أو راح والنزل ما يهيأ للضيف عند نزوله بالقوم وعن الترمذي عن أبي سعيد الخضري رضي الله تعالى عنه عن رسول الله صلى الله عليه وسلم انه قال إذا رأيتم الرجل يعتاد المساجد فاشهدوا له بالإيمان فان الله عز وجل يقول انما يعمر مساجد الله من آمن بالله واليوم الآخر الآية وقال

الترمذي حديث حسن وقد رأينا من اسلافنا من كان يلازم المساجد لا يخرج منها إلا لحاجة كوالدي رحمه الله تعالى فانه لازم المسجد الشريف الأموي في دمشق الشام مدة حياته لم يفارقه إلا لضرورة وكان يصلي فيه اماما أول ويجلس على التخت الذي كان فيه تجاه ضريح سيدنا يحيى عليه السلام في الجانب الشمالي حتى عرف التخت به ويقرئ عليه العلوم سيما الفقه والحديث ويفتي السائلين يقصد للفتوى من الجهات البعيدة وكثيراً ما يقصد لتعبير الرؤيا فقد كان رحمه الله تعالى له فيه اليد الطولى كالفقه الشافعي حتى انه كان يعبر عنه بالشافعي الصغير وكان لا يفتر عن قراءة القرآن أو الذكر أو الصلاة على النبي صلى الله تعالى عليه وآله وصحبه وسلم أو اقرأ العلم والفتوى ما رؤى ساكتاً ولا عابثاً وبقي على تلك الحال الحسنة إلى أن توفاه الله تعالى فرحمه الله تعالى رحمة واسعة (١١٩) ولا ريب ان عمارة المسجدين الحرامين مسجد مكة ومسجد النبي صلى الله تعالى عليه وسلم يحصل بانشاء هذه السكة ويزداد يوماً فيوماً وسواء كان الاعمار بالاصلاح والبناء أو بالذكر والصلاة والتعليم فيه فان للمسببين في انشاء هذه السكة والمنشئين لها أجر المعمرين للمسجدين الحرامين بكلا قسمي الاعمار من غير ان ينقص من اجر المعمرين شيئاً لقوله صلى الله تعالى عليه وآله وصحبه وسلم من سن حسنة فله أجرها وأجر من عمل بها إلى يوم القيمة فالمسببون لانشاء هذه السكة والمنشئون لها بالمال أو بالنفس والمعمرون للمسجدين الحرامين بالصلاة والذكر واشبههما وبالمال في الأجراء سواء من غير أن ينقص من أجر احدهم شيء فمن يعن على انشاء هذه السكة الحديدية الحجازية الشامية يكن معمرا للمسجدين الحرامين وقد رأيت ما أعد الله تعالى لمن يعمر مسجدا من المساجد من الأجر والثواب فما بالك بمن يعمر المسجدين الحرامين فأن الحسنة تضاعف فيهما إلى أمثال أمثالها أما الصلاة في مسجد مكة فتضاعف إلى مائة ألف وأما في مسجد المدينة فإلى ألف والمراد به المسجد الذي كان في زمانه صلى الله تعالى عليه

وآله وصحبه وسلم لا ما زيد فيه بعده كما رواه الإمام أحمد في مسنده والبيهقي في سننه وغيرهما عن عبد الله بن الزبير رضي الله تعالى عنهما ان رسول الله صلى الله عليه وسلم قال صلاة في مسجدي هذا أفضل من ألف صلاة فيما سواه من المساجد (١٢٠) إلا المسجد الحرام وصلاة في المسجد الحرام أفضل من مائة صلاة في مسجدي فكانت مكة أفضل من المدينة وهذا بناء على قول الإمام الشافعي وأبي حنيفة وأحمد رضي الله تعالى عنهم ومن وافقهم فيه وأما على قول الإمام مالك رضي الله تعالى عنه فالمدينة أفضل وهذا خلاف مشهور وكما تضاعف فيهما الحسنات تضاعف السيئآت حتّى ان الهم بالسيئة في غير الحرمين لا يكتب على صاحبه سيئة بخلافه في مكة قال الله تعالى ومن يرد فيه بإلحاد بظلم نذقه من عذاب أليم قال في الدر المنثور وأخرج ابن أبي شيبة وعبد بن حميد وابن المنذر عن مجاهد قال تضاعف السيئات بمكة كما تضاعف الحسنات وأخرج عن عكرمة قال ما من عبد يهم بذنب فيؤاخذه الله بشيء حتّى يعمله الا من هم بالبيت العتيق شرا فانه من هم شرا عجل الله له واخرج عن أبي الحجاج في الآية قال ان الرجل يحدث نفسه ان يعمل ذنبا بمكة فيكتبه الله تعالى عليه ذنباً وعن ابن مسعود في قوله ومن يرد فيه بإلحاد بظلم نذقه من عذاب أليم قال من هم بخطيئة فلم يعملها في سوى البيت لم تكتب عليه حتّى يعملها ومن هم بخطيئة في البيت لم يمته الله من الدنيا حتى يذيقه من عذاب أليم فيا طوبى لمن يوفقه الله تعالى للإعانة بانشاء هذه السكة اعماراً للحرمين اللذين تضاعف فيهما الحسنات ليكون له مثل اجر المعمر والله الموفق ويقول الحق وهو يهدي السبيل .

في ان إنشاء هذه السكة انفاق في سبيل الله وبيان أجره

(١٢١) لقد تحقق مما تقدم كون انشاء هذه السكة الحديدية من اعداد القوة للاعداء ومن اعمار المساجد المأمور بهما في القرآن المجيد على سبيل الوجوب والفرض والترغيب والأنفاق في كل منهما انفاق في سبيل الله .

وسبيل الله تعالى يطلق ويراد به الجهاد كقوله تعالى الذين آمنوا وهاجروا وجاهدوا بأموالهم وأنفسهم في سبيل الله ويطلق ويراد به وجوه البر كالصدقة الواجبة وهي الزكاة مثل قوله تعالى انما الصدقات للفقراء والمساكين والعاملين عليها والمؤلفة قلوبهم والغارمين وفي سبيل الله وابن السبيل فريضة من الله وقوله صلى الله تعالى عليه وآله وصحبه وسلم أنا آل محمد لا تحل لنا الصدقة وكالصدقة المسنونة كقوله تعالى مثل الذين ينفقون أموالهم في سبيل الله كمثل حبة انبتت سبع سنابل في كل سنبلة مائة حبة والله يضاعف لمن يشاء والله واسع عليم وقوله عز شأنه الذين ينفقون أموالهم في سبيل الله ثم لا يتبعون ما انفقوا منا ولا اذى لهم اجرهم عند ربهم ولا خوف عليهم ولا هم يحزنون .

ولا ريب ان اعانة المؤمن على الخير إذا كانت بالمال من وجوه البر الذي هو انفاق في سبيل الله فانشاء هذه السكة الحديدية الحجازية انفاق في سبيل الله بمعنى الجهاد لأنها من اعداد القوة للاعداء وانفاق في سبيل الله بمعنى وجوه البر والخيرات لإعمارها المساجد في الحرمين واعانة راكبيها (١٢٢) على العبادة بالزيارة والطواف واداء عمرة الإسلام والحج واقامة شعار الإسلام وتعاضد المسلمين وهذا كله من أعظم وجوه الانفاق في سبيل الله على ان المنفق فيها من حيث انها اعداد قوة للأعداء مجاهد كما هو صريح في نص القرآن قال تعالى الذين يجاهدون بأموالهم وأنفسهم في سبيل الله وقال عز وجل وفضل الله المجاهدين على القاعدين أجرا عظيما فسمى المنفق في الجهاد مجاهداً .

فالجهاد اما بالنفس أو بالمال والأول أفضل من الثاني وأفضل منهما الجهاد بهما معاً ففي الدر المنثور عن جماعة من الصحابة ان رسول الله صلى الله تعالى عليه وسلم قال من أرسل بنفقة في سبيل الله وأقام في بيته فله بكل درهم سبعمائة درهم ومن غزا بنفسه في سبيل الله وانفق في وجه ذلك فله بكل درهم يوم القيمة سبعمائة ألف درهم ثم تلا هذه الآية أي مثل الذين ينفقون أموالهم في سبيل الله كمثل حبة الآية وانما قدم تعالى في الآية المال على النفس لأن النفس تشح عادة بالمال

ولأن كثيراً من الناس لا قدرة لهم على الجهاد بالنفس ولأن الجهاد يتوقف عليه لاعداد القوة بل لا يمكن الجهاد بدونه خصوصاً في هذا الزمان فانه قد جرت العادة ان يقاتل الناس بالأجرة مع دولة لم يكونوا من تبعتها كما هو مشاهد معلوم فالمال في هذا الزمان يغني عنه الرجال لامكان استخدام الرجال بالمال وعدم امكان استخدام الرجال بدون المال .

فيلزم للدولة ان تكون دائماً غنية خزائنها مملوءة وهذا اعظم استعداد للدولة فالمال (١٢٣) هو الاستعداد فاذا كانت الدولة غنية كانت مستعدة بل في اعلى ذروة الاستعداد لأنه بالمال يحصل كل شيء ويكون الإنسان قادراً مع وجود المال على فعل كل شيء باذن الله تعالى فالدولة من باب أولى ولا يؤخر الدولة شيء أصلا مثل الاحتياج وعدم العدل فان المال والعدل قوام كل دولة فقدم تعالى المال في الذكر لذلك واهتماماً بشأن الذين لا قدرة لهم على الجهاد بالنفس فان اجرهم لا ينقص عن أجر المجاهدين بالنفس فعن زيد بن ثابت رضي الله تعالى عنه عن النبي صلى الله عليه وسلم قال من جهز غازيا في سبيل الله تعالى فله مثل أجره ومن خلف غازيا في أهله بخير وانفق على أهله كان له مثل أجره وروى أصحاب السنن الستة أن رسول الله صلى الله عليه وآله وسلم قال من جهز غازيا في سبيل الله فقد غزا ومن خلف غازيا في أهله بخير فقد غزا بل لو كان أحد جبانا وأراد الجهاد بالنفس واراد شجاع الجهاد ولا جهاز عنده وجهزه ذلك الجبان وانفق على عياله في غيابه وكفاه مؤنتهم وذهب ذلك الشجاع يقاتل كان الجبان القاعد أعظم اجراً مما لو ذهب هو نفسه سيما إذا كان يرجف العسكر بخوفه وجبنه فلربما يجب عليه ذلك ومثله ما إذا كان مريد الجهاد ذا عقل وتدبير لكنه فقير لا يقدر على الذهاب وآخر غني يقدر الا أن ذلك الفقير انفع للمصلحة منه فان الغني إذا جهز هذا الفقير يؤجر عليه أكثر مما إذا جاهد هو بنفسه وماله وأمثال هذا كثيرة والأمور بمقاصدها وترغيب الله تعالى في الانفاق في سبيله وذكر أجر المجاهدين (١٢٤) وتفضيلهم على القاعدين

في القرآن المجيد والحديث الشريف أكثر من أن يحصر قال الله تعالى وفضل الله المجاهدين على القاعدين أجراً عظيماً درجات منه ومغفرة ورحمة وكان الله غفوراً رحيماً وقال عز شأنه الذين آمنوا وهاجروا وجاهدوا في سبيل الله بأموالهم وأنفسهم أعظم درجات عند الله واولٰئك هم الفائزون يبشرهم ربهم برحمة منه ورضوان وجنات لهم فيها نعيم مقيم خالدين فيها أبداً ان الله عنده أجر عظيم وقال الله تعالى وما انفقتم من شيء فهو يخلفه وقال جل وعلا من ذا الذي يقرض الله قرضاً حسناً يضاعفه له ويغفر له وقال تقدس اسمه مثل الذين ينفقون اموالهم في سبيل الله كمثل حبة انبتت سبع سنابل في كل سنبلة مائة حبة والله يضاعف لمن يشاء وقال تبارك وتقدس الذين ينفقون أموالهم في سبيل الله ثم لا يتبعون ما انفقوا منا ولا أذى لهم أجرهم عند ربهم ولا خوف عليهم ولا هم يحزنون وقال صلى الله عليه وآله وصحبه وسلم النفقة في سبيل الله تضاعف بسبعمائة ضعف رواه البخاري في تاريخه وعن الطبراني عن معاذ بن جبل ان رسول الله صلى الله عليه وسلم قال طوبى لمن أكثر في الجهاد في سبيل الله من ذكر الله فأن له بكل كلمة سبعين ألف حسنة كل حسنة منها عشرة أضعاف مع الذي له عند الله من المزيد قيل يا رسول الله النفقة قال النفقة على قدر ذلك قال عبد الرحمن فقلت لمعاذ انما النفقة بسبعمائة ضعف فقال معاذ قل فهمك انما ذاك إذا انفقوها وهم مقيمون في أهلهم غير غزاة فاذا غزوا وانفقوا خبأ الله لهم من خزائن رحمته ما ينقطع عنه علم العباد وصفتهم فأولئك حزب الله (١٢٥) وحزب الله هم الغالبون والآيات والأحاديث والآثار في هذا الباب كثيرة فمن شاء زيادة على ما ذكرنا فليرجع إليها ولو لم يخرجنا ذكر أكثر من هذا عن القصد من تأليف هذه الرسالة لأتينا بما بقي بالمراد .

في ان إنشاء هذه السكة اعانة للمؤمنين وما في التعاون من الأجر

كنا ذكرنا طرفاً من الكلام على التعاون في مقالتنا اعظم المآثر

السنية وها نحن الآن نذكر ما يؤيد ذلك انشاء الله تعالى فنقول .

إن في انشاء هذه السكة الحديدية اعانة للمؤمنين على اداء فريضة الحج والعمرة وزيارة النبي صلى الله تعالى عليه وآله وصحبه وسلم والتجارة والصناعة والزراعة وتمدين المتوحشين واغناء الفقراء واشباع الجياع وثروة البلاد واحياء العباد إلى غير ذلك مما ذكرنا ويعلم باقيه منه فأن الذي ليس في قدرته الحج أو غيره مما ذكر أو في قدرته مع تحمل المشقة والزحمة في الطريق إذا تم إنشاء هذه السكة بحوله تعالى يحجون ويزورون ويتجرون ويفعلون ما يقصدونه في تلك البلاد بغاية السهولة والراحة وهذا اعانة من منشئيها سواء كان بالأمر أو بالنفس أو بالمال أو بالرأي والتشويق والتعاون على وجود الخير مندوب إليه شرعاً ومنصوص عليه في القرآن المجيد والحديث الشريف قال الله تعالى وتعاونوا على البر والتقوى ولا تعاونوا على الإثم والعدوان ومعصية الرسول وروى البخاري ومسلم والترمذي عن رسول الله صلى الله تعالى عليه وآله وصحبه وسلم أنه (١٢٦) قال من كان في حاجة أخيه كان الله في حاجته وروى مسلم عنه صلى الله عليه وسلم أنه قال من نفس عن مؤمن كربة من كرب الدنيا نفس الله عنه كربة من كرب يوم القيمة ومن يسر على معسر يسر الله عليه في الدنيا والآخرة والله في عون العبد ما كان العبد في عون أخيه ومن سلك طريقاً يلتمس فيه علما سهل الله له به طريقاً إلى الجنة وما اجتمع قوم في بيت من بيوت الله يتلون كتاب الله ويتدارسونه بينهم الا نزلت عليهم السكينة وغشيتهم الرحمة وحفتهم الملائكة وذكرهم الله فيمن عنده ومن بطأ به عمله لم يسرع به نسبه وروى الترمذي في صحيحه قال صلى الله عليه وسلم من نفس عن مؤمن كربة من كرب الدنيا نفس الله عنه كربة من كرب الآخرة ومن ستر على مسلم ستره الله في الدنيا والآخرة والله في عون العبد ما كان العبد في عون أخيه ومن أراد زيادة على ذلك فعليه بكتابنا أقرب القرب في تفريج الكرب فانشاء هذه السكة الحديدية اعانة للإخوان المؤمنين على اداء فريضة الحج

والعمرة والزيارة والتجارة وامثالها والله في عون المعين على انشائها ما دامت هذه السكة باقية وكذلك فيها تنفيس كرب السفر على الدواب أو مشياً على الأقدام وكرب الجوع والعطش والخوف وغير ذلك عن المؤمنين ولا ريب ان الله تعالى ينفس عن المسبب والمشارك والمعين على انشائها كربة بل كربات يوم القيمة .

في بيان ان في هذه السكة تعاضد المؤمنين وما فيه من النفع الدنيوي والاجر الاخروي

أعلم أن في إنشاء هذه السكة الحديدية تسهيل اتصال المؤمنين بعضهم ببعض (١٢٧) ولا ريب ان المؤمنين أخوة بالنص الصريح بالقرآن الصحيح قال الله تعالى انما المؤمنون أخوة والإيمان بالله تعالى ورسوله صلى الله تعالى عليه وآله وصحبه وسلم هو الرابطة الوحيدة لجمع رأيهم واتفاق كلمتهم وتوافقهم وتعاضدهم وفي التعاضد والاجتماع سيما على خليفة وأمير واحد كما هو الدين الإسلامي من الفوائد والنتائج الحسنة ما لا ينكره أحد .

قال الله تعالى على لسان سيدنا موسى عليه السلام واجعل لي وزيراً من أهلي هرون أخي اشدد به أزري واشركه في أمري وقال سبحانه وتعالى سنشد عضدك بأخيك وروى البخاري في صحيحه ان رسول الله صلى الله تعالى عليه وآله وصحبه وسلم قال المؤمن للمؤمن كالبنيان يشد بعضه بعضاً ثم شبك بين اصابعه ورواه مسلم في صحيحه أيضاً إلا أنه لم يرو ثم شبك وروى مسلم أيضاً عنه صلى الله عليه وسلم أنه قال مثل المؤمنين في توادهم وتراحمهم وتعاطفهم مثل الجسد إذا اشتكى منه عضو واحد تداعى له سائر الجسد بالسهر والحمى وعن أبي داود عنه صلى الله تعالى عليه وسلم انه قال ان حقاً على المؤمنين أن يتوجع بعضهم لبعض كما يألم الجسد الرأس . وأعظم واسطة لاكتشاف المؤمنين احوال بعضهم والوقوف على أخبارهم في البلاد البعيدة الشاسعة انما هو الحج ففي الحج فوائد دينية وسياسية تقدم ذكر بعضها وليس

هنا محل ذكر باقيها وهي معلومة لكل من له شعور بعلوم الدين واسرار القرآن وابنا انموذجاً منها في مقالتنا أعظم المآثر . (١٢٨)

وبالجملة ففي تعاضد المؤمنين وتعاونهم سر خفي بل جلي فيه قوام الدين والملك ولا ريب ان في التعاضد نجاة كبيرة من كيد الأعداء فتعاضد المؤمنين ظاهراً وباطناً بحيث يكونون كالعضو الواحد يمكنهم من كف اذى اعدائهم عن دينهم وملكهم وأنفسهم ويجلب لهم المنفعة التي لا تكون إلا به . والتعاضد المأمور به في الشرع لا يكون إلا باجتماع الرأي والكلمة وهذا أيضاً لا يكون إلا بالاجتماع على إمام واحد وأمير واحد والانقياد لأوامره ونواهيه كما هو مقتضى الشرع المحمدي الشريف فانه أوجب على المسلمين جميعهم ان يتبعوا إماماً واحداً وهو خليفة الرسول الأعظم صلى الله تعالى عليه وآله وصحبه وسلم روى ابن ماجه عن سيدنا عرفجة الاشجعي رضي الله تعالى عنه ان النبي صلى الله تعالى عليه وسلم قال من أتاكم وأمركم جميع على رجل واحد يريد ان يشق عصاكم أو يفرق فيما بينكم فاقتلوه فاذا كان المسلمون كلهم أجمعون سواء في اتباعه لا يقدر على مقاومتهم أحد وهذا ضروري لبقاء الأمة المحمدية لا مندوحة لهم عنها ويكفي هذا القدر في البيان هنا فانه معلوم لكل من رفع الغرض ونظر بعين الإنصاف وخلا من المرض فقد ضاق شبر عن مسير والله الموفق وإليه المصير .

شعر

(١٢٩) وبالتعاضد تلقي الخير أجمعه
وبالتفرق تلقي الشر والفشلا
فانبذ وراءك حب الذات منفرداً
فبالتعاضد كل يدرك الا ملا

هذا وكما ان في التعاضد منافع دنيوية لا تحصى فكذلك فيه أجور اخروية لا تستقصى وحيث كان انشاء هذه السكة الحديدية سبباً

للتعاضد كما قدمنا كان أجر ما نشأ عنه من النجاح الدنيوي والفلاح الاخروي للمتسبب والمعين بالمال والنفس والرأي والتشويق والله تعالى ولي التوفيق .

في وجوب طاعة أمير المؤمنين على كل مؤمن بالاعانة على إنشاء هذه السكة وحرمة مخالفته والتخلف عنه

طاعة السلطان حق واجب   جاءنا القرآن فيها والحديث
كل مسلم يخالف هـذا   فهو لا شك منافق خبيث

لقد اثبتنا ان انشاء هذه السكة الحديدية من اعداد القوة المأمورين بها في صريح القرآن المجيد أمر وجوب ومما يعين على التعاضد المرغب فيه شرعاً وعلى اداء فريضة الحج والعمرة والزيارة وعمارة المسجدين الحرامين وتوسيع نطاق التجارة والصناعة والزراعة وتسهيل ادخال المدنية بين الأمم الوحشية وتأمين السبل المخوفة وتسهيل الطرق الصعبة واعمار البلاد واسعاد العباد إلى غير ذلك من الأمور التي جاء بها هذا الدين المحمدي الحاوي العدل والفضل والطهارة والنظافة ولا ريب ان الحج احد الأركان (١٣٠) التي بني عليها الإسلام في قوله عليه وآله وصحبه الصلاة والسلام بني الإسلام على خمس شهادة أن لا إله إلا الله وان محمداً رسول الله وأقام الصلاة وايتاء الزكاة وحج البيت وصوم رمضان وقد ثبتت فريضته بالكتاب والسنة وهو معلوم من الدين بالضرورة ولا حاجة لسرد دلائل فريضته فانها جمة كثيرة كقوله تعالى ولله على الناس حج البيت من استطاع إليه سبيلا وقد اسلفنا ما في الحج والتعاون والتعاضد والانفاق في سبيل الله فلا داعي لإعادته وفيه الغناء عن ذكر غيره ويكفي المعتنى بشأنها والمعين على انشائها من حيث انها اعداد قوة قوله تعالى واعدوا لهم ما استطعتم من قوة ومن رباط الخيل ترهبون به عدو الله وعدوكم وقال عز شأنه يا أيها الذين آمنوا استجيبوا لله وللرسول إذا دعاكم لما يحييكم واعلموا ان الله يحول بين المرء وقلبه وانكم إليه تحشرون واخرج

ابن اسحاق وابن أبي حاتم في قوله تعالى لما يحييكم أي للحرب التي اعزكم الله فيها بعد الذل وقواكم بها بعد الضعف ومنعكم بها من عدوكم بعد القهر منهم لكم ولا مرية في ان اعداد القوة حكمها حكم الحرب لأنها واسطته التي يكون بها وفي ان الاستجابة لأولى الأمر إذا دعوا للحرب واجبة كالاستجابة لله وللرسول إذا دعوا له ومن حيث انها سبيل لعمارة المسجدين الحرامين قوله تعالى انما يعمر مساجد الله من آمن بالله واليوم الآخر وأقام الصلاة وآتى الزكاة ولم يخش إلا الله فعسى أولئك أن يكونوا من المهتدين (١٣١) فأن فيه التصريح بأنه من المهتدين باعتبار كونها سبباً لاعمار المسجدين الحرامين من حيث أنها لا يعمرها الا المؤمنون وقوله عز شأنه ما كان للمشركين ان يعمروا مساجد الله شاهدين على انفسهم بالكفر اولئك حبطت اعمالهم وفي النار هم خالدون الدال بالالتزام على ان الذين يمنعون من انشائها والمتسبب عنه عدم اعمار المسجدين لم يشهد القرآن لهم بالإيمان ومن حيث انها انفاق في سبيل الله قوله جل جلاله ومثل الذين ينفقون أموالهم ابتغاء مرضات الله وتثبيتاً من انفسهم كمثل جنّة بربوة أصابها وابل فأتت اكلها ضعفين فان لم يصبها وابل فظل ومن حيث انها اعانة للمؤمنين على البر والتقوى قوله تبارك اسمه وتعاونوا على البر والتقوى ومن حيث ان جزاءها من الله قوله تعالى من ذا الذي يقرض الله قرضاً حسناً يضاعفه له ويغفر له ومن حيث ان الارجاف فيها منع للخير قوله تقدس وعلا مناع للخير معتد اثيم وامثال هذه الآيات مما يرغب في انشائها ويصد عن الصد عنها كثيرة كقوله جلت عظمته ان الذين كفروا ينفقون أموالهم ليصدوا عن سبيل الله فينفقونها ثم تكون عليهم حسرة ثم يغلبون ومن حيث ان الامتثال في انشائها اطاعة لله ورسوله ولأمير المؤمنين قوله تعالى يا أيها الذين آمنوا أطيعوا الله واطيعوا الرسول وأولى الأمر منكم.

والأمر باطاعة أمير المؤمنين في اوامره ونواهيه بما جاء به الدين مطلقاً مما (١٣٢) اتفقت عليه المسلمون وجاءت الدلائل الصريحة

الظاهرة التي لا تحتمل التأويل بوجوبه على كل مسلم كقوله تعالى يا أيها الذين آمنوا أطيعوا الله وأطيعوا الرسول وأولى الأمر منكم وقوله تعالى ومن يطع الرسول فقد أطاع الله وقوله صلى الله عليه وسلم من أطاعني فقد أطاع الله ومن عصاني فقد عصى الله ومن يطع الأمير فقد أطاعني ومن يعص الأمير فقد عصاني وقوله عليه وآله وصحبه الصلاة والسلام طاعة الإمام حق على المرء المسلم ما لم يأمر بمعصية الله فإذا أمر بمعصية الله فلا طاعة له والأحاديث الواردة. بالنهي عن مخالفته جمة وافرة فمنها قوله صلى الله تعالى عليه وآله وصحبه وسلم ثلاثة لا تسأل عنهم رجل فارق الجماعة وعصى إمامه ومات عاصياً وأمة أو عبد أبق من سيده فمات وامرأة غاب عنها زوجها وقد كفاها مؤنة الدنيا فتبرجت فلا تسأل عنهم وقوله عليه وآله وصحبه الصلاة والسلام من خرج عن السلطان مات ميتة جاهلية وفي حديث آخر فانه ليس أحد يفارق الجماعة شبراً فيموت إلا مات ميتة جاهلية.

ولا شك عند المحققين ان المراد بأولى الأمر في قوله تعالى يا أيها الذين آمنوا أطيعوا الله واطيعوا الرسول وأولى الأمر منكم الإمام الأعظم ونوابه لا العلماء كما قاله بعض المفسرين ففي الدر المنثور عند قوله تعالى وأولى الأمر منكم واخرج ابن جرير عن ابن زيد قال قال أبي هم السلاطين قال قال رسول الله صلى الله عليه وسلم الطاعة الطاعة وفي الطاعة بلاء وقال لو شاء الله لجعل الأمر في الأنبياء (١٣٣) يعني لقد جعل إليهم والأنبياء معهم الا ترى حين حكموا في قتل يحيى بن زكريا انتهى عليهما السلام وأصرح منه قوله تعالى في قصة داود وقال لهم نبيهم ان الله قد بعث لكم طالوت ملكاً فكان الملك غير النبي لكن هذا في الأمم الماضية أما رسولنا صلى الله عليه وآله وصحبه وسلم فلم يكن معه ملك وان يكن اختار العبودية على الملك فكان الحكم له صلى الله تعالى عليه وآله وصحبه وسلم ولخلفائه الراشدين من بعده لا للعلماء ويمكن ان يكون قوله عليه الصلاة والسلام علماء أمتي

كانبياء بني اسرائيل دالا على هذا كما دل على غيره وذلك لأن العلماء مبينون للأحكام لا آمرون ولا منفذون فان الأوامر والنواهي بيد الإمام ولا يجوز الافتيات[16] عليه في الاحكام ويعين ان المراد بأولى الأمر في الآية الإمام ونوابه لا العلماء تتمة الآية وهي قوله تعالى فإن تنازعتم في شيء فردوه إلى الله والرسول ذلك خير وأحسن تأويلا وقوله تعالى فلا وربك لا يؤمنون حتى يحكموك فيما شجر بينهم ثم لا يجدوا في أنفسهم حرجاً مما قضيت ويسلموا تسليماً فدل ذلك على أن المراد بقوله وأولى الأمر الإمام لا العلماء لأن قوله فإن تنازعتم في شيء فردوه إلى الله والرسول وقوله فلا وربك لا يؤمنون حتى يحكموك فيما شجر بينهم ثم لا يجدوا في أنفسهم حرجاً مما قضيت صريحان في الحكم والقضاء فالرد حينئذ لله والرسول للقضاء والحكم فيه فالرسول صلى الله تعالى عليه وآله وصحبه وسلم يقضي ويحكم بشرع الله الذي أنزل عليه فرده إليه رد لله وليس العلماء حكاماً بل الإمام باعتبار انه خليفة الرسول صلى الله تعالى عليه وآله وصحبه (١٣٤) وسلم فكان هو ونوابه أولى الأمر المذكورين في الآية الكريمة والمأمورين فيها بطاعتهم فكانت طاعة الإمام خليفة الرسول صلى الله تعالى عليه وسلم واجبة من طاعة الله والرسول واما ان كان أولو الأمر علماء فطاعتهم واجبة لكونهم أولي الأمر لا لكونهم علماء كما في القضاة وأمثالهم واما إذا افتى العالم بأمر شرعي فيجب على من صدقه العمل بفتياه لأنها حكم الله تعالى لا لكونها أمره بخلاف ما إذا أمر ألوا[17] الأمر بما لم يخالف الشرع فإن اطاعتهم فيه واجبة للأمر فقط إذ قد يكون مندوباً في أصله فإذا أمر به الإمام يصير واجباً وهذا هو الفرق بينهما ثم بعد كتابتي هذا وجدت ان مذهب أهل الله السادة الصوفية نفعنا الله تعالى بهم في المراد بأولى الأمر في الآية الكريمة الإمام ونوابه كما قلناه وقال سيدنا قدوة العارفين الشيخ الأكبر في الفتوحات المكية في الباب السادس والثلاثين وثلاثمائة ما نصه فلما كان الناس شجرات جعل فيهم ولاة يرجعون إليهم إذا اختصموا ليحكموا بينهم

16 افتاآت or افتاءات Read

17 أولو Read

ليزول حكم التشاجر وجعل لهم إماماً في الظاهر واحداً يرجع إليه أمر الجميع لاقامة الدين وأمر عباده ان لا ينازعوه ومن ظهر عليه ونازعه أمرنا الله كما علم ان منازعته تؤدي إلى فساد في الدين باقامته وقتاله وأصله قوله تعالى لو كان فيهما الهة الا الله لفسدتا انتهى وكلامه هذا جدير بالنظر إليه بعين الدقة لأنه يشتمل على معان تجل عن الشبه ثم قال وقد أخذه من الكتاب والسنة وأمرنا الله تعالى ان لا نخرج يدا من طاعته ثم قال فحق الإمام أحق بالاتباع (١٣٥) قال الله تعالى يا أيها الذين آمنوا اطيعوا الله واطيعوا الرسول واولى الأمر منكم وهم الاقطاب والخلفاء والولاة وما بقي لهم حكم إلا في صنف ما ابيح التصرف فيه فان الواجب والمحظور من طاعة الله وطاعة رسوله فما بقي للأئمة الا المباح ولا أجر فيه ولا وزر فاذا امرك الإمام المقدم عليك الذي بايعته على السمع والطاعة بأمر من المباحات وجب عليك طاعته في ذلك وحرمت عليك مخالفته وصارحكم ذلك الذي كان مباحاً واجباً فيحصل للإنسان إذا عمل بأمره أجر الواجب وارتفع حكم الإباحة منه بأمر الذي بايعته فتدبر انتهى فثبت ان طاعة الإمام خليفة الرسول صلى الله تعالى عليه وسلم واجبة فيما فيه طاعة الله والرسول على العموم وسأولف في هذا الموضوع رسالة مستقلة انشاء الله تعالى وبانشاء هذه السكة على الخصوص لأنه لإطاعة الله والرسول في شيء مما يأمر به الخليفة أعظم من الاطاعة في أمره بانشاء هذه السكة باعتبار ما ذكرنا مما اشتملت عليه من الأمور التي أمر بها الشارع وأوجبها وحث عليها فكانت طاعة هذا الخليفة في انشاء هذه السكة واتمامها واجبة على كل مسلم بحسب اقتداره اما بالمال أو بالنفس أو بهما معاً حسبما يحكم عليه الشرع والله تعالى الهادي إلى سواء السبيل.

في بيان ما يلزم من الجمال للحجاج فيما بين ينبع والمدينة وللصعود لعرفات ذهاباً واياباً بعد إنشاء السكة

إن الجمال التي يؤجرها بدو الحجاز من ينبع إلى المدينة المنورة

للزوار والتجار والحجاج (١٣٦) يزيد عددها بعد مد السكة الحديدية أضعافاً مضاعفة وذلك لأن أهل الجهات الذين يمرون على ينبع إلى جدة اما ان يخرجوا إلى ينبع فيستأجرون مع القوافل إلى المدينة ومنها مع الركوب التي تخرج من المدينة إلى مكة أو مع الركب الشامي فإذا ذهبوا إلى مكة رجعوا إلى بلادهم من جدة ولا يعودون إلى المدينة المنورة ثم إلى ينبع وإما ان يذهبوا توا إلى جدة ومنها إلى مكة ثم مع القوافل التي تخرج من مكة للمدينة أو مع الركب الشامي ومنها إلى ينبع إلى بلادهم وهؤلاء الزوار انما يزورون مرة واحدة قبل الحج أو بعده حسبما يتيسر لهم ولا يزورون مرتين للمشقة وخوف الطريق بالركوب مع القوافل اما بعد وجود السكة الحديدية فحيث تحصل الراحة وأمن الطريق فيأتون كلهم إلى الينبع ومنها للمدينة فيركبون السكة منها إلى مكة ويرجعون عليها للمدينة ومنها إلى ينبع إلى بلادهم فيربح بدو الحجاز أصحاب القوافل من ينبع إلى المدينة ضعفي ما كانوا يربحون أولا إذا لم نلتفت للزيادة المحققة بواسطة راحة السكة وأمن الطريق بوجودها هذا من ينبع .

وأما من جدة فقد قلنا ان الذين يأتون مكة من جدة على أكثر ما يتصور الآن عشرون ألفاً وهؤلاء يبقون بعد مد السكة على حالهم الأولى بالنسبة لذهابهم من جدة إلى مكة ومنها إلى عرفات فلا يخسر بدو الحجاز الفائدة التي يستفيدونها من ايجارهم الجمال الآن قبل وجود السكة بل تزيد بالنظر لما يتأسس بواسطة السكة من الراحة (١٣٧) والأمن بين الحرمين فيزداد الواردون من جدة للحج طمعاً براحة الزيارة والأمن في الطريق وعلى وجود هذه الزيارة مدار الكلام هنا : قد فرضنا فيما اسلفنا ان عدد الواردين من جدة إلى مكة الآن عشرون ألفاً أكثر ما يكون ولا ريب ان رغبة المسلمين في زيارة النبي صلى الله تعالى عليه وآله وصحبه وسلم إذا وجدت الراحة وأمن الطريق تزيد وبقدر زيادتها يزيد الزوار فاذا كثر الزوار كثرت الفائدة لأهل الحرمين الشريفين من تجارة وغيرها وقد قلنا ان الذين يردون من

البر إلى مكة من أي جهة كانوا لا يحتاجون لاستئجار الجمال للذهاب لعرفة أو إلى المدينة المنورة لوجود دوابهم معهم وانما يحتاجها من أتى عن طريق البحر ولكن إذا وجدت السكة احتاج كل من يأتي عليها للحج من أهالي شمالي المدينة إلى القطب الشمالي سواء من البر أو البحر ان يستأجر من دواب بدو الحجاز للصعود لعرفات ولنبن كلامنا في بيان زيادة الفائدة من اجارة الجمال على ما قدمناه فنقول .

إن الذين يردون من بر الشام وجهاتها مع الركب الشامي الآن لا يزيدون على خمسة آلاف ولكن إذا وجدت السكة وتمت بمشيئة الله تعالى ودوام اقدام جلالة سيدنا أمير المؤمنين زادوا بالطبع اضعافاً مضاعفة فلو قدروا بثلاثمائة ألف لكان قليلا بل بخمسمائة ألف كان قليلا أيضاً بالنسبة لما هو متصور لما هو مطبوع في نفوس المؤمنين من الاشتياق الطبيعي الجبلي للحج والزيارة وان الذي يؤخرهم (١٣٨) بعد الطريق ومشقته وخوفه وزيادة المصارفات والاحتياج إلى التغيب عن الشغل والوطن مدة ليست بقليلة وما يصادفونه من الوقوع في ورطات المحاجر الصحية سيما في مثل الطور والوجه وما يتحملونه فيها مما لا يتصور كالاهانة والغلاء وعدم وجود ما يحتاجون إليه والتضييق الزائد إلى غير ذلك مما اشرنا إليه فبوجود السكة الحديدية المذكورة تنتفي هذه الأسباب كلها فيقبلون على الحج والزيارة حتى لا يتخلف أحد سيما إذا كانت الأجرة رخيصة فيقبل الناس من أقاصي بلاد الشام وحلب والموصل والاناضول والروملى والعجم وكردستان وبخارى وهكذا من جميع الجهات الشمالية حتى من السواحل ان شاء الله تعالى فان في المسلمين ولله الحمد كثرة واعتقاداً ولا يمنع أكثرهم عن اداء فريضة الحج والزيارة ويموت أكثرهم عاصياً بعدم اداء هذه الفريضة مع الاستطاعة إلا ما ذكرنا ومما يؤيد ما قلناه ان كثيراً ممن فرض عليهم الحج يؤدون فريضته ثم يقفلون راجعين لبلادهم من غير زيارة مع شوقهم الزائد لها وما ذلك الا لما يعلمون من تحمل المشاق في السفر من مكة للمدينة فيرجعون من مكة بعد أن يصلوا إليها لبلادهم

من غير زيارة .

فإذا فرضنا ان الحجاج الذين يركبون على السكة ثلاث مائة ألف على الأقل وكان يذهب نصفهم إلى عرفات ماشياً احتاج هذا النصف لجمال لتحميل حوائجهم وأكلهم وشربهم وخيامهم وأثاثهم إلى غير ذلك ولنفرض ان (١٣٩) كل ثلاثة يكفيهم جمل واحد كان اللازم لهم لتحميل حوائجهم المذكور خمسين ألف جمل وإذا فرضنا ان المائة وخمسين ألف الذين لا يذهبون مشاة يكفي كل اثنين منهم جمل لركوبهما وجمل لاثاثهما وحوائجهما كان اللازم لهم مائة وخمسين ألف جمل فإذا ضممناها إلى الخمسين ألفاً كان المجموع مائتي ألف جمل وهذا عدا الجمال التي تلزم للواردين من جدة فانها خارجة عن هذا العدد لأنها تبقى فائدتها لهم بعد وجود السكة كما هي قبلها فلا نطيل الكلام بضمها لها .

ثم إذا تمت هذه السكة فلا ريب ولا شك ان الحجاج المصريين لا يأتون من بلادهم على دواب بل يركبون في السكك الحديدية إلى السواحل ومنها إلى جدة على المراكب البخارية وانهم يزيدون اضعافاً مضاعفة عما هم عليه الآن وانهم يركبون على السكة الحديدية مستغنين بها عن الدواب فإذا كان كذلك يزاد ما يحتاج إليه اخواننا الحجاج المصريون من الدواب لنقل حوائجهم وخيامهم وأثاثهم من جدة إلى مكة أو من ينبع إلى المدينة ومن مكة إلى عرفة وأما من المدينة فيركبون على السكة وإذا فرضنا ان اخواننا المصريين يحتاجون إلى عشرة آلاف جمل كذلك كان ذلك مع ما مضى مائتي ألف وعشرة آلاف جمل وهؤلاء لغير الحجاج الذين يحضرون من جدة فلم ندخلهم في العدد كما ذكرنا لأنهم لا يزيدون ولا ينقصون وكذلك الحج البغدادي إذا تمت السكة على بغداد واتصلت بسكة بيره جيك ثم بسكة الشام لا يأتي على الدواب أحد (١٤٠) ولا تقدر الزيادة حينئذ ولكن لنقتصر الآن على ما ذكرنا بقى علينا ان نذكر الجمال التي يأتي عليها الزوار من ينبع إلى المدينة وبالعكس أعني يرجعون عليها من المدينة إلى ينبع

وقد قلنا انها بعد السكة تزيد عما كانت عليه قبلها ضعفين ولم نذكر قوافلها مع قوافل مكة لأنها ليس لها وقت معين بل تسير بحسب اللزوم وتارة تكون قليلة وتارة تكثر ولنفرض ان عدد جمال القوافل المذكورة الآن ألف وخمسمائة فيكون ضعفها بعد انتهاء السكة ثلاثة آلاف فتكون الجملة أربعة آلاف وخمسمائة ومثلها إياباً كان المجموع تسعة آلاف فتكون الزيادة ستة آلاف فاذا ضمت على ما ذكرنا كان الجميع مائتي ألف وستة عشر ألف جمل .

في موازنة واردات ايجار جمال القوافل ودواب الركوب المذكورة قبل السكة

لقد بينا أولا ان واردات جمال القوافل والركوب الآن قبل وجود السكة مهما بلغ خمس مائة ألف وستين ألفاً وثلاث مائة مجيدي .

منها خمس مائة وأربعون ألف مجيدي اجرة جمال القوافل والباقي وهو عشرون ألفاً وثلاثمائة مجيدي اجرة دواب الركوب وان المصارفات خمس مائة ألف وخمسة آلاف وستمائة واثنان وخمسون مجيدياً ونصف.

منها رسوم القوافل ثلاث مائة ألف وأربعة وستون ألفاً وخمس مائة مجيدي ومنها مصارفاتها ثمانية وتسعون ألفاً واثنان وخمسون مجيدياً (١٤١) ونصف ومنها ثمن الجمال التي تموت اربعون ألفاً وخمس مائة مجيدي ومنها مصارفات الركوب ألفان وستمائة مجيدي .

فإذا طرحت المصارفات والرسوم من الواردات كان الباقي بعد الطرح أربعة وخمسين ألفاً وستمائة وسبعة وأربعين مجيدياً ونصفاً .

هذا جميع ما يستفيده بدو الحجاز من الحجاج والزوار والتجار ولم اتعرض فيه لما تستفيده القوافل من ينبع إلى المدينة ولم ادخله مع الواردات قبل السكة بل تركته خارجاً عنها وذكرت الذي سيزيد عنه إن شاء الله تعالى .

في بيان اجرة الجمال المذكورة ومصارفاتها وما يبلغ مجموعها

لقد قلنا ان الحجاج بواسطة السكة يزيدون أضعاف ضعفهم الآن إن شاء الله تعالى ولا يمتري في هذا إلا مختل الشعور أو فاقد العقل أو ذو مرض في قلبه ختم الله على سمعه وقلبه وجعل على بصره غشاوة فإذا كان كذلك كانت زيادة الحجاج محتاجة إلى زيادة الجمال وبالضرورة إذا كثر الاحتياج غلا السعر فتكون الأجرة غالية بالنسبة لما هي عليه الآن .

وها هي الآن أجرة الجمل الواحد من مكة إلى عرفات ذهاباً واياباً من خمسة مجيديات إلى عشرة وقد تزيد على ذلك وهذا مع غير الركب الشامي أما معه فلا يؤجرون جمالا وحدها بل مع الخيمة وما يلزمها ويسمونها تعريفة وهي بخمسة وعشرين مجيدياً فلا ننظر إليها فإذا فرضنا أن أجرة الجمل الواحد عشرة مجيديات كان مجموع أجرة (١٤٢) مائتي ألف جمل وعشرة آلاف جمل مليوني مجيدي ومائة ألف مجيدي وإذا فرضنا ان أجرة الجمل الواحد من ينبع للمدينة الآن خمسة عشر مجيدياً تكون على الأقل بعد السكة لكثرة الزوار عشرين مجيدياً فإذا ضربناها في عدد الجمال كان الربح منها بواسطة السكة مائة وخمسة وثلاثين ألف مجيدي وذلك بعد اسقاط أجرة ثلاثة آلاف جمل باعتبار أن أجرة الواحد منها خمسة عشر مجيدياً كما كانت قبل السكة فإذا ضم ذلك إلى ما سبق من أجرة الجمال إلى عرفات كان المجموع مليونين ومائتي ألف وخمسة وثلاثين ألف مجيدي وإذا جعلنا لكل جمل كغيره مصرفاً عن اليوم ثلاثة غروش واعتبرنا أن مدة ايجارها للمدينة ذهاباً واياباً أحد عشر يوماً وضربنا الثلاثة المصرف بأحد عشر الأيام وضربنا الحاصل بعدد الجمال كان مصرفها عن المدة المذكورة عشرة آلاف وأربعمائة واحداً وعشرين مجيدياً وأما مصارفها في أيام ايجارها للصعود وإن كانت لا مصرف لها أو لها مصرف جزئي لا يستحق الذكر فلنفرضها مثل مصارفها في مدة ايجارها للمدينة فتكون مائة وثلاثة وتسعين ألفاً

وستمائة وأربعة وثمانين مجيدياً وسنقابل هذا بما يأخذون الآن من أجرة الجمال ونطرحه منه ونبين الموازنة والزيادة .

في موازنة واردات ايجاد الجمال ومصارفها بعد السكة المذكورة

لقد ذكرنا ان واردات ايجار الجمال لعرفات ستبلغ مليوني مجيدي ومائة ألف (١٤٣) مجيدي وان واردات ايجار الجمال بين المدينة المنورة وينبع الزائدة على وارداتها الآن مائة ألف وخمسة وثلاثون ألف مجيدي فيكون مجموعهما مليونين ومائتي ألف وخمسة وثلاثين ألف مجيدي .

وأما مصارفها فذكرنا أيضاً أنها للصعود قياساً على مصارفها للمدينة المنورة مائة وثلاثة وتسعون ألف مجيدي وستمائة وأربعة وثمانون مجيدياً وفيما بين ينبع والمدينة عشرة آلاف وأربع مائة واحد وعشرون مجيدياً .

فتكون جملة المصارفات المذكورة مائتي ألف وأربعة آلاف ومائة وخمسة مجيديات فإذا طرحنا المصارفات من الواردات كان السالم من الواردات مليونين وثلاثين ألفاً وثمانمائة وخمسة وتسعين مجيدياً .

فيما يستفيده الآن بدو الحجاز من اجرة الجمال وفي مصارفها

قلنا فيما تقدم ان أكثر ما يجتمع في قوافل مكة من الجمال لنقل الحجاج وغيرهم من مكة إلى المدينة سبعة وعشرون ألفاً وقد تكون أقل من ذلك بكثير وهو الغالب ولكن نفرض أنها دائماً كذلك وان أجرة الواحد منها للمدينة ذهاباً وايابا ثلاثون مجيدياً إذا قلت الجمال وكثر الزوار ولنغض النظر عن ان كثيرين منهم إذا لم نقل أكثرهم لا يرجعون إلى مكة بل يذهبون من المدينة إلى بلادهم عن طريق الشام او ينبع وأنه في أكثر السنين لا تبلغ الجمال هذا المقدار بل نصفه فإذا كان علينا ان نعتبر اجرة كل جمل عشرون مجيدياً (١٤٤) فإذا ضربت في سبعة وعشرين ألفاً كان حاصل الضرب خمس مائة ألف وأربعين ألف مجيدي وأما ما تستفيده من ركوب المدينة فقد اسلفنا

ان عدد الهجن فيها ألف وعدد الرهاوين مائة وخمسون وعدد الحمير خمسمائة وبينا ان اكثر الرهاوين الا ما ندر ملك لركابها وكذا عشر الهجن ثم ان اجرة الهجين الواحد من خمسة مجيديات إلى عشرين من المدينة إلى مكة ذهاباً واياباً وأجرة الرهوان من عشرين مجيدياً إلى ثلاثين وأجرة الحمار من خمسة إلى خمسة عشر فإذا فرضنا ان الهجن التي يحج عليها أهل المدينة المنورة في كل سنة ثمان مائة وأجرة الهجين خمسة عشر ريالا مجيدياً دائماً كانت أجرة الهجن اثني عشر ألف مجيدي وإذا فرضنا ان الرهاوين في كل سنة مائة وعشرون وان اجرة الواحد منها خمسة وعشرون مجيدياً كان مجموع اجرتها ثلاثة آلاف وخمسمائة مجيدي وإذا فرضنا ان الحمير اربع مائة واجرة واحدها اثني عشر مجيدياً كان مجموع اجرتها أربعة آلاف ثمانمائة مجيدي فتكون جملة أجرة الركوب في السنة عشرين ألفاً وثلاثمائة مجيدي .

وأما مصارفها فاعلم ان جمال قوافل مكة ازدادت على غيرها مصارف للرسوم فلها مصارف ورسوم دون الركوب فلا رسوم عليها .

فأما رسوم القوافل فهي .

الرسم المعين من قديم الزمان على كل جمل من الجمال	خمسة مجيديات
(١٤٥) للديوان ولعله مجلس البلدية	مجيدي واحد
للمطوف وهو الذي ينزل الحج في داره ويطوفه	ثلاث مجيديات
للرهنية وهو من يرهن نفسه عند أمير مكة تأميناً على الحاج	مجيدي واحد
للمقوم وهو من تكون أصحاب الجمال تحت إرادته	مجيديان
للخرج	مجيدي واحد

جملتها ثلاثة عشر مجيدي ونصف فاذا ضربت بعدد الجمال كان حاصل الضرب ثلاث مائة ألف وأربعة وستين ألفاً وخمس مائة مجيدي .

وأما مصارفها فلنفرض ان الجمل الواحد من جمال القوافل يحتاج في يوم إلى ثلاثة قروش صاغا وان مدة السفر ذهاباً واياباً ثلاثة وعشرون

يوماً يبلغ ذلك عن المدة المرقومة تسعة وستين قرشاً وهذا بما فيه اجرة خدامها فإذا ضربت في عدد الجمال بلغت مليوناً وثمانمائة وثلاثة وستين ألف قرش فإذا حولت مجيديات بلغت ثمانية وتسعين ألفاً واثنين وخمسين مجيدياً ونصفاً وكسوراً وهذا بقطع النظر عما تخسره البدو من موت الجمال بسبب السفر والتحميل والحط والترحال وسوء الإدارة والتعب والمشقة إلى غير ذلك ما بين واقع ومنكسر ومريض وهذا شيء ضروري مشاهد ولربما يقع الموت في عشرة من كل مائة في الطريق عدا ما (١٤٦) يمرض منها في الطريق ثم يموت بعد الرجوع للوطن فان هذا كثير والغالب ان يذبحوه ويأكلوه لليأس من حياته ولنفرض ان موت الجمال في الطريق وفي محلها بسبب السفر عشرة في المِاية تكون الخسارة الفين وسبعمائة جمل ولنتنزل إلى نصفها أعني في المائة خمسة تبلغ ألفاً وثلاثمائة وخمسين جملا فلو قدر ان قيمة كل جمل منها ثلاثون مجيدياً على الأقل مع ان البعض منها يساوي خمسين مجيدياً أو أكثر تبلغ قيمة هذه الجمال أربعين ألفاً وخمسمائة مجيدي وأما مصارفات الركوب فهي جزئية بالنسبة لمصارفات القوافل فإذا قلنا أنها تبلغ عشرة في المائة ما بين علف وموت وأجرة وغيرها تكون مصارفاتها الفين وستين مجيدياً.

ولا يقال ان هذه المصارفات كلها لا يلزم بل لا يجوز اسقاطها من الواردات لأنها تصرف عليها بكل حال لأنا نقول ان بدو الحجاز كغيرهم من البدو ويرعون جمالهم وبقرهم وغنمهم في البرية من الكلأ المباح لا يصرفون عليها شيئاً وأما في حال ايجارها فمحتاجة للعلف لأنها لا يمكنها ان ترعى لانشغالها وقت السير بالحمولة ووقت الحط بالراحة فلا يمكنها ان ترعى بل ولا تستطيع ان تقوم من تعبها سيما انها ليست معتادة على السير وممارسة على الحمل فيأخذها التعب حتى لا تقدر على الحركة ولو فرض انها يمكنها الرعي لا يكفيها بل تحتاج معه إلى علف فتكون لها قوة على الحمل وهذا معروف مشاهد فإن الجائع لا يقدر (١٤٧) على الشغل والحمل ولو في الناس فبالضرورة

يضطر اربابها لعلفها وكذا القول فيما يموت منها وان كانت الآجال كلها بيد الله تعالى فإن الله تعالى جعل لكل اجلا ولكل أجل كتاب لكنه تعالى اسند الأشياء في الظاهر إلى أسبابها الظاهرة فإذا تعلقت إرادته تعالى بايجاد شيء مرتب على سبب أوجد أولاً ذلك السبب والمسبب وربطه به ثم أنفذ فيه قضاه وأمرنا ان ننظر إليه بحكم الظاهر وهذا مقرر معلوم لا يحتاج إلى اطالة فإذا كان الصواب ان نضم ثمن الذي يموت منها في الطريق مع مصارفاتها ونسقطها من أصل وارداتها كما فعلنا وأما ما يربحونه الآن من ايجار الجمال إلى عرفات فلا يلزم التعرض له لأنه يبقى على حاله بعد وجود السكة كما كان قبلها لأن الحجاج الذين يأتون الآن من البحر عن جدة يبقون على حالهم ولو زادوا فان زيادتهم تزيد الواردات ولا تنقص فلا يلزم ذكرها .

في كيفية إيجار الجمال ومدتها للصعود من مكة لعرفة والرجوع إليها بعد السكة

إن مدة إيجار الجمال للصعود إلى عرفات وأيام التشريق والرجوع إلى مكة لا تزيد على خمسة أيام أو ستة لمن يبقى في منى إلى ثالث أيام التشريق كالسادة الشافعية وليس في هذا الإيجار مشقة على الجمال ولا على من معها فان الحجاج يخرجون من مكة يوم التروية الذي هو ثامن ذي الحجة الحرام إلى منى ويبيتون فيها كما هو السنة عن رسول الله صلى الله تعالى عليه وآله وصحبه وسلم عند السادة الشافعية (١٤٨) ومن وافقهم وفي يوم الصعود وهو اليوم التاسع يذهبون إلى عرفات فيصلون الظهر عند مسجد نمرة ثم يذهبون إلى عرفات بعد الزوال كما هو السنة أو يذهبون من مكة يوم التروية إلى عرفات ويبيتون فيها وهذا خلاف السنة كما يفعله الآن أكثر الحجاج احتياطاً منهم على زعمهم ليوافق الوقوف بعرفة يوم التاسع قطعاً بالإحتياط بوقوفهم يوم الثامن والتاسع لخوفهم ان يكون يوم التاسع في الظاهر يوم النحر الذي هو العاشر فيكونون بهذا الإحتياط وقفوا يوم التاسع

قطعاً وبتاً وعلى كل فانهم جميعهم ينفرون مساء ذلك اليوم بعد غروب الشمس ليلة عاشر ذي الحجة إلى منى لكن بعضهم يبيت في مزدلفة على السنة ويأخذ منها الجمار للرجم فإذا طلعت الشمس جاء عند المشعر الحرام وذكر الله تعالى كذكره آباءه أو أشد ذكراً ثم يذهب إلى منى كما كان يفعل رسول الله صلى الله تعالى عليه وآله وصحبه وسلم لطواف الأفاضة بخلاف مدة ايجارها إلى المدينة فإنها لا تنقص عن ثلاثة وعشرين يوماً وفي خلال هذا الإيجار لعرفات لا تحتاج إلى مصارفات كما تحتاج في ايجارها للمدينة إذ يمكن بعد ايصالها الحجاج لعرفة ان يذهب بها أهلها ويرعوها في الكلأ المباح وان احتاجت إلى علف ليلة أو ليلتين لا يستحق ان يذكر فتكون سالمة من المصارفات وبعضهم ينفر من عرفات بعد الغروب ويذهب توا إلى منى وقد يأخذون الجمار من مزدلفة وقد لا يأخذون ويبيت في منى وفي صباح اليوم العاشر يرجمون كلهم جمرة العقبة وهو الرمي الأول ويقصون أو يحلقون ويتحللون التحلل الأول ويلبسون ثيابهم ويضحون ثم يذهب (١٤٩) البعض إلى مكة ويطوف طواف الأفاضة ويسعى فيتحلل التحلل الثاني ويرجع إلى منى يبيت فيها ثلاث ليال على السنة أو ليلتين على الخلاف كما هو فعل الاكثر في هذا الزمان ثم يحملون حوائجهم وخيامهم وما معهم ويرجعون إلى مكة المكرمة فيطوف من لم يطف طواف الأفاضة ويسعى ويتحلل التحلل الثاني ويأخذ الجمال أربابها فغاية ما تمشيه الجمال في هذا الإيجار ست ساعات ذهاباً من مكة إلى منى ومثلها في ايابها وقد تزيد نحو ساعتين أو ثلاث في مجيئها يوم النحر إلى مكة ورجوعها إلى منى ومع هذا فقد ذكرنا مصارفاتها واسقطناها من وارداتها كما علمت.

فيما يستفيده بدو الشام من الحجاج الآن قبل السكة

قد ذكرنا ان بني صخر وولد علي من بدو الشام يحملون الحملة وهي الأحمال التي للحكومة من مزيريب إلى معان وهذه الحملة مائتا

حمل من الذخائر واجرة الحمل منها أربع مجيديات فيكون مجموع أجرة الحملة من مزيريب إلى معان ثمان مائة مجيدي ويحملون للتجار مائتي حمل أيضاً لكن أجرة الحمل ثلاثة مجيديات فيكون مجموعها ستمائة مجيدي ثم تضع الحكومة في معان نصف الحملة وتحمل بنو عطية ثلاث مائة حمل للحكومة والتجار إلى المعظم أجرة الحمل أربع مجيديات مجموعها ألف ومائتا مجيدي ثم تحمل الباقي اللبدة وأبو شامة والخريشا ومجموعه أربعمائة حمل من المعظم للجديد وأجرة الحمل أربع مجيديات أيضاً فتكون جملة الأجرة ألفاً (١٥٠) وستماية مجيدي وتضع الحكومة من الحملة فيها للرجعة والباقي يحمله الصخور والركاب الموجودون منهم في الركب وقد تحمل الأحراش من العقبة إلى المدينة ومن جملة الأحمال أحمال الماء التي تحملها الحكومة وتسمى افازة كما تقدم لسقي الفقراء والعسكر وغيرهم في المواضع التي يختبرون انها لا ماء فيها فيكون جميع ما يستفيده بدو الشام من اجرة الجمال من ركب الحج الشامي من الشام للمدينة أربعة آلاف مجيدي ولا يستفيدون منه شيئاً غير هذه الأجرة اصلا إلا إذا صادف مرور الركب على بيوتهم أو قريباً منها وكان الزمن ربيعاً فيه اللبن والسمن والخراف الصغيرة فانهم يبيعونهم منها شيئاً لا يلتفت إليه .

فيما يستفيده بدو الشام من الحجاج والزوار بعد وجود السكة

أعلم أنا ذكرنا فوائد من الفوائد التي ينجم عنها هذا الطريق بعد وجود هذه السكة وان أكثر هذه الاستفادة لبدو الشام لصلاح أراضيهم للزرع والغرس والاعمار وبسبب كثرة المارين عليهم وقرب الشام والحرمين بواسطة السكة تنفق بضاعتهم فيغتني أهل الحجاز بها عن واردات مصر ونجد وغيرها والشام عن واردات أرضروم والجهات الشمالية من غنم وسمن وغيرهما مما ذكرناه وهذه الفوايد لا يمكن تقديرها ولا يقابلها شيء من الفوائد فينبغي الاقتصار عليها لكن في مد السكة الحديدية من أرضهم واسطة لغناهم من جهة أخرى وهي

استخدامهم فيها فيربحون من معاشات استخدامهم فيها إذا خدموا بالصدق والأمانة أكثر مما كانوا (١٥١) يربحونه من أجرة الجمال بأمثال أمثال فينبغي أن يكتفي بما ذكرناه هنا عن غيره فان فيه كفاية لأولى الذكاء والعناية.

في الموازنة بين فائدة بدو الحجاز من اجرة الجمال قبل السكة وبعدها وبيان الربح التي تربحه بدو الحجاز بواسطتها

انما خصصنا بدو الحجاز بالذكر دون بدو الشام مع ان كلا من الفريقين لهما تعلق وفوائد بالطريق قبل وجود السكة وبعدها لما اشرنا إليه أولا من أن أصل موضوع التأليف على رد ما شاع ووسوس به من ان بدو الحجاز هم الذين يتضررون بوجود هذه السكة لعدم امكانهم حينئذ ايجار جمالهم وأما بدو الشام فلم نشركهم معهم فيها بذكر الموازنة بين حالهم قبل السكة وبعدها لما ذكرناه من أن فائدتهم من ايجار الجمال للركب الشامي الآن جزئية لا يلتفت إليها بالنسبة لفائدة بدو الحجاز منها ولما هو محقق من الفوائد التي سيستفيدونها بوجودها زيادة عما كانت قبلها اضعافاً مضاعفة إنشاء الله تعالى.

واردات أجرة الجمال بعد وجود السكة سالمة من المصارف مليونان وثلاثون ألفاً وثمان مائة وخمسة وتسعون مجيدياً.

واردات اجرة الجمال الآن قبل السكة خالصة في المصاريف أربعة وخمسون ألفاً وستمائة وسبعة وأربعون مجيدياً ونصف فإذا اسقطنا واردات الآن ما قبل السكة من الواردات بعدها كان الربح مليوناً وتسع مائة (١٥٢) وستة وسبعين ألفاً ومائتين وسبعة وأربعين مجيدياً ونصفاً.

وإذا حولناها ذهبات عثمانية على ان الذهب بمائة وقرشين ونصف كان الربح المذكور ثلاث مائة ألف وستة وستين وثلاثمائة وثمانية وعشرين ذهباً عثمانياً وثلاثة أرباع وإذا حولت قروشاً صاغاً باعتبار أن قيمة المجيدي تسعة عشر كان الربح سبعة وثلاثين مليوناً وخمس مائة وثمانية وأربعين ألفاً وسبع مائة وقرشين ونصفاً.

هذا الربح الذي سيكون إنشاء الله تعالى محققاً لأهل الحجاز من أجرة جمالهم عدا ما ذكرناه من الفوائد والحمد لله أولا وآخراً وصلى الله على سيدنا محمد وعلى آله وصحبه وسلم .

تمت

هَذَا كِتَاب

السَّعَادَة النَّامِيَة الأَبَدِيَّة

فِي

السِّكَّة الحِجَازِيَّة الحَدِيدِيَّة

أَثَر

السَّيّد محمد عَارِف بن السَّيّد أَحْمَد المنير

الحُسَيْنِي الدِّمَشْقِي عَفَى عَنْهُمَا

آمِين

Index

Numbers in parentheses refer to pages of this book (Introduction); other numbers are to pages of the manuscript (numbers in brackets at the beginning of each one in the text itself). Also see the Glossary.

'Aqaba, 10, 14, 24, 33, 150
'Aqaba Ibn 'Āmir, 115
'Aqaba al-Shāmiyya, 24
'Aqabat al-Kiswa *or* al-Shujūn, 20
Arabia, 139 (12, 13, 15, 17, 22, 25, 26); *see also* Hejaz, Najd
Arafat (Mount), 47, 60, 66, 74, 80, 86, 104–5, 116, 135–9, 141–2, 147–8
'Arīḍ, 16
'Ārif, Muḥammad, 1 (21–30)
al-'Arīsh, 23
al-'Asālī, 19, 20, 45–6, 48
'Asāliyya (place), 33; (tribe), 7
'Asfān, 16, 33
al-Ashja'ī, 'Arafja, 128
Asia Minor (8)
'Aṭiyya (tribe), 8, 149
Austro-Hungary (9, 11)
al-A'waj, 20
'Awf (tribe), 7, 33
Awlād Muḥammad (tribe), 7
Aydin (8)
'Ayn Tabra, 13, 33
Ayyūb (Companion of Muhammad), 93

Bāb al-Nabī, 48
Bāb al-Salām, 47
Badā'i', 11, 30
Badr, 12, 32, 34
Baghdad, 79, 100, 139 (8–11)
Baḥyawiyya (tribe), 7
Bajta, 20
Balkans (8, 12)
Balqā', 10, 18, 20, 106
Banū 'Amr (tribe), 7, 33
Banū 'Aṭiyya, *see* 'Aṭiyya
Banū 'Awf, *see* 'Awf
Banū Ayyūb (tribe), 7
Banū Ṣakhr (tribe), 8, 22, 45, 149, 150
Banū Shāma (tribe), 8, 149
Baqaliyya, 34
al-Bārida, 20
Barrāqa, 11, 30
Bashshar (tribe), 33
al-Bayhaqī, 115–7, 119
al-Bazzār, 87
Beirut, 37, 45, 57, 70, 106 (11, 20)
Beshikṭāsh Iskele, 56
Bilī (tribe), 7
Bīr 'Abbās, 12, 32
Bīr Darwīsh, 32
Bīr Ḥādiba, 17
Bīr Ḥiṣān, 15
Bīr Ḥufāt, 13, 33
Bīr Khilṣ, 15
Bīr Māshī, 13, 14, 33
Bīr Mubayrīk, 13, 33
Bīr Riḍwān, *see* 'Aqaba
Bīr Shaykh, 15
Bīr Tufla, 16
Bīr 'Urwa, 14, 75
Birejik, 79, 100, 139 (11)
Birkat Ṭabariyya (Lake of Tiberias), 22
Biyār 'Alī, 12–14
Biyār Ḥajar, 17
Biyār Nāṣif, 11, 30–1
Buḥayrat Lūṭ (Dead Sea), 22 (8)
Bukhara, 138
al-Bukhārī, Muḥammad Ibn Ismā'īl, 93, 118, 124–5, 127
Burckhardt, J. L. (26, 27, 30)
Burma (11)
Burton, Richard (26)

Cairo, 108 (12, 20, 30)
China, 79
Crete, 79

al-Dāghistānī, Shaykh Muḥammad, 74
Dakara (tribe), 7
Damascus, 6, 8, 9, 11, 17–19, 25, 36–9, 45, 46, 48, 49, 51, 58, 59, 61–7, 69, 70, 72–3, 84, 99–101, 105–8, 118, 139, 143, 150 (8, 11, 12, 14–18, 21–3, 25, 27–30)
Damascus Gate, 5, 19
Darwīsha, 64
David, 92, 133
al-Dayr, 106, 108
Der'a (15, 17)
Dhāt Ḥajj, 10, 24
Dhū'l-Nūn, 9, 18–20, 45
Didier, Charles (26)
Dolma Bahçe, 52, 54
Doughty, C. M. (27)

Jacob M. Landau is associate professor of political science, Hebrew University, Jerusalem. He is a native of Roumania and was educated at the Hebrew University (M.A. 1946) and the University of London (Ph.D. 1949). Professor Landau has written numerous articles for scholarly journals and has published the following books: *Parliaments and Parties in Egypt* (1954), *Studies in the Arab Theater and Cinema* (1958), *A Word Count of Modern Arabic Prose* (1959), *The Arabs in Israel* (1969), and *Jews in Nineteenth-Century Egypt* (1969).

Charles H. Elam edited the English portion of the manuscript. The book was designed by Richard Kinney. The type face for the text is Monotype Times Roman designed by Stanley Morison in 1931 and the display face is Bulmer originally cut by William Martin about 1790. The text is printed on an antique-finished paper, and the book is bound in Columbia Mills Bayside Vellum and Elephant Hide paper over binders' boards. Manufactured in the United States of America.